THE CORRUPTORS

BY Nicky Cruz

Satan on the Loose
The Corruptors

THE CORRUPTORS

BY Nicky Cruz

Satan on the Loose
The Corruptors

THE CORRUPTORS

by

Nicky Cruz

LONDON
Good Reading Limited

TO my dearest friends Becky and Hugh Cummings
who are beautiful Christian people.
They have been more than friends.
They have been like parents.

ACKNOWLEDGMENTS

Jeanie and Kirk Weyant

LaRue Price—my personal secretary who spent many long hours and much overtime in writing and reviewing, working directly with the publishers, and sacrificing time with her children during the past several months

Dear wife, Gloria, who has helped me so much and worked very closely with me.

Contents

Introduction

You may get mad at what I say in this book. Well, I didn't write it to make friends. I didn't write it to make enemies, either. I wrote it because I had to.

It started out a completely different book. But in the last year the world has changed so much. And I've changed. When Jesus spoke to me in a hotel room in Ottawa, Canada, what a difference it made in my life.

Now I see everything with new eyes.

Everywhere you look these days there is corruption and destruction. There are powers loose in the world that are out to get us. If you don't want them to destroy you and yours, let me show you what God has shown me.

Meet the *Corruptors.*

THE CORRUPTORS

1

Crash!

One of the fabulous stars of the entertainment world was Janis Joplin. She didn't just sing. When she got on a stage she was a whirling dervish in perpetual motion, twisting and rocking and shimmying until her gyrations and her lusty voice and the beat all blurred into one wild call to abandon. Janis's fans blew their minds. So many of them swarmed to see her sing and buy her records that all over the rock world Janis Joplin was queen of the scene.

It wasn't always so. As a teen-ager Janis felt fat and pimply and ugly. While she was in school, someone called her Ugliest Man on Campus. But then she learned to give the rock hounds what they wanted. Some people say she chased girls as well as men, tried all kinds of drugs and sex. Onstage she struck one listener like a lonely little girl telling dirty jokes. Offstage, she got deeper and deeper into trouble.

Janis Joplin soared clear to the top of the rock world. Then one night, after two drinks of vodka with friends, she shot some heroin in her hotel room. Returning to the lobby to purchase some cigarettes, she fell as she stepped back into her room, breaking her nose as she died. She was twenty-seven years old. Records show official cause of death as an accidental overdose of heroin.

Janis Joplin wanted desperately to reach the top of her world. She made it! But as she climbed onto her throne, her suicidal life-style brought her whole kingdom crashing down in a tragic end. *It took just five years to travel from superstar to death.*

You can spend your whole life searching for an impossible dream—you may even find it—and you can miss everything important. While I was in a city in the Southwest, a man in cowboy boots and a rancher's hat came to see me. "All my life I've wanted to do something worthwhile," he sobbed, "and now the years are running out and what have I got to show for it? A herd of range cattle not worth the land they graze on!" That rancher knew he had missed out on the most important things there are.

In the summer of 1973 Theodore and Jean Gilbert were having lunch in the New York hotel where they rented an apartment when there was a sound like an explosion. Jean put down her chicken sandwich and Theodore looked out into the hallway and gulped. The hall was gone. Outside the apartment door there was nothing but smoggy sky.

"Hey, Baby," shouted Theodore, "the building just fell down!"

Before it collapsed, the Broadway Central Hotel had been one of New York's finest buildings. For over a hundred years it had stood proud and tall, eight stories high, housing six theaters and more than three hundred tenants. It had been a landmark moldy with history. There Diamond Jim Brady had flashed his famous jewelry; there James Fisk, the railroad tycoon, was shot in a love triangle. There in recent years New York City housed many of its welfare patients, and drug addicts had sometimes roamed the halls.

Now, in a moment, the hotel's floors buckled, the walls ballooned out, the timbers popped and snapped, and in seconds three-fourths of the building collapsed like a house built with matchsticks. Fortunately, before the rest of the hotel fell into the basement, firemen arrived with cherry pickers and scooped the Gilberts and other tenants to safety. Then the remaining rooms and timbers shuddered and tore loose and crashed down into what was now only a heap of rubble. Some of the tenants were buried there. In the final collapse a baby was blown out of its carriage by the blast. The survivors called it a kaleidoscope of terror.

So, in barely the time it takes to read about it, the Broadway Central Hotel with its century of memories collapsed into a heap of bricks, wood, plaster, furniture, metal, glass, bodies, and dust. The whole thing was a kind of modern parable. The Broadway Central went from glory to disaster. The people in it at different times had really lived—they thought! There they had some of the highest experiences and greatest pleasures possible, and some of the lowest and worst. As the hotel neared its end, its imposing appearance was no more than that—a shell covering realities too weak to last. When the end arrived, everything collapsed into nothing.

Only a few years ago the world looked so good. Many kinds of diseases had been wiped out and people were living longer than ever before. The standard of living was rising; there were plans to wipe out poverty. Humans had explored the earth and were starting in on the moon and stars.

Today a lot of people are hungry and some are starving. The human life-span may be getting shorter again. We're running out of living space and food and fuel. There seems to be a shortage these days of nearly everything. The fight against inflation and pollution looks about lost. We are being shocked senseless by criminality in business, in labor, in the armed forces, in government—in everything. America used to tell other countries how to be like us. Now we're scrambling to get ourselves through the rest of the twentieth century.

No, it wasn't long ago that man thought he had conquered nature, space, the atom, the mysteries of the mind and the universe—everything but sin! Today how different everything is. Today's problems are hunger, shortages, pollution, violence, criminality, greed, chaos!

Whether it's the world, or the nation, or a life, everything can come crashing down to sudden destruction. I don't want to see it happen to anyone. So let's look at some of the causes.

Why did the Broadway Central Hotel collapse? The people who lived there said the walls shook every time a subway train went past. Fire Chief John O'Hagan said that the subways and the traffic in the streets weakened the building with their vibrations until it couldn't stand anymore and fell apart.

Isn't that what killed Janis Joplin? Bad vibrations that hit her again and again until she couldn't stand anymore and her life collapsed? Isn't that what's wrong with a lot of people today—and the world?

I know this—you can get so used to bad vibrations that you don't notice them. The people at the Broadway Central got so they hardly ever thought about it when a subway rumbled past. But everything takes its toll, whether you're aware or not, and the end can come mighty fast.

Today, when everything seems touched in some way by corruption, I can see the bad vibrations reaching into every corner of existence. It's going to take a lot of strength and stamina for anyone to *stand* when so much is shaking loose and falling apart.

But you can do it! I know that because I've felt the bad vibrations so often in my own experience, and I've learned how to survive. Here's what I've found out.

2

What Do You Put in Your Head?

A woman who opened her home to a number of foster-children had trouble with one of them over a certain movie. Ann insisted on seeing it. "Everyone else is going to see it," she said. "Why can't I?"

At the time, the woman was making Jell-O. "Ann," she asked, "Where's the garbage from the lunch dishes?"

"Under the sink. Why?"

"Because I want to use it. Please dump the garbage in the Jell-O."

"The *garbage?* It will spoil it! What do you want to put it in the Jell-O for?"

"If the garbage spoils it," said the foster-mother, "I can always throw the Jell-O out. But if you fill your head with garbage like that movie, I can't throw out your head."

A little later Ann turned down a friend's invitation to go with her to the movie in question. "My parents," she said proudly, "are very strict about what I see. Besides, why should I fill my head with that garbage?"

It's true. More garbage is being distributed today, in movie theaters and books and on TV and newsstands, than ever before in history. But if you think I'm going to say that you should never go to a movie, you're wrong. I know some fine Christian people who never go, and I admire them for their stand. They are saving themselves from a mental diet of garbage! However, I admit that there are some motion pictures I like. I know young people who were brought to Christ by seeing *The Cross and the Switchblade* and have met men and women who were inspired by the play or movie, *A Man for All Seasons*.

Even so, one fact we have to face is this: pornographic magazines, films, and shows make up one of the biggest business operations in the world today. In one recent year 200 million dollars worth of such smut was sold in America. In spite of governmental efforts to put some kind of lid on this dirty business, illicit sex seems to be a surefire success formula for the worst kinds of articles, books, and movies.

One of today's best-selling novelists writes such amateurish fiction that it would be hard to imagine anyone plowing through her books except for the sex that drips from nearly every page. Someone called this author's first novel a "candy box of vulgarity." Filled with sex perversion, drinking, and drug addiction, the book naturally became a popular movie. A magazine editor invited to watch the filming said about her visit to the movie set, "I heard more four-letter words in ten days on that set than I heard in four years at Sarah Lawrence."

The woods are full of people exploiting sex for money.

Books and magazines, movies, and even television shows seem to be built more and more often around sex and violence. One book claimed that it described more than a thousand seductions. Another advised young women on how to trap married men. Other books are billed as sex-filled, sadistic and orgiastic. A reviewer said of one novel, "Color this one dirty. It's been a while since I've seen so much filth outside the barnyard."

Across the nation and in many corners of the world, newsstands are filled with books and magazines that seem to have little to offer except large quantities of sex and nudity. Some of these are so vilely sadistic and pornographic that it is hard to understand how human beings can even prepare and distribute such literature.

But the pornography pushers are not all in the publishing business. Popular songs, often filled with double meanings, pound ideas about the delights of illicit sex and drugs into unsuspecting minds. All kinds of commercial products are tied to sex symbolism for quick success.

Advertisements are getting more and more suggestive. Travel ads promise that girls in bikinis will surround you the moment you arrive. An ad for alcohol pictures a blonde leaning back, glass in hand, and promises that if you mix her a Flaming Flimflam, "you might really stir up something." An ad for a bus line shows a couple snuggling close and suggests that if you go by Flatfoot Bus, "You'll make out better." A shaving cream company uses burlesque music as background for a shapely blonde's cry, "Take it off, take it all off!"—while an actor shaves off his stubble. There is bedtime perfume, and perfume that "makes things happen. What kind of things? That's her affair." For the men, there is an advertisement showing a girl about to get out of a well-used bed asking herself whether it was him, or his cologne. There is even one ad for "a topless car."

Remember, every time you buy a book, a magazine or a movie ticket that glorifies the world of smut, you're supporting the *smut business*. Boycott it by refusing to let your money be used to fill the pockets of the porn-producers.

Suppose the book or the magazine or the movie turns out differently from what you expected? You have a perfect right to walk out of the movie and demand your money back. Or to return the book or magazine.

Some people won't admit that this kind of thing is garbage. Or if they do, they may argue that what you read or see can't hurt you.

It can.

Do you remember Charles Manson? He and his friends were convicted of plotting some of the goriest murders in history, including Sharon Tate, the actress, and her friends. Charlie was fascinated by movies. While he and his gang lived on the Spahn Movie Ranch in southern California they made various motion pictures of their own. One was a pornographic movie in which, according to police, Manson used a machete to hack someone's arm. Another film was made of a group orgy celebrating the "initiation" of a fifteen-year-old girl. One of the girls involved said, "The whole scene was perversion like I've never seen before."

One of Manson's pals was Robert Beausoleil, who had played the part of Lucifer in an occult film called *Lucifer Rising*. At the time, Beausoleil has said, he believed he *was* the devil.

Sharon Tate, who was eventually murdered by Manson's friends, appeared in a number of occult movies. Her first major role was in the film *13* or *Eye of the Devil*. The technical adviser was a magician and occult leader who claimed he initiated Miss Tate into witchcraft during the filming of *13*. She played the part of a vampire in the movie *The Fearless Vampire Killers*.

Another actor in *The Fearless Vampire Killers* was the film's writer and director, Roman Polanski, who made a career of weird movies. He wrote the scenario for *Do You Like Women?*, a film about cannibals in Paris who cook and eat pretty young women. Polanski directed *Repulsion,* about a lovely manicurist who gets hallucinations and beats two of her men friends to death. Polanski also wrote and directed the screen version of *Rosemary's Baby,* a film about witchcraft. A consultant for this film was the notorious Satanist, Anton La Vey, who played the devil. After the film was finished, Sharon Tate married Roman Polanski.

In the summer of 1969 Charles Manson's followers crept into the Polanski home and stabbed Sharon Tate and four other people. Before they died, one of the victims asked one of the murderers, "Who are you?"

"I'm the devil," he answered.

A lot of people wondered why Manson's gang committed those horrible murders. I say *you are what you think about.* It wasn't a long step from all those movies about sex and the occult to that bloody death scene in Sharon Tate's bedroom.

In the past, movie stars took pride in their careers. Actors like Gregory Peck, Cary Grant, Gary Cooper, John Wayne, Spencer Tracy, Sidney Poitier, Jane Wyman, Bette Davis, Katharine Hepburn, Janet Leigh and Kathryn Grayson worked hard and long to create real drama and entertainment. Not so today! Now, often the first thing a would-be actor or actress is asked to do in an audition is to take off his clothes. All you seem to need is a good body.

So often that's true in music too. Some rock performances are nothing but invitations to lust. And a lot of modern music—like a lot of movies, television, radio, books and magazines—has become a giant propaganda campaign for drugs, adultery, and demonism. The music of the Beatles and the Rolling Stones helped glorify marijuana and hard drugs. George Harrison, John Lennon, Donovan, the Rolling Stones, Mia Farrow, and Shirley MacLaine created worldwide publicity for the Maharishi Mahesh Yogi. One rock group got so much press coverage that one of the performers said, "I don't see why they would take four mugs like us, who believe in fornication in the streets, and give us all that ink."

And the Rolling Stones have turned out songs with titles like "Let's Spend the Night Together," "Sympathy for the Devil," and "Their Satanic Majesty's Request."

The devil wants to take over your head. Is that what you want?

3

Violence Incorporated

When I was in the gangs in New York, blood and torture, fights and terror were my daily diet. After God reached down through David Wilkerson and lifted me up out of that way of life, I got a jolt when I learned how much violence there was *outside* the ghettos.

The last fourteen years have been a Roman circus of beatings, bombings, tortures, kidnappings, assassinations, massacres, and incredible crimes. Practically every year there has been a dramatic increase in burglaries, robberies, assault, rape, and general law-breaking. The number of crimes in America has more than doubled since 1960—and the sad fact is that most crimes are never reported.

Recently the young grandson of the billionaire J. Paul Getty was kidnapped and held for three million dollars ransom. When the family refused to pay, the kidnappers cut off the boy's ear. He was released when the ransom was put in the extortioners' hands. There seems to be no limit to the wickedness in the world today.

And inhumanity hasn't been cornered by gangsters and loners. Dozens of governments today condone torture to suppress dissent and get information. In Turkey, in Vietnam, and in many other places prisoners have been half-drowned, beaten to the point of

death, and tortured with electrical shocks by intelligence experts
—all in the name of freedom, security, law and order.

One thing I've noticed about the last fourteen years while crime
was increasing so rapidly has been the increase in movies and
TV programs, as well as books and articles in magazines, saturated
with violence. Many people have said there was no connection
between the two. I think they're dead wrong.

How can anyone fill his mind with beatings and killings and
crimes of all kinds and not be affected by it? After Robert Ken-
nedy was assassinated, a National Commission on the Causes and
Prevention of Violence was formed. The commission made a
lengthy study of violence and concluded that violence on TV
encourages violence in the streets. It recommended less program-
ming of violence, removal of violence from children's cartoon
shows, scheduling of crime shows only late in the evening, and
provision for attractive substitutes for the usual TV fare. That
makes a lot of sense.

I can't forget that it was soon after a TV station in Boston
broadcast a show about some teen-agers who set fire to an old
man, that several young people in that city surrounded a woman,
poured gasoline over her, and set her afire. She died after hours
of horrible suffering.

I'm not saying there's anything wrong with TV newscasts. I'm
saying TV should be controlled by parents in the home. Certain
programs should be off limits for children. Each father and
mother should know what their children can or cannot take. TV
serves a very good purpose in educating us on what is happening
in the world today. But like everything else, it can be used or
abused—it can inform or corrupt.

Sometimes when a rock group comes to town it's a signal for
lust and violence to break loose. Because of that some people
blame modern young people for today's violence. Don't think
they are the main cause. Most of the blood-and-thunder-and-sex
films and TV programs are produced not by young people but by
supposedly mature men and women who make their living that

way. I know from experience that some of these porn and violence merchants are "fine" people who live in excellent neighborhoods, belong to respectable organizations, support worthy charities, and raise "nice" families. And if you've ever seen the people buying tickets to a blue movie, you've noticed that many of them aren't young at all, but middle-aged and older. No, in the selling of sex and violence, no one age group has cornered the market. It reaches every part of our society. And it's a problem for all of us.

But I'm not thinking just of the things that make newspaper headlines. The spirit of violence is also the spirit of not caring when someone is in trouble. I think of all the older people suffering in dignified misery—I'll come back to them later. I think of all the people today without jobs and of the children and young people who tell me their parents don't seem to know they exist. I think of the people starving, as I write this, in Africa and Pakistan.

When we hear the morning newscast of things like this, do we *care?* Or do we just reach for another cup of coffee and forget those people are there?

The only real solution to any of our modern problems is to begin where they begin: inside. God knew what He was talking about when He said: "Keep thy heart with all diligence; for out of it are the issues of life" (Proverbs 4:23). Keep your heart warm and sensitive to human need. Keep it sound and straight and uncorrupted, and you've made a good start toward beginning to turn society right side up again.

So listen to what He says in the words of the Apostle Paul:

> Fix your thoughts on what is true and good and right. Think about things that are pure and lovely, and dwell on the fine, good things in others. Think about all you can praise God for and be glad about . . . . and the God of peace will be with you.
>
> Philippians 4:8, 9 LB

Instead of wasting your time on entertainment that leads straight downhill, read some of the great Christian books you can find these days in so many bookstores. Instead of getting curious about things better left unexplored, be curious about why the world is so twisted up and what God wants you to do about it. Think. Pray. Read the Bible. Get together with your Christian friends. Fill your mind and heart with things you can be glad about! Don't leave any room in your life for the things that tear down and corrupt. Let God make you a showcase of the things He wants to give everyone: peace and harmony and rightness and real joy.

4

The Spirit in the Bottle

One route to joy that millions of people try reminds me of a story Aunt Rosa used to tell. Tía Rosa, as we called her, lived all by herself in a tiny house in Las Piedras, Puerto Rico. But her heart was as big as her house was small. She wasn't really my aunt; all the boys and girls in Las Piedras called her that because she treated us all like members of her family. On hot days Tía Rosa gave us all delicious cookies and a cold fruit drink like lemonade, and told us stories. When I was small and I couldn't think of anything else to do I went over to her place sometimes and grabbed as many cookies as I could hold and listened.

The story I'm thinking of started out with a poor fisherman who always seemed to have bad luck. (My editor tells me this story came out of the *Arabian Nights* originally, but I'll tell about it as I remember it.) Every time this fisherman pulled in his net he got something he didn't want—once even a dead horse. But when he was about ready to give up, his net brought in an old copper bottle tightly corked. He pulled out the cork and thought the bottle was empty until smoke started pouring out, and *Wow!* The smoke collected overhead into the shape of a giant! Then the fisherman realized he had uncorked a spirit.

This spirit was a bad one. He told the poor fisherman, who was standing there shaking, that some bad person had put him in the bottle hundreds of years before, stuck in the cork and thrown him in the ocean. For the first century or two, the spirit thought of all the good things he would do for anyone letting him out. But as more centuries passed and he was still stuck, the spirit got more and more mad. Finally he decided he would kill the first person to let him out of his bottle-prison. So the fisherman found he was in worse luck than ever.

The fisherman thought fast. Then he told this giant spirit, boiling up into the sky over his head, that he just couldn't believe such a great being could get into that little bottle. The spirit went back inside to prove it, and the fisherman put the cork back in the bottle fast and threw the spirit back into the ocean.

I think of that story when I hear people worrying about drugs. Drugs are corrupting and destroying so many people today that it makes me sick to think of it. But the awful thing is that too many of the people who worry about drugs don't realize that the worst drug of all is getting into more and more homes, right here in America—Christian homes, too. It's a spirit that hides in a bottle and destroys the person who lets it out.

I mean *booze.*

Maybe you're thinking, "What do you mean, the worst drug of all? Surely you don't mean alcohol is as bad as the other awful drugs being taken today!" I do. I know what alcohol does. But this isn't just my own idea. In 1973 a federal commission finished a million-dollar, two-year study of drugs and reported that Drug Enemy Number One today is not heroin or marijuana or even LSD but *alcohol.*

The National Commission on Marijuana and Drug Abuse said that a lot of the information being given out about drugs today is so incorrect it should be stopped. And it said that a lot of the drug education may only stimulate interest in harmful drugs.

That checks with my own information. One father told me of his thirteen-year-old daughter's report on the drug instruction at her junior high school. She said, "The teacher told us that everyone in our school had tried some kind of drugs. I know that isn't true, because I don't even want to try drugs, and I know some of my friends have never tried drugs either."

That father was angry at his daughter's teacher, and I don't blame him. What a perfect method of tempting young people to try drugs! What boy or girl wants to be in the "inexperienced" minority? It's the same thing with sex. Every so often a school or a teacher somewhere does a little survey of the students' "sex experiences." What young person wants to admit being inexperienced?

The National Commission said the producers of alcohol ought to advertise the *dangers* of drinking, and should not slant their ads toward young people.

How I wish that recommendation were law right now! I'd love to see on every bottle of every alcoholic beverage, on every cocktail list in every restaurant and bar, and in every ad for anything alcoholic, the following warning—accompanied by a big red skull and crossbones:

DANGER

ALCOHOL IS THE MOST DANGEROUS DRUG KNOWN TO MAN. IT TWISTS MINDS. IT IS ADDICTIVE. IT KILLS. USE IT AT YOUR OWN RISK, TO THE MORTAL DANGER OF EVERYONE AROUND YOU.

I'm not going to tell anyone not to drink. It should be enough to point out some things everyone should know about this deadly drug. For one thing, alcohol can be very addictive. The physical risk of addiction to alcohol may be only moderate, but the psychological risk is very high. And it's so deceptive. People claim to drink for relaxation, to get rid of anxiety and tension and to get a feeling of peace and well-being. Before they know it, many drinkers are hooked. Today nine million Americans show all the symptoms of alcoholism, and *many of them don't realize it.*

Alcohol does relax—but it can break down your inhibitions—and moral values. It can also decrease your alertness, reduce your powers of coordination, slow down your thinking processes, and produce drowsiness, dizziness, blurred vision, slurred speech, stupor, nausea—and death. Addiction can reduce your life expectancy by ten years or more.

Like most drugs, it takes larger and larger amounts of alcohol to produce the same effects. Continued excessive use damages the stomach, liver, and brain. It can produce obesity, impotence, delirium tremens, and psychosis. Medical men used to believe that alcohol had some medicinal value. Today most realize it has *none*.

There has been considerable complaint about the amount of money the United States has spent in recent years on welfare, foreign aid, and space exploration. For welfare and space we have been spending about $10 billion a year. But we Americans spend $25 billion a year for booze. And the crime, accidents, and health problems caused by alcoholic misuse cost us countless billions more. Half the accidents in homes are connected with drinking. Many drinkers die every year from fires, falling, shooting accidents, drowning, choking, and freezing to death. Sandy Rogers, the soldier son of Roy and Dale Evans Rogers, tragically choked to death in Germany after his buddies enticed him into an unaccustomed drinking spree.

Heavy drinking lowers a person's resistance to pneumonia and other diseases. Alcohol is a major cause of twenty-eight thousand deaths each year from highway accidents. It is involved in nearly half the arrests, a fifth of the divorces, and a third of the suicides in this country.

Upton Sinclair, the brilliant social crusader and Pulitzer Prize winner, knew a lot of famous people who drank: Jack London, for example, one of the most colorful figures in American history. In his teens he shipped as a sailor to Japan. He panned for gold in the Klondike, became an oyster pirate, newspaper correspondent, and brilliant novelist. In his thirties he wrote his autobiography, entitled *John Barleycorn* because alcohol had played so big a part in his life. (He started drinking when he was five!) But in that book he denied that he was an alcoholic and boasted:

> I was never a drunkard, and I have not reformed . . . . I have decided coolly and deliberately that I should continue to do what I have been trained to want to do. I will drink—but oh, more skill-

fully, more discreetly than ever before. Never again will I be a peripatetic conflagration.

Jack London kept on drinking, kept on alternating between alcohol-induced euphoria and despair, and killed himself at the age of forty.

In his book *The Cup of Fury* Upton Sinclair tells of dozens of such well-known individuals, who all thought they could handle their liquor, but who became its helpless victims. One, not so famous but with a poignant story, was Sinclair's own father, who left home time and again hopeful and happy—and time after time had to be helped home by his teen-age son because he had become a staggering drunkard. Upton Sinclair lost to alcohol's clutches not only his father but three uncles and many friends— seventy-five in all. No wonder he hated and fought against drink all his life!

Once Sinclair went with a friend on a tour of New York behind the scenes. They went from one famous place to another. They stood offstage as the curtains went up on a famous Broadway play. They went into a bar and talked with a justice of the Supreme Court, a professional burglar, a skilled forger, and a New York politician under indictment for his crimes. They toured the night spots.

The thing that impressed Upton Sinclair about all these places was the number of men and women sitting by themselves, drugged, nearly asleep—"having a good time." Describing that night in *The Cup of Fury*, Sinclair adds:

And I thought how many wonderful things there are in this world, so much to do and so much to learn—and so much of it being lost in exchange for the measly, momentary "warm glow" of whiskey.

All my life I have been able to say that I am "drunk without alcohol." To me this universe is one vast mystery story, fascinating beyond any power of words to tell. If I could have my own way, I would stay here a million years to watch what happens.

I am anxious to know "what is going to happen next." I want to know more about what really happened in the past, and I read

5

This Chemical Age

When one of America's largest chemical manufacturers had a run on a certain poster its promotion department distributed, it was discovered that a lot of copies of this poster were being put on the walls of college students' rooms. The poster said in big letters: BETTER LIVING THROUGH CHEMISTRY.

The students, interested in LSD and other drugs, had a little different idea about the value of chemicals than the manufacturer intended!

But we *do* live in a chemical age. Today it seems like there's a pill for everything. Doctors prescribe pills to pick you up and pills to calm you down. There are drugs to make you happy, drugs to make you relaxed, drugs to help you loose weight and drugs to help you gain.

Sometimes I think that this is the generation that can't wait. When we get up in the morning, we can't wait to get going, so we reach for the coffeepot. If the caffeine in two cups of coffee doesn't stimulate fast enough, some people reach for their pickup pills. When we go to bed, we *have* to get to sleep the minute we turn out the lights. If we don't, we are tempted to reach for the sleeping pills.

This passion for speed is one of today's worst corruptors. Everything has to be instant. People used to be able to wait five or ten minutes to cook breakfast cereal. Now most of it is either "quick" (ready in three or four minutes), or "instant" (ready in seconds), or ready to eat. We demand instant breakfasts, instant potatoes, ready-to-eat dinners and ovens that cook everything quicker than quick. We take courses so that we can read with the "speed of light." We're always trying to shorten the time to get somewhere. Once there, we start figuring the fastest way home. And thousands who travel by plane try to obliterate even these few hours by steeping themselves in alcohol.

We live in a drug society! Drugs of all kinds are becoming more accepted every day. Some of these drugs are legal—and some are not.

One thing that stands out about the entertainment world of today is the amount of drugs in it. Janis Joplin was not the only star wiped out by chemicals. After Marilyn Monroe's sudden death, examination of her blood showed that she may have taken a bottleful of sleeping pills. Apparently barbiturates killed the Beatles' youthful manager, Brian Epstein. A good many rock entertainers have admitted that they rely on various drugs for a good performance. Some composers and writers depend on drugs to get "turned on."

But entertainers and creative people aren't the only ones involved with drugs. How shocked many of us were when Diane, the daughter of my dear friend Art Linkletter, jumped to her death from her fifth-story apartment due to an LSD flashback. That experience led Art to intensive research into the whole drug problem and he has campaigned hard to fight this modern menace.

There is so much misinformation today about drugs! If you doubt that, ask a friend to tell you which of the following is the most dangerous, and which the least:

> Glue vapor
> Amphetamines (stimulants, pep pills)
> Alcohol
> Cigarettes
> Barbiturates and narcotics
> Heroin
> LSD and related hallucinatory drugs
> Marijuana

Of course, there could be some debate about that. You already know where I rank alcohol, and how the Federal Commission on Drug Abuse rates it. Another expert is Samuel Irvin, professor of psychopharmacology at the Medical School of the University of Oregon. Professor Irvin specializes in studying the effects of drugs on the mind and body. He says that the intrinsic hazard potential is in *the exact order above*. Sniffing glue is the most dangerous, taking amphetamines the second, and so on down the list.

Let's go down the list ourselves.

Sniffing glue is unspeakably dangerous because the sniffer's first whiffs may be his last. Inhaling certain kinds of glue—and certain aerosol sprays—may irreversibly damage a person's lungs and brain, and even cause sudden death. These things should be kept far from anyone not wise enough to avoid experimenting with them.

Amphetamines are stimulants that can supply a quick pickup. They come in the form of benzedrine, dexedrine, pep pills, "speed," and so on, and are highly dangerous because it is so easy to become addicted—psychologically at the very least—and because of what they can do to a person. Although amphetamines are often prescribed for everything from depression to weight control, excessive use can cause hallucinations, convulsions, and even permanent mental disorders. About half the amphetamines get into the underground market, or are manufactured illegally, so they may be contaminated and therefore doubly dangerous.

Alcohol, the inhalants, the barbiturates, the tranquilizers and the narcotics (Demerol, hashish, heroin and other products of the opium poppy) are depressants. They relax—sometimes to the point of stupor, coma, and death. At the other end of the drug scale are the stimulants—the amphetamines, cocaine, synthetic antidepressants, caffeine, and nicotine.

Tobacco, like alcohol, is so widely used that most smokers would be very surprised if you called them drug addicts. But medically speaking, tobacco is indeed a drug, and cigarettes are among the most harmful substances used by man. The evidence has been piling up for years. In 1957 two scientists named Hammond and Horn presented to the American Medical Society a report they had made for the American Cancer Society. Hammond and Horn studied the smoking habits of two hundred thousand men for nearly four years. Their research showed many more deaths and diseases among the smokers than the nonsmokers. The more cigarettes smoked, the more deaths. When the heavy smokers cut down on their cigarettes, fewer of this group died. A very close correlation was found between cigarette smoking and lung cancer.

It was also discovered that the cigarette smokers died much more often than nonsmokers from emphysema, bronchitis, stomach ulcer, heart disease, hypertension, stomach cancer, and other diseases. These statistics held up regardless of the age, height, weight, IQ, location, education, background, or practically any other relationship of the smokers and nonsmokers. The one clear conclusion of all this research was that *cigarettes are one of the surest killers known.*

Similar investigations have been made in other countries. Research in England, Canada and various other nations shows the same relationship between cigarette smoking and all kinds of disease. Great Britain's Royal College of Surgeons has found that smokers may even be more accident-prone than other people. America's Public Health Service studied more than a million smokers and nonsmokers. It found out that the death rate for smokers is 68 percent higher than the incidence for nonsmokers. The rate is 980 percent higher for cancer of the lung, over 500 percent higher for bronchitis and emphysema! That scares me! I hope it scares everyone who reads this book enough so you'll never be addicted to those little white things that used to be jokingly called "coffin nails." Those two words turn out to be about as literal a description as you can find of the legal drug, the sneaky killer—tobacco.

Every time you puff on a cigarette you're taking into your lungs and bloodstream at least *fifteen known poisons and at least seven substances known to cause cancer.* (More poisons and cancer-starters are suspected but not yet completely proven so in laboratory tests.)

Every week a thousand Americans bleed or burn to death or

die in other ways from highway accidents. At least half those deaths are tied to alcohol abuse. Many of them may relate to smoking, since cigarettes decrease night vision. In any case, while cars kill a thousand people a week, cigarettes kill *seven thousand.* That's more deaths than from heroin!

You've heard of the horrible plagues and epidemics of the past —cholera, typhoid, and so on. Would you believe that all those epidemics in Western Europe since the start of the sixteenth century, and all the known epidemics of yellow fever in the history of the world, killed less people than cigarettes kill *every year* in this country? It's true! Please, don't let cigarettes become nails in *your* coffin.

Right here you may be wondering why I haven't said more about drugs like marijuana and LSD and heroin. I wish I had the space! There just isn't room in this book for all I'd like to say about such drugs. Let me mention, though, that David Wilkerson has put together a lot of valuable information about a good many dangerous drugs in his book *Hey, Preach . . . You're Comin' Through!* Read it for some good straight talk on the subject.

Let me just say this about marijuana, since there's so much talk today of legalizing it: **Pot is a corruptor, too.** For many young people, a stick of marijuana is often the first step down the awful trail toward hopeless addiction to the hardest and worst kinds of drugs. And recent medical evidence shows that steady marijuana smokers may become apathetic and confused, and suffer from personality changes and even brain damage.

About heroin, I hope by now everyone knows how dangerous it is. If everyone who has been ruined by heroin could come back from their graves and ghetto holes and speak, what horrible stories they could tell! Maybe such stories are summed up in these words which were found scribbled on a piece of paper in the pocket of a young woman who committed suicide:

> King Heroin is my shepherd.
> I shall always want.

He maketh me to lie down in the gutters.
He leadeth me beside the troubled waters.
He destroyeth my soul.
He leadeth me in the paths of wickedness.
Yea, I shall walk through the valley of poverty.
I will fear no evil for thou, Heroin, art with me.
Thy Needle and Capsule comfort me.
Thou strippest the table of groceries in the
    presence of my family.
Thou robbest my head of reason.
My cup of sorrow runneth over.
Surely heroin addiction shall stalk me all the
    days of my life, and I will dwell in the
    House of the damned forever.

The girl who wrote that was twenty-three when she killed herself. What a testimony!

It's really depressing to study the effects of practically any of these mind-bending substances. With the depressant drugs the results often are stupor, nausea, blurred vision, a thick tongue, confusion, impotence, unconsciousness, and finally death. With the hallucinogens and the stimulants the effects range from anxiety and panic to irritability, insomnia, delusions, damage to the mind and body, and again, death. It's destruction all the way!

And I'm not at all happy about reports that many young people today are turning away from illicit drugs to legal ones like alcohol. Their parents may be less worried, but the fact is, few people realize how dangerous alcohol and tobacco can be. The important thing to keep in mind is that they are *drugs*.

Let me tell you about Bart, who grew up in a university town in Europe. Through the students he was introduced early to various drugs.

When he was seventeen, Bart had a weird experience. Crossing a field, he suddenly had a vision of the sky splitting open and dropping balls of fire onto the earth, setting fire to everything they touched. Another time, driving along the Baltic coast, he felt that there was going to be an earthquake that would swallow him and everything around him.

Psychiatrists traced these hallucinations to Bart's experiments with drugs. For a time they felt he was schizophrenic, but in recent years, as he has left drugs behind, he has remarkably improved.

Bart said recently: "I don't trust a single thing that can alter the mind. I'm convinced now, from my own experience, that every single drug, including alcohol and pot, is extremely dangerous. Tell everyone you know, never fool around with your mind."

Yes, the whole drug business, legal or illegal, is one of the monstrous evils of our age. You could call this an age of drugs. Today there's a pill for everything. Doctors prescribe a pill to pick you up and a pill to calm you down. Millions of men and women are hooked on cigarettes and cocktails, on amphetamines to get going in the morning, and barbiturates to get to sleep, and don't even realize it.

Fortunately, many people are concerned about this problem of increasing drug addiction. (Though I don't hear as much alarm about the tendency in so many areas to lower the drinking age.) But how many are asking *why* so many turn to drugs? Why do we so often look at the *surface* of our problems, and so seldom at the real causes?

For one thing, there has been entirely too much publicity that has been more harmful than helpful. It's not enough to tell people how awful drugs are. They don't scare today any more than their grandparents and great-great-grandparents did when the preachers and temperance lecturers were all denouncing Demon Rum. Describing the awful effects of drugs like heroin and LSD has created a lot of unhealthy curiosity. It reminds me of the mother who told her children as she left them alone in the house, "Don't put any beans in your nose." The children would never have thought of such a thing if their mother hadn't given them the idea. As it was, they kept thinking of her parting words, and before long they found some beans. They had to find out what it felt like to stick beans up their noses, and when the mother got home every last child had beans stuck in his nose!

That's something like today's drug problem. All the publicity about crime and drug addiction and illicit sex and other related evils has led a good many people to try some of them to see what they might have been missing. That may be a stupid reaction, but I'm afraid it's also human nature. What we most need today is not so much more *information*—helpful as some of it may be, when properly presented—as more *desire to serve the Lord and help other people*. That's where every Christian can help.

To understand today's drug scene, let's look at what life was like when I was in the gangs of New York City. I *know* why so many of the gang members took pot and smack. Everyone in the gangs had this terrible feeling of emptiness, loneliness, sadness, and frustration. Drugs gave one kind of security and peace, and sometimes thrills which helped us forget the emptiness inside.

To many of us in the New York gangs, life often looked like one big hoax. We saw the hustlers and pushers driving around in Cadillacs, the cops and judges they paid off, and the decent people living in squalor and fear. We figured the one sure way to get ahead was to grab quickly all you could. It's not easy to see much future in that environment. So grab a reefer or a bottle or a needle and float off for a little while on some rosy cloud of temporary happiness! The tragedy of it all is that the trip is always so short, and you always hit so hard when you come down, and drugs write off your few chances to find anything better in life.

Our whole culture has a big empty spot in the middle. Unless Christ fills that spot, it's going to be filled with some counterfeit saviour.

Do you want to know why I don't need drugs of any kind? Because I've found a way to get everything they can provide, and much more. Would you like more energy, more zest in life, bigger thrills than you ever dreamed possible? One teen-ager who had been hooked on a number of drugs explained why he became interested in Christ. He met some young people from a Christian coffeehouse in New Milford, New Jersey. This is what he said about them:

> See, these kids came along and wanted to rap, and that was okay with me. I didn't mind—I was high on "coke." But five hours later my high was gone, and those kids were still high—on Jesus! Man, I tell you, that made me think. Now I'm all the way into Jesus, because He gives you a high that never lets you down.

But suppose you need a downer. Maybe you're too keyed up and you can't sleep. Don't reach for a sleeping pill. Instead, lie back and just meditate on the wonderful fact that the Lord is your Shepherd and Friend. You can never solve all your problems, but He can. Praise Him for that! Thank Him that He has everything under control. Let truths like that sink into your heart and mind, and you'll find a peace "which is far beyond human understanding," sweeping through your soul (*see* Philippians 4:7 TEV).

Dangerous as drugs are, there are worse problems today. Right now a good many young people are turning away from drugs. Many young people are very intelligent about the mind-benders; they know drugs can blow a mind sky-high. So the use of drugs may be decreasing.

Too many young people are turning instead to witchcraft and the occult.

6

The Occult

I wrote my last book *Satan on the Loose* because it has been impressed on me that one of the most corrupting forces in the world today is the occult. Fascination with this dark side of the supernatural is sweeping through every country and every area of life. Once such interest was limited to five-dollar fortune-tellers in back alleys and to séances in small dark rooms where desperately searching men and women tried to make contact with someone they had lost in death. Not any more! Today the occult is big business. Books, movies, games, schools—everyone seems to be trying to cash in on the tremendous interest in the supernatural.

It's very interesting that so many people who should know better are getting involved in the occult today. For many, God has been booted out the front door—but Satan and witchcraft and all the rest have sneaked in through the back door. On an airplane flight between Tucson and Dallas I sat next to a woman who was reading a book of astrology. When she saw me glance at her book she said, "You look like a Capricorn."

"You're right," I said, "but I have something better than astrology." Then I told her that I don't need to find out what influences the stars may have on my life, for I know the One who holds the stars in the hollow of His hand. This lady looked very uncomfortable as I talked about Jesus. I've found truth so often in what Paul said:

> Don't be teamed with those who do not love the Lord, for
> what do the people of God have in common with people of
> sin? How can light live with darkness? And what harmony
> can there be between Christ and the devil?
>
> 2 Corinthians 6:14, 15 LB

So many people who feel they are too modern or intelligent to
believe in the Bible, accept the most ridiculous things if they
have an occult label. The late Bishop James Pike at one time
seemed to be a serious Christian thinker. Then he began doubting
different things in the Christian faith. At one point he said that
he could *sing* the Apostles's Creed but that he could not con-
scientiously *say* it—because he could no longer accept what it said.

Bishop Pike may have first gotten interested in spiritualism soon
after he became an Episcopal priest. He heard strange noises in
his parsonage in Poughkeepsie, New York. Candles which he lit
were mysteriously extinguished, according to Hans Holzer, and
once he collided with a bat. Later, in New York and England, he
heard more strange noises and found books and other objects
inexplicably moved about behind locked doors.

Bishop Pike gave spiritualism and occultism a tremendous
boost when he took part in a television séance with the famous
medium, Arthur Ford. Through this and other dealings with mediums here and abroad, the Bishop exposed millions of people to
the false claims of this so-called religion which has often been
mixed up in all kinds of fakery and deceit. It seems a fitting end
to his career that when Bishop Pike was lost in a desert in Israel,
his wife contacted various mediums—some of whom said he was
alive and well, although it was soon discovered that he was dead.

When Bishop Pike questioned the Trinity he probably felt he
was being very modern, but actually I wonder if he was not slipping backward into the worst kinds of superstition. If I have to
choose between believing in the Trinity or believing in mediums,
I don't want to have to put my trust in mediums.

While I was writing this chapter, a friend brought me an
advertisement from a well-known book club. PUT THE POWER OF

THE OCCULT AT YOUR COMMAND! the advertisement says. There
follows a magical mixture of books, tarot cards, numerology
games, astrology charts, everything imaginable to involve people
in the occult. Everywhere things of this kind are coming out into
the open. In the streets of Rome and Los Angeles witches march,
demanding the right to practice their bestial rites openly. In England and Europe graves are opened, tombstones are broken,
churches are desecrated, debasing acts are performed. In America,
Satan is worshiped! More and more psychics are winning popular
approval. In California a man with allegedly psychic powers,
Uri Geller, recently came to Stanford University to try to prove
that his powers exist. It is claimed that Uri can read minds, bend
keys and snap spoons without touching them, and even repair
watches by unknown powers. He says that he does not think such
power comes from his mind: "I believe it is generated through me
by an intelligent power in the universe. I believe in God, but I
do not believe this is coming from God."

If Uri Geller's strange abilities come from some intelligent
power in the universe which is not God . . . *what is that power?*

In *Satan on the Loose* I mentioned the forms of the occult that
are ensnaring so many people today. I keep hearing of new examples all the time. A bright, attractive college student recently
reported her experiences as a witch. Ron Hutchcraft of *Campus
Life* interviewed this girl, Roberta Blankenship, and asked what
first attracted her to witchcraft. This was her answer:

> The funny thing is, I wasn't really attracted to it. It just sort
> of happened to me. It began at a junior high school slumber party
> when someone suggested we try a séance, just for fun. I didn't
> know how to run one, but I agreed to try. That night I began to
> realize some unusual power, and I decided to develop it. I started
> experimenting.

The occult power which Roberta was now contacting appealed
to her because she hated her environment and wanted revenge:

> My life at home was very violent. My mother and stepfather
> were constantly drinking and fighting, and it got pretty physical
> sometimes. I began to pity myself, and I lapsed into deep depres-
> sion, resenting my family. I wanted to hurt because I'd been hurt.

The séance led to more:

> My friends and I began to get little signs we were "making contact"—like a knock on the wall or something. Then we started to hear vocal correspondence . . . kids could recognize them as the voices of departed people. On some occasions there were visual formations—not solid figures, but with human features that identified them as male or female faces.
>
> The deeper we got into the occult, the more frightened the other kids became. Many were scared off.

But not Roberta. She enjoyed the strange powers.

> I led groups in the use of levitation and ouija boards. I stressed that we always use the ouija boards without hands to avoid human manipulation. This was no game to me.
>
> Soon I was into astrology and horoscopes. My girlfriends were impressed with these new fields, but I thought people were really being fooled by horoscopes—most were simple common sense and could apply to anyone. After astrology it was palmistry, Tarot cards, and the crystal ball.
>
> During this time I was having psychic visions that foretold the future. I even lost friends when the visions became true—they were getting very frightened of me. They heard me predict things like Robert Kennedy's assassination, my sister being hit by a car and numerous incidents in kids' lives. By that time, the word was really spread around school—Roberta is a witch.

Ron Hutchcraft asked Roberta whether she ever used her powers to hurt someone. Sometimes she did:

> . . . against people who were against me. I found I could cause accidents, illnesses and misfortune for people by using hexes. That is black magic. But I never *told* anyone about the hex—people can get psyched out by that and *cause* it to happen. I did it quietly and then sat back to watch my power work.

Roberta was invited to join a coven of witches, but refused because she felt their witchcraft was weak. The witches ascribed their power to the devil or some other deity; Roberta felt that her power was all her own!

Still, all that power didn't satisfy her. "My messed-up world wasn't changing. My home was still full of hate; I had no close friends. In fact, I attempted suicide."

At home, alone, she picked up a butcher knife to cut her wrists when she envisioned demons shouting with a single voice: "Roberta, you fool. *I* gave you all your powers." The demonic entity declared that Roberta was its slave as long as she lived, that she would not die until it was through with her. On that day Roberta Blankenship promised to worship and serve the devil.

But nothing she did helped make her into the kind of person she wanted to become. She was suspicious, violent, conceited, often depressed, and full of hate. "I trusted no one. . . . I got lonelier because of my hate. . . . I was sure that love was a lie."

Finally Roberta found a friend who loved her, a friend she could trust.

> I invited Christ into my life personally, and things really began to change. My hatred vanished, and an unexplainable love began to grow for the people I had hated. Because I stopped pitying myself, I was ready to reach out and help people.
>
> I found in Christ a Friend I could totally trust . . . Someone who really cared about me with no selfish motives. I reached the end of my loneliness and unhappiness and reached out to Him. And I discovered that Jesus is still the great Healer . . . not physically, in my case, but emotionally. He healed my wracked-up emotions.

Another thing Roberta found through Christ was more power. In witchcraft she had been obsessed with the idea of getting power; in Christ she found something far better:

> The Holy Spirit provides all of God's good power . . . but it's *power without bondage.* I lived all my life in the occult under an unseen whip that I wouldn't admit to. And I was responsible for many things that were wrong, things that hurt a lot of people. But Jesus offers forgiveness because He died for those things. In

essence, Jesus said after I trusted Him, "Roberta, don't look back."
You know, I never will.

Ron asked Roberta what she thought about young people who
fool around with séances, Ouija boards, and the like, with no intention of getting involved in anything evil. She said that she
knew there were such groups in many high schools, but she also
knew they were playing with something worse than fire:

> Take it from me, those things are much more than fun and
> games. They are the door to a strange world that sucks you right
> in. You taste a little—just for fun—and you want to come back for
> more. You just don't realize how deep you're going or how seri-
> ous it is. That's why the Bible says, "Don't give a place to the
> devil." He needs only a foothold to launch his takeover.

I've been impressed very much in the last few weeks with how
great the gulf is between Christ and Satan—and how sharply we
have to draw the line if we're going to be on the side of God and
Christ. Lois Hoadley Dick of Newton, New Jersey, has told of
her friend Janet who visited a gathering of spiritualists. Terribly
depressed when she arrived and sorry she had come, Janet started
repeating to herself the promise of 1 John 1:7, ". . . the blood of
Jesus Christ his Son, cleanseth us from all sin."

The leader tried several times to begin the séance, without
success. Finally he announced, "There is someone here who is
hindering the service. I cannot do anything until you leave." So
Janet got up and walked out. She realized she had come to a
place where she had no right to be, and apparently the spiritualists could not coexist with the blood of Christ.

Just before the Super Bowl football game in January, 1974, a
group of psychics and astrologers was asked who was going to
win—the Minnesota Vikings or the Miami Dolphins. There was
heavy enthusiasm for a Viking victory, based a lot on Coach Bud
Grant's star signs. "My vibrations tell me that his spirit is going
to prevail," said Houston occultist Sister Rainbow.

Well, those vibrations were wrong. The Vikings fought hard—

but what could they do against that unstoppable Dolphin machine? Some of my Christian friends and I often pray for the players as we watch games like that one. Admiring players on both teams, I wished there were some way *both* sides could win Super Bowl VIII. But of course only one team can win the Vince Lombardi Trophy, and the Dolphins' 24 to 7 victory proved once again that the psychics can be completely wrong.

It's a sign of the times that all that publicity was given to those psychics. Why should it be? Only because so many of us are so gullible that we'll listen to anyone who prattles about planetary conjunctions and mystical vibrations.

The movie *The Exorcist* is a shocking portrayal of the satanic possession of a twelve-year-old girl. Her face, her language and her actions become unspeakably repulsive as the devil takes control of her mind and body. Some of the people who stood in line for hours to see this picture said they wanted to see the child vomit on the priest; others, to see her masturbate with a crucifix. I wonder how many in the crowds who flocked to watch *The Exorcist* knew that it was based on fact. In 1949 a teen-age child in Maryland had a very similar possession, and the demon invader was finally exorcised by a Jesuit priest.

Just as *The Exorcist* was hitting the movie theaters, strange noises frightened workers remodeling a house in Texas. The house, known as "Devil's Corner," was said to have been used for pagan worship. A priest was called in to drive out the demonic presence.

And about the same time, a priest in California told of being called upon for help when a family was harassed by strange incidents. Fires started mysteriously in different parts of the home. Religious statues were destroyed. Knives and glasses sailed through the air when there was nothing to move them. Members of the family felt themselves seized by the throat and knocked unconscious. The priest performed the ceremony of exorcism fourteen times. The Archbishop of San Francisco said that after this the family found peace and relief.

The occult world is a many-headed monster, and every head sprouts from a single source—Satan. Don't fool around with astrology, reincarnation, gurus, spiritualism, inner visions, mystic auras, astral travel, Ouija, witchcraft, or anything of the kind. All of it is from below, not from above—from the devil, not from God.

Today I'm conscious as never before of the way the forces of evil are lined up against the powers of God. I predict that in the months ahead, occultism will enter more and more of our whole society. The stage is being set. In this twentieth century since Jesus came, a lot of people have turned from God to science to solve their problems. Now, with more and more shortages of the things we need, with our scientific achievements threatening to destroy us, men and women realize that science can't solve all their problems either, and they are looking for some other saviour. Strange occult forces beckon. I believe they will continue to trap many more victims. Don't let them trap *you!*

Take no part in the worthless pleasures of evil and darkness, but instead rebuke and expose them.

Ephesians 5:11 LB

7

A Necessary Evil?

While I was speaking at a church college, one student came to see me about a problem. He told me: "You know, in this school you can do just about anything you want to. I've slept with five different girls in the last month. I've got a hang-up on sex. I love it!"

"Sex is a wonderful gift of God," I said. "Why do you want to make it low and dirty?"

"But I don't," this young fellow said. "Sex isn't dirty!"

"Of course it isn't," I said. "Neither is a flower. But if you pull up a beautiful flower by the roots and drop it on your dinner plate, you won't want to eat from that plate until it's washed. There's nothing wrong with the flower—it's just in the wrong place.

"Sex outside of marriage is in the wrong place. I like sex as much as you, but I love Jesus! If you love Him, He has to be first. After you've had sex, how do you feel? During the experience you may feel great because your emotions take over. But afterward, when your mind and your conscience have a chance to get back to work, you know you've done wrong, don't you? You defiled yourself and the girl. Let God keep you clean!"

I know it's not easy to do that in this age, when the devil seems to be using every trick in his book to turn things around and make black look white, and young people especially are exposed to temptations of which our grandparents couldn't have dreamed. Recently a number of people were startled by the frank confessions of a teen-age girl. At thirteen, Joyce Maynard joined a youth group in a liberal church where the young people tried reading the Bible, but—as she reported in an article in the *New York Times Magazine* (April 23, 1972, "An 18-Year-Old Looks Back on Life")—"the Old Testament had no power. We gave up on Genesis and rapped, instead, with a casual college student who started class saying, 'Man, do I have a hangover!' "

Then the group discovered sensitivity training: "Now the group held weekly, nonverbal communication sessions, with lots of hugging and feeling that boosted attendance to triple what it had been in our old save-the-world days."

Marijuana, said Joyce, was smoked by nearly everyone in her high school. "Drugs took on a disproportionate importance. Why was it I could spend half a dozen evenings with someone without his ever asking me what I thought of Beethoven or Picasso but always, in the first half hour, he'd ask me whether I smoked?"

At eighteen Joyce Maynard entered Yale:

> The freshman women's dorm at Yale has no house mother. We have no check-in hours or drinking rules or punishments for having boys in our rooms past midnight. A guard sits by the door to offer, as they assured us at the beginning of the year, physical —not moral—protection. All of which makes it easy for many girls who feel, after high-school curfews and dating regulations, suddenly liberated. (The first week of school last fall, many girls stayed out all night, every night, displaying next morning the circles under their eyes the way some girls show off engagement rings.)
>
> We all received the *Sex at Yale* book, a thick, black pamphlet filled with charts and diagrams and a lengthy discussion of contraceptive methods. And at the first women's assembly, the discussion moved quickly from course-signing-up procedures to gynecology, where it stayed for much of the evening. Somebody raised her hand to ask where she could fill her pill prescription, someone else wanted to know about abortions. There was no standing in the middle any more—you had to either take out a pen and paper

and write down the phone numbers they gave out or stare stonily ahead, implying that those were numbers you certainly wouldn't be needing. From then on in it seemed the line had been drawn.

But of course the problem is that no lines, no barriers, exist. Where, five years ago a girl's decisions were made for her (she had to be in at 12 and, if she was found—in—with her boyfriend . . .); today, the decision rests with her alone. She is surrounded by knowledgeable, sexually experienced girls and if she isn't willing to sleep with her boyfriend, somebody else will. It's peer-group pressure, 1972 style—the embarrassment of virginity.

That's pretty frank language for a Christian book, isn't it? I've quoted it because for too long Christians have been so nicey-nice we haven't dared even talk about some of the real problems of life. And adults haven't had any idea what it's like to grow up in this sex-saturated age.

Let me throw out a few facts:

- A sign on the desk of a college dean asks passing students HAVE YOU HAD YOUR PILL TODAY?

- A college official, asked about students' sexual relationships, answers, "It's no concern of ours who sleeps with whom."

- It is the accepted thing in a number of universities for boys to sleep with their dates in their dormitory rooms on weekends.

- The book *The Student Guide to Sex on Campus* has received official approval on many campuses.

- Some parents let their teen-age children sleep at home with their friends of the opposite sex.

- Less than half of the teen-agers in America are virgins; 70 percent believe there is nothing immoral about sex before marriage.

- An increasing number of young women are having babies outside of marriage, while abortions are at an all-time high.

- Homosexuals and lesbians are making more and more blatant demands for acceptance, recognition, and "equal rights" to employment by groups (such as police and fire departments) which do not tend to welcome such people into their ranks.

- Venereal disease is spreading so fast that it is now recognized as a public epidemic.

- An article appeared in the March 28, 1974 issue of the *Raleigh Times,* a Raleigh, North Carolina newspaper, "Sex Offers Elderly Release From Anxiety." It stated that there should be a more tolerant attitude taken towards the patients in nursing homes. A room should be set aside for sex to offer the elderly the kind of relief that most people get from tranquilizers, alcohol, eating, and violent behavior. We should consider the therapeutic value of sex activity among the elderly. Tolerance should extend to homosexuality and sex between unmarried persons by mutual consent.

When I was speaking in New York recently I took a walk across town. Three young women in extrarevealing dresses smiled their invitations. A burly man and one with slim hips came down the street holding hands. A huckster blared from a doorway, "See the skin flicks. A live sex show after every movie. Everything you ever wanted to know about sex, performed before your eyes!" Bookshop windows were crammed with books and magazines so luridly explicit I felt embarrassed to be near them.

All this may be a bit more blatant in New York than in most cities, but the same kind of thing can be found in every part of the world. There seems to be a never-satisfied demand for more nudity, more sex, more perversion, more debasement. Movies, books, magazines, and shows banned a few years ago seem mild compared to what is produced and shown today.

I've already discussed the pornography so prevalent today. But don't blame the porn merchants alone for all this. Our whole society is sex-crazed, according to more than one observer, and I have to agree. Our moral standards keep slipping.

Venereal disease is on a rampage. Gonorrhea is becoming a national epidemic. Gonorrhea, sometimes called "clap" or "morning dew," can produce heart disease, arthritis, eye inflammation, blood poisoning, and pelvic and intestinal disease. A pregnant girl who has gonorrhea may give birth to a blind child.

The other leading venereal disease—which means disease spread through sexual relations—is syphilis, which is also approaching the epidemic stage. Syphilis may cause paralysis, insanity, blindness, heart disease, sterility, and even death. It too can produce blindness and other diseases in babies.

Venereal disease is passed from one person to another by sexual intercourse (and sometimes by contaminated hypodermic needles). VD is growing and spreading like a monster. It is destroying our teens.

There is a widespread idea today that sex isn't any more important than a handshake, and therefore that most of the laws and principles safeguarding marriage and the home are ready for the scrap heap. In one popular motion picture a group of college students is encouraged in sexual promiscuity by the administration; the words *marriage* and *adultery* are passed off as "no longer meaningful." When one student asks a faculty member why the teacher and her husband don't take part in the school's sexual experiment, she replies that it's up to the new generation to revolutionize sex: "We represent the past. You represent the future."

A British sex-education film aimed at adolescents shows a twenty-three-year-old teacher masturbating and generally endorses promiscuity.

Joyce Maynard is right. The whole idea of sexual purity is so often ridiculed today, and popping into bed with practically anyone is accepted so widely as good and right, that virginity seems embarrassing.

Well, what can we do about it? One of the problems is that Christians sometimes act as though sex is a *necessary evil*—something you have to admit is a fact, but something you say as little about as possible. I know of one young man who came to know the Lord and went to a Bible college. There, late one night, he

was sharing his problems and temptations with other students
and several ministers. This boy asked for prayer as he confessed
the temptations and pressures that came to him sexually. He was
stunned when there was a long silence, followed by several criti-
cisms for speaking so frankly. He was stunned most of all because
not a single person present would admit that he had any such
sexual impulses or needs.

So often sex is presented as though it's unnatural, or at best a
means to something else—so seldom as something God created,
right and beautiful in the proper setting—a tremendous gift.
Christian sex education is so needed today, and so seldom found!
When the Bible's teaching about sex is given, too often it is presented through the sins of David and Bathsheba, Solomon, Samson, and so on.

The church ought to emphasize instead the positive side of
sex! Think of the normal, happy married life of Abraham and
Sarah, Boaz and Ruth, Joseph and Mary. Think of Jesus' presence
at the famous wedding in Cana. Think of His words:

> But from the beginning of the creation God made them
> male and female. For this cause shall a man leave his father
> and mother, and cleave to his wife; And they twain shall be
> one flesh: so then they are no more twain, but one flesh.
> What therefore God hath joined together, let not man put
> asunder.
>
> Mark 10:6—9

That is beautiful! Sex at its best, as God meant it to be, is the
union and the sharing of two lives in a relationship so intimate
and wonderful that it is hard to describe. It is indeed a blessed
gift.

But pornographic pictures and movies make sex seem ugly
and dirty. They ruin its meaning. All these pictures make a big
thing of positions, of the sex act in itself. Such pornography stirs
the minds of the mentally ill and degrades the beauty of this
gift of God.

I am very disturbed at the attitudes of many people concerning this area. Sinners are not the only ones who know how to make love. Christians are not square! They have human desires and passions like anyone else. I don't have to pray before making love. I can enjoy sex as much as anyone. Sexual relations are very beautiful, thrilling and satisfying—with the right person.

The right person for me is my wife. The right sexual partner for you is your wife or husband. I'm not being preachy when I say that, but there are a lot of hang-ups in evangelists and pastors today. They get so involved in their work that they forget that they have a woman beside them; a woman (their wife) who has a right to be satisfied. They get so tired that they have no time for their wives. They feel so holy that they have no time to touch their wives. This is permissible if husband and wife are fasting, but man and wife should not separate themselves all of the time.

I admit that I can be tempted as much as anyone else. It's like going into a bank. I may wish I had all that money, but that's a long way from holding up the bank or walking out with a stolen roll of hundred-dollar bills in my pocket. I know that money belongs to someone else! I can appreciate the good looks of another woman, but she's not mine and sex outside of marriage is not right, and all the "new morality" in the world will never make it right.

I hear of so many hang-ups from Christian women. Some of them have the wrong concept of marriage. There is nothing in the Bible that tells you that you should do this or that, or that you should not do something else, in the privacy of your marriage. My wife has personal desires. I am her man. She desires to be touched and/or caressed by me. She knows that I am hers and she is mine. She does not have to ask me to make love to her, and she doesn't tell me that she wants me to make love to her: she just provokes me into it. She has no hang-ups in this area because she has a perfect right to be aggressive. Both partners should be aggressive—which makes for a more desirable relationship. There is nothing wrong with a good wife being a "tiger" in bed and a lady on the street. There is also nothing in the Bible that says

you should have sexual relations any number of times a month.
A couple may have sexual relations as often as they desire. The
Bible says to be considerate of the other person's body. Some of
the things a wife could do to "turn her husband on" is perhaps to
wear a sexy nightgown, have a fresh breath, and have a clean,
but not stifling, fragrance. Bad odors are repulsive.

Jesus does not teach us techniques. When two people are
joined together in the sight of God in holy matrimony, they become one. No position nor method of intercourse is wrong. It is
not my business to tell anyone how to make love—I'm only saying
that anything a husband and wife do during their intimate times
together is acceptable to God. You don't have to read a dirty
book or see a dirty film to get turned on. Some adults actually do
this and then switch husbands and wives to satisfy their physical
desires. This is all wrong!

Many books are written, filled with a lot of advice on how to
make love. I will not accept any such book nor watch any film
of this kind.

The intimate relationship between husband and wife in sex is
beautiful. There is nothing in any way filthy or ugly about it. The
human body is to be desired and enjoyed in the marital act. Sex
is like a fine dessert after a good meal—without any calories.

Thank God for this marvelous gift of sex. Don't let anything
cheapen it for you or yours. Real committed Christian marriages
witness to the fact that sex enjoyment went way up after Christ
was the center of their marriage. Many Spirit-filled Christian
couples are testifying to this great truth and witnessing to new
pleasure in sex life as their marriage in Christ grows.

Young Christian wives and husbands also witness to the teach-
ings of Jesus in the Bible that will make them more attractive to
each other. A man or woman who loves the Lord can be taught
by God Himself to be more beautiful to his or her spouse than
ever before.

8

Gay Isn't Happy

It was the end of a crusade I had held in a famous tourist city. Most of the young people who had come forward to talk to me had gone home. Then a teen-age girl I had noticed waiting at one side came up to me.

She was one of the most beautiful girls I have ever seen. While she began speaking, a reporter from the local daily kept looking at her as though he'd been bewitched. A cleaning man crossed the coliseum with his broom—and turned back, unable to tear his eyes away from this girl's face. Three young men who had started out the door came back and stared.

"Nicky," she said, tossing her long golden hair out of her blue eyes, "I dig guys. Girls too. What's wrong with that?"

"You mean sex?" I said. I knew what her answer would be.

"Sure," she said. "I'm bisexual. I like it. What's wrong with it?"

"Why do you ask me?"

"Well . . .", she stopped. "I liked what you said tonight. I guess the way I live doesn't fit, you know, what you said about accepting Jesus."

"You've got it!" I went over the Gospel again in a few words. "You'll have to choose between Jesus and whatever takes the place of Jesus in your life."

"It's not easy," she said with tears in the blue eyes. "I'd like to give my life to Jesus, but sex is so strong."

"Very strong. But if you take Jesus, you're not on your own. Keep close to Him, and He'll help you every step of the way."

I prayed with this girl. Before she stopped praying, she was crying, and there were tears in my eyes, too. I could feel God struggling with Satan for the soul of that girl, and it was a beautiful moment when she cried out, "Praise the Lord!" I knew she was delivered. A letter from her just a few days ago contained this sentence:

> Ever since that night I found Christ, there has been a real difference in my life. I've been tempted to go back to the old ways, many times, but every time Jesus has given me the victory. They say lesbians and gays can't be changed. Well, Jesus has made me a completely new person.

Homosexuality isn't new, but it used to be underground. Today it is coming out into the open. All over the world, gays are campaigning for recognition and acceptance. They have their own clubs and bars. They are turning out propaganda to make their twisted attitude toward life look normal and right. At a recent meeting of the National Education Association, one teacher announced a gay caucus.

And—God help us!—the homosexuals are even creating their own gay *churches*. When such a church was chartered recently in Boston, one minister stood with his arm around his homosexual lover, while another minister, a woman, embraced her lesbian mate. At the Communion service that followed, the gay lovers present were invited to take the Communion elements together.

The worshipers in a New York church were startled one Sunday morning to see behind the altar a large painting of two nude homosexual couples. The painting was there as a backdrop for a play about homosexuality that was performed soon afterward at the church.

Early in 1974 a national magazine printed a news item about a school for homosexuals that opened in San Francisco. This school has been flooded with requests for information on how to enroll. In the same magazine there was a news report about the gay "marriage" of two black men. Only a year before, the male "bride" had entered into another homosexual union that (like many such alliances) lasted only a short time.

Things like this are becoming so common nowadays that they are hardly news any more—unless they're connected with something supersensational. Recently the worst mass murders in history were uncovered near Houston, Texas. A detective said, "The place was wall-to-wall bodies." Investigators dug up the corpses of dozens of young men who had been homosexually assaulted and tortured. Soon after that, a nationwide homosexual ring was discovered operating out of another city. The operators published pictures and descriptions of young boys for the benefit of men all over the country who were the "customers." Some of the pictures found at the gang's headquarters had the word KILL written across them. The reason: these particular boys had been "uncooperative."

There's a tide of permissiveness today, a trend to accept any kind of sexual deviation and label it normal and right. I was asked to speak to my own state legislature recently when a bill was introduced to legalize practically all forms of sexual behavior except rape. Let me make it clear where I stand on such things. There is no question that in God's eyes homosexuality is not right, it is not just a sickness, *it is dead wrong.* That's what the Bible says in many references, and if you're a Christian you have to accept what the Bible says. Homosexuality is a sin—I'll say more about this later—and the wages of sin is death. Often, death very literally, as the news reports I've referred to show.

But homosexuality, like anything else, doesn't just happen. Why is it increasing today? One reason is what is happening in the home. Families are not what they used to be. Too many fathers, and mothers too, are gone from home too often. When a boy has no strong father to look up to and model his life after, when a girl doesn't learn from her mother how a woman should live, when children have to be on their own, emotionally, too early, they can become confused and grow up with distorted attitudes and confused values.

Right on! God hates homosexuality, but He loves homosexuals as much as anyone else. If you are not convinced whether homosexuality is right or wrong, let me tell you about two men who spent the night in a city with a wild reputation. The two visitors were straight. A lot of the men in the city were openly gay. When they heard that there were visitors in town, they shouted, "Bring out those men to us so we can rape them."

The man who owned the house where the visitors were staying told the gays, "Please, fellows, don't do such a wicked thing. Look —I have two virgin daughters, and I'll surrender them to you to do with as you wish. But leave these men alone!"

The gays wouldn't listen. So full of unnatural lust they weren't satisfied with the substitute, they tried to break into the house to attack the visitors.

What happened next you will find in Genesis 19: 10–25. (The above conversation is from the *Living Bible* paraphrase, verses 4–9.) Fire fell from heaven on that wicked city and it went up in smoke and destruction. If you wanted to see the city's remains today you would have to fly to Israel and look underneath the Dead Sea. The city's name was Sodom—a name forever after linked with depraved sex. The fate of the immoral cities of Sodom and Gomorrah is a warning of the fate that lies ahead for Sodomites, Lesbians, and others who cling to homosexual sin instead of to Christ.

If you want to know more about the real meaning of homosexuality, read the first chapter of Romans. There you'll see the descent of man into pride, idolatry and gross sin.

Because men are such fools, God has given them over to do the filthy things their hearts desire, and they do shameful things with each other. . . . God has given them over to shameful passions. Even the women pervert the natural use of their sex into unnatural acts. In the same way the men give up natural sexual relations with women and burn with passion for each other. [They] do shameful things with each other, and as a result they receive in themselves the punishment they deserve for their wrongdoing.

Romans 1:24, 26, 27 TEV

No, for anyone who takes God and His Word seriously, there is no question that homosexuality is a vile sin, utterly wrong.

Yet God loves every sinner. If you have been caught in the homosexual trap, you may already realize that it is a deadly trap and that few escape. I know of only one way out—through Jesus Christ! He is big enough and loving enough and strong enough to get you out and make you over. Turn to Him this minute, before it's too late. You'll be amazed at what He can do.

One thing about homosexuals that hits me is this: *gay isn't happy*. Of all the sad, hopeless, miserable people I've ever seen, the gays are among the saddest and most miserable. They may tell themselves they are really free and enjoying life, but deep down they know it's a lie. The real joy comes when they find Jesus.

A final word to Christians. Don't think that being a Christian lifts you above the homosexual temptations. I knew a preacher in a large northwestern city who testified how God had delivered him from homosexuality and other sins. Yet one day as I was sitting in his study talking with this man, he made advances which indicated that the demon of homosexuality was back in his life. I rebuked that evil spirit. This man confessed that slowly he had gotten further and further away from Christ, until finally his old habit had crept back into his life.

A few weeks later that preacher had a real experience with Christ. He confessed to Him his weakness and sin, and Jesus gave him complete, total victory over his old habit. Today he's one of the happiest men I've ever seen. He's found where real joy and satisfaction are—in God and Jesus and the Holy Spirit.

9

Religion

You may be surprised to find a chapter on religion in a book about corruption. Most people seem to think anything religious is good. That isn't necessarily so.

Only one step away from the occult are the pseudoreligions that seem to be blossoming all over the world today. Many of them are doing very well. The Process Church of the Final Judgement, one of the newest religions on the American scene, incredibly combines worship of Jesus with worship of Satan. Its members aggressively hunt for converts on city streets and college campuses, and it has already received so much support that it has leased a valuable building in the middle of New York City as headquarters. Obviously, all this wouldn't be happening if the Process leaders weren't very persuasive and if a good many people weren't ready for a completely new religion, even if it does make a god of the devil.

Every year the Eastern religions fare better in the Western Hemisphere. A whole procession of gurus from India have hit it big in the United States. One of the most successful right now is teen-aged Maharaj Ji, who had six American followers in 1971 and now has so many that his movement, the Divine Light Mission, has an annual budget of three million dollars and has "missions" in thirty-seven countries. (There are more than six million followers of Maharaj Ji in India alone.) To these followers, Maharaj Ji is "The Perfect Living Master." Rennie Davis, just a little while ago a radical revolutionary, is now a convert. He says Maharaj Ji appeared to him in a vision with the words, "I am your Lord," and Rennie is one of the many who have left all else to follow him.

Late in 1973, members of the Divine Light Mission rented the Houston Astrodome to praise Maharaj Ji and celebrate "Millennium '73" which was supposed to bring peace to the world through its teen-aged lord. The Mission plans to build its own divine city in this country, run on solar energy and designed to fulfill practically all its inhabitants' desires at the touch of a button.

Another popular new religion is Scientology, founded by an American science-fiction writer named L. Ron Hubbard. The basic philosophy here is dianetics, a sort of science-fiction version of self-psychoanalysis. Through certain routines—sold to initiates at fifteen dollars-and-up an hour—a person becomes *cleared* of his problems and hang-ups and is supposed to end up feeling good toward everybody and confident that he can do practically anything. From the appearance of some of the seedy-looking people I've seen handing out Scientology literature, I find it hard to believe they are *clears*. And as far as goodwill toward other people is concerned, both Scientologists and Maharajjiologists can be very vindictive toward anyone who criticizes—or even tells the truth about—their religion. One newspaperman was beaten up so severely after publishing an unfavorable story about Maharaj Ji that he had to have a steel plate put in his fractured skull.

When *Newsweek* said recently that the world seems to be looking for new gods to worship, it was commenting on one of the great movements of our time. Everywhere people are searching for something, someone to believe in, and they fill the empty place in the center of their hearts with whatever substitutes they can find for the God who is revealed in Jesus Christ. And I'm concerned about the many religions, new and old, that are luring so many people today. Christian churches are being crowded out by temples of Buddhism and Islam and other cults. A new Japanese religion, Soka Gakkai, has grown from five thousand members to ten million in less than thirty years. Another Japanese group making headway in America is the Church of Perfect Liberty, which lets its members have their cake and eat it too. This church teaches that playing golf is a way of self-improvement. Members don't need to skip church to play golf on Sunday mornings; they can do both at the same time!

On almost any city street or college campus today you can see Hare Krishna converts dancing and chanting, handing out literature and even food consecrated before their idols. I must say they show a lot of zeal and courage, to spend so much time dancing barefoot in their saffron robes, to shave their heads and paint their foreheads, and do more public witnessing every day than many Christian church members do in a lifetime. And it seems to be paying off. This religious order has grown so fast in one American city that it is shopping around for a building for its headquarters, and payment seems to be no problem.

A minister friend told me of running into a Hare Krishna group celebrating just off Times Square, which is sometimes called "the crossroads of the world." At an intersection, incense burned in front of what looked something like a large dollhouse with figures that looked like a doll and a toy elephant inside.

"What is that?" my friend asked one of the whirling Hare Krishna youngsters.

"That," she replied, "is God."

"*God?*" he asked.

"Yes. If you accept it, that is God. The two figures are the male and female personifications of the infinite force of the universe." Then, watching my friend's face and probably realizing he wasn't going to be a believer, she added: "But if you do not accept it, those are just two dolls."

"I got an eerie feeling," my friend said as he told me about the incident, "realizing that those Eastern idols were being worshiped in the middle of America's largest city!"

In Iceland there is a revival of the old worship of Thor, Odin, Loki, and other gods and goddesses of ancient Norse mythology. Before Christianity came to Scandinavia, human sacrifices were made to these gods. The new worshipers are trying to get permission to make sacrifices of horses and to brew their own spirits for their services, and have announced that their aim is to de-Christianize all Iceland.

It could spread. If you see a bunch of people in animal skins burning a horse on a funeral pyre and drinking aquavit, it may be just one more new-old religious gathering—this time out of Scandinavian mythology.

"So what?" you may ask. "These religions don't harm anybody, do they?" Don't be too sure about that. For example, Scientologists are taught: "Never fear to hurt another in a just cause." Doesn't that remind you a little of Adolf Hitler—or the Communists—or Watergate?

In the summer of 1973 a faith healer laid his hands on the head of an eleven-year-old boy with diabetes and someone shouted, "Praise the Lord! He's healed!" The next day when the boy went into the kitchen to take his regular insulin shot, his father broke the needle and threw it away. For a short time the boy was happy —no more shots, and he could eat all the cake and ice cream he wanted. But in two days he was dead.

I know God can do miracles, but it's dangerous to turn our backs on the tools of healing which He puts in our hands. God and medicine aren't enemies; they're allies in the fight against disease and death, as thousands of Christian doctors and their patients know. The wonderful thing about Christ's healing is that it begins where medicine ends. But it is a corruption of faith to reject God's gifts of medical and scientific knowledge.

So religion can be a corruptor and destroyer, too! The religious establishment ganged up with nonreligious groups to crucify Christ. Religion has bad things as well as good things connected with it. Wars have been started, "heretics" have been tortured, martyrs have endured agonizing deaths—all in the name of religion.

I'm not saying Christianity is perfect, either. The Christian churches have had their share of corruption down through the ages. At one time, when one church controlled most of Europe, there were so many orgies, prostitutes, bribes, illegitimate children, and murders even at the highest levels of church government that the period is often called the Rule of the Harlots. You can't say Roman Catholics had a corner on such things, either. Protestants have had their share of wars and tortures and heresy trials and brainwashing and corruption. And before the division between Protestants and Catholics, losing a religious debate could mean being thrown out of the country or being killed.

The thing that is important is not religion but *Jesus. He* is not a religion. *He* is a living experience. The one thing that can make our churches vital and real to people is to help them turn away from empty, dead religious traditions and controversies, to the *living experience of Jesus Christ*—as so many are doing.

There is one religious movement today that is amazing everyone who sees it—the Jesus Movement among young people all over the world. Many of these youngsters have turned away from the programs of the established churches, but have *turned on to Jesus.* Some have founded their own churches, electing their own deacons and elders and conducting their own services. Perhaps some of these groups have gone to dangerous extremes, but wherever I see people who love Jesus, I feel I'm among friends. To me the Jesus Movement is a marvelous example of how God's Spirit is working today, though often clear outside the organized churches.

In Ann Arbor, Michigan, the Word of God Community holds praise and prayer meetings every Thursday night; hundreds of young people attend regularly. One of the hymns they often sing goes like this:

> The Holy Ghost will set your feet a-dancing
> The Holy Ghost will thrill you through and through
> The Holy Ghost will set your feet a-dancing
> And set your heart a-dancing too.

It seems to me that's typical of the new Jesus Movement. There's not a thing dull or stuffy or stodgy about it. It sets hearts dancing! And it shows the *power* of the Spirit of God. Time and again, drug addicts who find Jesus through groups of this kind, gain deliverance from drugs so quickly that observers find it incredible.

Sometimes—though not always—addicts who come to Jesus kick their habits with no withdrawal symptoms whatsoever. When other young people see that happening, they don't need someone to convince them that Jesus is real and alive today. They *know* it! They have seen Him at work! I have, too.

And that's the whole key to "destructive" religion. When Jesus isn't a vital part of it, there can be a very corruptive influence.

It's amazing what most religions really think about Jesus and God and even about life. According to many of them, life is a pretty rotten deal controlled by inexplicable fate, with no real hope, no real security. God is only a name for some kind of abstract force or power. And Jesus is just one more teacher or guru or saviour. *All the non-Christian religions deny that He is the unique Saviour and God that He tells us He is.* All of them deny that Jesus is the only way to God, that His blood atones for our sins, and that He is the only genuine bridge between sinful humans and a holy God. They can't admit that Jesus is Lord of lords and King of kings.

Nearly every one of the new religions tries to drag Jesus down to a purely human level, to put Him on the same level as Buddha and Confucius and Mohammed and a whole group of other beings.

None of those religions helped me when I was hooked on hatred and crime. Most of them have great-sounding rituals and rules and good advice. But they don't show you how to find help when you're up against it. Jesus did and does, and that's why I'll stand with Him against anyone who denies what He says:

I am the Way—yes, and the Truth and the Life. No one can get to the Father except by means of me.

John 14:6 LB

Go in by the narrow gate. For the wide gate has a broad road which leads to disaster, and there are many people going that way. The narrow gate and the hard road lead out into life, and only a few are finding it.

Matthew 7:13, 14 PHILLIPS

Come to me, all of you who are tired from carrying your heavy loads, and I will give you rest. Take my yoke and put it on you, and learn from me, for I am gentle and humble in spirit; and you will find rest. The yoke I will give you is easy, and the load I will put on you is light.

Matthew 11:28–30 TEV

10

Money, Money, Money

After Bobby Fischer won the world chess championship, Russian newspapers denounced his delay in agreeing to a rematch with the Soviet champion. They said Bobby Fischer's only motivation was "money, money and money." They questioned his love of chess and called him a "chess-businessman"—probably the worst word anyone in a Communist country could use. As a matter of fact, Fischer seems to have been holding out for a million-dollar prize for the winner, and that looks like an awful lot of money until you start thinking of how much money so many other people with a lot less talent than Bobby Fischer are making.

When athletes and entertainers are paid many times more than presidents, when public officials become millionaires while in offices where it is said that the expenses are greater than the salary, when the highest-paid police in America are reported to make more than their salaries from bribes, when the primary (and practically only) consideration in business is profit, something is wrong. Money isn't the root of all evil, as some people think the Bible says. But "the *love* of money is a source of all kinds of evil" (*see* 1 Timothy 6:10 TEV—*italics* added). When anyone loves money instead of people and God, he's in deep spiritual trouble. Nobody can really afford to be motivated only by money, money, money.

And yet every one of us knows how important money is in

these days of shortages and inflation. We can't do without money but we have to learn to live with it and escape being corrupted by it.

Not long ago a woman telephoned me to ask for an appointment for her boss to see me. If you heard his name you would recognize him as head of one of the most successful businesses in his area. After he arrived, his uniformed chauffeur waited in the parking lot in an enormous Lincoln Continental during the visit.

"What's wrong with me?" the executive asked. "Every night this month I've lain awake for hours dreading the morning. A week ago I was in Chicago on a business trip and I had the strongest urge to throw myself out my hotel window. There's nothing I can think of that I couldn't buy if I wanted it—and there's nothing I want to buy."

It was incredible! Here was one of the richest businessmen I know, asking me, Nicky Cruz, a onetime slum kid, for help. What could I say? What would you have said to this man? Think that over while I mention a couple of other things about this subject of money.

You may be waiting for me to knock money. I'm not going to. I know how important it is—and so do you. You know you can't get along without that indispensable "green stuff." You can't do much of anything or go hardly anywhere, you can't live, and you can't even die decently without money. And let's face it, even in church you have to think about what to put in the collection plate.

In a way, money is life. It takes sweat and muscle power and brainpower to get money, and all kinds of good things in life are bought with money. There was a businessman named Russell Conwell who raised many thousands of dollars to found Temple University in Philadelphia, and in a famous speech, "Acres of Diamonds," he said:

> Money is power, and you ought to be reasonably ambitious to have it. You ought because you can do more good with it than you could without it. Money printed your Bible, money builds

your churches, money sends your missionaries, and money pays your preachers, and you would not have many of them, either, if you did not pay them. . . . The man who gets the largest salary can do the most good with the power that is furnished to him.

Of course, money doesn't necessarily do all that good. Here in America today we spend $40 billion a year to travel, $9 billion to eat out, $6 billion to drink, more than $3 billion in beauty shops. We spend more for liquor than for milk or education, more for tobacco than for bread, more for gambling than for meat, more than twice as much for jewelry and movies as everything we give to the churches.

These days you can even buy cosmetics for dogs. One chain of department stores offers poodle perfume, nail polish, and mascara—"for sophisticated dogs, slate gray to accent their liquid eyes."

Think of that the next time you break a ten-dollar bill!

But what I really want to say about money is to warn you to watch out for the power it can gain over you. It is important to have a job in which you can make a living and serve God. But too often making a living becomes the big thing in our minds. And then, to keep the paycheck coming, we can find ourselves in a corner where we think we must do something which we know deep down is wrong.

Have you heard about Frank Serpico? As a boy in New York he dreamed of helping people by becoming a policeman. Then when he got on the police force he discovered that too many of his buddies were taking bribes on the side. Some of them said they took only "clean" bribes. "Clean" meant payoffs for traffic violations or gambling or prostitution. "Dirty money" meant bribes from the drug business. (Some of the police, Serpico noticed, took payoffs from the drug pushers, too, when the bribes were big and juicy enough.)

Serpico didn't like any of this. He decided to live only on his policeman's salary, which was an embarrassment to others who received substantial portions of their income from the criminal world which they were supposed to police. When a special commission started looking into corruption among the police and Serpico was questioned, he told the truth. That, of course, was even more embarrassing to everyone involved in taking bribes or just looking the other way when the payola was distributed. Serpico heard that the word had gone out to get him. He got used to hearing threats like "if he isn't careful he'll be found face down in the East River."

Serpico went on about his business. Six months after he told the truth in a trial, he started out with two other policemen to capture a heroin pusher, in the Williamsburg section of Brooklyn. Dressed in high boots, dungarees, a turtleneck sweater and an old army jacket topped with a scarf, Serpico sauntered into the five-story building where the pusher worked. Underneath the army jacket Serpico had a Browning automatic and a .38. Inside a gas mask which he carried over one shoulder he had his service revolver.

Pretending to be in need of a fix, Serpico knocked on the pusher's door and said in Spanish, "I need something." Behind him his two police companions stood on the landing of the stairs. The door started to open and stopped, checked by a chain lock. Serpico charged into the door, snapped the chain—and found himself pinned, as someone inside jammed the door against him while the pusher raced into another room for his gun.

The pusher shot Serpico in the head while the other cops still stood on the stairs. After he crashed to the floor they appeared and eventually got him to a hospital.

Miraculously, Serpico survived. But during the long weeks in the hospital, the police on guard hardly ever spoke to him. He knew that a number of his fellow officers despised him. A nurse heard one guard say to his relief, "Don't talk to him. He's no good."

Frank Serpico got two sympathy cards while he lay in that New York hospital. One message was a get-well note with the printed hope that the recipient would RECUPERATE QUICKLY! The word "Recuperate" was crossed out and the sender had written in *Die!* The second card read: WITH SINCERE SYMPATHY but underneath was scrawled the regret: *That you didn't get your brains blown out, you rat. . . . Happy Relapse.* Finally, Frank Serpico left the police force. It wasn't too healthy for him around his old beat.

As I write this, a movie about Serpico has just been released. Nothing I've said here is an endorsement of the movie or a blanket approval of everything Serpico may have done. But it is my tribute to a man who had the guts to be a *man,* the strength to be honest when so many others had their hands out for bribes from crooks.

As far as I know, money never corrupted Serpico, but it can corrupt anyone, young or old. When one teen-ager took a job in a supermarket, his boss told him, "Charge the customers a few cents extra whenever you can get away with it. If they catch you at it, apologize and tell them you made a mistake." The boy did it because he didn't want to lose the job.

A secretary may say that her employer is in conference when he isn't because that is part of her job. A government official may falsify records because he understands that to be part of his duties. An engineer may do nothing about the defective steering in a certain automobile because he believes that his company wants him to cover it up. In every case, what is really happening is that something wrong is being done for the sake of money.

To get back to that businessman who came to see me: I found out that although he had a lovely home, a private plane, and considerable investments—all the things so many men and women pour out their lives for—he owned nothing really important. He hadn't been inside a church for years. His children were strangers to him. His wife had been showered with *things* but robbed of the personal attention and love she deserved. So she, like the children, had grown cold and hard toward this man. The result: depression and thoughts of suicide.

I talked with this man for some time. I said, "You have sacrificed your wife's happiness and your children's happiness. And you have lost the best things there are—love and faith and hope. But you still have one thing that you can't buy and you can't lose. Whatever you do, remember this: Jesus loves you!"

We prayed together, and when this businessman left, there

were tears in his eyes. I could see the love of God beginning to get through to him. He was beginning to discover the riches beyond money or price.

As I write this book, the ugly stains of Watergate keep spreading like a foul flood. What was Watergate all about? Money, money, money! So many dollars stuck to so many sticky fingers that laws, morality, and human decency were stepped on and left in the mud. Of course, a lot of things connected with Watergate were not new, but I doubt that ever before in history was so much money used to corrupt so many lives and institutions. Public Enemy Number One may well turn out to be the dollar bill. When one of the officials questioned by the Senate's Watergate Committee was asked why he thought so much corruption had come about, he replied in effect: "Too much money. There were so many millions of dollars with so little restraint on how they could be spent."

Today it seems like money can buy practically anything and anyone. One man protested about what he knew was going on in a certain charitable organization—what was going on bothered his conscience—but he admitted later, "Every time I said something, they shut me up with a raise."

Another man refused to be silenced. When he was ordered to falsify the tax records for a music company, he refused—and was fired. He learned that being true to your principles may cancel your paycheck.

For the worst example of all, look at the way organized crime corrupts everything it touches. Here is the love of money exposed in its nakedest, most horrible form—stopping at nothing from robbery and bribery to torture and murder—as its tentacles grab businessmen and their concerns, public servants and their governments, labor unions, every possible kind of person and organization.

Even the church—even religion! Yes, the love of money can corrupt the highest and best things of all. In the next chapter, I'll give you some examples.

11

The Jesus Money Tree

It's going to be hard to write this chapter, because it will seem to some people that I am knocking other Christian workers. I'm not. But God won't let me write this book without saying what He has told me, so here goes.

Let me start with Rick. The first time I saw him I was just getting started in my ministry. Fresh out of Bible college, I searched for a headquarters. God showed me the place: the middle of a ghetto in Los Angeles with about ten blacks and two or three Mexicans and Asiatics to every white person. There was an old white house on Twentieth Street that looked just right. Some people might call it a white elephant. I loved it because it had plenty of rooms! Rooms for wanderers and drug addicts to find a home and kick their bad habits; rooms where society's outcasts could live and pray and reach out for others; room for God to work.

Out of all the savings I had ever been able to put in the bank, I made the down payment for that first Outreach Center on Twentieth Street.

When we started, the air on Twentieth Street was filled with despair. I was a young Puerto Rican who could barely speak English and no idea of all I was getting into, but I had a vision and a hope. I knew what Jesus had done for me, and I knew what He could do for anyone I could introduce to Him.

Sometimes hope was about all I could offer the houseful of dropouts and addicts I gathered together in that crumbling old house. I remember once for a whole week all we had to eat were stale doughnuts donated by a local bakery. (To this day doughnuts don't get a bit of rise from me; if I were wrecked for a week on a desert island with no food but doughnuts, I don't think I'd eat a thing all week.) Those were the days when drug addiction was largely a ghetto problem; it hadn't yet reached into white suburban society to any great extent, and so many people didn't understand my vision (or chose not to). But on Sundays the members of our little household of hope would go out and speak in small churches, and Christians touched by the Spirit would give us small love offerings for our ministry, and bring us canned food.

But limited as the diet was in the old house on Twentieth Street, we lived life to the fullest degree. It was a house of lonely, hardened children of the streets struggling to get their lives together, knowing that this was the last stop on the way out. And little by little it happened. The Spirit of God reached into those wrecked lives and made them new again. I had been where those young people had been, and in my eyes every boy was me.

Rick had been in trouble with the law so much and busted so many times I think even he had lost count. He was living on Sunset Strip, on drugs, when he found our center. In all his eighteen years he hadn't been able to find an answer to his questions about existence. But he was tired of rebelling against the world and himself and God, and when he found our little community with a living Christ right in the middle of it all, he recognized immediately that Jesus was the answer to all his questions.

In a prayer room that had once been a bank vault, Rick turned his life over to Jesus Christ. He gave Jesus everything—his failures, his drug habits, his attitude (a penal-institution outlook, hardened by too many stretches in reformatories and prisons), his mind, body, and soul. And Jesus really saved him. Some people talk about being saved from sin. Rick *knows* he was completely transformed. "It was so great," Rick says now, "I could feel it in my bones, and I still can. Jesus reached me when no one else could."

Rick was one of those people, like St. Paul, who couldn't do enough for the Christ he had once kicked against. So when he met established Christians who "looked Christian" but didn't feel the pull he did to work every minute for the Saviour, he couldn't understand it. Rick entered Bible college so he could be prepared for full-time Christian work, and there too he was bothered by the apathy he found. The other students might study all day and then turn on the radio and take it easy in the evening. Not Rick! He wanted to be out witnessing every minute. "Man," he kept thinking, "there are people dying out there and they need Jesus. When are we going to put 'Go ye therefore' into high gear?" I remember that Rick told me he saw so many people looking at little hills when there were mountains to climb.

Then it happened. All of a sudden Christianity was kicked into high gear—no, not kicked, slammed. All over the world, thousands of people began finding Jesus. Junkies, cons, freaks, prostitutes, businessmen, secretaries, movie stars, housewives, high school and college students were being saved. At first Rick couldn't believe it. When he picked up a magazine with a photograph of hundreds of people being baptized in the ocean, Rick cried, "The revival! It's come!"

The next year books, magazines, television, movies, and newspapers were talking about Jesus. "Christian" became not how you look but *where you are at.* Jesus festivals were held, books and magazines began featuring Jesus and the Christian life, Christian music stood up and started dancing in the aisles!

But as the Christian revival has continued, some things worry Rick and me. At an evangelistic meeting one of the leaders was defensive about the fact that nearly everyone present was already a Christian. He said to me, "Brother, the Lord knew who needed to be here tonight." I don't accept that. I know that no effort was made to get unsaved people to come. I'm concerned at the indifference, the lack of direction in our spiritual enthusiasm.

On the other hand, there is the attitude that because you have come to a meeting, something is supposed to happen. I call it *spiritual bloodsucking*. People are invited to a meeting and then drained of everything the leaders can get out of them. It's like using Jesus to get money from people.

Often no one asks, "Why are we doing this?" Instead someone says: "Do it! It will work!" Some religious leaders seem to be selling Jesus the way a sharp salesman sells cars or real estate. Secondary things are put first and primary things seem to be forgotten.

In the evangelistic field today, to be successful, it seems that you have to have a different gimmick or ministry. Instead of preaching Jesus, some evangelists are always selling things. I know of one man who took the tent he had preached under and had it cut into pieces which he sold for a hundred dollars apiece. "The glory of God went through this tent," he claimed, "and you can buy a piece of it." Another evangelist claimed he could sell "angels of light." All kinds of psychological and advertising tricks are used to cheat credulous people.

Two salesmen for a commercial organization came to my office and tried to sell me on the idea of marketing a T-shirt with my name and these words printed on it: SMILE, JESUS LOVES YOU! They told me of the thousands of dollars I would make from this venture, but I sensed a satanic temptation. I thought of the time when Jesus went into the temple and cast out everyone who was buying and selling, and overthrew the money tables. I was led to rebuke these men for their scheme. I did not give my life to Christ for the purpose of making money. In our Outreach ministry, all receipts from crusades go directly to the organization to help with our work. Proceeds from the sale of books and records go directly for the ministry. We do not take any of this money for ourselves. (Royalties from my books, on the other hand, are set aside for my children's education. I do not want my children ever to feel that the Lord forgot to take care of them.) All offerings are turned over to the work of Nicky Cruz Outreach.

We need to be careful that in our honest enthusiasm we don't buy and sell and organize Jesus until we expect Him to react to what *we* want instead of what *He* wants.

And we need to be *very* careful not to make Jesus into a magic money tree. So often, successful entertainers and business-men are asked to give Christian testimony whereas a plain ordi-nary Christian who is not making all that money is completely overlooked—even though he might have a lot more to contribute, and much more valuable spiritual insight. It's not meant that way, I'm sure, but the impression is given that accepting Christ is a quick way to fame and fortune.

It isn't.

And how much harm some of these successful "Christian" per-formers do. There is one well-known religious music group, in-vited to a good many churches and evangelistic campaigns, which uses gospel music purely to make money. At one of their per-formances I noticed the eyes of some of these performers roving over the audience as they sang. Then, after the meeting was over, several of the singers took off on dates with the most attractive chicks. Some religious singers perform very well, and dress beau-tifully, but how they live is what counts. They know the words of the Christian songs, but if someone asked them how to find Jesus Christ, could they do it? I doubt it.

Religion is big business today! Sometimes I wonder about all those Christian buttons and bumper stickers and books and rec-ords. Where do all those profits go? Are these things being turned out for love of Jesus, or for love of the "almighty dollar"?

There is a lot of money in religion today. There is money in selling religious books—and some publishing houses are returning to religious books after once abandoning them for what they thought was more profitable. There is money in the occult and witchcraft, too, so some publishers go into that for the same reason.

Where does Jesus fit into all this?

God forbid that I should throw stones at any of the dedicated people who are distributing Christian books and music to so many corners of the earth. I salute them. I just don't want anyone to confuse God and mammon (money). Jesus warned long ago,

"Ye cannot serve God and mammon" (*see* Luke 16:13) and we still need that warning.

No, Jesus is no magic money tree. Instead of automatically showering money on us, He shows us what we could be doing for people in need—people like the *forgotten generation.*

12

The Forgotten Generation

Last Thanksgiving I was visiting some of the people in a home for the aged. One man I'll never forget. He was dressed up in a white shirt and tie, and his worn old trousers were pressed so neatly they looked as though they had just come from the dry cleaner. (I'd guess he had pressed them himself that morning.) "My son is coming to see me today," he told me proudly in his thin old voice.

All day long that poor old man sat in his room waiting for a son who never came. The last I saw of him that day, he was sitting there all by himself with a tray in his lap, chewing on a dry piece of turkey. He had been waiting all day, and at last he realized his son wasn't coming. There was such loneliness in his face! I could feel it for a long time afterward.

One of the worst things I see today is the way old people are treated. It starts early. By the time you reach forty you may be in trouble. Try getting a good job at that age or older! No way! Forty means you are over the hill as far as most jobs are concerned; the companies look for younger people they can start at lower pay.

If you are fortunate you will retire on a pension. A lot of people never get even a small one. A famous manufacturer closed his factory in one city and thousands of men who had worked there suddenly lost their jobs. Some of the workers were in their

sixties, too old to get a job anywhere else. All of them were left
with no pension, *nothing*—and one man would have retired in less
than a year.

One of the worst things about the inflation that is galloping so
fast these days is what it does to older people. The ones lucky
enough to have small pensions find that every week their few
dollars buy less and less. Some old people have to choose between food and fuel. On Christmas Eve of 1973 a ninety-three-
year-old man and his wife were found frozen to death in Schenec-
tady, New York. Four days before, the power company had
turned off their electricity because they hadn't paid their last bill,
and they couldn't start their furnace.

A lot of older people do not have enough money to buy bare
essentials. Some live on little besides stale bread and cheap
margarine. An old lady at a supermarket check-out counter found
she didn't have enough money to pay for the few things in her
arms, and she put back a can of cat food.

The check-out girl was sympathetic. "It's too bad," she smiled,
"you won't be able to bring that to your cat."

"I don't have a cat," the elderly woman said. "That was for me."

Some old people are forced to live on pet food.

Frankly, I don't understand the way so many senior citizens
are treated. From my earliest days I remember the love and honor
and respect I used to see showered on the old. My Grandfather
Ignacio lived in my childhood home, in spite of our big family,
until he died. Mom was always fixing chicken soup for him—and
other things he especially liked. All our elderly relatives were
cared for in the same way.

In Puerto Rico when I was young, that was the way most old
people were treated. They were loved and cherished and respected, and if an old person was neglected, everyone regarded
it as a scandal and shame. People tell me it used to be the same
way in the United States. Families had big houses and there was
generally room somewhere for Grandma or Grandpa when either
or both couldn't live alone any longer.

How different it is in so many places today! Houses aren't big enough anymore to hold an older relative, and the grandparents who live long enough to need care are often shunted off out of sight into nursing homes or other places for the aged. Modern children miss the great blessing of knowing their parents' parents, and they miss all the wisdom they could gain from this contact. Today's older generation misses the joy of entering into the life and growth of the younger generation.

When an elderly person chooses to live alone, that's a different matter. My own mother chooses to live with my niece in Las Piedras, Puerto Rico, but some of my brothers and their families live close by, and her children and grandchildren are always dropping in. My brother José Ramon lives in the house next to Mama and he keeps a watchful eye on her. My mother knows she is not neglected. She knows that any of us children would be glad to have her come and live with us anytime. During the summer months Mama sometimes comes to New York to visit. On those visits she spends one or two weeks with each of my brothers and my sister who live in New York, and each family fights to have her visit them first.

We have got to learn how to restore the honor and care we owe to the ones who loved us and sacrificed so much for us when we were young.

God expects that of us. He says, "Honour thy father and thy mother" (*see* Exodus 20:12) and He has never repealed that law. It is not honor to let an aged mother or father slowly starve—from lack of *either* food or affection—nor to hide them away in some institution and forget all about them.

Jesus tells us to love our neighbors as ourselves, and He does not say not to include our parents. And He set such a wonderful example Himself, for all time. Do you remember when He was dying, stretched out on that cross on Calvary? Nearly all the disciples had deserted Him at the end. One who stuck by Him right to the end was the disciple who loved Him so much, the Apostle John. Practically the only other one who dared to stand by Him at the cross, when everyone was ridiculing Jesus and spitting on Him, was His mother.

And while Jesus was dying there, bearing the sin of the whole world on His great shoulders, taking that awful burden on Himself, He was thinking about His mother.

Jesus didn't want His best friend to be left all alone and He didn't want His mother to be neglected. What a wonderful thing He did for both of them! He said to Mary, "Woman, behold thy son!" And to John, "Behold thy mother!" (*See* John 19: 26, 27.)

If Jesus could do that while He was dying the worst death the world has ever known, how can we neglect taking care of our own mothers and fathers?

Among Latins, old men and women are truly respected and honored. People admire their experience and wisdom and come to them for advice. In some of the so-called underprivileged countries, a child has a hard time when he's young, but as he gets older, things get better, until in old age he has the best, happiest time of his life. There is a lot of criticism about America's South, but I respect and admire the way most Southerners treat their older people, and that goes for both black and white.

Today many people practically idolize their children. Anything they want, they can have! Pain and suffering and problems we keep away from them—until they learn the hard way that there are such things. But the future they should anticipate with hope is often a time of dread, for even young children can sense the way most older people are treated. So life often ends in misery and depression and loneliness and sadness.

We reject old age today! Actors and actresses and the models who sell us products have to be young and exciting and wrinkle-free. We hide our old people out of sight. Why? Is it because the sight of the aged reminds us that *we too* must someday grow old and die? We've got to learn to be honest with ourselves and just and fair to the old.

What can we do for them?

We could see that the fixed incomes of the aged fluctuate in some way with inflation, so that their few dollars won't buy less and less.

We could reduce their taxes.

We could rethink our priorities. Education is certainly important for our children, but what would happen if every community
slowed down on its tax increases for new buildings and other
expenses for children's public education until more is done for
the aged?

A number of churches have homes for the elderly, and that's
good, but can we stop there? There are Christian ministries to the
young, the poor, the minorities, and all kinds of special groups,
but where is the ministry to the old? Who watches over their
welfare, spiritual or physical?

How I wish I could challenge everyone who reads this book to
start right now thinking and praying and *doing something about
our forgotten generation.*

The fact that a person has had sixty-five or seventy or eighty
birthdays should not mean that he or she has lost touch with life.
I believe that most older people are just as pleased with Christmas and Easter observances, with birthday parties and picnics
and good times as younger people. They like interest and attention and time and love just as much or more. And how often
no one meets these needs.

In one community a number of young people were assigned
specific older people for contact and help. Several teen-agers and
oldsters became fast friends!

Some churches today require each committee or group to
represent minority groups, the young, and so on. How about
making sure they also represent the old?

One thing is for sure. Unless the Lord returns first, every one of
us will one day be wrinkled and old. How will we feel then?
Will we be able to look back over our lives with satisfaction,
knowing we have given of our best for the generation that seemed
old when we were young?

13

Before the Fall—Pride

I was invited to speak in a certain city in May. A week before the date, I sent Bill Rhodes, one of my staff members, to check on the arrangements.

"Find out what they've been doing to advertise the crusade," I asked Bill. "Also how many prayer chains have been set up for support. Check on the size of the auditorium, the lighting—you know, all those little things that are so important to our crusades."

Bill went, but when he reported back to me he looked so dejected I couldn't understand it. "What's the trouble, Bill?" I asked. "You look as though you're ready to write a new song:

I have the gloom, gloom, gloom, gloom
Down in my heart!

"I suppose so," Bill said with a sigh. "I just can't take any more of what I've been through."

Bill explained. When he had arrived at the scene of my coming crusade, Bill had been treated, he felt, like dirt. There were good plans under way, but every suggestion Bill made to improve them was rejected outright. The local crusade committee took a totally negative attitude toward everything Bill said; nothing could be added to or taken away from their plans—not even the smallest detail.

Result: I had to go to the crusade site earlier than I had planned, simply to do what the committee hadn't let Bill do. Miraculously, the instant I arrived, I felt as though I was being treated like God. I made exactly the same suggestions Bill had, but this time everyone outdid himself to do what I asked.

It was too much for me. Reluctantly I took one of the committee members aside and told him how I felt about all this. "You have shamed me," I told him, "that you would treat another Christian brother as you treated Bill. You treated him completely different from me. Yet Bill works for me; he came here as part of the crusade, part of me, and you rejected him!"

The man looked down. I think he was beginning to realize what he had done and what it would mean. For it was quite clear by now that the men of the crusade committee had been guilty of one of the worst sins of all—pride.

Pride! It is so dangerous because it is so hard to recognize. We treat some people like pieces of furniture, instead of persons, because we are so wrapped up in our own affairs that we never think of how the other person feels. We discriminate shamefully. We go out of our way to praise and please one person while we practically step on another.

Even our prayers can be soaked in pride. One man of prayer gave God 10 percent of his income, fasted often, and would no more have committed adultery than he would have missed church. In his prayers this man was likely to say: "I thank you, God, that I am not greedy, dishonest, or immoral, like everybody else" (*see* Luke 18: 9–14 TEV). But God never heard those spiritually proud statements. We know that is one kind of prayer which God will not answer because Jesus told us so in this parable of the Pharisee and the tax collector. Look it up and you will find that Jesus tells us that God will listen more readily to the humble sinner who turns to Him than to the religious person who is filled with pride.

Pride corrupted the world in the beginning. Adam and Eve wanted to be as wise as God, and they set themselves above Him, listening to the devil's false promises instead of God's clear commands. But pride was around long before the Fall! That *super-*

corruptor Satan started out as one of God's highest angels. Somewhere along the line Satan developed delusions of grandeur and
coveted the throne of God for himself. His unchecked pride left
God no choice: He had to banish to the bottomless abyss the
devil and all the angels which got behind him. I wish they would
stay there! One day they will be sealed up forever, but right now
—as everyone who follows Jesus knows—those fallen spirits are
at work night and day trying to get you and me into their wicked
ranks. Since they cannot get to the Creator, they settle for His
Creation or the part of Creation that most touches His heart—
man!

Since God recently spoke to me in Ottawa, I have seen the
sin of pride so often! In the *name-droppers,* for instance. A man
may come up to me and say, "When I was talking to Billy
Graham and Senator Stennis recently, I thought of something
Pat Boone told me about how the Lord worked in the life of
Maria von Trapp." God forgive me if I judge people like this
wrongly, but I can't help being suspicious that for them I'm one
more name to add to their list, so that they can tell the next person they meet, "As Nicky Cruz told me the other day. . . ."

And then there are the people who get in touch with me (I
suspect) to make money. I am approached about so many money-
making schemes, you wouldn't believe it. I've turned them
down because I know if I started that route, at best I would end
up living for money and what it can buy, and that's not what
I've given my life to God to do.

It's all a form of the old, old appeal of pride—thinking of
things instead of people, thinking of yourself instead of others,
putting God last instead of first.

Pride is treating someone differently because he isn't *somebody*.
Pride is asking, "What's in it for me?" instead of, "How can I
serve the Lord in this situation?" Pride is an attitude—"I can't
benefit from knowing that person, or from talking to him or
spending my time with him—so I won't bother with him."

Pride is so widespread in the world today. The lust of the eyes
and the flesh and the pride of life are waiting to trip you up at

any time, and the only way to avoid those spiritual land mines is to ask God over and over to keep you straight and humble and dedicated to Him. So many people build their lives around pride. They spend so much time building themselves up, trying to create a false image, getting to know the right people, belonging to the right club—hoping this approach will give them the answers to their problems. It won't because it can't! Pride is one of the worst corruptors of all, and as I write these words I pray that the Lord will keep me from it, and save from it every person who reads these words.

Pride is such a sneaking temptation. You've heard of the fellow who was proud to say *he* wasn't proud! That's how tricky pride is. And it gets mixed up with so many other things. Nearly everyone could use more money or a nicer car or home and wants to be a success. The sin comes in when things like that become such a passion that we put them ahead of the things that are really important. And then we have to be the best politician, the most successful businessman, the finest athlete, the richest millionaire, the best singer in the choir, the hardest worker in the church! Yes, pride seeps into everything we do for the Lord, too, and we have to keep a constant watch against it.

So often in the churches, the poor family that comes to the Lord is overlooked while the banker, politician, or famous person who joins, is asked almost automatically to serve at the next election to the official board. And he may not have the spiritual background for this at all. Money counts for too much, even in the church! James asked, in effect, "Are you going to show more attention to the people of wealth and influence who may come to church than the poor and the really needy ones? The ones lowest down may rank highest in the eyes of God!" (*See* James 2:1-9.)

Our attitudes need changing and cleansing, so pride will not ruin all we do.

Even as I say this, I realize that it may look as though I'm up on a pedestal looking down on "the proud." I know how easy it is for pride to get into my own life. Let me try to be completely honest here. I know I take pride in myself and in the work God uses me to do. It seems to me only natural and right to take some degree of pride in accomplishment. I don't believe that kind of pride is wrong, if you keep in mind that you can't really accomplish anything without God's constant help. But if you forget His enabling, if you let pride *rule your life,* if you begin to think you're naturally better than somebody else—you're in deep trouble.

Let me make it clear what pride means to me. First of all, pride should not be confused with how you value yourself personally. The first thing that impressed me about the Lord was how He looks at every one of us as individuals. He loved *you* enough to give His life for you, and that means you're valuable! You can't get lost in the crowd. The Bible says that all the hairs of our heads are numbered. Think of it—every day some hair falls and new hair grows in, and the Lord knows all about what is happening! He *loves* us! If the Lord loves us, we should love ourselves and place real value on what we stand for.

I have been traveling extensively for almost ten years and I have to admit that the Lord has had to slap me down because of pride that sneaked into my life. I was preaching in Pittsburgh. I had grown aware of the uniqueness of my ministry, of how I had become something of an adult and teen-age idol. I knew how to present myself in a way that made people put me in their mental Hall of Fame. I had prayed before the meeting, but it had been a selfish prayer, more asking God to "Give me. . . ." than I like to remember. Everything went well in my meeting until the most important part of all, the altar call. At that point I began to choke and could hardly get out the words. I was humiliated.

After the meeting was over, when I returned to my hotel room, I felt that I had received a slap from the Lord. It was as if I had been in a rumble and lost the fight. I felt ashamed.

But I needed that rebuke. I learned that God can pop the balloons of our pride and cut us down to size.

As the Bible puts it so well, pride goes before a fall (*see* Proverbs 16:18 and 29:23).

And pride can corrupt your calling. That's what I want to tell you about next.

14

Don't Corrupt Your Calling

Soon after David Wilkerson brought me to Jesus, I went to Bible college in La Puente, California. After I graduated, the first job I got was in a restaurant in Oakland. I had a few months —five, to be exact—and then I would be off with my new bride, so in the meantime I got a job as a busboy. That's right, a busboy! I cleaned tables, swept floors, washed dishes. The restaurant was one of the nicest eating places in Oakland, right on Jack London Square. People with money, and many celebrities, came there to dine and drink. (Maybe I should put that the other way around, and say they *spent money like crazy and drank like fish*.)

The atmosphere was not exactly healthy, morally or spiritually, for a Christian right out of Bible college. It was certainly a challenge to everything I had learned and called for every scrap of spiritual protection I could find. I thank God that He was with me, because I knew this was where He wanted me to be for a while, even though deep in my heart I knew that He was calling me into a definite future ministry.

At the restaurant worked another busboy who was also from Puerto Rico. His name was Roberto. I discovered he was constantly watching me. Puerto Ricans are very emotional people and Roberto was no exception to the rule. Before long I learned exactly how he felt about me.

Often Roberto and I ate lunch together in a side room after

the main push at lunchtime was over and we could have a little breather. One day as I was thanking God for the food, Roberto started laughing.

"Why are you talking to yourself?" he asked.

I stopped in the middle of my prayer and I explained that I was thankful for everything Jesus gave me, and so I thanked Him for food and everything else. I said I knew Jesus personally, that He was right there with us, and I made it clear I was very serious about my faith.

Roberto sat there stunned. I knew he had been making fun of me before. To him it had been a funny sight to have someone talking to someone who wasn't there. The idea that Jesus was there in the room shook him up. Roberto didn't know what to say.

The next couple of days Roberto watched me constantly. Wherever I went in the restaurant, whatever I did, I could feel Roberto's eyes on me, and I knew he was thinking and wondering. I took Roberto to my heart in prayer, and I shared what I knew about Jesus whenever I had the chance. I told him about the old days of witchcraft and fear in Puerto Rico, and the gang days in New York, and what Christ had done for me—and was doing every day. Roberto looked and listened.

Only one week later Roberto came with me to church. At the close of the service, when the invitation was given to come forward and accept Christ, Roberto went forward and knelt down at the altar and gave his life to the Saviour.

That was just the beginning. Most Puerto Ricans have large families, and counting all his brothers and sisters there were at least fifteen in Roberto's. Through Roberto's newfound faith, every last member of his family, including his grandfather and grandmother, accepted Jesus.

Three days after Roberto's conversion I left my job as a busboy to begin my own ministry. At the same time, Roberto quit to enter Bible college. Today he is a minister of the Gospel, giving all his time and effort to bringing Jesus to others.

What a blessing Roberto brought me! No matter how unknown I was at the time, no matter how insignificant I might be in anyone's eyes—and to many of the people I served, I was just a robot, moving food and dishes—I knew I had done something eternally important. It didn't matter now what happened. I knew that God was in control, and that He would honor me if I honored Him. It didn't matter whether anyone else knew what happened. Lives had been changed, and would be changed, for the Lord. I came to that job a plain, straight Christian who loved Jesus. I was in the right place at the right time, and I left at the right time.

I began speaking to the Spanish-speaking churches in the area, and I found many hearts hungry for the Word. There were tremendous numbers of sincere people who listened, as Roberto had, to my simple message of Jesus and His love and power. The burden to share Him grew deeper and deeper within me. I became very happy in those years of growing and sharing, and I never questioned God.

And little by little I changed from a nobody to a somebody. God opened door after door, and the name Nicky Cruz became one which people started talking about.

When you become a "personality" it is easy to forget how your work began. How do you keep yourself humble when you see your name all over a city like a movie star's? How do you make the right decision when someone does something wrong to you, or forgive when you don't feel like forgiving? These are questions I never find easy to answer. Prayer is constantly needed so as not to fall into temptation and pride. It is so easy to lose the burden God gave you, to lose sight of your calling, to forget that the Lord has brought you so far. There is a deep need to come closer and closer to Jesus every day, and never to forget Him.

I have such beautiful memories, as I think back, of all Jesus has done for me. I think of all the friends who pray for me. I look for such people wherever I go. They are part of my life. Without them and Jesus I couldn't do a thing. I try not to forget these partners in my ministry and their love and prayers.

People often ask me, "Nicky, how did you get to where you are today?" It has not been *my* doing. Whatever I have done is a tribute to Jesus and my partners in prayer.

But I want to emphasize this. While I was attending Bible

college, I wanted to become a missionary in South America. It
seemed like the natural thing to do, and what God would have
me do. I knew Spanish, I was Spanish, I came from a Latin
American country, so what else could God want me to do?

I announced my conclusion to the dean of the school, and I
will always remember what he said:

> Nicky, the will of God is not always what we want, or even
> what we may be quite sure is right. The best way to fulfill the
> will of God in your life is to serve Him totally every day. God
> may want to send you to South America. He may want to keep
> you right here in California. I have an idea that He has a great
> ministry ahead for you. But I learned long ago that the Lord's
> ways are greater than our ways, and often far different from any-
> thing we can think or dream. Let it be the center of your ambi-
> tion to give Him all your energy each day of your life, and He
> will take you where He wants you to go.

How true I have found those words of that wise man of God.
I have made it my ambition to serve God to the best of my ability
every day, day by day, and moment by moment, and God has
done for me more than I could ask or think.

It is so easy to fail in this area. We tend to take our eyes off
the sky and look at the mud below. No one should ever corrupt
the value of the calling of God in his life. Neither should we
limit it, or be tempted into fanaticism. We must learn to know
ourselves and to know God, and as we make serving Him every
day the center of our ambition, He takes care of the rest.

It is easy to dream of the green pastures on the other side of
the fence. People write to me so often to the effect: "If only I
didn't have this job (or this wife or husband or this problem)
how I would love to serve the Lord as you are doing."

My dear friend, don't corrupt your calling. God has put you
where you are just as He led me years ago to work as a busboy.
If I hadn't been true to Him there, none of the other wonderful
things that followed would have happened. Roberto wouldn't be
bringing men and women and boys and girls to Jesus today, and

so many opportunities for God would have gone right down the drain.

Happiness in hardship—what a blessing! I remember the tough times which David Wilkerson went through when he was first trying to get hold of us gang people in New York. So often he was down to his last dollar! But he never let the hardships stop the work he knew God had called him to do. I didn't know it in the beginning, but I know now that David had three very important things in his life that kept him from getting discouraged and quitting.

One was *faith*. Like the David in the Bible who killed the giant Goliath, David Wilkerson trusted that God would do His part if he did his. Sometimes I used to wonder why he prayed so much. Now I know that he kept his faith strong with much praying and reading the Bible. Another thing David Wilkerson had was a *positive attitude*. He expected to reach his goals, he never let negative ideas get the upper hand, he expected great things from God, and attempted great things for God. A third thing in David Wilkerson's life was his *relationship to his wife*, Gwen. She had the beautiful habit of helping him forward instead of pushing him down, and she was a real fellow worker with him in the Lord. So David Wilkerson didn't corrupt his calling!

(Let me add right here that one of the corruptors I often come across today is the attitude of the wife who does keep pushing her husband down. I don't think some women realize that they are doing this, but *they do it*—and their husbands know it! Please, ladies, be encouragers to your husbands, not discouragers. Remember that you are one of the biggest reasons behind whether your husband is a success or a failure, happy or depressed.)

I remember my own early experiences in Teen Challenge. In the beginning we did not have a car, and that first winter I walked through the snow to visit my old buddies from the gang. My salary was twenty-five dollars a week, and yet there was so much satisfaction from working in the ministry of Christ! My

heart filled with thanksgiving every time a young man or woman
was saved.

Have you heard of Sonny Arguinzoni? When he began his
ministry in Los Angeles, he lived in one of those low-rent building projects where his life and the lives of his family were often
in danger. Sonny didn't have enough money to pay the rent
much of the time, or to buy food or clothes for his children. Once
Sonny's assistant pastor went to preach in a church that wanted
to know about the work, and they gave him a love offering.
When they counted it they found it came to twenty dollars! Both
Sonny and his assistant needed that money for rent, but Sonny
gave it to his assistant.

Today Sonny Arguinzoni's ministry is unique in every way. It
is one of the most outstanding examples of spiritual outreach in
the whole Los Angeles area. The Drug Addicts' Church—Victory
Temple, the women's home (some of the women have their children with them), the men's home, the ranch—these are all places
where the Spirit of God is at work. I cry inside when I see Sonny
preaching and leading this ministry. There are some who criticize
Sonny and say, "He has it made!" I believe the critics are jealous
of Sonny Arguinzoni's success. He is a success in every respect,
but the critics don't know what it took when Sonny was starting
his ministry.

Another man who has come through unbelievable hardship is
Luis Rosario, the director of our Outreach center in Puerto Rico.
Luis has a lovely home, neat and clean as can be. But there is
not a wasted nickel in anything Luis and his wife do. They have
never bought new furniture. Luis has taken things that were
given to him and painted and repaired them until they look like
new. This way he feels he is free from debt to work more freely
for the Lord.

Luis is right. I do not believe that ministers should get in debt
or that they should always be wanting what other people have.
That's a good way to let Satan gain dominion over you! Luis has
been faithful in his ministry, and faithful waiting on the Lord to

supply every need, never questioning his calling. To me that is the mark of a healthy spiritual giant. To people like that I take off my hat. They can identify with suffering and need because they have experienced it themselves. Why shouldn't they enjoy success when it comes? And why shouldn't they find success in the Lord's good time?

I am hurt and concerned about the outlook of some Christians and even some ministers in relation to others who prosper. There is evident a sense of pessimism, cynicism, jealousy, and resentment when someone succeeds spiritually or financially. So many ask, "Why not me?" They forget that these successes were often happy and grateful and joyful people even when they didn't have so much. They took a positive attitude toward the little things, believing that the Lord can bless a little today as He blessed the fishes and the bread in Galilee. The successful ones who have come through difficulties take the attitude, "Now that I have it, I must be careful." The critics are often so negative they wouldn't be satisfied with anything. They forget to count their blessings and are always in the turmoil of dissatisfaction and complaining.

Don't corrupt your calling. Be content with the thing God has called you to do whether it's a big thing or a little thing. Praise Him for your opportunities, right where you are, right now.

15

Corruptor Number One

At this point you may be wondering why I haven't said something about one of the specific forms of corruption about which *you* are most concerned. I wish I had room! I could fill a book ten times the size of this one with just a few of the things that could be written about corruption and destruction, and I still wouldn't have done much more than scratch the surface. So let me see if we can't get down to basics.

When I was quite small, I can remember hoeing some weeds in my father's garden and thinking that I was doing a good job. I got rid of a whole row of weeds—at least I went down the row of beans and chopped off every weed in sight. When I got to the end of the row I stopped and looked back, pretty proud that all the weeds were gone. Then I noticed my father watching me. He came over to where I was leaning on my hoe and asked, "Are you finished, Nicky?"

"Sure!" I said. "Look, Father, the weeds are all gone!"

"No, Nicky," my father said. "Look." He knelt down in the garden and poked his finger into the ground. "See this root? As long as you leave the roots, the weeds will keep growing. It's not enough to chop off the tops. You must cut deep into the ground and kill the roots if you want to keep the weeds from growing."

So far in this book we have been chopping down some bad corruptors. But what about all the others? What about getting rid of corruption for good? How about killing the *root!*

Some people may think it just happens that there are so many corruptors in the world. They think it is human nature or an accident that so many good things are spoiled by so many bad things —pride, greed, violence, and all the rest. I say that if you see many plants of a weed growing close together, you know they come from the same root. And if you see the same kinds of corruption spoiling things in every part of the world over hundreds of years, they must grow out of one root.

To put it another way, when a number of women in Boston were all strangled in the same way, the police concluded that the murders were all committed by the same person. They were—by the Boston Strangler. When people all over the world are destroyed morally and spiritually in the same basic way, sensible people should conclude that the destruction must come from one source. The Bible says that source is the devil—the biggest corruptor of all times.

A lot of people get uptight if you mention Satan. That name may bring a mental picture of someone with horns, a tail, and a pitchfork, but I'm not talking about a fantasy. The devil is a reality.

To understand him, you've got to go back to the beginning. Originally, as many Bible passages show, Satan was one of the highest and most beautiful angels in heaven. He was close to God. He must have wanted to be bigger than God. And at some point before the earth was created, Satan swelled with pride. He conspired with other angels to try to overthrow God and take His throne. Naturally, the plot failed. When God saw the wicked pride in that powerful being, He cast him and the other evil angels clear out of heaven.

Satan had once been one of the most beautiful angels in heaven. His name in the beginning was Lucifer—angel of light. So when God made the world and planned for man to be happy in it and lead a beautiful life there, the devil was watching and waiting to spoil it all, just as he had tried to spoil heaven.

God took His time in separating the land from the water, creating the birds, the fish, the plants and trees, and He took just pride in everything He made. Finally He made human beings in

His own image, as the crowning glory of His work. Of all the creatures God ever made, only man was made in His image. This shows how highly He thought of mankind. When God had completed His creation, He looked upon it and said, "This is good!"

God created Adam from the dust of the earth and placed him in a situation where he could really make a difference. He learned to call everything by name—the cattle, the birds, and every beast (*see* Genesis 2:20). The first man was his own computer. God gave him the mind to acquire knowledge and the wisdom to do all this. And God had beautiful communication with Adam. There was fellowship all the time, especially in the evening, in the cool of the day when God walked through the Garden of Eden and talked with that man who is the ancestor of us all.

But God felt that man needed a companion. He put Adam to sleep and out of his side He took a rib and of it created a woman to be this companion. The two were very happy. God gave them His law and revelation to guide and inspire them. They had the privilege of doing whatever they wished. They could eat anything in Eden but one thing—God told them not to eat of the fruit of the tree of knowledge of good and evil.

Then the battle started! Satan never rests in peace. He is always planning, plotting, conspiring against God. Satan wanted to hurt God, and the best way to accomplish that was to get at the being of which God was most proud, and that was man. From that day, the witchcraft started. Satan himself entered a serpent that was in the garden. Never in history has there been another record of a serpent speaking, but this serpent talked to Eve and she replied.

Satan guessed that the woman in Eden was weak. (Men are generally considered the stronger, although in some ways women appear tougher than men.) But the devil knew that the best way to get at Adam was through Eve. And his first step was to inject his personality into her mind. He tried to give her the idea, "You think that God told you not to eat that fruit because doing that would make things go wrong. But I promise you, eat it and you'll be as intelligent as God. You'll be able to see yourself as you are —and you will know good and evil, just like God."

It was a low trick, half truth and half lies, like all of Satan's deceptions, but Eve fell for it, and Adam fell, and as a result all mankind fell. From that day forward death came into the world through sin.

Adam and Eve were deceived by the devil, but there was some truth in his deception. After that, they could really see themselves. Their eyes were opened and they saw their nakedness before each other and before God. They felt ashamed!

Although Adam and Eve discovered the form of the human body, there was nothing wrong with this discovery in itself, but in this case, Adam and Eve made the big mistake of letting pride take over. They let sin control them, they fell, and were cast out of the garden.

Men have never been satisfied. They are always wanting to *do their own thing.* Man wants to build his own kingdom and be his own god. The generations have proved that. There was a time when the people of God, the Israelites, were slaves in Egypt. God sent them a liberator when the people asked for someone to bring them out of bondage. And God found Moses to do it. Moses talked with God. He believed so strongly in his heavenly Father that he refused to compromise with sin. Moses was the kind of man which God could use, and Moses took the people out of slavery.

There was a festival—a celebration—when the Israelites had crossed the Red Sea. Festivals didn't start with Woodstock and Watkins Glen. Moses' sister Miriam took a tambourine and danced. Everyone was dancing and happy. There were so many beautiful feelings resulting from this freedom, from no longer living in fear and captivity. The festival went on while Moses went up into Mount Sinai to pray and to receive the Lord's guidance. He was there many days, and while he was gone, Satan got busy again. This time he injected into the people's minds a dissatisfaction with their leader and he gave them the idea that they should have a god they could see and touch. So when Moses finally came down from the mountain with the Ten Commandments, the people were dancing in lust and worshiping an idol

they had made with their own hands. Moses could not endure
this. He became so indignant that he smashed the Commandments, engraved on stone tablets by God Himself (*see* Exodus
32: 1–19).

A number of times after that, Satan filled the people's minds
with rebellion, discontent, grumbling, criticism, and unbelief.
Once this brought a plague of serpents among them. At another
time, God would have destroyed them all had not Moses inter-
ceded to win their forgiveness by God. Again and again, the
Israelites went their own way instead of God's and it was only
His patience and love which kept them from destroying themselves.

For centuries after, there was revealed the same story of sin,
punishment, and finally repentance and deliverance. The famous
Samson was known not only for his superhuman strength, but
for his moral weakness. Delilah was one of the women whom
Samson loved. She was paid a high price to learn from her lover
the secret of his great strength. While he was sleeping, Delilah
cut Samson's hair and turned him over to the Israelites' enemies,
the Philistines, who gouged out his eyes and put him in prison.
During a great pagan festival, Samson was brought out of prison
in chains to amuse the Philistines in the temple of their god
Dagon. At that moment, this tragic hero prayed for the restoration
of his lost strength and pulled down the temple. It is written that
those Samson killed in his death were more than all the enemies
he had killed in his lifetime (*see* Judges 16). Once again, Satan
almost seemed to get the best of God's people, but at the last
moment, God's side won the final victory.

On another occasion, God used a woman named Deborah to
deliver His people from their enemies. She was a prophetess and
judge with unusual talents for executive and military leadership.
Deborah commanded the Hebrew general Barak to gather his
troops and fight the opposition Canaanites. Reluctantly, Barak
carried out his mission with Deborah at his side and the enemy
was routed (*see* Judges 4).

The people asked God to give them a judge and prophet, and

He gave them Samuel, one of the great men of God. Samuel was used by God to tell the old priest Eli that his house would be punished for the sins he had permitted his sons to commit (*see* 1 Samuel 3:11–18).

Still dissatisfied and envious of the kings who led other nations, the Israelites asked God for a king of their own. This hurt God, for He had been more than a king to His people, but He answered their demand. Their first king was Saul, a handsome, tall, egocentric, and worldly man who "spelled trouble" early in his reign. Saul was dependent on Samuel at first. He was confused and didn't know how to rule as a king and soon refused Samuel's help when the prophet tried to counsel him. After Samuel died, Saul went to a witch and tried to communicate with the departed prophet (*see* 1 Samuel 28:7–19). This was one of the early recorded instances of alleged communication with the dead. The devil must have laughed with much glee as Saul was deluded into seeking false ways out of his difficulties.

Then God gave to the people—David, a beautiful man and king. He was human and made many mistakes, but God loved him because he was sincere and honest. He didn't try to hide anything. When David saw the lovely Bathsheba bathing, he was so overpowered with desire that he sent for her and eliminated her husband by putting him on the front lines of the army, where he was killed in battle. Soon Bathsheba bore David's illegitimate child. But David didn't try to cover up his sin permanently. He wept many bitter tears over this tragic affair, and when he turned to God in true repentance, God forgave as He always does those who honestly turn to Him (*see* 2 Samuel 12:13).

There were both good and bad kings after that, but the people got tired of all of them and asked God again for a prophet. So He sent them not one prophet, but a number of them. Usually these men of God—Isaiah, Jeremiah, and others—were rejected and sometimes killed by the people, who did not really want to hear what God had to tell them. When Isaiah began to preach the truth and tried to bring the people together, they turned against him and according to ancient legend, this great prophet was finally sawn in half.

The last great prophet—the man who closed the Old Testament age and ushered in the age of Christ—was John the Baptist. John proclaimed His Coming and His Kingdom and really preached the Word of God! But what happened when he criticized the personal life of Herod Antipas, the head of the government? King Herod was committing adultery with his brother's wife, Herodias, and John had the guts to preach against that illicit passion. Herod was disturbed, but since he was somewhat in awe of the Baptist was not sure what to do. So furious was Herodias, however, that she searched for revenge through her daughter Salome. When Herod so admired her dancing that he promised her anything she wished, Salome, coached by Herodias, asked for the head of John the Baptist (*see* Mark 6: 17–28). So Satan managed to get rid of that prophet, too.

Give me! All through history, inspired by Satan, people have been asking God, "Give me, give me, give me." And God, the long-suffering, patient One, has been giving, giving, giving—and time after time Satan has laughed, because God seemed to be playing into his hands. Satan must have thought many a time, "Now, God, I've got You."

At last God had given men everything possible—His best gifts, His best servants. There was only One left for Him to give—His only Son, Jesus. God did not hold back His last, dearest possession. He saw the opportunity to save mankind, and so He sent Jesus to earth. The Saviour came willingly, eager to show what it is like for God to live on earth. He healed the sickness and wounds of many who lived in poverty and who had been falsely led by the wrong guidance, the wrong religion, into a wrong way of living.

When Jesus came to earth, the devil must have rubbed his hands and cried, "I've got You now, God! I'm going to hurt You real bad. I'm going to put the whole world out of balance. *I'm going to let You see Your Son tortured to death on a cross.*" When that happened, God found it unbearable to look on the sight. He had to turn His face away—He couldn't watch His Son going through that agony. There was the torture of the nails and the suffering and the physical exhaustion, but on top of all these, there was the pain that was even worse—the bearing on His body of the sins of the whole world. Jesus died that slow, horrible death for your sins and mine.

When Jesus hung on the cross He prayed, "Father, forgive them; for they know not what they do" (Luke 23:34). And He was so concerned about His disciples and His mother (*see* John 19:26, 27). Here we see Jesus' great compassion for man. He saw that His disciples were going through a time of anguish and loneliness. That was why He had been so concerned to promise them the Holy Spirit (*see* John 14:16–20). The Spirit would be another Friend and Comforter. He would strengthen them and give them courage and power. Without the Holy Spirit, we are as weak as kittens—with Him, we are stronger than lions.

We should be so grateful to Jesus for sending the Holy Spirit! And for going away to prepare a place for us, and promising to return (*see* John 14:3). I definitely believe in the Second Coming of our Lord Jesus Christ. Jesus explained it, the Bible says it, and I believe in Jesus and the Book.

While Jesus was dying, the devil must have been thinking, "Now I'm going to take over. I'll be able to rule the whole earth!" But all his plans backfired. For three days it looked as though Satan had beaten God. But on the third day Christ returned from the dead. The Resurrection proved that God lives and that Jesus is eternal, and that the devil can't win unless we let him. Death was conquered right there when Jesus rose.

Without the Resurrection, there would be no need to be a Christian. Any old religion would do! The real answer to Buddhism and all the other cults and superstitions is *Jesus.* Jesus Christ is greater than any false god. He came from the One God, He *is* God, and His Resurrection proves it.

With the Holy Spirit, we have God's best Gift in our daily personal lives. Before He left this earth, Jesus looked ahead and saw that His disciples would need divine power. So He instructed them on how to receive the Holy Spirit (*see* Acts 1:4–8). God and Jesus were way ahead of the devil. Satan was counting on getting rid of Jesus, but he couldn't have guessed that Jesus would return from the dead, and he never could have imagined what the Spirit would do.

We need the Spirit of God to live a full, powerful Christian life. Remember that the devil always tries to attack God through man—through you and me. That is his psychology and his technique. But, praise God!—with the protection of the Holy Spirit, he can't hurt us. With the Spirit's aid we can have complete communication with God. Through Jesus Christ we can talk with God—go straight to God to learn His will. We don't need anyone to intervene between God and ourselves. We can go into a corner, or any other place, and we can have this wonderful relationship with Jesus.

That is why I am so happy that Jesus took over after man sinned. Right at the beginning, back in Eden, God foretold that there would always be war between man and the serpent. But He promised that the serpent would bruise the heel of the woman's seed—and "it shall bruise thy head" (*see* Genesis 3:15). It happened! Satan struck at the seed of the woman—Jesus—and He stepped right on the serpent's head. Everything the devil tried to do backfired.

Jesus won!

16

Meet My Psychiatrist

Psychiatry is a big thing today. Among the jet set, it is as fashionable to be analyzed as it is to have your children's teeth straightened.

But I want to say right out: Medicine is a very good thing, a gift from God that we should all be thankful for. However, psychiatry doesn't have all the answers.

Not long ago the evening news program in one large state told a story tragic enough to wring tears from a stone. A psychiatrist who had been feeling very depressed left his office, went home, took a gun and murdered his wife and his sixteen-year-old daughter. The telecast ended with the camera zooming in on that teenage girl's room. Millions of viewers saw her bullet-riddled body slumped on the floor in a pool of blood. Then the camera moved to the book that had fallen from her hands. It moved close-up, so everyone could see the words on the cover: THE LONELY NOW —NICKY CRUZ.

How thankful I was that the young girl knew the Physician with the real power to heal.

As you know if you've read my other books, when I was president of the Mau Maus and the judge turned me over to the court psychologist, that expert failed. He tried hard to figure out what made me a gang leader, but I don't think he ever got near the real truth. So he finally gave up and told me I was doomed.

119

I know of some psychiatrists who solve one problem by creating another. One man struggling with sex temptations was advised to do whatever he felt like doing. Another man was so depressed he had the urge to throw himself in front of a train. He went to a psychiatrist who told him he ought to visit a prostitute. I say such advice is dead wrong.

In the last few years a number of psychiatrists have admitted having sex relations with their patients. After four women got involved in this way and then were abandoned by their psychiatrist-lover, one tried to commit suicide, two went into a deep state of mental depression, and the husband of a fourth patient killed himself after he discovered what his wife had been doing. Some therapy!

Dr. E. Fuller Torrey of the National Institute of Mental Health says that psychiatrists are in many ways like witch doctors. In his recent book, *The Mind Game,* Dr. Torrey says that both psychiatrists and witch doctors depend a lot on the patient's confidence and faith, both build up that confidence by projecting an image of expert ability, and both get cures in their own cultures which neither one could accomplish in the other's culture. What the psychiatrist achieves with his diploma, according to Dr. Torrey, the witch doctor achieves by rattling his gourd.

Even so, a *good* psychiatrist can help a lot of people. He listens to you—and in these days it's hard to find somebody who will simply listen to what you want to say. He accepts you as you are, not as you could or should be. He helps you sort out your feelings and problems. He helps you understand them. He helps you accept yourself, and your situation in life, and the people with whom you have to live or work. He gives you a new perspective on things. At best, your psychiatrist helps you move up to a better level of existence. He helps you make the best of yourself and your circumstances.

I'd like to introduce you to my own Psychiatrist. The One I have always listens to me. I can get an appointment with Him any time of the day or night. After an hour with Him I'm never told, "The time is up. Come again next week." My Psychiatrist always listens for as long as I want.

He accepts me. He knows all my weaknesses and mistakes, but no matter what I do, He never turns me off. He is never threatened by what I say or feel.

And He leads me to more than understanding. He does more than help me make the best of things. He makes me into a better person, able for anything. He does more than that. Sometimes He changes my circumstances, so the problems I was trying to cope with simply disappear.

Other psychiatrists charge fees that are out of sight for a good many people. My Psychiatrist never charges a cent.

A psychiatrist is a healer of the mind and spirit. My Psychiatrist is the Great Physician. Unlike some medical doctors, He has no hopeless cases; He never fails.

Soon after I found God at that amazing meeting David Wilkerson had in the St. Nicholas Arena years ago, I turned myself in to the police. I found myself standing before the same judge who had sentenced me before. He asked, "What are you doing here?"

"Your honor," I said, "about three days ago I gave my life to Jesus."

The judge's jaw fell open. He looked as though he was trying to figure out what I was saying but couldn't comprehend it. Obviously he couldn't believe it. All he seemed to be able to say was: "*What?*"

I said, "Your honor, about three days ago I gave my life to Jesus."

The judge said, "Sit down and wait right here."

I waited there in the courtroom for about forty-five minutes, wondering what was happening. The judge had disappeared into his chambers. I discovered later that the judge had telephoned the court psychologist who had said to me only a few weeks before, "Nicky, you're doomed. There's no hope for you."

About the time I felt like getting away from that courtroom as far as I could possibly get, the court psychologist walked in. I jumped to my feet.

"Doc," I said, "do you remember what you said to me the last time I saw you?"

"Yes, I remember."

"I've got good news for you, man! Three days ago I turned my life over to Jesus. I don't know too much about this Jesus stuff yet, but I can tell you one thing. I've never been so happy in my life as I have been for the last three days. I've been reading this Bible I have here. Listen to this!"

I opened my Bible to the first page and I read the whole first chapter of Genesis to the psychologist. When I got to the end of the chapter and stopped, he said: "Nicky, that's beautiful. I hope you make it."

The court psychologist, meant well. He had done his best. But he had to give up when it came to changing my life. He couldn't touch what the Great Psychiatrist did for me—in an instant!

And still does for me.

A good psychiatrist may be able to do one thing for you. Whatever your problem is, depression or marriage difficulties or something else, he may help you solve it. But then he turns you loose and that's the end.

Jesus never turns you loose. He is *a very present help,* as David knew (*see* Psalms 46:1).

Jesus didn't just lift me out of my troubles and then turn me loose. I need Him all the time—and He's there every time I need help.

I had a rough time writing *Satan on the Loose.* When I decided to write that book, I knew something about what I was going to be up against. I had watched my father, a witch doctor all his life, face all the powers of the demonic world when he decided to become a Christian. I knew how viciously those powers were still attacking my mother, a medium until she, too, became a Christian. Before writing that book I had been like a freed prisoner of war. Christ had redeemed me from captivity to Satan, and I had worked with Him to redeem other captives.

But in *Satan on the Loose* I was attacking Satan directly, exposing his sneaky plans to win the world completely to his horrible domination, and I knew that he was going to use every trick in his book against me.

He did.

When I started writing *Satan on the Loose,* I learned what it means to have the gates of hell wide open and feel the breath of Satan blowing in your face. I knew I would need superhuman power to face that ancient enemy—but I felt my energy drained away before I could get in my first blow. You know how sometimes you jump out of bed eager to start a new day? Well, the first morning after I started working on that book, I woke up exhausted. It was as though I could barely pull on my shoes—or open the Bible—or pray. God seemed a million miles away. I didn't feel like doing a thing.

Gloria, always very sensitive to my spiritual needs, asked, "What's wrong, Nicky?"

And I didn't even feel like telling her. I felt lost in a spiritual fog, and it seemed as though there was no way to get out. I was drained of energy and even of hope.

For eight months, while I plodded ahead with *Satan on the Loose,* I felt as though I was in one of those nightmares where you try to move and cannot. Once, when I was a boy in Puerto Rico, I dreamed I was Tarzan of the Apes. I dreamed that a gigantic jungle cat was in a tree over my head, crouched ready to spring at me—and I was frozen like a statue, unable to make a single move. Well, it was like that for eight months while I wrote *Satan on the Loose.* I felt like a powerless pygmy in the grip of a supernaturally strong, giant enemy.

I knew that anyone who gets into witchcraft or the occult has to be on guard against attacks on his mind and his sanity. When I felt so depressed, and I couldn't seem to find any way out, I wondered if Satan was winning his battle against my mind. I felt that I was getting into depths where Gloria couldn't help me, where no one on earth could help.

Outwardly I think I appeared happy and normal to most

people. But deep inside I was sad and depressed and I felt an incredible demonic weight on my soul. Sometimes I found myself sitting for hours, looking out the window, seeing nothing of the bright world outside but envisioning the darkness and hopelessness of the world of Satan. It was a weight and a feeling so powerful that I couldn't seem to find any way on earth to shake it off!

I kept wondering, *Why do I feel this way?* I searched my memory. It was real turmoil—I knew something was wrong with my spiritual life, but I just couldn't seem to find the cause—or the cure. The awful darkness seemed to be blotting out everything I should have known. I felt as though I was in a pitch-dark room at midnight with no way to find a light. I couldn't put my finger on what was wrong.

As those periods of depression and blackness swept over me and I stared out the window, I struggled against powers and forces that I could feel almost physically. I tried to pray, but it seemed like too great an effort even to call to God for help.

Then the Great Psychiatrist came to my rescue. Out of nowhere came the words: "Ask, and it shall be given you; seek, and ye shall find . . ." (Matthew 7:7). It was like a lifeline flung to someone drowning! I cried out in my heart: "Jesus, help me!"

And the miracle happened. Like the sun burning through fog, the Light of the World cut through the darkness and drove it back. My half-frozen heart began to warm in that wonderful sunlight. Joy and hope flooded through my being, and I knew that once more Satan was on the run.

One of my sessions with the Great Psychiatrist was while I was driving down the Los Angeles Freeway in 1966. I had just finished a youth crusade in Santa Ana. Three thousand people had listened to my testimony. When I invited them to accept my Saviour, hundreds crowded forward. It was thrilling for me, Nicky Cruz, once a gang leader, to be used that way by the Lord!

I thought of the European tour I had taken the year before. There had been some fabulous crusades in some of the biggest cities in Europe. London was especially fascinating. There I spoke in the great Royal Albert Hall. All around me, filling the arena in front of the speaker's platform and in tier upon tier filling that enormous building, the youngsters and oldsters of London listened to the message. There were girls in mini-mini-skirts, young gentlemen with long wavy hair and ruffled shirts who looked as though they had stepped out of the eighteenth century, and tough-looking molls and skinheads who were probably as much at home on the streets of London as I used to be on the streets of New York. When these young people came forward to accept Christ, I knew He was using me in ways that I never would have dreamed possible a few years before.

There was a feeling of excitement and anticipation before each of those meetings. When I spoke, I held nothing back. I lived all over again my desperate life of crime in the gangs, my discovery of Christ, my new life since. As those seeking Christ knelt under the hot glare of the overhead lights, I could feel the cool wind of the Spirit of God moving in their hearts, soothing their feverish spirits and implanting His new life within them. Communicating Jesus in this way was one of the most exalting experiences I have ever had.

Now, at Santa Ana, the same thing had happened all over again. Members of the runaway generation by the dozens were coming Home, finding the peace and security they had been searching for so desperately, in their Father's loving arms.

But going back over these scenes of triumph as I drove my Pontiac down the Los Angeles Freeway brought me some very mixed emotions. In a way it had been a thrilling thing to be able to lead so many young people to Christ. But I took no pride in my shameful past. There may be individuals who glory in violence or blood. It may well be that many youngsters who come to my meetings get a vicarious thrill out of hearing the details of the bloodshed and lust and anarchy that were once part of my life.

I don't. The fact is that it is very painful for me to talk about the muggings and murders and robberies and gang fights in my past. For me, preaching is harder than any of those gang battles. Whenever I step into a pulpit, or onto an evangelistic platform, I sense the cosmic conflict that is really taking place.

I know that Jesus is there, looking at all those people with His infinite love for every last one of them and longing to bring them to Himself. And I know that Satan is there too, desperate to keep all those thousands in his own clutches, ready to try anything to prevent them from turning to Christ. I can practically see Christ on one side, the devil on the other, struggling for the eternal soul of each person there. And I realize that what I say can tip the balance toward heaven or hell!

Realizing all that, I can't rattle off my life story like a salesman's spiel. I feel that I have to put everything I've got into it, and so I live all over again those moments of crime and lawlessness that are now so shameful for me to think about. If you think that isn't hard, ask yourself this question: How would you feel if you were asked to reveal in public all the lies and wrong desires and shameful things in your own past life? How would you like to do this, not once, but over and over again?

All these things crowded through my mind as I drove down the freeway toward the home I then had in Los Angeles. I implored:

Lord, do I have to go through these experiences time after time? I thank You that I can identify with the sins and the problems of so many young people. You know how I rejoice that I can share Your vibrations of truth and freedom. I praise Your name that You can use me so often to bring so many young people to You. But it's such agony to live through some of these things, over and over! Do I have to keep doing it night after night, week after week? Isn't there some other way? Lord, You know I won't put on an act to play with people's emotions. You know that I can't be a robot, saying something I don't feel. When I tell what You did for me, I have to do it honestly, with all my feelings. You know it hurts because I do give myself 100 percent!

I felt torn apart. I wept from a broken heart. As I drove along the crowded freeway, tears kept filling my eyes.

All of a sudden I found myself almost fighting with the Lord. I was hurt. "Lord," I sobbed, "do people come to my meetings

to find You, or do they come just to see a real live gang leader? Is this what You want of me, to become a public spectacle?"

For half an hour I poured out my heart.

Then the answer came.

Suddenly I felt a chill. I knew that Someone was there in the Pontiac with me. I became ashamed of the way I had been talking to Him. I knew He deserved every shred of my love and respect, and I'd been talking to Him like a teacher scolding a bad student.

I felt the Great Psychiatrist close to me.

Jesus spoke. It wasn't an audible voice. It was simply the Son of God speaking in my heart, in His quiet, beautiful way:

Nicky, this is why I picked you up out of the streets of New York. This is why I cleansed you and gave you new life. It is that you may share it with others. That you may tell everyone, good or bad, dirty or clean, wise or foolish, about Me. I know your feelings. Do not feel sorry for yourself. Do not rebel against what I ask you to do. Rejoice that you can be My witness at such a time as this.

I knew the Great Psychiatrist had heard all my questions, understood my agony, knew my rebellion. I knew that He had borne the torment with me, that He had accepted it into Himself and cleansed and forgiven and healed my hurts.

These words leaped into my mind:

I can do all things through Christ which strengtheneth me.

Philippians 4:13

My grace is sufficient for thee; for my strength is made perfect in weakness. Most gladly therefore will I rather glory in my infirmities, that the power of Christ may rest upon me.

2 Corinthians 12:9

The Lord knows that I cannot go into a pulpit without giving myself completely. He knows that when I speak it is a real experience for me. And because He knows my weakness, He goes into the pulpit with me, and truly His strength is perfected in my weakness.

I cannot understand how anyone can speak from a pulpit without Jesus. How can anyone speak about Him if He is not real to the speaker at that moment?

Once I sat in an airplane next to a man with a clerical collar. He was interested in my work, he said, because he believed in a relevant Gospel. But when I talked about Christ he moved slightly away from me and looked at me as though I were deranged. He didn't seem to have any idea of what it is like to have Jesus in the pulpit beside you. He didn't understand me, and I couldn't understand him.

I'm thankful that my Saviour did not save me and then forget about me. He keeps on saving me, from myself and from all kinds of impossible situations. I can do anything I have to do through Him.

It still tears me up to tell about my old life. But the Great Physician heals the wounds. I'm still aware that many of my listeners may be there for the thrill of blood and lust. But if Christ can use it all for His glory, I'm content.

I still worry that Nicky Cruz may be exalted instead of Jesus Christ. I want to ask you who read this to pray that He will always be the one I praise. But I realize now that as long as I trust Him, He can keep me in the right place. Now, with Paul, *I am sure that God who began the good work . . . will keep right on* helping me grow in His grace (*see* Philippians 1:6 LB).

I'm sure that as long as I live, I'll have problems. But I also know this: *With Jesus as my Psychiatrist, I'm ready for anything.*

17

Straight Is Beautiful

These days, if you don't smoke grass you may feel like a freak. Well, let me tell you that the *real* freaks are the acid freaks and the pot smokers and the troublemakers. They are the ones who get the headlines. The drug addicts, the revolutionaries, the protesters, the crooks, the heavies, the kidnappers, the killers —they're the ones that make the news. But the straights and the squares—the people who build up instead of tearing down, the ones who hold things together, who quietly go about their business doing good things—these are the people who really count. Freakiness and crookedness get talked about, but *straight is beautiful*.

I've seen that so often. Frank wanted to make a career in business and politics. When he started working for a chain of supermarkets he advanced fast, but the work just didn't satisfy him. In his heart he knew he was going to have to do more in life than make money. He came to work on my staff, and there he met Elizabeth.

Elizabeth had been brought up in a church in Indiana. But she was not content with just supporting her church. She wanted to find some Christian action, so she too found her way to the headquarters of Nicky Cruz Outreach. When Elizabeth met Frank, it didn't take long for the two to discover that they both had the same deep desire to go all out for Christ. Between them they have been a tremendous help in my work. And both Frank and Elizabeth will testify that nothing is more exciting than such 100 percent service.

It is a beautiful thing to see Jesus take someone who has been wrecked from drug abuse, or heading straight downhill in some other way, and change him totally. But I believe we often forget that the same power of Christ is often at work in Christians who have long lived quiet, peaceful lives, like Frank and Elizabeth. The same miracle of new birth has happened to them! When a caterpillar turns into a butterfly, it's a miracle of nature. But the same power of God is at work when a flower unfolds from an unpretentious little bud.

The change of personality, habits, and character is so evident when a *freak* of some kind is converted that the salvation of a *straight* may look like a lesser miracle. But if that's the way we look at it, we are wrong. For then, not only are we belittling Christ's omnipotent work, but we are downgrading those whose confession of Christ is just as real and just as life-changing as anyone's, though perhaps not quite so dramatic.

The change in my own life, from ghetto gang leader to evangelist and youth worker, along with many experiences since and many observations of American young people, has made me keenly aware of that misconception.

I have seen so many young people, eyes aglow, clamor to a stage to shake hands or get the autograph of Nicky Cruz. Some of these youngsters will not listen for five minutes to a parent or pastor or Sunday-school teacher talk about spiritual things. Yet they will stand in line for an hour, sit on the floor for two hours, and wait backstage for an hour more, just to have me sign my name in a book.

I know why some of this happens. A good many young people feel: "You've been there, Nicky. You know what I'm facing. You know what life is like for someone my age." There's truth in that. The Apostle Paul gave his testimony time after time, for the benefit of those who could identify with him. I've given my own testimony many times in my talks and my books. Thousands of people have told me that through my life story they saw themselves and their need for Christ. Yet I shudder at the thought that anyone's past experiences are glorified more than the Lord who brought about those experiences.

Perhaps, as I have been told so often, it is better for young people to have a Christian hero than some other kind. The fact is, this is a generation without heroes. So many of the inspiring figures of past years are now dead or gone from center stage. The astronauts were popular for a time, but how many people even knew the last team of astronauts was in outer space? Political heroes have turned out in so many cases to be frauds and phonies. Who can anyone look up to? But I don't want to be idolized. I will feel uneasy until I know that all the credit for changing a life like mine goes to Christ and His power and glory.

The One to look up to is not on earth but above. The Bible tells us to continue *looking unto Jesus the author and finisher of our faith* . . . (Hebrews 12:2). He is the One who saved us and will keep us going to the end!

The freaks and heavies—where are they now? I'll tell you where they are. Some of them are dead. Many more than I like to think about are buried from New York to Miami to Los Angeles, dead from drug overdoses, suicide, disease, or run-ins with the law. Some are behind bars for committing horrible crimes. Some have syphilis and other diseases. Some have suffered irreversible damage to the mind. Some are homosexuals. Some have turned to witchcraft and the occult. Others are lost in religions that they think will give them peace, although they will never find it without the Prince of Peace.

"I've got to find my identity," one young woman told me on the way from her parents' home to a New Mexico commune. Identity! Today you could hardly tell her from thousands of other young women like her—old before their time, worn and battered by life, the sparkle gone from their eyes, about as attractive as old shoes.

Come with me to a hippies' hangout in a midwestern town. A lot of them look like vegetables. They just aren't functioning anymore. They go through the motions of living, but they are zombies—dead on their feet, their souls are gone and they don't even know something is missing. Here's a gang of them sitting in a circle in this decrepit old house where they live. They pass a stick of marijuana around the circle and think they're having fun. No way! All of them look half-dead-to-the-world. This is being together? Where is the excitement, the joy?

Get me straight—it takes guts to stay away from situations like that and to know how to say *no!* Joseph worked for a man with a lot of money and a beautiful wife. One day while Joseph was alone in the house with his employer's wife, she tried to get him to go to bed with her. Joseph had the guts to say no. He just went on about his work trying to ignore her invitation for two reasons. One: He knew it wouldn't be fair to his employer. Two: He knew it would be a sin against God.

But Joseph's temptation, like most temptations, didn't go away. The woman kept trying to seduce the young man, and when he wouldn't give in she got angry. She waited until there was no one around and then she made a last try. "Come to bed with me," she whispered in Joseph's ear as she tried to pull him into her bed. Joseph managed to flee from her but the woman held on to his jacket, and when her husband got home she got her revenge.

"Look at what that Hebrew servant you like so much tried to do!" she screamed, waving the jacket in her husband's face. "While you were gone he came into my bedroom and tried to rape me, and when I screamed he ran away and left his jacket behind!"

The husband was so angry that Joseph went to prison—but the Lord was with him. The whole story is in your Bible, Genesis 39. Joseph had guts! He always stuck to his principles, and eventually, even though he was in a foreign land, he rose to the second-highest position in the government of Egypt, and when hard times came along he saved his people and his own family from starving.

Be proud of who you are, and be yourself. Stand for your principles even when it is hard.

I begin laughing when I see people who want to look like heavies. On a plane, I watched a lady who must have been well over fifty years old, strutting around in a tight sweater, dark glasses, and a miniskirt. She went around calling everybody "Honey" and she seemed to be trying to act like a starlet. I noticed that even when this woman crossed her legs, nobody seemed to be turned on. The fact is, people laughed at her. Young people are not at all the only ones with hang-ups. Corruption is in no way limited to teen-agers. Whatever your age, you can *choose* whatever you want to be: heavy or straight. And you will find if you choose to be straight, the pay is better. Your riches will be things money can't buy and nothing can take away, ever.

There are so many straight people whose lives show so clearly how completely Christ *does* save and keep! Take Park Tucker, brought up in the coal mines of Wilkes-Barre, Pennsylvania. By the time he was twenty-two, he was an old hand in the mines. He was working a quarter of a mile under the ground when the mine caved in. Two of his friends were killed instantly. A huge rock snapped Park's left arm, and with other rocks piling up around him, Park made God a promise: "If You save my life, I'll give it all to You."

When the rescuers got through the cave-in, they found him the only man still alive. He had to spend the next year in a hospital, but Park Tucker came through—and kept his promise. He went back to grade school—a giant among small children. He went through high school and college, struggling every minute, working his way. He got through and became a minister and then a chaplain in the federal penitentiary in Atlanta, Georgia. There he brought Christ to thousands of convicted prisoners.

You hear so much today about corrupt politicians, it's easy to get the idea that everyone is a crook. Everyone isn't! Look at Orrin G. Judd, a federal judge who often works sixty hours a week. When he learned of complaints against a home for retarded children, he visited it himself and ordered sweeping

changes in its administration. Judge Judd is a Christian, active
in his church and the American Bible Society. He, too, proves that
straight is beautiful.

Take Kenneth Taylor. I'm pretty sure that at no time in his
life would he have come any closer to experimenting with drugs
or other freaky experiences than jumping into a pit of cobras.
For a number of years he was an editor for Moody Press, writing
Christian books in his spare time and raising a family. A straight,
ordinary Christian!

One day during family devotions Ken realized that his children
weren't getting much from the reading of the Bible, with all its
"thees" and "thous." On the train to work he started putting the
Bible into language his children could better understand. They
liked it, and after he had rephrased the Epistles of Paul, Ken
Taylor tried it on a publisher. And another. And another. Every
single publisher turned it down. "What do we need of one more
translation of the Bible?" they asked. "There are more than
enough already!"

Taylor took his life's savings out of the bank, borrowed some
more money, and printed his own *Living Letters*. He got a few
orders. Taylor printed more copies and rephrased more of the
Bible. Before long the work was taking so much time he resigned
his editorial job and put all his efforts into what is now *The Living Bible*—one of the most successful, best-selling versions of the
Bible since the *King James Version*.

The next time you open *The Living Bible*, thank God for
straight, "ordinary" Christians like Kenneth Taylor, whose most
dramatic experiences are simply doing the marvelous things to
which God leads them. The world is full of people like that—
and the most exciting, most satisfying thing you can ever do is
to let God open the doors and light the paths for your own
journey in the light.

No one else on earth has *your* problems and *your* circumstances. But Christ is big enough to take them all and make
them work for you! Out of the most unlikely challenges He can

produce the most surprising results. With Him in control, you may have plenty of difficulties, but He can help handle them all!

If you are straight and you are determined to *stay* straight and clean, you'll find that you are often tempted and criticized, even persecuted. You'll always be under pressure to give in here, to compromise there, to be like others who walk a low road instead of the high road with Jesus. You may have a tough time of it.

18

The Love Explosion

While I was speaking in a beautiful southern city, I came across a newspaper article on venereal disease, which today has become a fast-growing epidemic. The article mentioned a woman with VD who had been intimate with six different men. Those six had sexual contact with eleven other women. Three of the eleven had relationships with nine other men. So all together this one woman infected with VD was spreading the disease to twenty-six other people.

You could call that a "love explosion," but that would be cheapening the word *love*. So let me tell you about the real love explosion that is happening everywhere today.

Suppose you tried your hardest to reach just one person in the next week with the Good News of Jesus' love. That wouldn't be impossible, would it, if you really worked and prayed to bring that person to Jesus? Suppose you succeeded so well that the new Christian brought one more in the following week, and each new convert brought one more each week. At the end of the second week, there would be four of you in love with Jesus. The third week there would be eight, the fourth week sixteen—the number would double every week, and in ten weeks there would be over a thousand new Christians. By the twentieth week, over a million! It may sound impossible, but it could happen. In fact, it is happening!

A lot of people today are wondering why the Jesus People are multiplying so fast. There's your answer. *It takes just one man or woman, boy or girl who loves the Lord to produce a spiritual explosion to shake the earth.*

At the beginning of this century some zealous Christians had the slogan, "Evangelize the world in this generation and bring back the King!" Since they didn't do it, some people got discouraged and said it could not be done. *It can, and it's happening. Get on the bandwagon!*

Let me tell you how I saw God working in a community I'm going to call Elm City. It began in disappointment. I had been looking forward to holding a series of meetings in another city in May of that year. The meetings were cancelled—just like that. "They didn't give any reason at all," my secretary, Jeanie Weyant, told me. "They just said that circumstances beyond their control made it necessary to withdraw their invitation."

It was hard to understand. I knew some of the unbearable problems in that city, and I had hoped that by speaking there I could be used by the Spirit of God to drive at least the tip of a wedge into that mess of corruption, to give Him a fighting chance. With all its crimes and problems, a city is a strategic center; win a place in it for Christ and you can mold a large part of a nation. So I was deeply disappointed when the cancellation came. But I have learned that God always has a plan better than you can imagine, and I felt a deep peace despite the change.

Meanwhile (as I learned later), in another state, a woman of whom I had never heard felt a strange urgency to pray for her nephew. I will call her Mary Dugan. As Mary later told her nephew, although she could not explain it, she found no rest until she went into her bedroom and poured out from her heart a prayer that God would use her nephew in a special way.

The following morning about ten o'clock Mrs. Dugan was with a group of women in a neighborhood Bible-study class. Again she felt the inexplicable burden of prayer, and she asked the women to join her in prayer for her nephew.

That morning her nephew John Barker was at his desk in the insurance company of which he is president. John is an executive who gives tremendous efforts to his growing business, but that morning he was not thinking of business.

A strange vision came before his eyes. Elm City, where he lives and works, is a historic city of about a hundred thousand people. A year before, a beautiful new civic center had been built there. John had never been inside the million-dollar coliseum, but now he saw it in his mind's eye—filled with people.

They overflowed the oval amphitheatre and stood in the aisles. They were listening to stirring music and forceful preaching of the Gospel. At the invitation, crowds came from all over the vast arena to form a great swelling throng waiting to receive Christ into their lives and hearts.

John Barker had been concerned for some time about Elm City's inability to handle a steadily growing increase in drug addiction, sexual promiscuity, venereal disease, and general deterioration and corruption. A teen-ager in John's own well-to-do neighborhood, Bill Robertson, had wandered down the street only the week before, looking dazed and disoriented. John learned from his own son that Bill was going around with a group of young people rumored to use both marijuana and speed.

Unknown to John Barker, on the day of his waking vision, three boys at the Elm City High School were talking about Bill Robertson. "He's going downhill fast," said one boy.

"Yeah," said another, "but what can you do? He won't listen to anyone."

The third boy said, "We could pray."

And they did—the two boys who happened to be Christians, that is. Not with any fanfare, and usually silently, they asked God to do something to help their friend.

John Barker shared his vision with some other Christian businessmen. They talked and prayed and checked schedules. The next day John called my office.

"I've never done anything like this before," he said, "but some of us in Elm City believe you should come here to hold some evangelistic services. We are ready to rent our civic center this spring, on faith alone—believing that it will be filled and the expenses will be met if you can come."

I explained that most of my meetings are booked far in advance, and that my spring schedule had been completed some time ago. I was honored at the invitation, and I hoped Mr. Barker would understand.

"Nicky," said John Barker, "we were hoping you could come the one spring weekend there is an opening at our coliseum— May sixth and seventh."

Those two days were the ones that had just been cancelled from my engagement calendar.

I accepted. During the next few weeks, while I was crisscrossing the country on other speaking missions, John Barker and his friends were putting their money and their hearts and hands and mouths where their faith was.

They signed a contract for the rental of the Elm City Coliseum for May sixth and seventh.

They put posters all over Elm City: NICKY CRUZ IS COMING.

They got thousands of dollars worth of free time on radio and television in their area, filling it with spot announcements, interviews, and all kinds of publicity about the upcoming crusade. They arranged for the showing of the videotape *No Need to Hide* on May second, the Tuesday evening before my first crusade meeting. In that TV special, Art Linkletter takes me back to my old haunts and we talk about my life and work; as a videotape and a film it has been shown thousands of times.

Plans were made to distribute thousands of copies of my life story—both the original book and a dramatization in comic book form—in all the schools within a hundred miles of Elm City.

They invited the local ministers' association to help with the crusade; especially, they sought the pastors' help in counseling and in telling their congregations about the meetings.

They ran into heavy trouble. The ministers' association voted not to support the crusade. Many of the schools in the area refused to permit the distribution of my books to the students. On May second FBI Director J. Edgar Hoover died, and the whole hour that had been reserved for the showing of *No Need to Hide* was used instead for a memorial tribute to Director Hoover.

John and his friends prayed as soon as the first roadblock appeared, and they kept praying as new ones developed. *Other things began happening.*

A black boy had an argument with a white boy in one of the public schools where distribution of my book had been banned. Another black boy came to the first youngster's aid, two white youths jumped in, and in minutes there emerged what looked like the beginning of a race riot. That week the school board rescinded its ban on *Run Baby Run.*

Word came from another school that there was no objection to distribution of my book on a one-to-one basis. John's friends took stacks of the books home, and Christian young people in the school presented copies personally to everyone who wanted a copy.

In a third school the superintendent telephoned to say that he himself would see that the books were distributed. He did—hundreds of copies.

While the ministerial association never reversed its vote, individual ministers began calling John Barker to say they would participate personally in the crusade. Then they and many of their church members came to classes to learn how to present Christ personally to anyone who would come forward at the evangelistic crusade.

The director of the local TV station moved *No Need to Hide* to the hour that normally carried "Hawaii Five—O."

"We couldn't have hoped for a better time," John's friend Joseph Giles exulted as he told me the story later. "More people watch 'Hawaii Five—O' than any other program!"

When I arrived on Saturday at the Elm City airport, John was there with two of his business friends to drive me to the motel where they had made reservations for me. At lunch they reviewed what they had done, and afterward we went to the civic center to look things over.

Ed Jones, one of John's co-workers, stood beside me as I

looked over the vast coliseum from the speaker's platform. "It
holds about eleven thousand people," Ed said. "We have done
everything in our power to fill these seats. A group of us walked
off the area, section by section, and we claimed every section of
it for Jesus Christ. Now it is up to God."

I checked the microphone and the lighting system. As I looked
out over the vast arena, it came to me that the portable seats in
the center section were too close to the platform. What if God
took these humble men at their word, as they had taken Him
at His, and sent a multitude of inquirers forward that night to
find their Saviour? There was space there for perhaps four hundred seekers. What if the Spirit of God doubled that number?

"Those first three rows of seats," I said, "please take them all
out."

A workman asked if the seats could be put lengthwise down
the sides of the building, and of course that was fine.

One of the best music groups I know met me in Elm City.
I first came across the Singing McCrarys in a church in Los
Angeles, and now I have them at my crusades whenever someone
like Pat Boone hasn't signed them up first.

Alfred McCrary plays a vibrant bass guitar. Howard McCrary
plays the piano. Sometimes Howard plays the piano with one
hand and a keyboard instrument called the clavinet with the
other, adding a very bouncy effect to the group's singing. Sam
McCrary sings with his brothers and their lovely sisters, Linda
and Charity.

The McCrarys are young, they are alive, they are with it, and
the radiance of the glory of God shines from their faces when
they are on a platform. They were in Elm City for a week before I arrived, singing and playing in the schools and churches
and helping prepare for the crusade.

That first night of the crusade, the coliseum was filled with
thousands of people—especially young people—as the McCrarys
started to sing. They did "Let It Be" and other popular numbers.
Then they swung into "Rock of Ages" and other familiar hymns.

When they got to "How Great Thou Art," eight thousand people stood up to sing with them, clapping their hands and tapping their feet to the powerful melody, and the music seemed to soar right up to "seventh heaven."

As I waited to speak, I looked at the sea of faces stretching away before me. Busloads had come in from all the surrounding areas, and the parking lot outside was jammed with cars. There were plainly-dressed country people in the audience, men and women who looked well-to-do, and cripples in wheelchairs. They were black and white, young and old. In one section lounged a group of hippies. Teen-agers were everywhere, as well as children of all ages. I thought of the problems and needs of all these people, and as always at such a time I asked God for the words to make Jesus Christ real to them.

I told them what Jesus meant to the streetwalker taken in the act of adultery, and to the hippie usually known as the prodigal son. I spoke of what He means to prodigal sons and daughters I have met myself—runaways, drug addicts, the whole lost generation of this age—I testified to what Jesus means to me.

I said, "I don't care how you look. You can look like Tarzan if you want. You can walk like Jane, you can smell like Cheetah, but Jesus loves you."

This is the big message I always try to make the heart and center of what I say—the love of Jesus. I know how great it is in my own life, and how much He can mean to anyone. I tried to show how beautiful Jesus is.

At the end I asked those who were willing to make a stand for Jesus Christ to stand up and be counted. I do *not* ask for "every head bowed, every eye closed," when I make an appeal for decisions. Deciding for Christ takes courage, and I don't want those I bring to Him to start off ashamed to let people see what they're doing. So I asked those who had decided, to stand and come forward.

At first no one moved. Then a boy who looked about twelve came across the open space to the platform where I stood. That started it. From then on there were lines of people winding down the sides of the amphitheatre, all over that great building, making

their stand, coming to find Reality. The McCrarys led in the singing of "Just as I am, without one plea," and as long as the singing
went on, those lines continued to surge forward. At last the whole
space at the front of the stadium was filled, and people were
backed up the aisles.

There were teen-agers, boys and girls, men and women. One
young lady had mascara running down her cheeks. I saw a number of youngsters hugging each other in joy. Men and women
wiped their eyes and blew their noses.

One young fellow stood by himself, solitary among the seekers,
his blond curly hair cascading to his shoulders. I learned later
that he was Bill Robertson.

Personal workers, trained for exactly this occasion, led the
seekers to counseling rooms—but they overflowed these rooms,
and all over the platform small groups talked and prayed together, going through the four spiritual laws outlined by Campus
Crusade for Christ. As decisions were witnessed and sealed in
prayer, tears gave way to laughter and heavenlike joy. Young
people embraced in spiritual ecstasy. For two hours the counseling and rejoicing continued while many crowded around me to
shake my hand, to ask questions, to request prayer for loved ones.

When I thought of what this was going to mean in the lives
of those who crowded around me, I too found myself close to
both tears and great joy. Some of these young people had already
started down the horrible trail of carnal indulgence, drug addiction, lawlessness; now they had taken a fork in the road onto
higher ground. Some were at a crossroads, and they had turned
toward Jesus instead of the devil. What wonderful things God
had wrought!

Mary Dugan was in the audience that night, watching the
fruit of her prayer. John Barker sat on the platform as chairman
of the crusade. After it was all over he said, "It has all happened
just as I saw it at my desk three months ago."

One of the Christian businessmen said: "Elm City hasn't had
anything like this since Billy Sunday held an evangelistic campaign here. We've been living too long in the past. It's time we

let the Spirit of God move us into His program for the twentieth century."

At the final rally of our crusade, the Sunday afternoon of May seventh, thousands again filled the coliseum and hundreds came forward for more decisions for Christ. Before I left Elm City, John Barker and his friends were making plans for the opening of a Nicky Cruz Outreach Center there. With men like that, and with God's Spirit moving as He is today, what an explosion of love can reach out to every man and woman and young person on this planet!

As I said earlier, the real corruptors are the things within us —our inmost attitudes and desires. Only one thing can clean up the spring of corruption in everyone's heart, as I discovered through David Wilkerson years ago. That's why every piece of mail that goes out of my headquarters in Raleigh, North Carolina, is stamped with the words: REMEMBER, JESUS LOVES YOU!

Let me add God's own message about this from the *Living Bible* paraphrase of Romans 13:8–10.

Pay all your debts except the debt of love for others— never finish paying that! For if you love them, you will be paying all of God's laws, fulfilling all His requirements. If you love your neighbor as much as you love yourself you will not want to harm or cheat him, or kill him or steal from him. And you won't sin with his wife or want what is his, or do anything else the Ten Commandments say are wrong. All ten are wrapped up in this one, to love your neighbor as you love yourself. Love does no wrong to anyone. That's why it fully satisfies all of God's requirements. It is the only law you need.

Yes, my friend, whoever you are, wherever you may be when you read this: Remember—Jesus loves *you!*

19

When God Breaks Through

Some time has elapsed since the events of the last chapter. But this book would not be complete unless I shared some very special experiences with you.

Flashing through my mind, many things have bothered me about my ministry. It started out slowly, steadily, and spontaneously, but with the pressures of success seems to have taken on a more mechanical nature.

I can see many ministers, evangelists, and other Christians going through such heavy trials that they do not feel the Lord in their life, and the only thing to hold on to is faith in Christ. Through many dark personal experiences, I found myself thinking that somehow God was trying to change my ministry. I was functioning like a personality and fighting deep down to be just a person. Many times I was fighting because of a young staff with lots of problems. Some young people have been sharp and smart but could not handle pressures in the ministry. I opened my organization to them, but I felt some of them used this ministry to develop their own ministry. That hurt me very much. The Bible tells us "For where your treasure is, there will your heart be also" (Matthew 6:21).

I'm an evangelist, a minister, not an administrator. I know the calling of the Lord. He wants me to present the Gospel. I have seen Him perform many miracles and change lives of many, and

147

now it seems like things are getting a little sour. I traveled so much in 1973—more than 300,000 miles. I began to drift away from many of the things that I should have been on top of. I didn't see Gloria or the children very much. I know this was hard on them. We were drifting further and further apart. I began to distrust people, did not know who my friends were nor whom I could trust. I was aware that evangelists go through pressures of gossip and unfaithfulness in their own organizations. That hurts. My Board of Directors began to see my pressures and my fatigue. As they tried to relieve the pressures, more was being put on me. It is hard when you have to do something and have to agree with others. God gave us good men, men of integrity and I respect them very much. I went through heavy periods of strain and at one of my last meetings, I was coming up from that type of pressure. I came with enthusiasm for a better organization and to pray for a more mature staff. I had a different feeling in my mind and I had a need that was heavy on my heart and they knew of that need.

Edward Birch, as I'm going to call him, seemed to be throwing cold water over everything I proposed. "All this sounds to me like laying out more money," he said. "Where could we find any more than we've already obtained for administrative purposes?" As Director Birch went on, I felt that I was being judged for things that had been beyond my control. There was an apparent harshness in his attitude that made me feel stupid and guilty. It seemed to me that if I was being judged by this man, it was with no compassion at all. I knew Mr. Birch liked to run a tight business, but I wasn't prepared for the apparent fury of his attack on my proposal. I try never to hate anyone, yet a feeling close to hatred and bitterness came over me as he spoke. Eventually my board gave me all the backing I could ask, but at the end of that meeting I felt as depressed and lifeless as a zombie. It was a feeling like trying to fly across the country with no airplane.

I was supposed to leave immediately after the Directors' meeting for a three-day crusade in Canada, but I made up my mind not to go. I felt so depressed. I didn't want to go anywhere. I drove straight home and told Gloria I wasn't going to Canada, dropping my arms down beside me in disgust. "I can't do it," I said. "I just don't feel like going anywhere right now."

Gloria was silent for a moment. Then she said, "Nicky, there will be people in Ottawa waiting to hear you. They have nothing to do with how you feel."

That did it. I knew that Gloria was right, that I couldn't back out of a scheduled crusade just because I was feeling low. By now I had only five mintues to get ready! I called Eastern Airlines and they held my plane for at least twenty minutes until I got aboard. (Right here I want to express my appreciation to Eastern, to Delta Airlines, and to other airlines that have gone out of their way to help me so many times.)

During my engagement in Ottawa I felt completely uninspired. No one at the crusade realized how I was suffering as I spoke; they saw me smiling, but I was only performing. I knew how to perform. I watched the people at the crusade enjoying it all, and I felt like an actor playing a part. After the altar call I felt as though I was putting my hands on empty heads, because I knew my heart wasn't in it. If anyone had known what was really going on he would have knelt down and prayed for Nicky.

Rick Johnson, one of my dedicated fellow workers from the Outreach staff in Raleigh, came with me on this Canada crusade. One of the fine Christians in Ottawa took us both to our hotel, where we checked in at about 2:15 in the morning. We had to get up at 6:00 A.M. to catch a 7:30 plane to Toronto, so I called the hotel operator and asked her to wake me in time. Normally I like to have a hotel room to myself, but I knew Rick was concerned about me so I asked him to stay with me during the few hours before we left. I went to sleep, a very deep sleep.

Sunlight pouring through the hotel windows awakened me at 7:45 the next morning. Turning in disgust to the telephone that should have awakened me earlier, I realized that I had given the operator the room number 1213 instead of the right one— 2213. Rick was still sleeping. I woke him and said, "We've missed our plane, Rick. I'm going home." But I found there was no flight with the right connections for some time, so I decided to rest awhile longer and I went back to sleep.

I woke up with tears in my eyes and a tremendous desire to pray, but I felt that I had no power to do it. Rick was asleep. I got on my knees and groaned a prayer without words; something inside me was crying out to God. I felt great pain. I am not a new Christian. I have been growing in the Lord for many years. But I felt the kind of first-love yearning for Christ that a new Christian often feels. My eyes were swollen and red with my emotion and my chest hurt. My body was not ready for such a strong presence of God. He let me know He was there. The whole room glowed with the presence of Jesus. Jesus was like a friend as He sat on the bed next to me. I began talking to Him as I would talk to my wife or my mother. I did not hear a loud voice —there was no need for that. He was there sitting next to me. Never had this happened before. I began to talk to him.

"Jesus, thank You for walking down the streets of New York City, thank You for picking me up with Your strong arms—out of that bondage of sin. Thank You for everything You have done, but Jesus, I'm going through very painful moments now."

Jesus answered, *I know, Nicky.*

I said, "I have done many things wrong, Jesus, and You have helped me through."

I know, Nicky, Jesus said.

"Christians including Dave Wilkerson told me—'Nicky, Jesus loves you.' Even in the Bible You tell me that You loved me first. I have been walking with You, Jesus, for fifteen years and it is now August 1973, and until now, I never knew how much I loved You. I love You Jesus, I love You now, not that You love me, but because I love You. I tell You, I love You, I love You, I love You, I love You."

I began to express my feelings to Him, "Lord Jesus, I have bitterness and hate in my heart and it will destroy me. You are the Great Physician, Lord, and I beg You Lord, with Your hands, heal me inside now."

He told me, *Yes, Nicky, I will do that.*

I felt like I was sleeping, my body felt new, I felt like singing. I was so blessed by God as He took all that hatred away. I did not have that feeling anymore. I began to pray for my wife and my children. Jesus told me that He was going to make me cancel all my crusades so that I could take care of myself and my family.

I said "Jesus, many of these things, I did not ask You to do, but, thank You Lord, for all these blessings." I began to talk to Him about my staff. There had been too much misrepresentation of the whole situation. Pride had possessed many of them. I said, "Lord, if You want them to be removed, do it, but bring more people who can deal with heavy situations."

He said, *I will do it, Nicky.*

I said, "Lord, if anything displeases You, put a stop to it, anything, Lord, any misuse of money in the office or home. Be the guest of my office and my home all the time. Heal the sickness of many souls. Take this nightmare of darkness and terror and these tormenting events of doubt. Take this feeling of insecurity out of my mind."

He replied, *I will do it, Nicky.*

I was still pouring my heart out to Jesus as I confessed to Him my calling. I said, "Lord, You called me into Your ministry. You made it grow. You've given me so much, and I'm thankful. Now please take over once again. You have the wisdom that I don't have. Show me what to do next. You are Love. You are Light. Help me to have the love and the light I need. Help me to grow in the Spirit. Give me Your blessing, Lord, and make me a blessing to everyone I meet. Show me Your glory."

I asked Him to bless Gloria and my little girls. Gloria was pregnant at this time and I asked Him to give us a beautiful baby, the last one, a beautiful, healthy baby. I forgot to ask Him for a boy and we have a beautiful baby girl, Elena Mia. I prayed for my entire family, my supporters, my Board of Directors and I prayed for Mr. Birch. I asked God to take out of my heart every bit of wrong resentment that might be there toward him or anyone else.

I asked the Lord to take care of my ministry and He said He was going to change it. He said: *I want you to trust Me and when*

I finish you are going to see My Glory. I can do all things. I control you, you do not control Me. I will heal the sicknesses of the soul, mind, and body. I have resources of power to fill the restless heart with My Holy Spirit. I told Him about this book. He told me to throw away the first eight chapters and rewrite it. (This I have now done.) He said, *I will bless this book abundantly.* I said, "Thank You, Jesus."

I asked Him to give me grace about pressure in crowds, to help me function as a person and not a personality. I asked Him to give me happiness and He did. I asked Him to take care of the Centers, the financial situation, and all the changes taking place in our organization, and He did.

Wonderful things began happening as I called out to the Lord from my knees. I began to have the strongest feeling of the warmth of His loving presence. Light seemed to be filling the room—light not from this earth, but from clear beyond it.

I began to see things I had never realized before. Things clicked into place in my mind. A memory came back to me from my childhood in Puerto Rico. While I was a small boy there was often a flock of chickens in my parents' backyard. One day I noticed that when the rooster got mad, he was likely to stab out with his beak at whatever chicken was closest. But with the hens it was different. One hen ruled the roost when the rooster wasn't around. This hen pecked at another one when she was angry, and that one would peck at still another, and so it went down the line. There was a thin, scraggly little chicken at the bottom of the heap that always got it last of all. She was a sad sight; there wasn't anyone else she could peck at.

I realized that I had been caught in a sort of pecking order, too. Smarting from hurt feelings, I'd been taking my feelings out on those "below" me. I promised God that with His help I wouldn't do that again.

While I was praying and meditating, Rick woke up and felt the presence of the Lord. He couldn't believe it. He began receiving such a blessing that he was crying, and he began to pray with a beautiful spirit of compassion and humility and dedication. I prayed, too, but now it was mostly praise and thanksgiving for God's infinite love and all His promises and power and guidance. I thanked Him for Rick and for all the many people who make the Outreach possible. And as I prayed, love filled my heart for each person I named, including Mr. Birch. I suddenly felt very thankful for that man's financial wisdom and his concern for keeping our Outreach ministry sound and solvent.

I looked at my watch. I had spent almost three and one-half hours with Jesus in person. What a great joy, what a great thrill! He really healed me. Jesus really healed me.

I knew something was happening to me that I had never felt before. The promise of the Twenty-third Psalm came into my mind:

The Lord is my shepherd; I shall not want.
He maketh me to lie down in green pastures:
  he leadeth me beside the still waters.
He restoreth my soul . . . .
I will fear no evil: for thou art with me . . . .
  my cup runneth over.
Surely goodness and mercy shall follow me all the days of
  my life: and I will dwell in the house of the Lord for ever.

And I remembered Jesus' parable of the shepherd with a hundred sheep (*see* Matthew 18:12–14). When one of the sheep got lost, the shepherd left the other ninety-nine sheep behind and looked everywhere until he found the lost one and brought it safely home. From my study in Bible college I knew how a shepherd in the Holy Land would take care of a lost lamb. He would hold the little lamb close to his chest for two weeks. The lamb comes to love the warmth and tenderness of the shepherd's body. The shepherd would hold the lamb and look after it and feed it all through the day and sleep with it through the night. Finally he would let the lamb go, but it would have learned its lesson: it would never leave the shepherd more than a few feet away.

Some words came back to me from a wise old teacher in Bible college:

In the Holy Land, when a lamb strays like that, sometimes the shepherd breaks the lamb's leg. Then he carefully sets the broken limb and keeps it in splints and bandages. He carries it tenderly in his arms and lets the lamb get used to the warmth and even his heartbeat. He cares for it this way until it is completely healed and strong again. He does it in love, to teach the lamb a very important lesson—and to save its life.

As I thought of all this, I made a startling discovery.

THE SHEPHERD HAD JUST BROKEN ME.

I realized that Jesus had broken my pride, my roughness, my bad thoughts, my defensiveness. He had been rebuking me, and He had healed me. There was oil for my wounds, heavenly balm for my bruises. I felt His loving arms holding me. And I felt the beauty of His holiness and purity.

It's hard to put this into words, but at the same time I felt how important it is to take a clear-cut stand for the Lord. I saw how foolish it is to compromise your Christian testimony or fool around with anything wrong. I felt the truth of the message:

. . . God is light, and in him is no darkness at all.

If we say that we have fellowship with him, and walk in darkness, we lie, and do not the truth:

But if we walk in the light, as he is in the light, we have fellowship one with another, and the blood of Jesus Christ his Son cleanseth us from all sin.

If we say that we have no sin, we deceive ourselves, and the truth is not in us.

If we confess our sins, he is faithful and just to forgive us our sins, and to cleanse us from all unrighteousness.

1 John 1:5–9

Cleanse us from all unrighteousness! That's what God wants us to do. To make His children spiritually strong and whole, free from corruption of any kind. To use us to bring His other children Home.

As all this came to me in that hotel room, there was such a time of praise! I wish I could share it with you, but some things just cannot be put into human language.

Let me just say this, though: Jesus was there in that hotel room, and I knew it and Rick knew it. The glory of those hours is with me now, and will stay with me.

Now I know how Moses felt when he took off his shoes at the burning bush. I left Ottawa with a new vision of holiness unto the Lord. I feel more deeply than ever before how vital it is to be completely dedicated if you want to do the Lord's work. I have a new passion now, to make every word count. One day I'll be passing on from earth to heaven, and I want to be sure that my work and my words will go on for the Lord.

After we returned to Raleigh, Rick and I shared some of our experiences at our staff prayer meeting. Rick's wife, Sarah, who was also on our staff at the time (right now she's looking after a new baby), told us: "You know, while you two were in Ottawa, I was praying and I felt the same burden for complete consecration."

It's a long way from corruption to consecration—like the distance between darkness and light, or sickness and health, or death and life. The one is the complete opposite of the other. Yes, the one is the *only* answer to the other.

No sensible person would choose sickness instead of health, or death instead of life. Then why do the *corruptors* have such a hold on the world? Maybe because the people trapped by them don't know what glorious freedom they could have in Jesus.

And anyone who finds how great He is, drops the corrupting things the way a young man leaves the toys behind, when he grows up, and turns to the things of manhood and reality.

But so many people are still playing with things that aren't important at all. As I think of the years ahead, I see unbelievable changes taking place all over the world. I am convinced that the foundations of our faith, our homes, and our society will be shaken as never before. Many things that are precious to us will almost disappear from sight.

There may be less drug addiction in the next few years. However, although we have become more educated about drugs, we will still have to live with it. There will also be an incredible increase in addiction to witchcraft, spiritualism, Satanism, Eastern religions and false gods, although more ministers are getting together to fight the occult, and the blood of Christ will be applied to every Christian. There will be a veneer of peace in the world, but underneath there will be more spiritual conflict and anguish than ever before. There will be widespread revolt against every form of moral restraint.

Some people think the pendulum will swing back soon toward the way things used to be. *I don't.* I see ahead of us more sensuality, more nudity, more sexual perversion, more open attacks on the home and the family and God and the church and government. I believe it's going to become harder and harder to be faithful to Jesus Christ. I see evil becoming so attractive that many are deceived and corrupted. I believe TV and movies will bring about this corruption. I see the powers of the demonic world openly displayed and applauded. In these last days there will be more divorces than ever before. Satan is going to be attacking Christian marriages more and more.

Ahead of us there is chaos and revolution. Problems that our physicians and psychiatrists thought they had under control will become too much for them. Shortages and inflation will increase until only the few will be able to buy what they want. A depression will sweep over the whole civilized world.

The people of God will be tested as never before. This is not a vision nor a prophecy but the experience of traveling and being sensitive to our environment and this world, and I believe that many educators and ministers feel as I do.

I personally feel that there will be a tremendous love between

Catholics and Protestants in these last days in the name of Jesus. I believe they will all sit down together at the "banquet table" singing and praising the Lord, shouting *Hosanna* to Jesus Christ, the Son of the Everlasting God.

BUT JESUS LIVES! HE AND THE HOLY SPIRIT WILL GIVE STRENGTH AND BLESSING TO EVERYONE WHO FOLLOWS HIM. PRAISE HIS NAME!

If you would like more information about our work, write to: Nicky Cruz Outreach, Box 27706, Raleigh, North Carolina 27611.

Postscript

At 5:40 this afternoon, April 30, 1974, I put the last touch on this book. I now have the most beautiful staff, just as God promised me. He has sent me fellow workers as talented as they are dedicated. Jim DeVries, employed for twelve years by Sarns, Inc. in Michigan as production manager, is my executive director. LaRue Price is my personal secretary. She holds prayer meetings for our staff in the office and has opened the Outreach offices to the public. People call in constantly for prayer and we pray with them over the telephone. I was deeply touched recently when I talked personally with a lady who phoned in long distance. This woman had been trying to reach me for several days while I was away ministering in a crusade. She told me that she was a hustler and had syphilis. We prayed together over the telephone and we were so broken by the Lord that we both began to cry. Some days later I got a letter from this lady testifying that she had accepted Christ and had been proven completely healed by her physician. She wrote that her husband, with whom she had been having so many problems, had also found Christ and that they now have a very beautiful marriage. These are just a few of the blessings that I had been missing.

When God breaks through I become very happy, and He has broken through, my friend—I **LOVE YOU.**

Your friend and servant,

Nicky Cruz

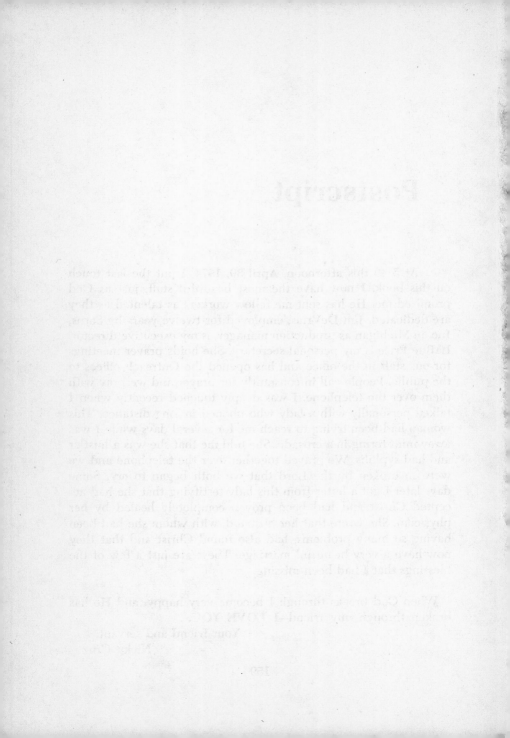

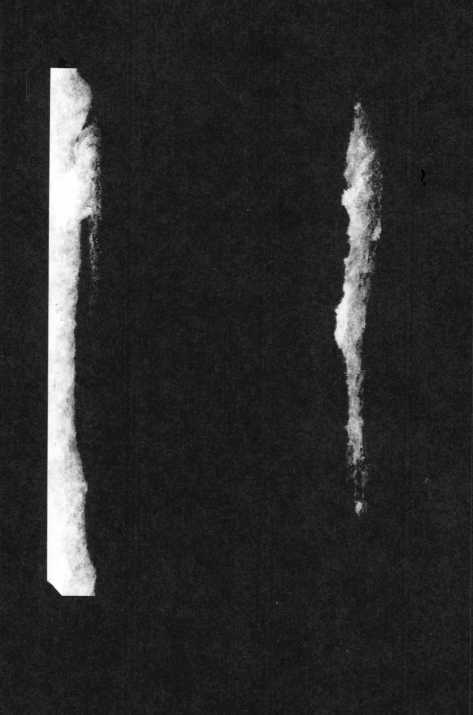

Also by Peter May

PETER MAY
ENTRY ISLAND

Quercus

First published in Great Britain in 2014 by

Quercus
55 Baker Street
7th Floor, South Block
London
W1U 8EW

A CIP catalogue record for this book is available
from the British Library

ISBN 978 1 78206 220 2 (HB)
ISBN 978 1 78206 221 9 (TPB)
ISBN 978 1 78206 222 6 (EBOOK)

10 9 8 7 6 5 4 3 2

Typeset by Ellipsis Digital Ltd

Printed and bound in Great Britain by Clays Ltd, St Ives plc

For Dennis and Naomi

Gus am bris an latha agus an teich na sgàilean

Until the day breaks and the shadows flee away

Song of Solomon 4:6
(often used in Gaelic obituaries)

PROLOGUE

It is evident from the way the stones are set into the slope of the hill that industrious hands once toiled to make this pathway. It is overgrown now, the shallow impression of a ditch on one side. He makes his way carefully down towards the remains of the village, pursued by the oddest sense of treading in his own footsteps. And yet he has never been here.

The silhouette of a broken-down drystone wall runs along the contour of the treeless hill above him. Beyond it, he knows, a crescent of silver sand curls away towards the cemetery and the standing stones on the rise. Below him, the footings of blackhouses are barely visible among the peaty soil and the spikes of tall grasses that bend and bow in the wind. The last evidence of walls that once sheltered the families who lived and died here.

He follows the path between them, down towards the shingle shore where a ragged line of roughly hewn stones vanishes into waves that cast their spume upon the pebbles, frothing and spitting. They are all that remain of some long-forgotten attempt to build a jetty.

There were, perhaps, ten or twelve blackhouses here once. Thatched roofs curved over thick stone walls, leaking peat smoke through cracks and crevices to be whipped away on the icy edge of winter gales. In the heart of the village, he stops and pictures the spot where old Calum lay bleeding, his skull split open, all of his years and heroism erased by a single blow. He crouches down to touch the earth, and in doing so feels a direct connection with history, communing with ghosts, a ghost himself haunting his own past. And yet not his past.

He closes his eyes and imagines how it was, how it felt, knowing that this is where it all began, in another age, in someone else's life.

CHAPTER ONE

The front door of the summerhouse opened straight into the living room through a fly-screen door off the porch. It was a large room occupying most of the downstairs footprint of a house that the murdered man used for guests who never came.

A narrow corridor at the bottom of the staircase ran off to a bathroom and a small bedroom at the back of the property. There was an open fireplace with a stone surround. The furniture was dark and heavy, and took up most of the floor space. Sime thought that although the house itself had been remodelled, this must still be the original furniture. It felt like stepping back in time. Generous old armchairs with antimacassars, worn rugs strewn across uneven but freshly varnished floorboards. Heavy-framed oil paintings on the walls, and every available space cluttered with ornaments and framed family photos. It even smelled old in here, and made him think of his grandmother's house in Scotstown.

Blanc fed cable off into the back bedroom where he would set up his monitors, and Sime lined up two cameras on tripods to focus on the armchair facing the window, where the newly widowed woman would be well lit. He set his own chair with its back to the window so that his face would be obscured to her, but every micro sign to flit across her face would be evident to him.

He heard floorboards creaking overhead and turned towards the staircase as a policewoman came down into the light. She looked bewildered. 'What's going on?'

Sime told her they were setting up for the interview. 'I understand she's upstairs,' he said. The officer nodded. 'Send her down, then.'

He stood by the window for a moment, holding the net curtain aside, and remembered the words of the sergeant enquêteur who had met them at the island's only harbour. *Looks like it was her that did it.* Sunlight caught his face so that it was reflected in the glass, and he saw his familiar lean features beneath their tumble of thick blonde curls. He saw the fatigue in his eyes, and the shadows that hollowed his cheeks, and he immediately jumped focus to gaze out across the ocean. The longer grass along the cliff's edge was dipping and diving in the wind now, white-tops blowing across the gulf from the south-west, and in the distance he saw an ominous bank of dark cloud bubbling up on the horizon.

The creak of the stairs brought his head around, and for a moment that seemed like an eternity his world stopped.

She stood on the bottom step, her dark hair drawn back from the delicate structure of her face. Pale skin stained by dried blood. Her bloodied nightdress was partially covered by a blanket draped around her shoulders. He could see that she was tall and holding herself erect as if it were a matter of pride not to be cowed by her circumstance.

Her eyes were a dark, crystal-cut blue with darker rings around the pupils. Sad eyes filled with tragedy. He could see the shadows of sleeplessness smudged beneath them as if someone had drawn charcoal-stained thumbs across the skin.

He heard the slow tick, tick of an old pendulum clock on the mantel, and saw motes of dust suspended in the light that slanted through the windows. He saw her lips move, but there was no sound. They moved again in silence, forming words he couldn't hear, until he became aware suddenly of the irritation in her voice. 'Hello? Is there anyone home?' And it was as if someone had released the pause button and his world wound back up to speed. But the confusion remained.

He said, 'I'm sorry. You are . . . ?'

He saw her consternation now. 'Kirsty Cowell. They said you wanted to interview me.'

And out of his turmoil he heard himself saying, 'I know you.'

She frowned. 'I don't think so.'

But he knew he did. Not where, or how, or when. But with an absolute certainty. And that feeling he had experienced on the plane returned to almost overwhelm him.

CHAPTER TWO

I

Hard to believe that just a few hours ago he had been lying in his own bed over a thousand kilometres away in Montreal, arms and legs tangled among the sheets, sweating where they covered him, freezing where they did not. His eyes then had been filled with sand, and his throat so dry he could barely swallow.

During the long night he had lost count of the number of times he had glanced at the digital display on his bedside clock. It was foolish, he knew. When sleep would not come, time crawled with the unerring pace of a giant tortoise. Watching its painful passage only increased the frustration and reduced the odds of sleep even further. The faintest of headaches lay just behind his eyes as it did every night, increasing in its intensity towards morning and the pain-killer that would fizz furiously in his glass when it was time at last to rise.

Rolling over on to his right side he had felt the empty space beside him like a rebuke. A constant reminder of failure.

A cold emptiness where once there had been warmth. He could have spread himself across the bed, warming it from the heat of his own body, but he felt trapped on the side where he had so often lain in simmering silence after one of their fights. Fights, it had always seemed to him, that he never started. And yet through all the sleepless hours of these last weeks, he had begun to doubt even that. Harsh words endlessly replayed to fill the slow, dark passing of time.

Finally, at the very moment he had felt himself slipping off into darkness, the trilling of his cellphone on the bedside table had startled him awake. Had he really drifted off? He sat bolt upright and glanced at the clock, his heart pounding, but it was still just a little after three. He fumbled for the light switch, and blinking in the sudden glare of the lamp grabbed the phone.

From his riverside apartment in St Lambert, it could take anything up to an hour and a half during rush hour to cross the Pont Jacques Cartier on to the island that was Montreal City. But at this hour the huge span of arcing girders that straddled the Île Sainte Hélène fed only a trickle of traffic across the slow-moving water of the St Lawrence River.

As the lights of empty tower blocks rose up around him, he swung on to the off-ramp and down to Avenue de Lorimier before turning north-east on Rue Ontario, the dark silhouette of Mount Royal itself dominating the skyline in his rear mirror. The drive to 1701 Rue Parthenais took less than twenty minutes.

The Sûreté de Police was housed in a thirteen-storey tower block on the east side of the street with views out towards the bridge, the TV station and the mountain. Sime took the elevator up to the *Division des enquêtes sur les crimes contre la personne* on the fourth floor. It never failed to amuse him how the French language needed nine words where one in English would do. Homicide, the Americans would have said.

Capitaine Michel McIvir was returning to his office with a coffee, and Sime fell in beside him as he walked along the corridor past framed black-and-white photographs of crime scene investigations from the fifties and sixties. McIvir was barely forty, just a handful of years older than Sime, but wore an air of authority that Sime knew would never be a fit for him. The capitaine glanced at his sergeant enquêteur with shrewd eyes.

'You look like shit.'

Sime grimaced. 'That makes me feel so much better.'

'Still not sleeping?'

Sime shrugged, reluctant to admit the extent of his problem. 'Off and on.' And he quickly changed the subject. 'So why am I here?'

'There's been a murder on the Magdalen Islands, out in the Gulf of St Lawrence.' He called them by their French name, Les Îles de la Madeleine. 'The first in living memory. I'm sending an initial team of eight.'

'But why me? I'm not on the rota.'

'The murder took place on l'Île d'entrée, Sime. Better known to its inhabitants as Entry Island. The Madelinots are French-speaking for the most part, but on Entry they speak only English.'

Sime nodded, understanding now.

'I've got a light aircraft standing by at St Hubert airfield. It'll take about three hours to get out to the islands. I want you to lead interrogations. Thomas Blanc will monitor. Lieutenant Crozes is your team leader, Sergeant Superviseur Lapointe on admin and logistics.' He hesitated, uncharacteristically. It did not go unnoticed by Sime.

'And the crime scene investigator?' He posed it as a question, but already knew the answer.

McIvir set his mouth in a stubborn line. 'Marie-Ange.'

II

The thirteen-seater King Air B100 had been in the air for over two and a half hours. During that time barely a handful of words had passed among the eight-officer team being sent to investigate the Entry Island murder.

Sime sat on his own up front, acutely aware of everything that set him apart from his colleagues. He was not an habitual member of their team. He had only been attached because of his linguistic background. The others were all French in origin. Each spoke English, to a greater or lesser extent, but none was fluent. Sime's heritage was Scottish. His ancestors had arrived speaking Gaelic. Within a couple of generations the language of home had all but died out, to be replaced by English. Then in the 1970s the government of Quebec had made French the official language, and in a mass exodus half a million English-speakers had abandoned the province.

But Sime's father had refused to go. His great-great-grandparents, he said, had carved out a place for themselves in this land, and he was damned if he would be forced off it. And so the Mackenzie family had stayed, adapting to the new francophone world, but holding on to their own language and traditions in the home. Sime supposed he had much to thank him for. He was equally at home with French or English. But right now, aboard this flight to investigate a murder on a distant archipelago, it was what set him apart. The thing he had always wanted to avoid.

He glanced from the window and saw the first light in the sky to the east. Below them he could see only ocean. They had left the tree-covered Gaspé Peninsula behind them some time ago.

The stooped figure of Sergeant Superviseur Jacques Lapointe emerged from the tiny cockpit clutching a sheaf of papers. He was the man who would facilitate everything. Accommodation, transport, all their technical requirements. And it was Lapointe who would accompany the body of the victim back to Montreal for autopsy in the basement of 1701 Rue

Parthenais. He was an older man, somewhere in his mid-fifties, with big-knuckled arthritic hands and a spiky black moustache shot through with silver.

'Okay.' He raised his voice to be heard above the roar of the engines. 'I've booked us into the Auberge Madeli on the Île du Cap aux Meules. That's the main administrative island, and it's from there that the ferry leaves for Entry. About an hour for the crossing.' He consulted his notes. 'The airport's on Havre aux Maisons, linked to Cap aux Meules by bridge, apparently. Anyway, the local cops'll meet us there with a minibus, and it looks like we'll be just in time to catch the first ferry of the day.'

'You mean they'd have sailed without us?' Lieutenant Daniel Crozes raised an eyebrow. The team leader was almost the same age as Sime, but a little taller and possessed of dark good looks. Somehow he always managed to maintain a tan. Quite a feat during the long, cold Quebecois winters. Sime was never quite sure if it derived from a bottle or a sunbed.

'Not on your life!' Lapointe grinned. 'It's the only way of getting a vehicle over there. I told them I'd sink the fucking thing if they didn't hold it for us.' He inclined his head to one side. 'Still, it looks like we won't be disrupting the schedules. And it does no harm to keep the locals on side.'

'What do we know about Entry Island, Jacques?' Crozes asked.

The big man pulled on his moustache. 'Not a lot, Lieutenant. Main industry's fishing. Dwindling population. All English-speakers. Fewer than a hundred, I think.'

'One less now,' Crozes said, and there was some muted laughter.

Sime glanced across the aisle and saw Marie-Ange smiling. With her short, brown, blonde-streaked hair and lean, athletic figure, there was something almost boyish about her. But nothing masculine in her liquid green eyes, or the full red lips she stretched across the white teeth of that disarming smile. She caught him looking at her, and the smile immediately vanished.

He turned back to the window and felt his ears pop as the small aircraft banked to the right and began its descent. For a moment he was dazzled by a flash of red sunlight reflecting off the ocean, before the aircraft banked again and he saw the Îles de la Madeleine for the first time. A string of big and small islands linked by causeways and sandbanks, lying on an axis that ran from south-west to north-east. Oddly, it formed an overall shape not unlike a fish-hook, and was perhaps around sixty kilometres in length.

As they turned to make their final descent towards the airstrip on the Île du Havre aux Maisons, the pilot told them that if they looked out to their right they would see Entry Island sitting on its own on the east side of the Baie de Plaisance.

Sime saw it for the first time, silhouetted against the rising sun and lying along the horizon with its two distinctive humps like some toppled Easter Island statue, almost lost in a pink early morning mist that rose from the sea. And quite unexpectedly he felt a shiver of disquiet down his spine.

III

Sime stood stamping on the quayside, breath billowing about his head in the early morning light as Lapointe reversed their minibus on to the *Ivan-Quinn* ferry. Flight cases packed with their equipment were strapped to the roof. Sime wore jeans, leather boots and a hooded cotton jacket, and stood a little apart from the others. Not a space that the casual observer might have noticed, but to him it felt like a rift as deep as the Grand Canyon. And it was more than just language that separated them. Blanc crossed the divide to offer him a cigarette. Had he known him better, he would have known better. But Sime appreciated the gesture.

'Gave it up,' he said.

Blanc grinned. 'Easiest thing in the world.'

Sime cocked a quizzical eyebrow. 'Is it?'

'Sure. I've done it hundreds of times.'

Sime smiled and they watched in silence for a while as Lapointe manoeuvred into the tight, two-vehicle car deck. He glanced at his co-interrogator. Blanc was six inches smaller than Sime, and carrying a good deal more weight. He had a head of thick, curly black hair balding on top, a monk's tonsure in the making. 'How's your English?' Sime said.

Blanc pulled a face. 'I understand it okay. But I don't speak it so good.' He nodded his head vaguely beyond the harbour wall. 'I hear these Entry islanders refuse to speak French.' He snorted. 'I'm glad you're doing the talking.' Sime nodded. Blanc would sit with two monitors and a recorder at the end of a cable in another room and take notes while Sime conducted the interviews on camera. Everything was recorded these days.

Lapointe was parked up now, and the rest of them walked up the vehicle ramp and on to the ferry, squeezing down a narrow corridor to the seating area in the bow. Sime let them go and climbed the stairs to the top deck, skirting the wheelhouse to make his way to the front of the boat. There he leaned on the rail beneath a torn CTMA flag, and counted three cruise ships berthed at various quays.

It was another ten minutes before the ferry slipped out of the harbour, gliding past the outer breakwater on a sea like glass, to reveal Entry Island in the far distance, stretched out on the far side of the bay, the sun only now rising above a gathering of dark morning cloud beyond it. The island drew Sime's focus and held it there, almost trancelike, as the sun sent its reflection careening towards him, creating what was almost a halo effect around the island itself. There was something magical about it. Almost mystical.

IV

None of them knew if the ferry was usually met by this many people, but the tiny quay was crowded with vehicles and curious islanders when the ferry berthed at the harbour on Entry Island. Sergeant Enquêteur André Aucoin from the Sûreté on Cap aux Meules was there to meet them. Middle-aged but lacking experience, he was overawed by the arrival of real cops from the mainland, but enjoying his fifteen minutes in the sun. This was his first murder. He sat up beside Lapointe in the front of the minibus and briefed them on it during their bumpy ride across the island.

He pointed to a huddle of buildings above the road just past Brian Josey's restaurant and general store on Main Street. 'Can't see it from here, but that's the airstrip up there. Cowell had his own single-engined plane that he used to fly back and forth to Havre aux Maisons. There's easy access from there by scheduled flight to Quebec City or Montreal for business meetings. He kept a Range Rover here at the strip.'

'What business was he in?' Crozes asked.

'Lobsters, Lieutenant.' Aucoin chuckled. 'What other business is there on the Madeleine islands?'

Sime noticed the thousands of lobster creels heaped up against brightly coloured wooden houses and barns set back from the road and dotted about the rolling green pasture of the island interior. There were no trees, just telegraph poles leaning at odd angles, and electric cables looping from one to the other. A late cut of summer grasses had produced big round hay bales that punctuated the landscape, and in the distance he saw the spire of a white-painted wooden church, the long shadows of gravestones reaching down the slope towards them in the yellow early light.

Aucoin said, 'Cowell ran half the lobster boats in the Madeleines, landing around fifteen million dollars'-worth a year. Not to mention the processing and canning plant he owned on Cap aux Meules.'

'Was he from the islands?' Sime asked.

'A Madelinot born and bred. From the English-speaking community at Old Harry in the north. But his French was good. You wouldn't have known he wasn't a native speaker.'

'And his wife?'

'Oh, Kirsty's a native of Entry Island. Hasn't been off it, apparently, in the ten years since she graduated from Bishop's University in Lennoxville.'

'Not once?' There was incredulity in Crozes's voice.

'So they say.'

'So what happened last night?'

'Looks like it was her that did it.'

Crozes spoke sharply. 'I didn't ask for your opinion, Sergeant. Just the facts.'

Aucoin blushed. 'According to Kirsty Cowell there was an intruder. A guy in a ski mask. He attacked her, and when the husband intervened he got stabbed and the intruder ran off.'

He couldn't hide his disbelief and his own interpretation slipped out again. 'It's pretty weird. I mean, I know you guys are the experts, but you just don't get break-ins here on Entry Island. The only way on and off since the air service got cut is by ferry, or private boat. It's unlikely that anyone could motor into the harbour and out again without someone noticing. And there's only one other jetty on the island. A small private quay that Cowell had built at the foot of the cliffs below his house. But the currents there make it pretty treacherous, so it's hardly ever used.'

'Another islander, then,' Sime said.

The look that Aucoin turned in his direction was laden with sarcasm. 'Or a figment of Mrs Cowell's imagination.'

They left the lighthouse on their right and turned up the hill towards the Cowell house. Most of the homes on the island were traditional in design, wooden-framed with shingle-clad walls or clapboard siding beneath steeply pitched shingle roofs. They were vividly painted in primary colours. Red, green, blue, and sometimes more bizarrely in shades of purple or ochre, window and door frames picked out in white or canary-yellow. Lawns were well maintained. A local preoccupation, it seemed, and they passed several islanders out with their lawnmowers profiting from the autumn sunshine.

The Cowell house itself stood out from the others, not only in size but in design. It was out of place, somehow, like an artificial Christmas tree in a forest of natural pines. It was not of the island. A long yellow-painted building of clap-board siding with a red roof broken by dormers and turrets and a large arched window. As they pulled around the gravel path at the cliff side, they saw that there was a conservatory built along almost the entire south-facing length of it, windows looking out across a manicured lawn towards the fence that ran along the cliff's edge.

'It's bloody huge,' Lapointe said.

Aucoin blew air through pursed lips, savouring the impor-tance that his local knowledge gave him. 'Used to be a church hall,' he said. 'With a bell tower. Over on Havre Aubert. Cowell had it cut in three and floated across on barges brought up specially from Quebec City. They reassembled it here on the cliffs, then finished it inside and out to the high-est specs. The interior's quite amazing. Had it done for his wife, apparently. Nothing was too good or too expensive for his Kirsty, according to the neighbours.'

Sime's eyes wandered to a smaller property no more than fifty yards away. It stood a little lower on the slope, a tradi-tional island house, blue and white, with a covered porch that looked out over the red cliffs. It seemed to sit on the same parcel of land. 'Who lives there?'

Aucoin followed Sime's eyeline. 'Oh that's her place.'

'Kirsty Cowell's?'

'That's right.'

'You mean they lived in separate houses?'

'No, that's the house she grew up in and inherited from

18

her parents. She and her husband both lived in the big house that Cowell built. They had the old place renovated. Used it as a summerhouse, or guest house, apparently. Though according to the folk we've spoken to, they never had any. Guests, that is.' He glanced back at Sime. 'She's in there just now, with a policewoman. Didn't want her messing up the crime scene.' If he expected some kind of pat on the back, he was disappointed when it didn't come. He added, 'At least, not any more than she already has.'

'What do you mean?' Marie-Ange spoke sharply and for the first time. Suddenly this was her territory.

Aucoin just smiled. 'You'll see, ma'am.' His importance to them would pass quickly. He was determined to make the most of it while it lasted.

They parked outside the house next to what was presumably Cowell's Range Rover. Patrolmen from Cap aux Meules had hammered in stakes and stretched crime scene tape between them as they had no doubt seen in the movies. It fluttered and hummed now in the stiffening breeze. Marie-Ange got her trunk down from the roof and changed into a suit and hood of white tyvek, slipping bootees over her trainers. The others pulled on plastic overshoes and snapped their hands into latex gloves. Aucoin watched with admiration and envy. Marie-Ange chucked him some shoe covers and gloves. 'I know you've probably tramped all over the place already, but let's try not to fuck it up any more than you already have.' He blushed again and glared at her with hate in his heart.

19

The team moved carefully into the house through sliding doors that took them into a tiled sun room with a hot tub. They passed through it to the conservatory lounge, which was littered with recliners and glass tables, one of which was smashed. Shards of broken glass crunched underfoot. Then up two steps to the main living space, avoiding a trail of dried bloody footprints.

A vast area of polished wooden floor delineated a space that rose up into the arched roof. A large dining table and chairs stood off to the left, and at the far side an open-plan kitchen was partitioned from the main entrance by a standing dresser. A staircase dog-legged up to a mezzanine level on the right, and to their left another three curved steps led up to a sitting area with a grand piano and three-piece suite set around an open fireplace.

Almost in the centre of the floor a man lay on his back, one arm thrown out to his right, the other by his side. He was wearing dark-blue slacks and a white shirt that was soaked in blood. His legs were stretched straight out, slightly parted, his feet in their Italian leather shoes tilting to right and left. His eyes were wide open, as was his mouth. Unnaturally so. But the most striking thing was the way his blood was smeared across the floor all around him. In streaks and pools and random patterns. Bloody footprints seemed to circle him. Naked feet, which had left a trail leading away from the body towards the kitchen and then back, fading on the return before picking up fresh blood to track away to the conservatory and down the steps. The main body of blood was almost dry now, oxidised, sticky and brown in colour.

'Jesus!' Marie-Ange's voice came in a breath. 'When you said mess you weren't kidding.'

Aucoin said, 'This is how it was when we arrived. Mrs Cowell claims she attempted CPR and tried to stop the bleeding. Without success.'

'Obviously.' Marie-Ange's tone was dry.

Aucoin shifted uncomfortably. 'The footprints are hers. She ran over to the kitchen to get a towel to staunch the flow of blood. One of my men found it lying out there in the grass at first light. When she couldn't revive him she ran down the hill to a neighbour's house for help.' He paused. 'That's the story she told them, anyway.'

Marie-Ange moved around the body like a cat, examining every pool and spatter of blood, every footprint and smear on the floor. Sime found it difficult to watch her. 'There are other footprints here,' she said. 'The tread of a shoe.'

'That would be the nurse. She came when the neighbours called. She had to ascertain that he was dead. Then she called us.'

'If the wife attempted CPR she must be covered in blood herself,' Crozes said.

'Oh yes, sir, she is.' Aucoin nodded gravely.

'I hope you haven't allowed her to wash or change.' Marie-Ange cast him a look almost as acid as her tone.

'No, ma'am.'

She turned to Lapointe. 'We'll need to have her photo-graphed and medically examined, checked for fibres and injuries. I'll want samples from beneath her nails. And you'll need to bag her clothes and take them back with you to Mon-treal for forensic examination.' She returned her attention to Aucoin. 'Is there a doctor on the island?'

'No, ma'am, just the nurse. There's two of them. They come week about.'

'She'll have to do then. And I guess I'll have to be the examining officer, since it's a woman.'

Blanc said, 'Was there any sign of a break-in?'

Aucoin's laugh was involuntary. But he quickly caught himself. 'No. There would be no need to break in. No one on the island locks their doors.'

Lieutenant Crozes clapped his hands. 'Okay, let's get started. Have you interviewed the wife, Sergeant Aucoin?'

'No, sir. I took statements from the neighbours, that's all.'

'Good.' Crozes turned towards Sime. 'Why don't you and Blanc set up in the summerhouse and take an initial state-ment before we do the medical exam?'

CHAPTER THREE

The sound of her voice was almost hypnotic. Monotonous, unemotional. She recounted the events of the night before as if she were reading them off a printed account for the umpteenth time. And yet the images they painted for Sime were vivid enough, filled as they were with detail that he supplied himself from his own picture of the crime scene.

But it was a picture that came and went, in sharp focus one moment then blurred the next. Everything about her distracted him. The way her hair fell to her shoulders, limp now but still animated by a natural wave. So dark it was almost black. The strangely emotionless eyes that seemed to drill right through him, to the point where he had to break contact and pretend he was thinking about his next question. The way her hands lay folded in her lap, one inside the other, long elegant fingers pressed together with tension. And her voice with its lazy Canadian drawl, not a hint of French anywhere present in its intonation.

The clouds he had seen earlier were massing now out in the gulf to the south of the islands, and the sun came and went in fleeting moments that fired up the ocean in occasional patches of dazzling light. He felt as much as heard the wind beating against the house.

'I was preparing for bed,' she said. 'Our bedroom is downstairs, at the far end of the house. French windows open on to the conservatory, but the lights were out there. James was upstairs in his study. He had arrived home not long before.'

'Where from?'

She hesitated momentarily. 'He'd flown over from Havre aux Maisons and picked up his Range Rover at the airfield. He always leaves it there.' She paused to correct herself. 'Left, I mean.'

Sime knew from professional experience how hard it was for someone to refer suddenly to a loved one in the past tense.

'I heard a noise in the conservatory and called out, thinking it was James.'

'What kind of noise?'

'Oh, I don't know. I can't remember now. Just a noise. Like a chair scraping on tiles or something.' She interlaced her fingers in her lap. 'Anyway, when he didn't respond I went to take a look, which is when a man lunged at me out of the darkness.'

'Did you get a look at him?'

'Not then, no. As I said, it was dark. He was just a shadow coming out of nowhere. He was wearing gloves, though. I knew that because one of his hands was in my face and I could feel and smell the leather.' She shook her head. 'It's strange the things you're aware of in moments of stress.' Now it was she who broke eye contact, and her gaze seemed to drift off into the middle distance as if she were trying to reconstruct the moment. 'I screamed and punched and kicked, and he tried to pin my arms to my side. But we fell over a chair and landed on one of the tables. Glass. It just gave way beneath us and shattered on the floor. I think I must have landed on top of him because for a moment he seemed incapable of moving. Winded, I guess. And then I saw the blade of his knife catch a reflection from the light in the living room. And I was on my feet and running for my life. Up the steps into the living room, screaming for James.'

Her breathing increased with the pace of the storytelling, and he noticed how the colour rose on her cheeks and around her eyes as she turned them back on him.

'I could hear him right behind me. And then felt the force of his shoulder in the back of my thighs. I went down like a ton of bricks. Hit the floor with such a force it knocked all the air out of my lungs. I couldn't catch a breath, couldn't scream. There were lights flashing in my eyes. I tried to wriggle free, get on to my back so I could see him. And then I did. He was on his knees above me.'

'Your first good look at him.'

She nodded. 'Not that I can tell you much. He wore jeans, I think. And a dark jacket of some kind. And a black ski mask pulled over his head. But, really, Mr Mackenzie, my whole focus was on the knife in his right hand. It was raised high and just about to plunge down into me. In that moment I was sure I was going to die. And everything suddenly became clear, like I was watching an HD movie in slow-motion. I could see every reflected surface of the room along the length of that blade. The stitched leather fingers around the haft. A strange intensity in the eyes behind the slits.'

'Colour?'

'His eyes?'

Sime nodded.

'I suppose I should remember. They just seemed dark. Black. Like maybe the pupils were fully dilated.' She drew a deep breath. 'And then James was there behind him, both hands around the wrist of the knife hand, pulling it back, dragging him away from me. I saw him try to pull off the mask, and the man swung a fist into his face, and they both staggered off across the floor. Then they went over with a terrible crash, and the other man was on top.'

'What did you do?'

She shook her head. 'Nothing that made much sense. I ran across the room and jumped on the man's back. Like I had the strength to stop him! I was punching and kicking and screaming, and I could feel James bucking beneath us both. Then an elbow or a fist, or something, came back and caught me full on the side of the head.' She raised a hand to pass fingertips delicately over her right temple. 'I've heard of people seeing stars. Well, I saw stars, Mr Mackenzie. My head was filled with the light of them. And it stole all the strength from my arms and legs. I went over on my back and thought I was going to be sick. I was completely helpless. I heard James shouting, and then a terrible gasp, and a thudding like punches, and then the man ran past me, back down the steps and out through the conservatory.'

Sime watched her closely. From an initially detached retelling of a traumatic event, she had become fully, emotionally, involved. He saw fear and apprehension in her eyes. She was wringing her hands in her lap. 'And then?'

It was some moments before she responded, as if dragging herself back from her memory to the present, and something about her whole body went limp. 'I managed to get to my knees, and I saw him lying on his side, all curled up, almost in the foetal position. He had his back to me, and it wasn't until I got to him that I saw the blood pooling on the floor. He was still alive, clutching his chest like he was trying to stop the bleeding. But I could see it pulsing through his fingers with every fading heartbeat. I tried to get to the kitchen for a towel to staunch it myself, but I slid on his blood with my bare feet and fell. It was like the floor turned to glass beneath me and I was slithering and sliding about like an idiot. Panic, I guess.'

She closed her eyes, and behind her flickering lids he imagined her visualising the moment. Reliving it. Or making it up. He was not yet sure which. But he knew already that he wanted her story to be true.

'By the time I got back to him, he was going. I could hear it in his breathing. Rapid and shallow. His eyes were open, and I could see the light going out of them, like watching the sun set. I knelt in his blood and pushed him over on to his back. I really didn't know what was the right thing to do, so I shoved the rolled-up towel into his chest to try to stop the blood from coming out of it. But there was so much of it already on the floor. And then there was this long breath that came out of his open mouth. Like a sigh. And he was gone.'

'You told the neighbours you tried to revive him with CPR.'

She nodded. 'I've seen it done on TV. But I'd no real idea what to do. So I just pressed with both hands on his chest, again and again, as hard as I could. Anything to try to restart his heart.' Now she shook her head. 'But there was nothing. No sign of life. I must have pumped his chest for two minutes, maybe more. It seemed like a lifetime. Then I gave up and tried mouth to mouth. I pulled his jaw down and held his nose and blew air into his mouth from mine.'

She looked at Sime, tears gathering in her eyes from the memory. 'I could taste his blood. It was on my lips and in my mouth. But I knew in my heart it was no good. He was gone, and there would be no bringing him back.'

'And that's when you ran to the neighbours' house?'

'Yes. I think I must have been pretty hysterical. Cut my feet on broken glass on the way out. Couldn't tell which was his blood or mine. I think I scared the McLeans half to death.'

The tears in her eyes spilled as she blinked, and rolled down her face in the tracks of their predecessors. And she sat staring at Sime as if waiting for the next question, or perhaps daring him to contradict her. But he simply returned her stare, half lost in the visualisation of her account, part of him in conflict with the scepticism his experience and training as a policeman engendered, part of him lost in human empathy. And still he was gripped by the compelling and discomposing sense of knowing her. He had no idea for how long they sat in silence.

'Am I disturbing something here, Simon?' Marie-Ange's voice dispelled the moment, and Sime turned, startled, towards the door. 'I mean, is the interview over, or what?' She spoke in English, standing with the screen door half open and looking at him curiously.

Sime got to his feet. He felt disorientated, confused, as if he had somehow lost consciousness for a moment. His eye was drawn by a movement in the hallway beyond the stairs, and he saw Thomas Blanc standing there, an odd look in his eyes. He nodded mutely, and Sime said, 'Yes, we're finished for now.'

'Good.' Marie-Ange turned toward Kirsty Cowell. 'I want you to come with me to the medical centre. We'll take some photographs, the nurse will conduct a physical examination, and then you can get cleaned up.' She looked at Sime, but he avoided her eye and she turned back to the widow. 'I'll wait for you outside.' She let the door swing closed and was gone.

Sime glanced towards the hallway, but Blanc had returned to the bedroom.

Kirsty stood up, fixing him with a strange, knowing look. 'Simon, she called you. You told me your name was Sheem.'

He felt unaccountably embarrassed. 'It is. The Scots Gaelic for Simon. Spelt S-I-M-E. At least, that was my father's spelling of it. It's what everyone calls me.'

'Except her.'

He felt the colour rising on his cheeks and he shrugged.

'Lovers?'

'My private life has no relevance here.'

'Ex-lovers, then.'

Perhaps, he thought, fatigue and stress were simply making her blunt. She didn't even look interested. But still he felt compelled to respond. 'Married.' Then he added quickly, 'Past tense.' And finally, 'This interview's not over. I'll want you back after your medical exam.' She held him in her gaze for a long moment before turning to push through the screen door and out on to the porch.

Sime followed a few moments later to find Marie-Ange waiting for him. The murdered man's widow had climbed into the back of the minibus, Lapointe at the wheel, engine idling, the purr of its motor carried away on the wind. Marie-Ange stepped close to Sime in a gesture that might almost have seemed intimate had her body language been less hostile. She lowered her voice. 'Let's just get the ground rules straight right now.'

30

He looked at her with incredulity. 'What rules?'

'It's simple, Simon.' She had reverted to his formal name since the break-up. 'You do your job, I'll do mine. Except for when there's a cross-over we have nothing to talk about.'

'We've had nothing to talk about for months.'

Her voice reduced itself to a hiss barely audible above the wind. 'I don't want us getting into any fights. Not in front of my team.'

Her team. A reminder, if he needed it, that he was the outsider here. Her eyes were so cold he almost recoiled and he remembered how she had loved him once.

'There won't be any fighting.'

'Good.'

'But you can come and get the rest of your stuff any time you like. I really don't want it lying around the apartment.'

'I'm surprised you noticed. You hardly ever noticed me when I was there.'

'Maybe because you never were.'

She let that one go. 'You know what's interesting? I don't want the stuff. Don't miss it. Don't miss us. Why don't you chuck it in the trash?'

'Like you did with our marriage.'

'Don't give me that. You're a cold fish, Simon. You know? Got nothing to give. My only regret is it took me so long to realise it. Leaving you was the best thing I ever did. You have no idea how free I feel.'

All his hurt and betrayal was evident in the sad brown eyes that held her in his gaze. Although he had often wondered if there was someone else, she had always denied it. Everything was his fault. The fights, the silences, the lack of sex. And now it was he who was paying the price of her freedom. 'I hope you enjoy it, then,' is all he said.

She held his eye for just a moment before turning to hurry down the steps to the waiting minibus, and he saw Kirsty looking at him from beyond the reflections on the window.

CHAPTER FOUR

It had been only too easy for him to lose confidence in himself after a series of relationship failures. The point had been reached when he had begun to believe that he was the problem.

And that was the place he had been in when Marie-Ange came into his life.

A painful, lonely place. Approaching thirty years of age he had a handful of clumsy relationships behind him, and saw only a long succession of empty nights stretching ahead. It was clear to him then that his job was going to be his life, his future. And that he would become so impossibly set in his ways that in the end sharing it would cease to be an option.

He had always been self-sufficient, even as a child. He'd had few friends and no inclination to share, even then.

His apartment before meeting Marie-Ange had been a joyless place. He had never taken the time to decorate or furnish it beyond basic requirements. The only picture that hung on the wall was a landscape painted five generations earlier by an ancestor who had come to Canada and made something of a reputation for himself as an artist. Not that Sime was particularly attached to it. It had come from his parents' house after their accident. His sister had taken most of their stuff, but thought that Sime should have the painting. Hanging it on the wall had seemed like the best way of keeping it out from under his feet. Marie-Ange had never liked it.

For a time she had tried to turn the place into a home. Nest-building. But each of them made so many compromises, that in the end neither felt comfortable in it.

The condo was on the third floor of an apartment block in St Lambert. It had three bedrooms, and would have made an ideal first home for a couple wanting to start a family. That thought had always been in the back of Sime's mind when he took it on. He had been in a relationship then that had lasted nearly a year, a record for him, and they had been going to move in together.

Then suddenly she was gone. Without a word. And Sime never did know why. Which is when the self-doubt had started creeping in.

Meeting people had never been easy for him. A policeman's hours, almost by definition, are antisocial. Even harder was maintaining a relationship, because there was never any guarantee what time you would be home, or sometimes what day. Sime had never really got involved in the social life of the Sûreté, like so many of his colleagues. It had just seemed too incestuous. So the dating agency had been something like the last hope of a desperate man.

It was a friend from his academy days who first suggested it, and at first Sime had been violently opposed to the idea. But it worked away at his subconscious over several weeks, slowly breaking down all his arguments against it. And finally his resolve faltered.

It was an online agency. He had to verify for them who he was, of course, but beyond that complete anonymity was guaranteed. They provided him with a fictitious dating name that he could choose to dispense with, or not, after their first meeting.

Sime spent a whole evening filling in the questionnaire on the website, trying to answer as honestly as he could. And then when he reviewed his answers decided nobody in their right mind would want to date him. So he was both surprised and a little shocked when the agency said they had come up with a match, and that if he wanted, she would be happy to meet him.

Sime had faced down murderers, been shot at, disarmed a man with an automatic rifle on a killing spree, but he had never felt as nervous as he did the night of his first date.

They had arranged to meet in a Starbucks on Avenue du Mont-Royal Est. Sime arrived early, afraid that he would get snarled up in traffic and be late. The place was quiet when he got there and ordered a grande caramel macchiato. He sat near the window so he could see customers come and go.

Which is when he saw Marie-Ange crossing the street outside. He knew her, of course. She was one of the department's crime scene specialists, though they had never actually worked together. Sime turned away so that she wouldn't see him sitting in the window, but was horrified when she pushed open the door and headed for the counter. He almost cringed with embarrassment at the thought she might discover that he was there on a blind date set up by an internet dating agency. It would have been all over the division the next day. He fervently hoped that she was just in for a take-out and wouldn't notice him.

But he had no such luck. She picked up her skinny latte from the barista and turned to look straight at him. Sime wanted the ground to swallow him up. She seemed almost startled, but there was no way of avoiding the fact that they had seen each other. So she smiled and came over to sit down at his table. Sime did his best to return her smile, but felt it was more like a grimace.

'Hi, Sime. Fancy meeting you here.'

He blurted, 'I'm waiting for someone.'

'Oh?' A wry smile spread itself across her face and she pushed up one eyebrow. 'Hot date?' In contrast to his agitation she seemed unnaturally relaxed.

'Sort of.'

'Anyone I'd know?'

'I shouldn't think so.'

'Can't be anyone in the force, then. I only seem to know cops these days.'

'Yeah, me too.'

'Except for your date.'

Sime tried to seem amused. 'Yeah. Except for my date.'

A silence settled awkwardly between them and they sipped on their respective plastic lids. She glanced at her watch and Sime stole a look at her. He had never really paid her much attention before. She was just one of the guys, the short hair and boyish figure contributing to that sense of her. But he saw now that there was a wonderful depth to the green of her eyes, a finely angled jawline and rather full lips. At second glance she was really quite attractive. She looked up and caught him watching her.

'What time's your date?'

'Seven.'

She sighed. 'Pity. You could have taken me to dinner. I've got nothing else to do tonight.'

And suddenly he thought, yes! I would much rather have dinner with you. With someone I didn't have to pretend with. Someone who already knows me. Who knows I'm a cop, and what that means. He raised his eyes towards the clock on the wall. It was still only 6.55. He stood up. 'Let's do that.'

She frowned. 'Do what?'

'Have dinner?'

She laughed. 'What about your date?'

Sime shook his head and glanced nervously towards the door in case she would suddenly turn up. 'Never liked her much anyway.' He held out his hand. 'Come on.'

She laughed again and took it and stood up. 'Where are we going?'

'I know a great little place over on Rue Jeanne-Mance.'

They sat and talked that night in a way they never did again. In some strange sense Sime felt suddenly unchained. The wine helped loosen ingrained inhibitions, and he found himself sharing all those little fears and foibles that he had kept locked away from the world, guarding them carefully, because sharing your weaknesses makes you vulnerable. But he didn't feel at risk, because she unburdened herself too. Told him all about her failed teenage marriage, the uncle who liked to stroke her budding breasts when she was just thirteen, her mother's battle with alcohol and then breast cancer.

Sime told her about his parents dying when a bridge over the Salmon River collapsed as they were driving across it. About his difficulty socialising with other kids at school. His ineptitude with girls.

All of which, in retrospect, seemed pretty depressing. But they laughed a lot as well. Funny stories accumulated over nearly ten years in the force, and it was late by the time they were on their second digestifs. Sime was feeling mellow, and the alcohol made him bold enough to confess finally that the real reason he had been at Starbucks that night was to meet a woman found by an online dating agency.

Marie-Ange's smile faded and she looked at him with curious eyes. 'Seriously?'

He immediately regretted telling her.

'And you stood the poor woman up without even giving her a chance?'

Sime had a rush of guilt that made it hard to meet her eye. 'Was that really bad of me?'

She pursed her lips and nodded. 'I gotta tell you, Sime, it was pretty mean. Especially since I was the woman you stood up.'

Sime's jaw dropped, and he must have presented such a look of shock that she laughed so much the tears ran down her cheeks. It took him only a moment to realise the truth. That each of them had stood up their blind dates in favour of someone they already knew. And that the someone they already knew had, in fact, been their blind date.

In the end their laughter had forced the owner of the restaurant to ask them to leave. They were annoying the other customers.

They had gone back to Sime's apartment, and that night had the best sex of their future relationship. Pure lust, like Sime had never known before. They had been married within six months.

But the truth he had learned since then was that you can't build a whole relationship on the basis of one night. And that what might seem like a good match to a computer doesn't always work in life.

CHAPTER FIVE

I

The wind was gathering strength out of the south-west, sweeping up over the clifftops and flattening every growing thing in its path. The sun, veiled at first by high cloud, had now been swallowed by storm clouds rapidly approaching across the slate-grey swell of the ocean. But the air was warm, soft on the skin, and Sime sat among the tall grasses bowing all around him, just metres from the edge of the cliff. He could hear the waves breaking below, and had a sense of being fully exposed to the power of nature. Both at one with it, and completely at its mercy. He felt almost ghost-like, insubstantial, lost somewhere in a life gone wrong.

How was it possible that his relationship with Marie-Ange had been so easily found and so painfully lost? Affection exchanged for enmity. The fulfilment he had felt in those heady early days replaced by an aching emptiness. It occurred to him that neither of them had ever really loved the other. It had been need more than love. And that like a hunger satisfied, the need had simply passed.

At the start she had filled a gaping hole in his life. He had known from his early teens that he was somehow different from others. That there was something missing from his life. Something he had never quite identified or understood. And for a few short years it seemed that Marie-Ange had fitted into that missing piece of him, making him complete in some way. For her part, he suspected she had been driven by some mothering instinct, wrapping arms around the little boy lost. Which was no basis for a relationship. And so it had proved.

For a moment he closed his eyes and let the wind caress him. If only he could sleep, he was sure that much of this torture would pass. He was so tempted simply to lie down in the grass, with the sound of the wind and the ocean in his ears, the sense of coming storm still some way distant. But as his lids shut out the light, the face of Kirsty Cowell came to him in the dark. As if she had always been there. Just waiting for him.

'You all right, Sime?'

The voice, raised above the wind, startled his eyes open and he looked up, heart pounding, to see Lieutenant Crozes standing over him. 'Sure,' Sime said. 'Just listening to the wind.'

Crozes stared out over the ocean. 'The forecasters say there's one helluva storm coming.'

Sime followed his gaze to the accumulation of clouds, black, contused and devouring the sky as they approached. 'Certainly looks like it.'

41

'The remnants of Hurricane Jess, apparently.'

Sime had been only vaguely aware of TV news items about the hurricane that had torn up the eastern seaboard of the United States. 'Really?'

'Downgraded to storm status now. But they're calling it a superstorm. It's going to be touch and go whether we get off the island tonight.'

Sime shrugged. He didn't much care one way or another. Wherever he laid his head for the night he knew he wouldn't sleep. 'How's the door-to-door going?'

Crozes expelled air through pursed lips. 'Like getting blood out of a stone, Sime. Oh, everyone's nice enough. Lots to say but nothing to tell. Not to us, anyway. And no one's got a bad word about Kirsty Cowell.'

Sime got to his feet, brushing dead grasses from his trousers. 'Why would they?'

'Well, they wouldn't. She's one of them. An islander born and bred. But although no one's saying it, seems clear they all think she killed him.'

Sime looked at him, startled. 'Why?'

Crozes shrugged. 'That's what we need to find out.' He turned and nodded down the hill towards a green-painted house not a hundred yards away. 'While she's with Marie-Ange and the nurse it might be an idea if you and Blanc interviewed the neighbours. According to Aucoin they were the first ones on the scene.'

Fine spits of rain stung their faces.

II

The McLeans were an odd couple. They sat nervously in the Cowells' summerhouse. No doubt they had been in it many times, but today they were like fish out of water. Uncomfortable and uncertain in foreign surroundings. Agnes, as near as Sime could guess, was around seventy. Harry a little older. She had an abundance of white hair like cotton wool, crimped around the sides of her head and piled up on top of it. He had almost none, a bald brown head spattered by age. They seemed very small to Sime, like little shrunken people.

'I couldn't say exactly what time it was.' Agnes had a shrill voice that dipped and dived like a butterfly on a summer's day. 'We were asleep.'

'What time do you normally go to bed?'

'About ten usually.' Harry's nicotine-stained fingers turned his wedding ring around as his hands lay in his lap. He would doubtless have been happier to have a cigarette in them.

'So it was after ten, and sometime before midnight?'

Agnes said, 'It was about ten past twelve when I first noticed the time. And that was after we'd called the nurse.'

'And it was the nurse who called the police?'

'Yes.'

'Tell me what happened when Mrs Cowell came to your door.'

The elderly couple glanced at each other as if to reach agreement on who would speak first. It was Agnes who did so. 'She came hammering at the door in the dark. It was like World War Three. I'm surprised she didn't do damage to her hands.'

'So that's what woke you?'

'Me, not him.' Agnes snatched a quick look at her husband. 'It would take more than a world war to rouse him from his slumbers. I had to shake him out of his sleep.' He glared back at her. 'But he was awake soon enough when we opened the door to her.'

'Like an apparition, she was,' Harry said, his beady blue eyes opening wide with recollection, like flowers in sunlight. 'Just in her nightdress. All white and insubstantial-like, nearly see-through. I mean, with the moon up behind her like that it was plain she was buck naked beneath it.'

Now it was Agnes who glared at him. But he was oblivious, still reliving the moment.

'And she was just covered in blood. Man, I've never seen anything like it. On her hands and face and all over her nightdress.'

'She was hysterical,' Agnes butted in. 'Just kept screaming, help me, help me, he's dead, he's dead.' She cast a withering glance at her husband. 'And, of course, he has to ask who. As if it wasn't blindingly obvious.'

'Wasn't obvious at all.' Harry frowned. 'Could have been anyone.'

Sime said, 'So what happened then?'

'We followed her up to the house,' Agnes said. 'In our

44

dressing gowns. Harry got a flashlight and his shotgun. And we found Mr Cowell lying in all that blood in the middle of the floor.'

'She said she was attacked and Cowell tried to save her.' Harry couldn't hide his scepticism, and Sime was quick to pick up on it.

'But you didn't believe her?'

Harry said, 'No,' and Agnes said, 'Yes.' Both at the same time. She glared at him again.

'Why didn't you believe her, Mr McLean?'

'Harry . . .' There was a clear warning in his wife's tone.

But he just shrugged. 'Well, who could blame her? The man was a cheat and a liar, and everyone knew it.'

Sime frowned. 'What do you mean?'

'Well, he up and left her just a week ago, didn't he? For some floozy over on Grindstone.' And as an afterthought he added, 'That's Cap aux Meules to you.'

III

They sat in the minibus on the crest of the hill, looking down on the Cowell house and the lighthouse beyond. L'île du Havre Aubert, the nearest of the islands in the archipelago, was almost obscured by the flurries of rain that blew in across the bay. Blanc sat in the front passenger seat, the window down, his cigarette smoke whisked away by the wind. Lapointe was hunched over the steering wheel munching on a sandwich that left crumbs clinging to his moustache. Crozes, Marie-Ange and Sime sat in the back. Two of the team were still out, tramping door to door and no doubt getting soaked. Marie-Ange's crime scene assistant was taking photographs before they moved the body.

'As soon as the Cowell woman is washed and changed I want you to ask her why she didn't tell us she'd just split with her husband.' Crozes was chewing absently on a finger-nail.

Sime washed down a mouthful of baguette with coffee from a plastic cup and nodded. For some reason it was almost a source of comfort for him to know that Kirsty Cowell's had not been a happy marriage either. It gave them something in common. It also gave her a motive for murder.

'You should maybe have a word with the nurse first.' All heads turned towards Marie-Ange. She shrugged. 'She's not a local, but she's familiar enough with the island and every-one on it to know where most of the bodies are buried.' She smiled wryly. 'So to speak.'

'Are you thinking of any bodies in particular?' Crozes said.

She trapped him in the gaze of her green eyes and he looked momentarily discomfited. 'We got to talking after she examined Mrs Cowell. Seems there's a fisherman lives some-where up near the school had a real grudge against Cowell. Claims he stole his father's boat.'

Crozes made a thoughtful moue with his lips and turned to Sime. 'You and Thomas better talk to him, then, Sime. If you think it's worth it we can bring him in for formal interview.'

Thomas Blanc flicked his cigarette out into the early afternoon and saw it snatched away by the elements. He scratched his tonsure. 'Suppose Mrs Cowell was telling the truth,' he said. 'Why would this guy attack her if it was Cowell he had the grudge against?'

The minibus rocked as a sudden gust of wind lifted up over the cliffs and hit the side of it with the force of a physical blow. A moment of sunlight washed across the island, as if in the stroke of an artist's brush. And then it was gone.

'Well maybe he had something against the wife, too,' Crozes said. 'That's what you guys need to find out.'

CHAPTER SIX

I

The island health centre was located in a white-trimmed yellow hut that stood on the right-hand side of Big Hill Road fifty metres up from the island grocery store. To call it a road was a misnomer. It was an unmetalled track full of potholes. The sign outside the centre read *Centre de santé et de services sociaux des Îles*, even although no one on the island spoke French. Further evidence of the schizophrenic nature of the province to which the island belonged was to be found in street names preceded by the French *Chemin*, and followed by the English *Road*.

The nurse was in her late thirties, an embodiment of that schizophrenia. She was a native French-speaker from Cap aux Meules, but spent every other week living and speaking English on Entry Island. Sime noticed that there was no ring on her wedding finger. She perched on the edge of her desk and looked worried. 'You won't tell anyone I told you this, will you?'

'Of course not,' Blanc said. He was more comfortable now

that they were speaking French again. 'Anything you tell us is in complete confidence.'

She wore jeans and a woollen jumper and folded her arms defensively across her chest. Dark hair showing the first signs of grey was drawn back severely from a high forehead and a face devoid of make-up. 'His name's Owen Clarke. A bit of a brawler. I mean, nice guy and all, but turns kind of sour with a drink in him. I've treated injuries inflicted by those big split knuckles of his often enough. Nothing serious. But these are hard men here. Some of them spend six months at a stretch fishing away from home. You can't blame them for letting off a bit of steam now and then.'

'What sort of age is he?' Sime asked.

'I guess he's in his forties now. Got a teenage boy called Chuck. Not a bad kid, but looks to be following in his father's footsteps. In temperament, I mean. Not on to the boats. Like most kids on the island these days, all he wants is to get off it.'

She glanced from the window, almost longingly Sime thought. On a clear day she could probably see home on Cap aux Meules from here.

'Strangely enough it's the mother who rules the roost in the Clarke household. Owen's a big brute of a man and Chuck's not far behind him, but Mary-Anne's the pack leader.'

Blanc was playing absently with an unlit cigarette in his right hand, turning it over between three fingers like a magician performing a trick. It kept drawing the nurse's eye as if she were afraid he might light it up. He said, 'So what was his beef with Cowell?'

'Something to do with his boat. I don't know the details. But his father used to own it. And now Cowell does.' She caught herself. 'Did. And Owen skippered it for him.'

Sime said, 'And you think Clarke might have been capable of killing him?'

'I didn't say that,' she said quickly. 'Just that there was no love lost.'

'You were the first on the scene,' Blanc said. 'After the McLeans, that is.'

'Yes.'

'And Cowell was dead when you got there.'

She bit her lip softly, and Sime could see the troubled recollection in her eyes. 'He was.'

'How did you verify that?'

'Sergeant, nobody who'd lost that much blood could still be living.'

'But you were able to determine what caused the bleeding?'

'Only the pathologist can tell you that.' She sighed and relented a little. 'He appeared to have three stab wounds in his chest.'

'So it must have been a pretty frenzied attack.'

She shook her head. 'I have no idea. I treat cuts and bruises and hand out advice to pregnant moms, Sergeant. All I can tell you is that at least one of the wounds must have punctured a lung, because there was a lot of frothy, very red oxygenated blood.'

Blanc raised his cigarette as if to put it in his mouth, then seemed to think better of it and lowered it again. 'What kind of state was Mrs Cowell in when you got there?'

She raised her eyeline and her focus drifted off to relive the moment. 'Almost catatonic.'

'The McLeans said she was hysterical.'

'Not by the time I got there. She was sitting on the edge of one of the chairs in the conservatory just staring into space. I've never seen a face so white. It made a shocking contrast with the blood on it.'

Blanc flicked a glance at Sime then back to the nurse. 'Do you like Mrs Cowell?'

She seemed surprised by the question. 'Yes, I do.'

'Do you think she killed her husband?'

Colour rose on her cheeks and she pushed herself away from the edge of her desk and stood up. 'I have no idea, Sergeant. That's your job.'

Outside, the wind whipped the hair on Blanc's head almost straight up in the air. He turned to Sime. 'I suppose we'll have to talk to this guy Clarke. But something tells me it'll be a wild-goose chase.' He turned his cigarette around one last time and it snapped in half. The tobacco it spilled in the wind disappeared into the fading afternoon.

II

The minibus bumped and rattled over the pitted and uneven surface of School Road, the twin paps of Big Hill and Cherry Hill rising up to their right above scattered plantations of stunted pine. Blanc smoked at the wheel, and Sime wound down the window to let in some air. The rain of earlier was intermittent now, and smeared in streaks across the windscreen with each passage of the wipers.

The school was housed in a long, low shed with windows all along one side and sat in the valley beyond the nearest plantation. Built at a time when the island population might well have been double its present number, Sime doubted if it was attended by more than a handful of children these days.

They turned off on a rough track before they got to the school, and strained up the slope to a purple-painted house on the rise. A white picket fence enclosed an overgrown garden, and they found Clarke in a breeze-block hut at the far end of it, directed there by an elderly lady who answered their knock on the front door. Not his wife, Sime thought.

Piles of lobster creels lay around the hut like seaweed washed up on the shore. They were piled six or seven deep, a hundred or more of them, linked by rope and pegged to the ground to keep them from being carried off by the winter gales.

There were no windows in the hut, the only light provided

by a single naked bulb hanging from the darkness of the roof space. The air was filled with cigarette smoke and the hum of a large chest freezer that stood against the rear wall, and Sime detected a background perfume of stale alcohol. The walls were hung with nets and tools and ropes, batons of wood two metres long stacked up along one wall. A profusion of white and pink buoys hung from the roof like fungus growing from its timbers.

Clarke was hunched over on a stool at a workbench beneath the light bulb, eyes screwed up against the smoke from the brown-stained cigarette that burned in the corner of his mouth. A half-drunk bottle of beer stood at one end of the bench, and Clarke was attaching netting to the frame of a newly built lobster trap. The table and floor were covered in sawdust, and a rusted fretsaw hung from a vice bolted to the bench next to the beer.

He laughed when they told him why they were there. A laugh that seemed filled with genuine mirth. 'And you think I killed him? Goddamnit, I wish I had. He sure had it coming.' He sucked smoke into his lungs and blew it at the light bulb, momentarily clouding its glare. Most of his lower front teeth were missing, and he hadn't shaved in at least a week. A cat watched them with studied disinterest, curled up inside a cardboard box that stood on an old wooden cabinet cluttered with the detritus of a chaotic life.

Blanc deferred to Sime, since they were back in English-language territory. But he used Clarke's cigarette as a pretext for lighting one himself, and the air grew thicker. The three men eyed each other warily like so many faces peering through fog. 'What exactly was it that you had against Mr Cowell, sir?'

Clarke guffawed. 'Sir? Hah!' Then his smile faded, the fleeting light in his eyes replaced by a dark hatred. 'I'll tell you what I had against the bastard. He stole my father's boat and killed him in the process.'

'How so?'

Clarke dropped his cigarette on the floor and extended a foot to crush it. Then he took a swig of beer and held the bottle in his hand as he leaned forward into the light. 'This is a hard fucking life, man. You spend your winters cooped up here, months on end with nothing better to do than listen to the goddamn womenfolk chewing your ear off. Drives you stir-crazy. Snow and cold. Endless damn darkness, and days on end sometimes when the ferry doesn't come 'cos of ice in the bay, or winter storms.'

He took a long pull from the neck of his bottle.

'When the spring comes you gotta prep the boat, then you're out fishing. Short lobster season here, too. Two months only, from May first. Out at 5 a.m. for the flare going up, and then you're off. Long hard days, and dangerous too. When those creels leave the boat they're linked by rope. Long damn coils of the stuff. Get your feet tangled up in that and you're in the water in a heartbeat. Those things are heavy, and they pull you right down. Man, you're drowned before you know it.' For a moment he couldn't meet their gaze. 'Brother went that way. There one minute, gone the next. Not a damn thing I could do about it.'

And Sime saw in shining eyes a hint of tears that were quickly blinked away.

'We spend three, four months up in Nova Scotia most years. See, it's a small window of earning opportunity we got, and you have to make it last through long idle winters. That's why it was important to my old man to have his own boat. To work for himself. Sell at the best price. He spent his whole damn life out there fishing, just so he could pass that boat on to me.' He paused. 'Well, me and Josh. Only Josh is gone. Near broke my old man's heart, too. So it was just me. And I was everything to him, you know? I was the reason he did it. Then Cowell goes and takes it all from him. In the blink of an eye.' His lips curled as he spoke, as if he had a bad taste in his mouth.

'How did he do that?' Sime said.

Clarke thrust out his bristled jaw defiantly, as if challenging them to contradict him. 'You have bad years, you know? It happens. And we had two of them. One after the other. No way to make it through the next winter. So the old man borrows money from Cowell. The boat's his security. But he knows he'll pay it off next season. Trouble is Cowell charged twice as much as the banks.'

'Why didn't he just borrow from the bank, then?'

Clarke scowled. 'Bad risk. No choice. Cowell or nothing.

Then just before the spring season my old man goes and has a heart attack. Doc tells him he can't go to sea, so it's just me. And I can't bring in as much as we did together. So we don't have enough to pay off the loan and Cowell calls it in. And when we can't cough up he takes the boat. Thinks he's doing me a favour by letting me skipper it, too.' He blew his contempt through loosely puckered lips. 'Took away everything my old man worked for all his days. That boat was his pride and joy. And he wanted it to be mine.' He pulled up phlegm from his throat to his mouth and spat it on to the floor. 'He was dead within the month.'

He drained his bottle and then stared at it, as if seeking inspiration in its emptiness.

'If that boat was mine now, I'd have something to hand on to my own son. And maybe he wouldn't want to leave.'

A long silence hung as heavy as the smoke that moved in slow, shifting strands around the light bulb. Finally Sime said, 'Where were you last night, Mr Clarke?'

Clarke raised dangerous eyes to fix Sime in their glare. He spoke slowly, suppressing his anger. 'I was at home. All night. You can ask my wife, or my mother.'

'We will.'

He pushed himself back from the bench and sat up straight. 'I guess the good thing is that when you people go, you'll take Cowell with you, and he won't be back. See, I really don't care who killed him. As long as he's dead.' He smiled grimly at the expression on the faces of the detectives.

'There's no law nor nothing on this island. People make their own justice. We're free.' He took a roll-up from a tin and lit it. 'This is our place. And you can all go to hell.'

III

Old Mrs Clarke sat at the dining-room table, her downturned mouth and sad eyes reflected in its polished surface. Entering the Clarke household had been like stepping back in time. Frilly yellow net curtains gathered around the windows. Floral striped wallpaper covering the walls above dark wood panelling. The floor laid with a dull green linoleum. Plastic ivy with red flowers draped around a profusion of mirrors that somehow seemed to light the room even in the fading afternoon. Every surface and every shelf groaned with ornaments and framed family photos.

The old lady herself wore a long red blouse over a straight blue skirt that modestly covered her knees. Bloated feet at the end of corned-beef legs were squeezed into shoes that must once have fitted but now looked painfully small. Her face behind thick round glasses was pale, almost grey, and looked as if it had been moulded from putty.

'I was just making up the message list,' she said, indicating a printed sheet of grocery items and a scrap of lined paper covered with shaky scribbles. The wind outside whistled around the windows and door frames.

'Message list?' Sime said.

The old lady chuckled. 'Messages we call them. Shopping you would say. I phone in my grocery list to the Co-op on Grindstone every two weeks and they send them over on the ferry next day. That's my job. Chuck's job is to go and fetch them. Not much to ask a grown boy, but it doesn't stop him complaining.'

'You live here with your son and daughter-in-law then?'

'No. They live here with me. Though you'd not know it to hear the way her ladyship calls the shots around the place. Not that I pay a blind bit of notice. They'll get the house soon enough. I'm not long for this world.'

Sime glanced at Blanc, who seemed confused. 'You look well enough to me, Mrs Clarke.'

'Appearances can be deceptive, son. Don't believe everything you see.'

The door from the hall flew open and a small, square woman in her forties with cropped, red-dyed hair stood glaring at them. Sime glanced from the window and saw a car at the gate where there hadn't been one earlier. They had not heard it arrive above the clatter of the wind. Mary-Anne Clarke, he presumed.

'What the hell do you want?' she said.

'Mrs Clarke?'

'My house, I'll ask the questions.'

Sime began to understand why Owen Clarke hated the winters. He showed her his Sûreté ID and said, 'Detectives Mackenzie and Blanc. Just trying to establish the whereabouts of your husband yesterday evening.'

'He didn't kill that weasel Cowell, if that's what you're thinking. Wouldn't have the balls for it unless he had half a pint of whisky in him. And then he wouldn't be capable of it.'

'Do you know where he was?'

'He was right here at home. All night.' She glanced at her mother-in-law. 'That right, Mrs Clarke?'

'If you say so, dear.'

Mary-Anne swung her gaze back towards the two policemen. 'Satisfied?'

'Jesus, Sime,' Blanc said as they closed the garden gate behind them. 'If I was Clarke I wouldn't be able to wait till that flare went up on May first.'

Sime grinned. 'Are you married, Thomas?'

Blanc cupped his hands around the end of a cigarette to light it, and Sime saw the smoke whipped away from his mouth as he lifted his head. 'Tried it once and didn't like it.' He paused. 'Didn't learn my lesson, though. Second time I got snared. Three teenage kids now.' He took another pull on his cigarette. 'Guess there's not much point in pulling him in for a formal interview.'

Sime shrugged, disappointed somehow. 'Guess not. For the moment anyway.'

Blanc looked at his watch. 'Probably just got time to interview the Cowell woman again before the ferry leaves.' He raised his eyes to the sky. 'If it leaves.'

They were upwind of the quad bikes and so didn't hear them until they swung into view. Five of them, engines screaming. Sime and Blanc turned, startled at the sound of throttles opening up to give vent to pent-up horsepower. They came, almost from nowhere it seemed, up over the brow of the hill, one after the other to start circling the two police officers.

Just kids, Sime realised. Fourteen, fifteen, sixteen-year-olds. Two girls, three boys. Sime raised his voice. 'Cut it out!' But it was lost in the wind and the roar of the engines.

Rain had begun to fall in earnest now, and Sime and Blanc were trapped by the circle of bikes, unable to reach the shelter of the minibus. The teenagers were laughing and hollering above the noise. Sime stepped into the path of the nearest bike to break the circle and for a moment thought it was going to run him down. But at the last moment it turned sharply away, overturning and sending its rider sprawling into the grass.

The others pulled up abruptly and Blanc went over to the fallen biker to take his arm and drag him to his feet. He was a sullen-faced boy who looked like the eldest of the group. His hair was shaven at the sides and gelled into spikes on top. 'Damned idiot!' Blanc shouted at him. 'Are you trying to kill yourself?'

But the boy never took his eyes off Sime. Humiliated in front of his friends. 'No, he's the one trying to do that.'

A sharp, shrill voice cut across the noise of wind and

motors. 'Chuck!' Everyone turned towards the house. Mary-Anne Clarke's dyed hair looked incongruously red in the sulphurous light. She stood in the doorway, and there wasn't one among them, adult or adolescent, who didn't know that she was not to be argued with. 'Get yourself in here. Now!'

Reluctantly, and with the worst possible grace, Chuck righted his quad bike with the help of one of his friends and turned a sulky face towards Sime. 'You leave my dad alone. He'd nothing to do with killing that fucking man.' And he climbed back on the bike, revving its motor several times, before driving it away around the back of the house. His mother went inside and closed the door. The other kids gunned their engines and wheeled away up the hill, kicking up mud and grass in their wake.

The rain was coming in waves now, blown in on the wind. And Sime felt it burning his face.

CHAPTER SEVEN

The imminent weather event had now leached most of the light out of the sky. There was a strange ochre quality to it, and it was dark enough in the summerhouse to warrant the use of electric light to record the second interview with Kirsty Cowell.

The wind had reached something approaching storm force. Shutters were rattling and shingles lifted on the roof. It was nearly as noisy inside as out. The rain was still coming in bursts and flurries. Just an advance guard. But the main body of it was visible out across the water, like a black mist, and it was on its way.

Sime sat again with his back to the window but with his face lit now by the overhead light. It left him feeling more exposed than he would have liked. A digest of the nurse's medical examination of Mrs Cowell lay across his knees. His face was pink from the sting of the rain. He had dried his hair with a towel, but it still felt damp.

'Why did you not tell me that you had broken up with your husband?'

Her face remained expressionless. 'You didn't ask.'

'You do yourself no favours, Mrs Cowell, by withholding information.'

She said nothing, and he examined her face. With the blood washed away, and not a trace of make-up, he saw now that she was a handsome woman without being beautiful. And oddly, even more familiar. She had a strong bone structure with slightly high cheekbones, and a full wide mouth. Her nose was a little broader than it might have been in a perfect world, but not disproportionate to the rest of her face. She had a well-defined jawline that culminated in a slightly pointed chin, but her eyes were still her most striking feature. They were fixed on him now, cool and wary. Her hair, wet from her shower, hung in limp ropes down to her shoulders, and she wore a simple pair of cut-off jeans with tennis shoes and a sweatshirt that seemed several sizes too big. There was light bruising on her left cheek and right temple.

'Tell me why he left you.'

'I'm tempted to tell you to ask him that.' She paused. 'But I'm sure you already know that he was having an affair with another woman.'

He wondered if perhaps her hostility was a shield against the humiliation she must surely feel at having to discuss the failure of her marriage with a stranger – he could imagine how he himself might feel if the roles were reversed. Or whether she was just wary of being caught out in an inconsistency. 'I'd like to hear your version of events.'

She sighed, resigned to the inevitable. 'He was spending more and more time away on business, Mr Mackenzie. As I'm sure you've been told, I have not left the island for many years, so I never accompanied him on any of his trips.'

'Was it unusual for him to be away so often?'

'No, he left the island frequently. Almost daily during the lobster season, but was never gone for long. It was the amount of time he was spending away from the island that was new. Whenever I asked about it, he just said it was the increasing demands of the business. But business had never been that demanding before, and he was quite capable of running it all from his upstairs office in the house.'

'So you challenged him about it?'

'No.' Her tiny laugh was facetious. 'Like a fool I believed him. I had no inkling of the truth until a neighbour returning on the ferry from Cap aux Meules one day told me she had seen him there.'

'And he was supposed to be somewhere else?'

'Montreal. He had phoned me just the night before. From his hotel, he said. The one he always stayed in. He wanted to warn me that he was going to be delayed for a couple of days in the city and wouldn't be home until the end of the week. So when I heard he was just across the water I knew he'd been lying to me.'

'What did you do?'

'I waited until he got home, and I asked him how it had gone in Montreal. Wanting to give him every chance to tell me a change of plans had brought him back to Cap aux Meules and he just hadn't had the opportunity to tell me.'

'But he didn't.'

She shook her head. 'He even told me about the meal he'd had the previous night in his favourite Montreal restaurant, La Porte in Boulevard St-Laurent.' She closed her eyes and for just a moment Sime felt released from their hold. When she opened them again they were burning like ice. 'I told him I knew he'd been on Cap aux Meules, and I watched the colour drain from his face.'

'What did he say?'

'He was pathetic. Floundered around trying to find some excuse, some reason to explain why he'd been in one place when he said he'd been in another. And then suddenly he just gave up. Knew it was hopeless, I suppose. Admitted that he'd been lying. That there was someone else. That he'd been having an affair for months. And that somehow it was all my fault.'

'How was it your fault?'

'Oh, I was cold and distant, apparently.' Accusations that were only too familiar to Sime. 'And my biggest crime of all? Refusing to leave the island. Like he hadn't known that from day one of our relationship.' She was breathing hard now, and Sime could feel her pain and anger in the memory of the confrontation.

'When did all this happen?'

She closed her eyes again, drew a deep breath, and it was as if a cloud of calm descended upon her. Her lids fluttered open and she looked at him candidly. 'About ten days ago, Mr Mackenzie. He moved out and in with her last week.'

Evidently the wounds were still fresh. 'Did you know her?'

'Not personally. But I knew of her. Everyone knows of her.'

'Who is she?'

'Ariane Briand. She's married to the mayor of Cap aux Meules.'

Sime gazed at her thoughtfully. Suddenly there was another jilted lover in the frame, and he wasn't quite sure why he felt a sense of relief. 'Why did your husband fly back to the island last night if he had already left you?'

'Because there's a ton of his stuff still in the house. He came to pack some cases.'

'Did you know he was coming?'

She hesitated only briefly. 'No,' she said.

He glanced at the medical report on his knees. 'You realise the fact that he'd just left you could be interpreted as a motive for murder.'

'Not by anyone who knows me.' It was a plain, simple statement of fact. He looked at her for a moment and realised that this was meant for him. And she was right. He knew not the first thing about her.

He lifted the medical report from his knees. 'It says here there is ample evidence of bruising and scratching about your body, as if you'd been in a fight.'

'I *was* in a fight! For my life.' Anger flared briefly in her eyes. 'It's hardly surprising I'm scratched and bruised. And I have no motive for murder, Mr Mackenzie. If you want to know the truth, I'd grown pretty much to hate the man. I would never have wanted to see him hurt, but I was happy that he was gone.'

Sime raised an eyebrow in surprise. 'Why?'

'When we first met he pursued me . . .' she searched for the right word, 'relentlessly. I was his obsession. He sent me flowers and chocolates, wrote me letters. Phoned me a dozen times a day. He used his wealth to try to impress me, his passion to seduce me. And like an idiot I fell for it. Flattered by his attention, all the grand gestures. He swept me off my feet. I had just graduated from university. I was young, impressionable. And coming from the island, probably not very sophisticated, certainly not very experienced. So when he proposed to me, how could I refuse?'

She shook her head in sad recollection.

'Marry in haste, they say, and repent at leisure. Well, I certainly had plenty of time for that. A real relationship's based on trust and understanding, the sharing of little things. Moments of happiness and laughter. Realising you've both just had the same thought, or were about to say the same thing. James and I shared nothing, Mr Mackenzie, except the same space. And even that, less and less often. I grew to realise that his emotions were without substance. His obsession was with himself, not me. He'd be telling me about some big contract he'd signed, some export deal to the US, and I'd realise he was watching his own reflection in the window as he told me. Playing to his own imagined gallery. Posing for photographs that weren't being taken. He was in love with the idea of me, but I was just another trophy in a life that was all about him. His image. His perception of how others saw him.'

Lightning forked out of the sky across the gulf, and the distant rumble of thunder punctuated the silence in the room. Sime waited for her to go on.

'You must understand that when I found out that he was having an affair, my overwhelming emotion was one of relief. Of course I was hurt. How could I not feel some sense of betrayal? But when he left, it was as if I had got my life back again.'

And Sime remembered Marie-Ange's words: *Leaving you was the best thing I ever did. You have no idea how free I feel.*

'He was gone, Mr Mackenzie. Why would I want to kill him?'

After the interview Sime left Blanc to dismantle their equipment, and found Kirsty Cowell standing out on the stoop. The rain was blowing horizontally off the gulf and into the porch. But she didn't seem to mind. She stood facing the wind and rain, something defiant in her stance, arms folded, face lifted slightly, rainwater running off it like tears. He stood beside her and felt the rain in his own face.

'It's going to be bad,' she said, without turning to look at him.

'So I'm told.' The roar of the sea breaking over rocks at the foot of the south-facing cliffs below was almost deafening, and he had to raise his voice to be heard. 'I'd like you to stay here tonight. Unless there's somewhere else you want to go.' He nodded towards the house that Cowell had built. 'That's off-limits.'

'I'll stay here.'

'An officer will be posted in the big house overnight.'

She turned to look at him. 'Am I a suspect?'

'You're not under arrest, if that's what you mean. The officer will be there to maintain the integrity of the crime scene.' He hesitated. 'Do you have any friends, or relatives, that you'd like to come and stay with you?'

She shook her head. 'I have plenty of acquaintances, Mr Mackenzie, but I have never made friends easily. And my only surviving relative is my cousin Jack. But he lives over on Havre Aubert and works shifts in the salt-mine up north. We really have very little contact, and almost nothing in common.'

Again she turned her gaze on him, and he found it hard to stop himself feeling some kind of emotional response.

'I'm not going to leave the island, if that's what you're worried about. I haven't left it in more than ten years, and I have no intention of leaving it now.'

'Why?'

'Why what?'

'Why won't you leave the island?'

She shrugged her shoulders. 'I had to, of course, when I was younger. When my parents sent to me secondary school on Prince Edward Island. And then again when I went to university in Lennoxville. Which was fine, as long as my folks were still here. But my mom died during my final year. Cancer. And my dad went not long after. Just couldn't face life without her, and gave up the fight. I haven't been off the island since I buried him back there in the churchyard.'

She smiled. The first one Sime had seen. But it was sad.

'It used to drive James mad. Oh, in the beginning he thought it was delightfully eccentric. Exotic, even. The two of us holed up here together, him flying off to conduct his business wherever it took him, then returning to this love nest he had built for us.' She glanced wistfully towards the big house. 'Where his love would always be waiting. The one constant he could always rely on.' She turned her back on the weather and leaned against the rail, gazing up at the house where she had been born. 'What he didn't know was that when he was gone I hardly ever slept in his bed. I came over here. Like coming back to the womb. There is comfort and love in this house, Mr Mackenzie. The house that James built is cold and empty. Which is how it made me feel.'

She sighed deeply and turned to look at Sime once more.

'Of course, he tired of my eccentricity soon enough. It frustrated him, became a source of friction. He liked to travel, you see. To dine in fine restaurants. And he had always wanted to go to Europe. None of which was possible with a stupid wife who wouldn't leave a tiny island in the middle of the Gulf of St Lawrence.'

She stopped now, searching his face, a slightly puzzled look creasing around her eyes.

'Why is it so easy to talk to you?'

Sime smiled. 'That's my job.'

'And that's why I am telling you things I've never told anyone in my life?'

His eyes never wavered from hers. 'You still haven't told me why you won't leave the island.'

Her eyes drifted away then, to find focus somewhere in her thoughts. 'Maybe that's because I can't.'

'Can't or won't?'

'Can't, Mr Mackenzie. You see, I have no real idea why. It's just a feeling I have. Very powerful. Something inside me that I can't explain. My mother was the same. Hated to leave the island. And it killed her in the end. She wouldn't go over to Cap aux Meules to see the doctor, so they didn't find the cancer until it was much too late.' She refocused on her interrogator. 'It's like . . .' she searched for words to give form to the thought, '. . . like I'm waiting for something. And if I leave I might miss it.'

He raised his right hand to sweep wet hair back from his forehead and saw more than heard her gasp. She reached out to take his hand in both of hers and turn the back of it towards her. She canted her head to one side and a frown formed between her brows.

'Where did you get this?'

Sime took his hand away from her and looked at the gold signet ring on his third finger. He had been wearing it for so long he had almost forgotten it was there. 'Why?'

She took his hand back and ran her thumb over the engraved surface of the oval red stone set into the gold. 'It's carnelian.'

'What's that?'

'A semi-precious stone. Very hard. Ideal for engraving.' She glanced up, the strangest look in her eyes. Confusion. Even fear. 'You know what the engraving is?'

She was still holding his hand. He looked at the ring again. 'To be honest, I've never really thought about it. Looks like a crooked arm holding a sword.'

'Where did you get it?' she asked again. More insistent this time.

He pulled his hand away. 'It was my father's. Passed down through the family, I guess. I got it when he died.'

She stared at him for a long time with a strange, silent intensity, then looked down again at his hand. 'I have a pendant,' she said. 'Bigger. But oval, and set in gold, with exactly the same symbol engraved in the carnelian. I'd swear it was identical.'

Sime shrugged. 'It was probably fashionable at some time in history. I bet there's thousands of them out there.'

'No.' Her contradiction was sharp and its vehemence startled him. 'It really is identical. A family crest of some sort. I've looked at it hundreds of times. I can show you it.'

In spite of his curiosity, Sime was wary of indulging her in this bizarre turn of events. 'I don't think that would serve any purpose. And, anyway, you can't go back into the big house for the moment. Not while it's still a crime scene under investigation.'

'I don't need to. The pendant's here. I brought most of my personal stuff back into the summerhouse after James left. Including my jewellery box.' She turned and hurried into the house. Sime stood for a moment with the rain whipping in under the eaves, and felt infused by the oddest sense of uncertainty. He had already been unsettled by his sense of knowing her. Now this. He looked at the engraving on the ring. It could only be some kind of bizarre coincidence. He pushed through the screen door back into the sitting room as Blanc brought the flight cases containing the monitors through from the bedroom.

Kirsty ran down the stairs holding a polished wooden box inlaid with mother-of-pearl. She set it on the coffee table in front of the fireplace and knelt to open the lid. Blanc glanced from Sime to Kirsty and back again, the almost imperceptible raising of one eyebrow asking his silent question. Sime's response was the merest of shrugs. Both men turned their heads at the sound of her gasp of frustration.

'It's not here.'

The curiosity that Sime had felt out on the porch was replaced now by a burgeoning cynicism. He walked over to the coffee table and stood above her as she knelt in front of it, searching through the clutter of jewellery inside the open box. Then in frustration she tipped its contents out on the glass tabletop. Rings and bracelets, necklaces and pendants, brooches, clasps, dress pins, all rattled across the glass. Silver, gold and platinum set with precious and semi-precious stones. Some of the items were modern, others clearly from a bygone age.

She tried to sort through them with clumsy, trembling fingers, until he saw her upturned face filled with confusion. 'I don't understand. I've always kept it in here. Always. And it's gone.'

Sime was aware of Blanc looking at him. He said, 'What you may or may not have done with an item of jewellery is of no concern here, Mrs Cowell. Murder is.' He paused. 'We'll see you in the morning, weather permitting.'

CHAPTER EIGHT

I

There were fewer people on the quayside for the departure of the ferry that afternoon than had met it in the morning. But it was probable that the weather had more to do with it than any lack of curiosity on the part of the Entry islanders. The *Ivan-Quinn* was rising and falling dangerously, even in the sheltered waters of the harbour, and Lapointe had difficulty reversing their minibus up the ramp to the car deck.

James Cowell was zipped into a white plastic body bag and lay on the floor between the seats. Nobody had spoken a word on the drive across the island to the harbour with his body lying among them like a ghost. And now everyone was keen to get into the bowels of the ferry and out of the rain. Except for Sime. His jacket already soaked through, he climbed slippery rusted steps to the upper deck and made his way along a narrow walkway to the stern of the boat. From there he could see over the interlocking concrete fingers that made up the breakwater, back across the bay towards Cap aux Meules. It was already almost lost in rain and low cloud. Just a sliver of blue and gold lay along the horizon behind it. The sea in between looked angry. Rising and falling in foaming slabs of grey water like molten lead.

A klaxon sounded as the ramp was raised, and the ferry slipped its mooring to round the breakwater and head out into the advance legions of the coming storm. Waves broke over the bow as soon as she escaped the comparative shelter of the island.

Sime held on to the white-painted rail and watched as Entry Island slowly receded behind them. Incongruously, the sun had slipped beneath the line of cloud in the west, sending out the last of its light to illuminate the contours of the island against the blue-black sky behind it. Before suddenly it was gone, and the island was swallowed by the rain and mist.

Sime let go of the rail with his right hand and lifted it to examine his ring. Its history went back several generations, he knew, but he had no idea of its original owner. He became aware of Lieutenant Crozes approaching, and grabbed hold of the rail again. Crozes stopped next to him, his waterproof jacket zipped up to the neck, a baseball cap pulled low over his forehead. His hands were thrust deep in his pockets, and he was managing somehow, with feet planted wide, to move his body to the rhythm of the boat and stay balanced. An experienced sailor, Sime thought.

'So what do you reckon?' he shouted above the wind and the sea.

'About the wife?'

Crozes nodded.

'Hard to say, Lieutenant. She has motive, certainly. And she's the only witness. Her scratches and bruising are compatible with the story she tells. But they could just as easily have been suffered during a struggle with her husband. Though he was a fit man by the look of him, and she's slight built. An unequal struggle, you would have thought. Makes you wonder how she could have got the better of him.'

Crozes nodded again and seemed to thrust his hands even more deeply into his pockets.

'But if we're just looking at motive,' Sime added, 'then there's also the cuckolded husband. Mayor Briand at Cap aux Meules. We're going to have to talk to him.'

'Yes, we are. I've already briefed Sergeant Arseneau to go find him as soon as we get back. We can interview him tonight or first thing tomorrow at the local Sûreté. But the minute the ferry has docked I want you and Blanc to go and talk to Madame Briand. The local boys have got an address for us.'

Sime glanced at him and saw that his face was set. Whether against the weather, or some other obstacle to their investigation it was impossible to tell. But his mood was clearly black.

Crozes said, 'Trouble is, as Blanc pointed out, if we buy the wife's story that she was the object of the attack, and not Cowell, why would either Briand or Clarke attack her?'

Sime nodded. 'What does Marie-Ange say?'

'That there's no evidence of a third party at the crime scene. She's collected blood samples from the broken glass in the conservatory, hair and fibres from the body and the surrounding floor. They'll go back to Montreal with Lapointe and the body for analysis. But not tonight. And maybe not in the morning either. Everything's being locked down tight for this storm. The airport's been closed. It's unlikely that anyone or anything's going to get on or off the Madeleines in the next twenty-four hours. Including Cowell and our samples.'

They stood for a moment in silence watching how the boat carved a green channel that fanned out in their wake, rising and falling among the waves. Then Sime felt Crozes turn his face towards him. 'Blanc said she was troubled by a piece of jewellery that's gone missing.'

Sime nodded.

'What's all that about?'

Sime turned his head to look at him. 'It's the weirdest thing, Lieutenant. The moment I set eyes on her I could have sworn I knew her from somewhere.'

Crozes frowned. 'And do you?'

Sime shrugged helplessly. 'I can't imagine how.'

'And the jewellery?'

'A pendant. An oval of red carnelian set in gold, and engraved with an arm holding a sword.' He raised the back of his right hand so that Crozes could see his ring. 'Exactly the same as this. So she said.'

Crozes examined it for a moment before Sime had to clutch the rail again to steady himself. 'But she can't find it?' the lieutenant said.

'No.'

Crozes was silent for several long moments. Then, 'Seven billion people in the world, Sime. Everyone's bound to look like someone. And don't let her fuck with your mind. If she killed her husband it's going to be hard enough to prove it as it is. She's nobody's fool, and who knows what kind of mind games she's capable of. Just make sure you don't lose your focus.'

II

The Briand house was set off the road in amongst woods a little over a kilometre south of the police station on Cap aux Meules. On the short drive down the Chemin de Gros-Cap coast road, with Thomas Blanc beside him in the passenger seat, Sime felt the pull of the steering wheel as the wind battered in off the Baie de Plaisance and buffeted the high side of the minibus. Entry Island was lost in the storm somewhere out there across the bay, hunkered down against the full force of it. He caught Blanc looking at him. 'Are you okay?' the older man asked.

'I'm not going to fall asleep at the wheel if that's what you're worried about.'

Blanc grinned. 'That's not what I meant.' He hesitated. 'Just . . . you know . . . you and Marie-Ange.'

Sime's smile faded. 'I'm fine.' Then, quickly changing the subject, 'What's Crozes like to work for?'

Blanc gazed thoughtfully through the rain-spattered windscreen. 'He's a good cop, Sime. But it's all about him. He's going places. You know,' He lifted his eyes towards the heavens, 'fast track to the top. Every case is important to him. Every conviction another step up the ladder. Do a good job and he'll back you all the way. Screw it up and he'll drop you right in it. Just don't ever make the mistake of thinking he's your friend. He's not.'

Sime nodded. He knew the type. And he knew, too, that Crozes would want this particular case wrapped up as quickly as possible. It would be the view from Montreal that a murder on an island with a population of a hundred, more or less, should be a straightforward matter. Besides which, keeping a team of eight detectives for any length of time on the Madeleine islands would be a costly business. And these days the bottom line was all important. 'I guess Ariane Briand will be a French-speaker,' he said. 'Maybe you should lead the interrogation.'

'If you like.' Blanc shrugged indifferently, but Sime knew it was what he wanted.

Sime spun the wheel and they turned into the Allée Robert-Vigneau, which developed into little more than a pot-holed track caught in their headlights as it cut into the pine plantation that stretched across this south-east corner of the island. A few hundred metres along it they turned right at a

80

mail box into a short pebbled drive that led up to a house surrounded by tall trees that swayed dangerously in the wind. Sime pulled into a parking place out front and they stepped down from the vehicle.

The Briand house was impressive, not typical of the classical island house. It was wooden, of course, but the roof was steeply pitched in the Scandinavian style, and much of the front of the house was glass. A security light came on and Sime saw their reflections in the glass as they walked up to the front door. An odd couple. One tall, lean, a little stooped, the other small and rotund, with a mop of curly dark hair fringing his bald patch. Like cartoon characters out of a graphic novel, he thought.

Blanc rang the bell twice, and when there was no reply knocked firmly on the glass. Sime stepped back and looked up at the house. There were no lights on anywhere. 'No one home,' he said. Through the trees, the lights of a neighbouring house twinkled in the gathering darkness. 'Let's see if the neighbours know where she is.'

Bracing themselves against the rain, the two men ran through the trees, following a path that took them into the neighbour's garden. Another security light flooded the patio, and a black SUV stood in the drive, its engine ticking, still hot. Sime rang the bell and a middle-aged woman wearing a sweatshirt and tracksuit bottoms opened the door, peering cautiously out at the two sodden strangers caught in the rain and the glare of her security lamp. Blanc fished out his ID and pushed it towards her. 'Sûreté, madame. We're looking for Madame Briand next door. Any idea where we can find her?'

'Oh, she's not at home,' the woman said.

'I think we'd already established that.' Sime's voice was laden with sarcasm, but it was lost on her. Dark eyes filled with intrigue opened wide. This could only be to do with the murder on Entry Island.

'Ariane flew out this morning to the mainland,' she said, as if imparting some important confidence. Then her face clouded. 'Not sure where she went, though. Or when she'll be back.'

Sime and Blanc exchanged looks.

III

The team was eating in the La Patio family restaurant next to the Auberge Madeli when Sergeant Enquêteur Jacques Arseneau returned with the news.

Two groups, four in one and three in the other, were squeezed into adjoining stalls. Sime and Marie-Ange sat in different groups, ostentatiously avoiding each other. The thirteen thousand inhabitants of the Madeleine Isles had been warned all evening in TV and radio broadcasts to stay indoors and the restaurant was empty, apart from one chef in the kitchen and a single server.

Arseneau came in dripping and battered, divesting himself of his jacket and baseball cap and cursing the weather. He squeezed into the end of one of the stalls.

Crozes looked at him. 'So what did Mayor Briand have to say for himself?'

'Not a thing, Lieutenant. He's not in the islands. Flew out this morning, apparently, for a bunch of political meetings in Quebec City. His secretary doesn't even know where he's staying. Seems it was a last-minute decision to go, and he made his own reservations.'

Silence settled like dust on the group, and all faces turned towards Crozes. He seemed impassive, but Sime noticed that the skin had darkened around his eyes. Perhaps none of this was going to be as quickly and easily resolved as he might have hoped. He chewed thoughtfully on his lower lip. 'Seems a bit strange, doesn't it?' he said. 'The . . . what was the phrase you used, Sime . . . ? Cuckolded husband? And the other woman. Both leaving the islands the morning after the murder.' He turned to Arseneau. 'Get on to Quebec City. Tonight. I want Briand found.'

The meal passed in relative silence, Crozes's mood transmitting itself and affecting the others.

After they had eaten they adjourned to the bar. A bowling alley that linked the hotel to the restaurant was closed because of the weather. From the bar they could see through windows to the empty aisles simmering silently under half-lighting. There was a spooky quality to the abandoned alleys, an almost ghostly quiet in the absence of players. By contrast, the noise outside was frightening. The wind was hurling bins and traffic signs across the car park with lethal force, and traffic lights swung violently on their overhead stanchions.

Sime excused himself and walked alone along the length of a deserted corridor to his room next to reception. His eyes were heavy and stinging. His mouth was dry again, and his tongue felt huge in it. Every muscle seemed to ache, as if stretched to breaking point. All he wanted to do was lie down and close his eyes.

In his room, sliding glass doors opened on to the car park at the front of the auberge. The wind was bowing the glass. He pulled heavy curtains across them to shut out the night, but it barely reduced the noise. If he wasn't so tired he might have been apprehensive.

He sat in the dark for the next half-hour with his laptop open on the dresser, searching the internet for information about Entry Island. There wasn't a lot out there. A dwindling population of just over a hundred at the last count, a school in danger of running out of pupils. There were two stores, a restaurant, an Anglican church, a museum, the school and a post office. It was just two kilometres wide, and three long. The winter was prolonged and brutal, and when the bay froze over as it often did, the ferry couldn't sail and the islanders were cut off, sometimes for long periods. He closed the laptop and wondered why Kirsty Cowell was so determined to stay there. The explanation she had given him seemed less than convincing.

He turned on the TV and lay on the bed in the dark. Although he was desperate to sleep he had no expectation of it, and didn't bother to undress.

He listened to the rain hammering against the sliding doors. It almost drowned out the frenetic commentary on an otherwise dull ice hockey match. He wondered how it must be for Kirsty Cowell alone out there in that clifftop house, fully exposed to the fury of the storm. While just fifty yards away the home she had shared with her obsessive husband stood empty. Except for the cop who kept guard over the scene of his murder. Sime wondered how many unhappy memories of the couple's ill-fated marriage had been subsumed by that house, become a part of its fabric, like the grain in wood.

He supposed that the house would be hers now. A house in which she couldn't bring herself to stay alone when Cowell was gone. And it occurred to him that she stood to inherit not just the house, but all of his wealth. The fifteen million a year in lobster income. The processing plant here on Cap aux Meules. As powerful a motive for murder, perhaps, as betrayal. There must surely be a will. Something else to check out tomorrow.

His aching eyes searched the ceiling for the cracks and stains that might occupy his mind in the long sleepless hours to come. He had developed an ability to make endless pictures out of shapeless blemishes on walls and ceilings. Exercising his imagination to fill in the time. Even the flickering light sent around the room by the ever-changing images on the TV screen could conjure up its own shadow theatre.

But tonight his lids were just too heavy. They fell shut, and there, once more in the darkness, he found her. Watching him, holding him in her eyes. And for a moment he thought he saw her smile . . .

CHAPTER NINE

I hear voices. Strange accents. I am lost among a sea of faces that I can't quite see. As if I am looking at the world through a veil of gauze. I see myself now. Younger. Seventeen perhaps, or eighteen. I can feel my confusion, and at the same time watch myself with a peculiar objectivity. Both spectator and player. I wear the oddest clothes. Breeches held up with braces, a stained white shirt without a collar, a three-quarter-length jacket, heavy leather boots that seem too big for my feet.

I feel cobbles underfoot, and blackened sandstone tenements rise around me. There is a river, and I see a paddle-steamer ploughing its way past the quay towards a low, arched stone bridge that spans the leaden flow. Somewhere beyond the tenements on the far bank I see a church steeple prick the sky, and clouds of smoke and steam rise into the blue from a railway station almost immediately opposite. I can hear the trains spitting and coughing as they idle against their buffers.

It feels like summer. The air is warm, and I am aware of the heat of the sun on my skin. The gauze dissolves now, bringing sharper focus, and my objectivity slips away. I become conscious of tall-masted sailing ships moored along the quayside. The sea of faces around me shifting and undulating as this current of humanity ebbs and flows, carrying me along like a piece of flotsam.

But I am not alone. I feel a hand in mine, small and soft and warm, and I look back to see Kirsty Cowell, apprehensive, unsettled by the lack of control we seem to have of our destiny in this crowd. She is younger, too. A teenager. I call to her above the voices that fill the air. 'Don't let go, Ciorstaidh, stay close to me.' And from somewhere, far away, in my unconscious world, I realise I am calling her by her Gaelic name.

A space opens up around us, and I see a boy with a cloth cap and ragged shorts. A pile of newspapers is draped over one arm, a folded copy raised in his other hand. He is chanting some incomprehensible refrain. Over and over. Someone snatches a paper and slips coins into his hand. Kirsty takes one too, letting go of my hand to unfold it. I see its banner. The *Glasgow Herald*. And before she opens it up, the date: July 16th, 1847.

'It's Fair Friday,' she says. 'No wonder it's so busy.' But for some reason this means nothing to me. I am gripped, I realise, by a sense of urgency. Of time running out. Somewhere I can hear a clock chiming the hour.

'We're late. We can't afford to miss the boat.'

She slips the newspaper under her arm and takes my hand

again, our free hands occupied by the carrying of small cardboard suitcases containing God knows what. Her face is shining, excited. She wears a tunic buttoned up over a long dress that flares and falls to the cobbles, but her black hair tumbles free across her shoulders, swept back from her face by a soft breeze.

'We're looking for the *Eliza*, Simon. A three-master. We've time enough. They said she wouldn't be leaving the Broomielaw till a quarter past the hour.'

I push up on to my tiptoes to see across the heads on the quayside. There are three boats tied up to giant iron capstans. And I see the name I am looking for painted in black and gold across the stern of the furthest. *ELIZA*. She seems huge to me, a confusion of masts and rigging and furled canvas sails.

'I see her. Come on.'

And, pulling Kirsty behind me, I push off through the bodies of men, women and children scrambling anxiously to secure their places on these wind-driven time capsules, to be carried off to new lives in other places.

But then I hear voices raised in anger, lifting above the others. Cursing and blaspheming and brimming with violence. A large group is gathered around a stand of trolleys laden with bags. An argument has led to a fight, and I can see fists flying. Top hats skiting away across the cobbles. The crowd ahead of us surges back, like displaced water, and my grasp of Kirsty's hand is broken.

'Simon!' I hear her scream, panic in her voice. I heave against the bodies that have separated us, only to see her carried away by a current stronger than both of us, fear in her eyes, a hand hopelessly grasping at the air above her head before she is lost from sight. 'Get to the boat.' Her call is barely discernible above the roar. 'I'll meet you there.'

The shrill sounds of whistles pierce the air, and I see uniformed constables ploughing through bodies, batons swinging. Another surge sweeps me away, and I realise that my only hope of finding her again is at the *Eliza*.

I am determined now, driven by anger and fear. I am young and strong and fight my way through the panicked hordes, head down, using my shoulders to clear the way ahead. And when next I look up the *Eliza* is towering over me, and I realise it must be high tide. The crowd is funnelling like water on to the narrow gangplank that leads up to the deck, marshalled by sheriff's officers.

Hands grasp my arms and my shoulders, propelling me forward, and I go helplessly with the flow, craning my neck and turning to look left and right above their heads to catch a glimpse of Kirsty.

We spill out on to the deck, hundreds of us it seems, and I elbow my way to the side of the boat from where I have a view of the gangplank and the crowded quay. I have seen sheep herded this way before, but never people. And never so many in one place and at one time.

I scan the faces that fill my field of vision, apprehension

rising like bile as I fail to find her. I have been pushed further and further along the deck, and away from the rail. Voices rise above the melee, and I am aware of the gangplank being pulled aboard.

Total panic fuels my fight through protesting voices back to the embarkation point, and I see dockers loosing ropes as thick as a man's arm from the loops that secure them to their capstans. More voices raised from above turn my head upwards in time to see vast sheets of canvas unfurling to catch the breeze, and I feel the ship lurch for the first time beneath my feet.

'Ciorstaidh!' My voice tears itself from my lungs and I hear her call my name in reply, so far away I fear I am just imagining it. I reach the rail in time to see that the *Eliza* has slipped her berth and is pulling out now into the main channel of the river where the water is deeper and the current runs fast.

And there, among the faces of the crowd on the quay, the pale upturned face of the girl I love. My sense of disbelief and dismay is almost overwhelming.

'Ciorstaidh!' I scream again. And for a fleeting moment I consider jumping overboard. But like most islanders, fear of water has always robbed me of the ability to swim, and I know I would be leaping to certain death. 'Wait for me!'

I can see the fear and consternation in her face as she pushes through the crowds, trying to keep up with the *Eliza* as she drifts away. 'Where?'

I have no idea. I search desperately in my confusion to find a single rational thought to hang on to. And fail. 'Wherever you are,' I shout through my hopelessness, 'I'll find you. I promise!'

And I watch helplessly as her face recedes from view, blurred and lost among my tears, as I realise it is a promise I can never keep.

CHAPTER TEN

I

Sime awoke calling her name. Hearing it rip from his throat. He sat bolt upright on the bed, and felt the sweat trickle down his face. And yet he was shivering with cold. His breath came in short rasping bursts, and his heart felt like someone hammering at his ribs from the inside, trying to break their way out.

It was just a dream, but so vivid that the same hopeless impotence felt by Simon when his lover faded from view lingered in his own consciousness like a black cloud of depression.

It was the first time he had dreamed it, but this was a story he knew. He pulled his knees up to his chest, leaning his elbows on them and closing his eyes. And for a moment he was transported in his mind back to childhood. To his grandmother's house on the banks of the Salmon River in Scotstown. An old timber house built in the early twentieth century and made gloomy by three tall trees that loomed darkly over it.

He could almost smell it. That perfume of old age and dampness, of dust and history that permeated every corner. And he could hear her voice. Low, almost monotone, and always with an underlying sense of melancholy as she read to him and his sister from the diaries.

He had not thought once about those memoirs in all the years since, and yet he seemed to recall them now with great clarity. Not in every detail, but with a striking sense of place and story. The story of his ancestor's life, begun on his voyage across the ocean. The man after whom Sime had been named, whose story had ended in a tragedy that his grandmother had always refused to read them.

Why had this moment suddenly forced its way into his consciousness? The tragic separation of Simon and Ciorstaidh on the quay at Glasgow. And why had his subconscious mind cast himself and Kirsty Cowell in their respective roles? He shook his head. A head that ached. He had no answers and felt almost feverish. Then it occurred to him that if he had dreamt, then he had slept. Although it hardly felt like it. He glanced at the bedside clock. It was just after 1.30 a.m. The television still sent shadows dancing around the room. The ice hockey match was over, but the channel had now surrendered its night-time hours to telesales of a machine for sculpting abdominal perfection. He could have slept for no longer than the real-time passage of his dream.

He slipped off the bed and went through to the bathroom to splash his face with cold water. When he looked up he was almost startled by the pale, haggard young man staring back at him from the mirror. Under the harsh electric light every crease and shadow on his face seemed darker and more deeply etched. His soft brown eyes were weary and pained, the whites shot through with red. Even his curls seemed to have lost their lustre, and although his hair was fair, almost Scandinavian blonde, he could see the grey starting to grow in at the temples. Shaved short at the sides and back, but allowed longer growth on top, it gave him a boyish appearance, which seemed incongruous now with the tired blanched face whose reflection he could hardly bear to look at.

He turned away to bury his face in a soft towel and went back through to the bedroom, dropping his clothes on the floor behind him as he went. He found a fresh pair of boxers in his bag and slid between cold sheets, turning on to his side and drawing his knees into the foetal position. He had slept once already tonight, albeit for less than an hour, and he so much wanted to return to his dream, to manipulate it as is sometimes possible when you are consciously dreaming. To achieve what his ancestor had been unable to do in life. To change its outcome. To hear her voice and find her on the boat, and release himself from that unkeepable promise.

For a long time he lay, eyes closed, with kaleidoscope colours appearing like inkblots behind his lids before vanishing again into darkness. He turned over and focused on his breathing. Slow, steady. Letting his mind and his thoughts wander. Trying to relax his body, let the weight of it sink into the bed.

And then he was on his back. Eyes open and staring at the ceiling. And although every part of him cried out for sleep he was wide awake.

It was possible that he had drifted off into periods of semi-consciousness, but it didn't feel that way. Unable to prevent himself, he had followed the painful passage of time through the digital figures that counted away his life during the small hours, the wind and rain raging without cease outside the glass doors of his room. Four, five, six o'clock. Six-thirty now, and he felt more tired than when he had lain down the night before. The headache was there, as it always was, and he finally rose to drop an effervescent painkiller into his plastic cup and listen to it fizz. It seemed impossible now to face the day without it.

Back in the bedroom he picked his clothes off the floor and slowly got dressed. His cotton hoodie, which he had hung over the bath the night before, was still damp. But he had brought nothing else, and so pulled it on anyway. He slid open the glass doors and slipped out into the car park. The first grey light of dawn was seeping through clouds so low they were scraping the surface of the island, propelled by a wind that was not yet spent. The tarmac was littered with the debris of the storm. Upturned garbage cans, their contents carried off into the night. Roof tiles. The branches of pine trees from the plantation that grew all around this island conurbation. A child's trampoline, all buckled out of shape, had been plucked from a garden somewhere and come to rest lodged between a pickup truck and a saloon car. The cross above the steeple of the ugly modern church building across the street had snapped at its base and hung precariously from the roof, attached only by its lightning conductor.

And still the air was not cold. The wind, though little diminished, was soft in his face, and he breathed it in deeply, letting it fill his mouth. Between the hospital and the church, a broad street led down towards the bay, and he could see the ocean piling in along the island's shoreline in huge green breakers that broke in fearsome froth around the curve of the coast. He crossed the road and walked towards it, hands thrust deep in his pockets, and stopped and stood for a long time on the slope of the hill just watching the power of the sea below him as the day began to make some impression on the storm.

Crozes was sitting in the breakfast room on his own, nursing a coffee. Two slices of hot buttered toast lay on the plate in front of him, a single bite taken. But he was no longer chewing when Sime came in, and he didn't appear to have an appetite for the remainder.

Sime poured himself a coffee and sat down opposite, placing his mug on the stained expanse of white melamine that lay between them. Crozes looked up from his silent thoughts. 'Jesus, man, did you sleep at all?'

Sime shrugged. 'A bit.'

Crozes scrutinised him carefully for some moments. 'You should see a doctor.'

Sime took a sip of his coffee. 'Already have. He gave me some pills. But they just make me drowsy during the day, and don't help me sleep at night.'

'Didn't sleep much myself last night. With all that damned noise. I thought the roof was going to lift off the hotel, or the windows were going to come in. They were creaking like they were ready to shatter.' He took a mouthful of coffee. 'I got a call about fifteen minutes ago. The King Air got struck by debris on the apron at the airport during the night. Damage to the windshield, apparently. If they can't fix it here, they're going to have to send over a replacement aircraft with the parts. Upshot is, we ain't getting off the islands today. So the body and all the other evidence is going to have to sit on ice till we can get us back in the air.'

'Tough break.'

Black eyes darted quickly in Sime's direction, as if perhaps Crozes suspected sarcasm. Both men knew it would reflect badly on Crozes if their investigation dragged on beyond a day or two. He delved into his pocket to retrieve a set of car keys and tossed them across the table. 'Lapointe has rented us a couple of vehicles. Those are for the Chevy. It's out front. Take it and go talk to Kirsty Cowell's cousin, Jack Aitkens. If you think it's worthwhile, bring him back to the station here on Cap aux Meules and we'll video a formal interview.'

'What do you think he might be able to tell us?'

Crozes tossed a frustrated hand into the air. 'Who the hell knows? But I've been looking at the tapes. She's a weirdo, right? The Cowell woman. Maybe he can give us some insight into her personality, her relationship with the husband. Anything that'll give us something more than we have.'

'You've reviewed the interview tapes already?' Sime was surprised.

'What else was I going to do? Couldn't sleep and it seemed like the best use of the time. I got Blanc out of his bed to set it up for me.' He glanced a little self-consciously at his junior officer. 'Guess I'm beginning to learn how it feels to be an insomniac like you.'

Sime lifted the keys from the table and stood up. He drained his mug of coffee. 'Do you have an address for the cousin?'

'He lives at a place called La Grave, on the next island down. Île du Havre Aubert. But he's not there right now.'

Sime cocked an eyebrow. 'You have been busy.'

'I want this done and dusted, Sime. And I want us out of here by tomorrow, at the latest.'

'So if he's not at home where will I find him?'

'He's working the night shift in the salt-mines at the north end of the islands. He's off at eight.' He glanced at his watch. 'If you hurry you should be just in time to catch him.'

II

The road to Havre aux Maisons took a diversion to avoid road-works where they were building a sleek new bridge to link it to Cap aux Meules. Sime drove through water-filled potholes, past shacks that advertised themselves as restaurants, or bars, or nightclubs. Flimsy, storm-battered structures painted in garish colours that belied the seedy night-time entertain-ment they offered the youth of the islands.

As he drove north through Havre aux Maisons, the land levelled off and the pine plantations and all signs of human habitation disappeared. Roadside reeds were flattened by the wind, and sand from the long, narrow strip of dunes on his right blew in swirls and eddies across the surface of the road. And all the time, sitting out across the bay, the shadow of Entry Island lurked in his peripheral vision.

The sky, at last, was beginning to break up, shredded by the wind to reveal torn strips of blue, and release patches of unusually golden, shallow-angled sunlight to fan out across the islands from the east.

The sea vented its wrath all along the shore, breaking in spume-filled spray over the causeway that linked Cap aux Meules and Île de Point-aux-Loups. Wolf Island was, in fact, a small cluster of islands in the middle of a long sandbar that linked the southern isles with a loop of three large islands at the north end of the archipelago. On his left the gulf stretched away to the unseen North American continent. On his right, the emerald-green waters of the Lagune de la Grande-Entrée were calmer, protected from the surging waters of the storm by a sandbar that ran parallel to the one on which they had built the road.

As he approached the final stretch of the sandbank on the west side, he saw the tanker terminal off to his right, where huge ships docked several times a week to fill their holds with salt. A long shed with a silver roof caught flashes of sunlight from the broken sky. A concrete pier extended out into the lagoon where a red-and-cream tanker was now docked, an elevated length of covered conveyor belt feeding salt into its belly.

The conveyor tracked back along the line of the shore for nearly a kilometre to the tower of the mine shaft itself, where a high fence topped by barbed wire delineated the secure perimeter of the mine. Thirty or forty vehicles were parked along the fringes of a muddy, semi-flooded car park. Sime parked up and found his way into the administration block where a secretary told him that Jack Aitkens would be off shift in about twenty minutes, if he would care to wait. She waved him towards a seat, but Sime said he would wait in his car and walked back out into the wind. It had been hot and claustrophobic in there. And he found it unimaginable that people could spend twelve hours a day underground in dark confined spaces. It would be worse than a prison sentence.

Sime sat in the Chevy with the engine running, hot air blowing on his feet, a window open to let in air. He gazed across the waters of the lagoon towards rock that rose almost sheer out of the sea, and the brightly painted houses that ran along the strip of green that topped it. Hardy folk, these. Fishermen mostly, the descendants of pioneers from France and Britain who had come to claim these uninhabited and inhospitable islands and make them their home. Until their arrival, only the Mi'kmaq Indians had ventured here on seasonal hunting forays.

Sime felt the wind rock his car as it blew in gusts across the open water, fading only a little now in strength. And he let his mind drift back to the diaries. Somehow it seemed important to understand why his subconscious had picked that particular moment from them to animate his unexpected dream.

It was odd. He could only have been seven or eight when their grandmother first read them the stories. Sitting out on the front porch in the shade of the trees during the hot summer holidays, or huddled around the fire on a dark winter's evening. He had lost count of the number of times he and Annie had asked her to read them again. And being the same age as the young boy described in the first of them, Sime had always remembered it in great detail.

But somehow it wasn't his grandmother's voice that he had heard. Not after being drawn into the story. It was as if his ancestor himself had read it out loud, as though he had been speaking directly to Sime and his sister.

CHAPTER ELEVEN

When I was very young, it seemed I knew lots of things without ever really remembering how or where I learned them. I knew that my village was a collection of houses in the township they called Baile Mhanais. And if I were to try to spell it in English now it would look something like Bally Vanish. I knew that our village stood on the west coast of the Isle of Lewis and Harris in the Outer Hebrides, and I remember it was at school that I learned that the Hebrides were a part of Scotland.

The teacher was sent by the Church, which seemed to think that it was important for us to learn reading and writing – if only so we could read the Bible. I used to sit and listen to that teacher, overwhelmed by everything I didn't know. At eight years old, my world seemed such a tiny place in the greater world beyond, and yet it filled my life. It was everything I knew.

I knew, for example, that there were nearly sixty people living in my village, and almost double that if you took account of the crofts that extended north and south along the shore on either side. I knew that it was the Atlantic Ocean that beat its relentless tattoo on the shingle shore below the village, and I knew that somewhere far away on the other side of it was a place they called America.

On the other side of the bay, fishermen from Stornoway sometimes laid out their catch of whitefish on the rocks to dry in the sun. They paid the children of the village a penny each to spend the day there and scare away the birds.

There was a jetty, too, built by the estate before Langadail was bought by its new owner. My father used to swear that the new laird spent nothing on improvements and that the place would go to rack and ruin.

There were a dozen blackhouses in our village. They sat at angles to each other on the slope, and my sister and I often played hide and seek among the dark alleys between them. Each house was built with the byre at the bottom end to let the animal waste drain out. At the end of each winter I would help my father break down the gable at the end of our house to shovel the cow shit on to a cart and haul it to our wee strip of land to use as fertiliser. It was always shit and seaweed we used to grow barley. And the thatch from the roof, blackened and thick with the sticky residue of peat soot, that we laid on the lazy beds with kelp to feed the potatoes. The oats seemed to grow fine without any encouragement. We reroofed each spring with fresh sheaves of barley stalks, then covered the thatch with fishermen's netting and weighted it down with hanging stones. The smoke from the peat fire somehow managed to make its way through the roof eventually, and the few hens we owned found warmth and comfort in winter by roosting in it.

The walls of our blackhouse were thick. Two walls really, drystone-built, with earth and rubble in between, and turf on top to soak up the water that ran off the roof. I suppose that to someone who wasn't accustomed to it, the sight of sheep grazing along the top of the walls might have seemed a bit odd. But I was used to seeing them up there.

All these things I knew because they were a part of me, as I was a part of the community of Baile Mhanais.

I remember the day that Murdag was born. I'd been sitting that morning with old blind Calum outside the door of his house near the foot of the village. Protective hills rose up to the north and east, though we were exposed to the weather from the west. The ridge beyond the bay provided a little shelter from the south-westerlies, and I suppose that my ancestors must have thought it as good a spot as any for the settling of their village.

As always, Calum wore his blue coat with its yellow buttons, and a time-worn Glengarry on his head. He said he could see shapes in the daylight, but not a thing in the darkness of his blackhouse. So he preferred to sit outside in the cold and see something, rather than be warm inside and see nothing.

I sat often with old Calum and listened to his stories. It seemed there was very little he didn't know about the people there, and the history of Baile Mhanais. When he first told me that he was a veteran of Waterloo, I didn't like to say that I had no idea what a veteran was, or what Waterloo might be. It was my teacher who told me that a veteran was an old soldier, and that Waterloo was a famous battle fought a thousand miles away on the Continent of Europe to defeat the French dictator, Napoleon Bonaparte.

It made me view old Calum in a different light. With something like awe. Here was a warrior who had defeated a dictator and he lived in my village. He said he had fought nine battles on the Continent, and was blinded in the last by his own misfiring flintlock.

It was cold that morning, with the wind blowing down from the north, and there were spits of rain in it with a hint of sleet. The winter could be wicked sometimes, and mild at others. My teacher said it was the Gulf Stream that stopped us from being under permanent frost, and I had a picture in my mind of a hot stream bubbling through the sea to melt the ice of the northern oceans.

I heard a voice carried on the wind. It was my sister, Annag. She was just over a year younger than me, and I turned to see her running down between the blackhouses. She wore a pale-blue cotton skirt beneath a woollen jumper that my mother had knitted. Her legs and feet were bare like mine. Shoes were for Sundays. And our feet were like leather on the soles.

'Sime! Sime!' Her little face was pink with exertion, her eyes wide with alarm. 'It's happening. It's happening now!'

Old Calum found my wrist and held it firm as I stood up. 'I'll say a prayer for her, boy,' he said.

Annag grabbed my hand. 'Come on, come on!'

And we ran together, hand in hand, up between the blackhouses, past our stack yard and into the barn at the back. We were both still wee and didn't have to stoop to enter the house, unlike my father, who had to duck every time or crack his head on the lintel.

It was dark in here, and it took a moment for our eyes to grow accustomed to the light. The floor was rough-cobbled with big stones, hay stacked high at one end, and the potato store boxed off in almost total darkness at the other. We ran through into the tiny space between the fire room and the byre, startling the hens. There were two cows in the byre at that time, and one of them turned to low mournfully in our direction.

We crouched down behind the chicken wire at the door and peered into the fire room. The iron lamps that hung from the rafters gave off the stink of fish liver oil, cutting through the acrid peat smoke that rose from the fire in the centre of the room.

It was full of people. All women, except for my father. Annag clutched my arm, tiny fingers bruising my flesh. 'The midwife came ten minutes ago,' she whispered, and paused. Then, 'What's a midwife?'

There had been enough births in my short life that I knew the midwife was the woman who came to help with the delivery. But, actually, she was just one of our neighbours.

'She's come to take the baby from *mamaidh*'s belly,' I told her. And I saw her bent over the prone figure of my mother in the box bed at the far side of the room.

I am not quite sure now how I could tell, because there was no outward sign of it, but there was panic in the fire room. Silent panic that you could feel, even if you couldn't hear or see it. Water was boiling in a pot hung from the chain above the burning peats. The other women were busy washing bloody rags and my father stood looking on helplessly. I had never seen him so powerless. He had a word for every occasion, my father. But right then he had nothing to say.

I heard the midwife urging, 'Push, Peigi, push!' And my mother screamed.

One of the neighbours gasped, 'It's coming out the wrong way.'

I had attended many animal births and knew that the head should come first, and straining my eyes through the smoke and shadows I could see the baby's arse between my mother's legs, as if it were trying to climb in and not out.

One at a time the midwife carefully freed the baby's legs, then turned and twisted to release first one arm, then the other. It was a girl. A big baby, but her head was still inside my mother, and there had been a dreadful tearing of the flesh. I could see blood on my mother's legs and on the hands of the midwife. I could see it soaking into the sheets.

There was sweat glistening on the face of the birthing woman as she tilted the baby up, one hand searching for its upturned face, trying to ease it free. But still the head wouldn't come.

My mother was gasping and crying, and the neighbours were holding her hands and softly urging her to be calm. But everyone in the room knew that if the baby's head were not freed quickly, the newborn would suffocate.

Suddenly the midwife leaned over, cradling the baby's body in one arm, her free hand feeling across my mother's belly for the head inside of her. She seemed to find it, and took a deep breath before pushing down hard. And, 'Push!' she shouted at the top of her voice.

My mother's scream brought soot dust tumbling from the rafters and turned my blood cold. But in the same moment, my new little sister's head popped out, and with a sharp smack on her bloodied arse she drew breath and echoed her mother's cry.

But my mother was still in distress, and the baby was taken quickly away, wrapped in blankets. Fresh sheeting was brought to try to stop my mother's bleeding. The midwife caught my father's arm and he dipped his head to hear her whispered advice. Her face had the white pallor of the dead.

My father's eyes burned like coals and he came running for the door, almost falling over Annag and me as we tried to scramble out of his way. He yelled out and grabbed me by the collar of my threadbare tweed jacket, and I thought I was in trouble for being where I shouldn't. But he brought his big whiskery face down next to mine and said, 'I want you to go for the doctor, son. If we can't stop the bleeding your mother's going to die.'

Fear shot through me like a bolt from a crossbow. 'I don't know where the doctor lives.'

'Go to the castle at Ard Mor,' my father said, and I heard the anxiety that choked back the words in his throat. 'They'll get him quicker than any of us. Tell them your mother'll die if he doesn't come fast.' And he turned me around and pushed me out, blinking, into the daylight, charged with the saving of my mother's life.

Propelled by a mixture of fear and self-importance, I ran pell-mell up the slope between the blackhouses and on to the path cut into the hillside. I knew that if I followed it far enough, it would take me to the road that led to the castle, and although I'd never been there I had seen it from a distance and knew how to find it. But it was a long way. Two miles, maybe more.

The wind hit me as I crested the hilltop and nearly knocked me off my feet. I felt the rain spitting in my face, as if God was contemptuous of the efforts of one small boy to save his mother. That, after all, was His business.

There was no way I could keep up that pace, but I knew that time was of the essence, so I slowed to a trot that would eke out my reserves of energy and at least get me there. I tried hard not to think as I ran, switching my focus between the path ahead and the bleakness of the rocky, treeless hills that rose around me. Low clouds bumped and bruised the land, and the wind whipped through my clothes, tugging at the nails I used as buttons to keep my jacket shut.

Vistas appeared and disappeared. I spotted the curve of a sandy cove between a spur of hills. In the distance dark purple mountains were ringed by clouds, and through an opening to my left I saw the standing stones on the rise beyond the big beach that we called simply Traigh Mhor. And still I ran. Settling to a pace that numbed my thoughts and calmed my fears.

At last I saw the road winding across the hills ahead of me. It was rutted and muddy, rainwater gathering in cart tracks and potholes. I turned north on to it, splashing through the puddles, feeling my pace slow as my strength was sapped. The land seemed to fold itself around me, closing off the sky. I could remember seeing men labouring to build this road, but the stones they laid were lost in the mud, and the ditches they dug were full of water.

I pumped my arms as I ran to try to get more air into my lungs, and then I came to a sudden standstill as I rounded a blind bend in the road. Ahead of me a horse-drawn trap was overturned in the ditch. The horse lay on its side, still attached to the trap, whinnying and struggling to get to its feet. But I could see that one of its hind legs was hopelessly broken. They would shoot the poor beast for sure. But there was no sign of a driver or passengers.

The rain began to fall in earnest as I approached the upturned vehicle. I jumped down into the ditch, which was half-hidden by the trap, and there sprawled among the roots of dormant heather lay a little girl, blue skirts and black coat fanned out around her, black hair pinned up under a royal blue beret. Her face was deathly pale, and the contrast with the bright red blood oozing from the gash at her temple was stark. Lying beside her, on his back in the ditch, was a middle-aged man, his top hat resting some feet away. His face was completely submerged, and somehow magnified by the water. Bizarrely his eyes, like saucers, were wide open and staring up at me. I felt myself trembling with the shock of it, realising that he was quite dead and that there was nothing I could do.

I heard a tiny voice moan, then cough, and I turned my attentions back to the little girl in time to see her lids flicker open and reveal the bluest eyes.

'Can you move?' I asked her.

But she looked back at me with vacancy in her face. A little hand reached up to grab the sleeve of my jacket. 'Help, help me,' she said, and I realised that she was speaking English, which I couldn't understand any better than she understood my Gaelic.

I was afraid to move her in case there was something broken and I did more damage. I took her hand and felt the chill in it, and I knew that I couldn't leave her there in the cold and the wet. I had seen how exposure to the elements could take a life in no time at all.

'Tell me if it hurts,' I said to her, knowing she couldn't understand, and she looked at me with such confusion in her eyes that it almost brought tears to mine. I slipped one arm beneath her shoulders, and the other into the crook of her knees, and carefully lifted her up into my arms. She was smaller than me, younger by maybe a couple of years, but still she was heavy, and I could not imagine how it would be possible to carry her all the way to the castle. But I knew I must. And now I felt the weight of responsibility for two lives in my hands.

She did not cry out, so I was encouraged to believe that nothing was broken. She flung both arms around my neck to hold on to me as I climbed back up on to the road and started off again at a trot. I had gone no more than a couple of hundred yards before the muscles in my arms were screaming with the pain of supporting her weight. But I had no choice other than to carry on.

After a while, I fell into a loping rhythm, somehow managing to keep my forward momentum. From time to time I looked down at her. Sometimes her eyes were closed and I feared the worst. At others I caught her gazing up at me, but she seemed almost fevered and I was not sure if she really saw me at all.

I was at the end of my tether, ready to drop to my knees and give up, when I rounded another bend, and there ahead of me was Ard Mor. The castle sat on a spur of land that jutted out into a rocky bay. Lawns extended from the front of it to a crenellated wall with cannon aimed across the water, the hill rising steeply behind it. The road wound down to a clutch of estate workers' cottages, and a stone archway led to the castle grounds.

The sight of it gave me fresh energy, enough of it anyway to stagger the final few hundred yards, past the cottages and through the arch to the big wooden front door of the castle itself. Laying the little girl down on the step in front of me I pulled the bell ring and heard it sound somewhere distantly inside.

It is hard to describe the maid's expression as she opened the door, her pink face wide-eyed with astonishment above her black blouse and white pinny.

And then, it seemed, I lost all control of events, as servants were called to carry the little girl into the castle, and I was left standing in the big stone-flagged hall as people ran around like mad things. I saw the laird on the stairs, his face pale and etched with concern. I heard his voice for the first time. But I didn't understand his English.

No one paid me the least attention and I began to cry, desperately afraid that I had failed my mother and that she was going to die because I had been deflected from the purpose of my errand. The maid who opened the door hurried across the flags and knelt beside me, consternation in her eyes. 'What's wrong?' she said to me in Gaelic. 'You have done a brave thing. You have saved the life of the laird's wee girl.'

I clutched her hand. 'I need the doctor to come.'

'The doctor's been sent for,' she said reassuringly. 'He'll be here in no time.'

'No, for my mother.' I was close to hysteria then.

But she didn't understand. 'Whatever do you mean?'

And I told her about my mother, and the birth of my little sister, and the bleeding. Her face paled.

'Stay here,' she said, and she hurried away up the big staircase.

I stood there for a miserable eternity, until she returned at a run and knelt beside me again, a warm, comforting hand brushing the hair from my eyes. 'As soon as he has seen to Ciorstaidh, the doctor will go with you to Baile Mhanais.'

I felt a huge wave of relief. 'Ciorstaidh,' I said. 'Is that the name of the laird's daughter?'

'Aye,' she said. 'But they call her by her English name. Kirsty.'

I'm not sure now how much time it took for the doctor to come and see to Ciorstaidh. But as soon as he was done we set off on his horse, back along the road towards my village. At the overturned trap we stopped. The horse was still alive, but had almost given up the struggle. The doctor took a look at the man in the ditch. He stood up, grim-faced. 'Dead,' he said. Though I could have told him that. 'Ciorstaidh's tutor from Glasgow. Only been here six months.' He got back on his horse and half turned to me. 'If you hadn't brought her back to the castle, son, she'd have died out here from the exposure.'

He hit the horse's flank with his crop and we set off at a gallop, until we reached the turn on to the path and had to slow to let the horse pick its way gingerly among the stones and heather roots, before descending the hill finally to the village.

Somehow, it seemed, they had managed to stop my mother from bleeding any further and she was still alive. The doctor was led into our fire room, and Annag and me were hustled outside to wait in the rain. But I didn't mind. It seemed that I had saved two lives that day, and I related the whole story to my wee sister, all puffed up with pride in the telling of it.

Then my father came out, and the relief on his face was visible to both of us. 'The doctor says your mother should be all right. She's weak and she's going to need rest, so it'll be up to all of us to fill her shoes for a bit.'

'What's the baby called?' Annag asked.

And my father smiled. 'Murdag,' he said. 'After my mother.' He put a hand on my shoulder. 'You did well, son.' And I felt such pleasure in the light of his praise. 'The doctor tells me you carried the laird's daughter all the way back to Ard Mor. Saved her life, without a doubt.' He pushed his chin out and let his eyes drift thoughtfully across the hillside above us. 'The laird will owe us for that.'

I can't remember exactly how long afterwards it was that the new term at school began. Sometime after the New Year, I suppose. I do remember being on the path to the schoolhouse that first day, passing below the church that served the townships of Baile Mhanais and Sgagarstaigh. The school sat out on the machair overlooking the bay on the far side of the hill and the strips of farmed land that rose beyond it. There were usually around thirty of us who attended, though that number could vary depending on the needs of the croft. But my father always said that there was nothing more important than a good education, and so he hardly ever kept me away.

My mother had made a good recovery, and baby Murdag was doing well. I'd been up at first light that day to fetch in a creel of peats and fill my stomach with the potatoes we'd left roasting among the embers of the fire overnight. Then when the fire was blazing my mother had boiled up more tatties, which we had with milk and a little salted fish. So with a full belly, I didn't feel the cold too badly, barely noticing the crust of snow crunching beneath my bare feet.

When I got to school I was surprised to find that we had a new teacher: Mr Ross from Inverness. He was much younger than the other one, and he spoke both English and Gaelic.

When we were all seated at our rough wooden desks he asked if there was anyone among us who spoke English. Not a single hand was raised.

He said, 'Well, who among you would like to speak English?'

I looked around and saw that once again, there were no hands up. So I put mine in the air, and Mr Ross smiled at me, a little surprised, I think.

It turned out that we were all going to have to learn the English. But I was the only one who wanted to, because I knew that if I was ever going to talk to that little girl whose life I'd saved, I'd have to learn to speak her language. Because there was no way the daughter of the laird was going to learn to speak the Gaelic.

CHAPTER TWELVE

I

'Are you the cop?' The voice startled Sime out of his recoll-ections, and it took a moment to clear the confusion that fogged the transition in his mind from a nineteenth-century Hebridean winter to this salt-mine halfway across the world on the Îles de la Madeleine.

He turned to see a man stooped by the open window, peer-ing in at him, a long face shaded by the peak of a baseball cap.

Almost at the same moment, the ground shook beneath them. A rumbling vibration, like a series of palpitating heart-beats. 'What in God's name is that?' Sime said, alarmed.

The man was unconcerned. 'It's the blasting. Takes place fifteen minutes after the end of each shift. They leave it to clear for two hours before the next shift moves in.'

Sime nodded. 'The answer to your question is yes.'

The man ran a big hand over a day's growth on his jaw. 'What the hell do you want to talk to me for?' His brows knitted beneath the skip of his cap as he glared in at Sime.

'I take it you're Jack Aitkens?'

'What if I am?'

'Your cousin Kirsty's husband has been murdered on Entry Island.'

For a moment it seemed as if the wind had stopped and that for a split second Aitkens's world had stood still. Sime watched his expression dissolve from hostility to surprise, then give way to concern. 'Jesus,' he said. 'I need to get over there straight away.'

'Sure,' Sime said. 'But first we need to talk.'

II

The walls of Room 115 in the police station of the Sûreté de Québec on Cap aux Meules were painted canary-yellow. A white melamine table and two chairs facing each other across it were pushed against one wall. Built-in cameras and a microphone fed proceedings to Thomas Blanc in the detectives' room next door. A plaque on the wall outside read *Salle d'interrogatoire*.

Jack Aitkens sat opposite Sime at the table. Big hands engrained with oil were interlinked on the surface in front of him. His zip-up fleece jacket was open and hung loose from his shoulders. He wore torn jeans and big boots encrusted with salt.

He had removed his baseball cap to reveal a pale, almost grey, face, with dark, thinning hair that was oiled and scraped back across a broad, flat skull. He nodded towards a black poster pinned to the wall behind Sime.

URGENCE AVOCAT gratuit en cas d'arrestation.

'Any reason I might need a lawyer?'

'None that I can think of. How about you?'

Aitkens shrugged. 'So what do you want to know?'

Sime stood up and closed the door. The noise from the incident room along the hall was a distraction. He sat down again. 'You can start by telling me about what it's like to work in a salt-mine.'

Aitkens seemed surprised. Then he puffed up his cheeks and blew contempt through his lips. 'It's a job.'

'What kind of hours do you work?'

'Twelve-hour shifts. Four days a week. Been doing it for ten years now, so I don't think much about it anymore. In winter, on the day shift, it's dark when you get there, it's dark when you leave. And there's precious little light underground. So you spend half your life in the dark, Monsieur . . . Mackenzie, you said?'

Sime nodded.

'Depressing. Gets you down sometimes.'

'I can imagine.' And Sime could hardly imagine anything worse. 'What size of workforce is there?'

'A hundred and sixteen. Miners, that is. I have no idea how many work in administration.'

Sime was surprised. 'I wouldn't have guessed from the surface there were that many men down there.'

Aitkens's smile was almost condescending. 'You couldn't begin to guess what's down there from the surface, Monsieur Mackenzie. The whole archipelago of the Madeleine islands sits on columns of salt that have pushed up through the earth's crust. So far we have dug down 440 metres into one of them, with another eight or ten kilometres to go. The mine is on five levels and extends well beneath the surface of the sea on either side of the island.'

Sime returned the smile. 'You're right, Mr Aitkens, I would never have guessed that.' He paused. 'Where were you on the night of the murder?'

Aitkens didn't blink. 'What night was that exactly?'

'The night before last.'

'I was on night shift. Like I've been all week. You can check the records if you like.'

Sime nodded. 'We will.' He sat back in his seat. 'What kind of salt is it you mine?'

Aitkens laughed. 'Not table salt, if that's what you're thinking. It's salt for the roads. About 1.7 million tons of it a year. Most of it for use in Quebec or Newfoundland. The rest goes to the States.'

'Can't be very healthy, down there twelve hours a day breathing in all that salt.'

'Who knows?' Aitkens shrugged. 'I've not died of it yet, anyway.' He chuckled. 'They say that salt-mines create their own microclimate. In some Eastern European countries they send people down the mines as a cure for asthma.'

122

Sime watched his smile fade and waited while Aitkens grew slowly impatient.

'Are you going to tell me what happened out on Entry Island or not?'

But Sime was not ready to go there yet. He said, 'I want you to tell me about your cousin.'

'What do you want to know?'

'Anything. And everything.'

'We're not close.'

'So I gather.'

Aitkens gave him a look, and Sime could see the calculation in his eyes. Had Kirsty told him that? 'My father's sister was Kirsty's mother. But my father fell for a French-speaking girl from Havre Aubert and left Entry Island to marry her when he was barely out of his teens.'

'You don't speak English, then?'

'I grew up speaking French at school. But my father always spoke English to me in the house, so it's not bad.'

'And your parents are still alive?'

He pressed his lips together in a grim line. 'My mother died some years ago. My father's in the geriatric ward of the hospital. Doesn't even know me when I go to see him. I have full power of attorney.'

Sime nodded. 'So basically you and Kirsty grew up in two very different linguistic communities.'

'We did. But the differences aren't just linguistic. They're cultural, too. Most of the French-speakers here are descended from the original seventeenth-century settlers of Acadia. When the British defeated the French and created Canada, the Acadians got kicked out, and a lot of them ended up here.' He grunted, unimpressed. 'Most of my neighbours still think of themselves as Acadians rather than Quebecois.' He started picking the grime from beneath his fingernails. 'A lot of the English-speakers got shipwrecked here on the way to the colonies, and never left. That's why the two communities have never mixed.'

'So you didn't have much contact with Kirsty when you were growing up?'

'Hardly any. I mean, I can see Entry Island from my house at La Grave. Sometimes you feel you could almost reach out and touch it. But it was never somewhere you would drop by casually. Of course, there were occasional family gatherings. Christmas, funerals, that sort of thing. But the English-speakers are Presbyterian, and the French mostly Catholic. Oil and water. So, no, I never really knew Kirsty that well.' He stopped picking at his nails and stared at his hands. 'In recent years I've hardly seen her at all.' He looked up. 'If I didn't go to see her, then she certainly wouldn't come and see me.'

Sime wondered if he detected a hint of bitterness in that. But there was nothing in Aitkens's demeanour to suggest it. 'From what you know of her, then, how would you describe her?'

'What do you mean?'

'What sort of person is she?'

There seemed to be a fondness in his smile. 'You'd be hard pushed to find a more gentle person on this earth, Monsieur Mackenzie,' he said. 'Almost . . . what's the word . . . serene. Like she had some kind of inner peace. If she has a temper, then I've never seen her lose it.'

'But you said yourself, you haven't really seen her that much over the years.'

Which irritated him. 'Well, why the hell are you asking me, then?'

'It's my job, Monsieur Aitkens.' Sime sat back and folded his arms. 'What do you know about her relationship with James Cowell?'

Aitkens made a noise somewhere between a spit and a grunt to express his contempt. 'Never liked the man. And never could figure out what it was he saw in her.'

'What do you mean?'

'Oh, no harm to Kirsty. I mean, she's a good-looking woman, and all. But weird, you know?'

And Sime remembered Crozes's description of her – *She's a weirdo, right?*

'Weird in what way?'

'This fixation she has with staying put. Never leaving the island. Not Cowell's thing at all. He was all fancy cars and airplanes, big houses and expensive restaurants. I was at the wedding. He had a big marquee erected over on the island, a company brought in from Montreal to do the catering. As much champagne as you could drink. Flash bastard! More fucking money than sense. Full of himself, too. Thought he was better than the rest of us because he'd made a pile. But he was just another islander. A fucking fisherman who got lucky.'

'Looks like his luck ran out.'

Aitkens inclined his head a little. 'How did he die?'

'According to Kirsty she was attacked by an intruder at the house. When Cowell intervened he got stabbed to death.'

Aitkens seemed shocked. 'Jesus! An intruder? On Entry Island?' Then he had a further thought. 'What was Cowell doing there, anyway? I heard he'd left her.'

'What, exactly, did you hear?'

'Well, it was pretty much common knowledge. Whatever his obsession was with Kirsty it seemed to have burned itself out, and he'd found somebody else to lavish his millions on. Ariane Briand, wife of the mayor here on Cap aux Meules. It's been quite a scandal!'

'You know her?'

'Hell, yeah. I was at school with her. A few years older, but I didn't know a boy then who didn't have the hots for her. I mean, a real looker she was. Still is. And much more Cowell's style than Kirsty. Kicked the mayor out, apparently, and Cowell moved in.' He snorted his derision. 'But just a temporary arrangement for sure. You can bet your bottom dollar that Cowell would have had plans for something much bigger than the Briands' little house in the woods.'

Sime nodded. 'Like the house he built on Entry Island.'

'Something even flashier, I would have thought. You set the bar that high, you can hardly start lowering it.'

Sime stroked his chin thoughtfully and realised he hadn't shaved that morning. 'I suppose she'll inherit,' he said.

Aitkens cocked his head and frowned at Sime. 'You don't think she did it?'

'We don't think anything yet.'

'Well, you're wrong if you do. I mean, she wouldn't kill him for his house or his wealth. She'd have got the house and half his money in any divorce settlement anyway. Cowell could hardly have taken the house with him, and no way would he have wanted to stay in it.' He spread his big hands out wide. 'And anyway, what would she do with all that cash? There's nothing to spend it on over there on Entry.' His eyes suddenly strayed towards Sime's right hand resting on the table in front of him. 'That's an interesting ring. Can I see it?'

Surprised, Sime held out his hand for Aitkens to take a look.

The salt-miner nodded. 'Beautiful. It's carnelian, isn't it? Had one similar once, only the stone was sardonyx. Kind of amber with white stripes. Nice phoenix engraved in it.' His face clouded. 'Left it in the washroom at the mine one time after washing my hands. Realised five minutes later and went back for it. Gone.' His lips curled in contempt. 'Some people are just dishonest.'

Sime said, 'Is this one familiar to you?'

127

Aitkens frowned. 'Yours? Should it be?'

'Your cousin said she had a pendant. Same colour, same crest.'

'Kirsty?' His eyebrows shot up in surprise. 'And did she?'

'I don't know. She couldn't find it.'

Aitkens frowned. 'That's weird.' And it was the second time he'd used the word in connection with his cousin.

III

Sime and Thomas Blanc walked with Crozes across the car park behind the police station, towards the *sentier littoral* and the beach beyond. The wind had dropped considerably, but was still strong, snaking through their hair and tugging at their jackets and trousers. The sun formed a reflective bowl of golden light in the sea that cradled the silhouette of Entry Island across the bay. Everywhere Sim went on the Madeleine Isles, Entry Island was disconcertingly present. It seemed to follow him, like the eyes of the Mona Lisa.

'Arseneau still hasn't found Briand yet,' Crozes said. He was anxious to rule him either in or out as a suspect and irritated by the delay. 'And I'm not sure we've learned anything very much from Aitkens.'

'Aitkens is right about the money, though, Lieutenant,' Blanc said. 'It doesn't seem like much of a motive for the Cowell woman killing her husband.'

'Yes, let's not lose focus. We're talking about someone

whose husband had just left her for another woman. And you know what they say about a woman scorned . . .' Crozes scratched his chin. 'I don't think money comes into it.'

As they reached the coastal path, they fell silent until a young female jogger had passed and was out of earshot.

Crozes turned and looked back towards the one-storey, red-brick building that housed the police station. 'I've requisitioned a fishing boat to take us back and forth to Entry Island so we don't have to rely on the ferry. I sent some of the guys over with the minibus on the *Ivan-Quinn* this morning. Marie-Ange needs to complete her examination of the crime scene, and I think we should talk to the widow again.'

Blanc said, 'Do we have a new line of questioning?'

Crozes nodded, 'What we talked about yesterday. If she's speaking the truth, and she was the object of the attack rather than Cowell, then maybe she has some idea who might bear her a grudge.'

Sime said, 'Aitkens will probably want to come with us.'

'Then let him. Might be interesting to see if he provokes an emotional reaction.'

His cellphone warbled in his pocket. He fished it out and turned away to take the call. Blanc swivelled his back to the wind and cupped his hands around a cigarette to light it. Then he glanced at Sime. 'So what do you reckon?'

'About who killed Cowell?'

'Yep.'

Sime shrugged. 'Still wide open, I'd say. What about you?'

Blanc drew on his cigarette and let the wind draw the smoke from his mouth. 'Well, the statistics tell us that more than half of all murders are committed by someone known to the victim. So if I was a betting man my money would be on her.'

'Shit!' Crozes's voice cut across the wind and turned their heads towards him as he thrust his phone back in his pocket.

'What's up, Lieutenant?' Blanc said.

'Could be this is going to get more complicated than we thought.' He pushed a pensive jaw out towards the silhouette of the island across the bay. 'Seems some guy's gone missing on Entry Island overnight.'

CHAPTER THIRTEEN

I

The crossing from Cap aux Meules took well over an hour in the boat that Crozes had requisitioned. It stank of fish and afforded little protection from the elements.

The sea was still tormented, and the wind strong enough to make their passage across the bay unpleasantly slow. Sime and Blanc huddled in a dark, cramped space below deck, salt water sloshing around their feet, the perfume of putrefying fish filling their nostrils and making their stomachs heave with every lurch of the boat. Crozes seemed unaffected, sitting lost in thought alone on a rusted cross-beam at the stern. Jack Aitkens spent the crossing in the wheelhouse chatting to the boat's owner as if he were out for a sail on a sunny Sunday afternoon.

Arseneau met them at the harbour, and while Aitkens was sent to sit in the minibus the sergeant enquêteur briefed them on the missing man. They stood in a huddle at the end of the quay, braced against the wind, and Blanc made several attempts to light his cigarette before giving up.

'His name's Norman Morrison,' Arseneau said. 'Aged thirty-five. And . . .' he hesitated, unsure of what was politically correct, '. . . well, a bit simple, if you know what I mean. One sausage short of a fry-up as my old man would have said.'

'What's the story?' Sime asked.

'He and his mother live alone up on the hill there. He went out after their evening meal last night to lash down some stuff in the yard. Or so he said. When he hadn't come back in after half an hour, his mother went out with a flash-light in the dark to look for him. But he wasn't there. And no one's set eyes on him since.'

Crozes shrugged. 'Anything could have happened to him in a storm like that. But what's the connection? Why should we be interested?'

Sime could tell from Arseneau's demeanour that he was about to drop a live grenade into the briefing. 'Apparently he was obsessed by Kirsty Cowell, Lieutenant. Fixated on her. And if we're to believe his mother, Cowell did more than just warn him off.'

Crozes did not take the news well. Sime watched as his jaw clenched and his mouth set in a grim line. But he wasn't going to be deflected from his predetermined course. 'Okay, we'll take Aitkens up to the Cowell house first. I want to see how she reacts to him. Then you can take us on up to the Morrison place.'

*

She was waiting on the porch of the summerhouse watching as they drove up the hill. She wore a white blouse beneath a grey woollen shawl pulled tight around her shoulders, and pleated black jeans tucked into calf-length leather boots. Her hair was blowing out in a stream behind her, like a tattered black flag, furling and unfurling in the wind. It was the first time that Sime had set eyes on her since his dream, and against all of his instincts he felt himself unaccountably drawn to her.

Jack Aitkens was the first out of the vehicle as they pulled up, and he ran across the lawn to take his cousin in his arms. Watching from a distance Sime felt the oddest twinge of jealousy. He saw tears glistening on Kirsty Cowell's face and after a brief conversation with her Aitkens came back to the minibus.

He lowered his voice, and it carried more than the hint of a threat in it. 'She tells me you've already grilled her twice.'

'Interviewed her,' Sime corrected him. 'And I'd like to talk to her again.'

'Is she a suspect or not? Because if she is, she's entitled to an attorney.'

Crozes said, 'As of this moment she is a material witness, that's all.'

Then Aitkens swung hostile eyes in Sime's direction. 'In that case your interview can wait. I'd like some time with my cousin, if that's all right with you.'

He didn't wait for their permission, but turned and went

back to the house, taking his cousin's hand and leading her down the steps from the porch in a wash of watery sunlight that suddenly played itself out across the cliffs.

The four policemen watched them start off up the slope together and Crozes said, 'I don't like that man.'

But Sime knew that Crozes wouldn't like anyone who stood in the way of a speedy resolution to their investigation.

II

The Morrison family home stood at the end of a gravel track that turned left off Main Street before the church and followed the contours of the island through the valley to the high ground below Big Hill. It was years since it had been painted, and its clapboard siding was a pale bleached grey. The shingles on its Dutch gambrel roof were only slightly darker. A number of outbuildings stood in various states of disrepair, and a rusted old tractor was canted at an odd angle in the backyard, one of its wheels missing.

A cultivated area of land behind the house ran down the slope of the hill, and a handful of sheep stood grazing among the long grass. From its elevated position it commanded a spectacular view south and west towards Havre Aubert and Cap aux Meules, and Sime thought it must have taken some battering from the storm during the night.

He let his eyes wander across the ravaged slopes below him. Some of the hay bales they had seen on their first visit were gone, shredded by the storm. But there didn't appear to be much damage to property. Flimsy though these brightly painted houses looked, they had clearly stood the test of time in a climate that was seldom forgiving. They ranged in silhouette along the rise, showing the same defiance as owners who stood firm in defence of their language and culture, determined to stay put at all costs. But with a dwindling school population and lack of jobs, it was clear the island was dying. It made it all the more inexplicable that a young woman like Kirsty Cowell should choose to stay when most of her generation had already gone.

Sergeant Aucoin and half a dozen patrolmen from Cap aux Meules, along with a group of islanders, stood in a knot on a gravel turning area just beyond the house. They shuffled impatiently in the wind, anxious to get their search under way. Morrison had been missing for more than sixteen hours now. But Crozes didn't want them trampling over what might be evidence until he'd had a chance to assess the situation.

'Sime!' On hearing his name Sime turned to see Crozes approaching with Blanc in tow. 'We're getting conflicting stories about this guy.' He nodded towards a blue-and-cream house about fifty metres away along a pebble track. 'The neighbours have been telling the local cops one thing, the mother something quite different. You'd better talk to them.'

*

'Only reason we stayed was to raise the kids here.' Jackie Patton ran dishwater-red hands over her apron and caught a stray strand of hair with her little finger to loop it back behind her ear. She left a powdering of flour on her cheek and on the soft brown hair at her temple. She had a square face, fair skin splattered with freckles, and there was a weary acceptance in her eyes that life had not gone as planned. She was not ugly, but neither was she attractive. 'Soon as it was time for the big school, we was gonna be up and away. Figured we owed it to the kids to give them the kind of upbringing we had on the island. Nothing better.' She sprinkled more flour on the dough on her worktop and flattened it out again with her rolling pin. 'Now they're gone, and we're still here.'

Crozes, Blanc and Sime were squeezed into her tiny kitchen, standing around a small table at its centre. They very nearly filled it. Mrs Patton's focus was on the short pastry she was preparing for her meat pie.

'We lost count of the number of jobs Jim applied for. Trouble is, twenty years of fishing for lobster only qualifies you to fish for lobster. So he's still out every May first on the boat and I'm stuck here counting the days till the kids get back for the holidays.' She looked up suddenly. 'They should have locked him up years ago.'

'Who?' Sime said.

'Norman Morrison. He's not right in the head. The kids used to go over there when they was younger. He was like one of them, you know, a big kid himself. Then he starts making this city on the ceiling.'

Sime frowned. 'What do you mean?'

'Oh, you'll see it for yourselves when you go over to the house. I figure it's probably still there. See, his bedroom's right up in the roof. Low ceiling and all. And with him being tall like that he could stretch up and reach it.'

She stopped to gaze out the window. The Morrison house stood at a respectful distance in stark profile against the water of the bay and the islands of the archipelago beyond.

'It was quite something. Took talent to do that. And some imagination. I mean, damn near the whole island has traipsed in there to see it at one time or another. Amazing what a simple mind can make of not very much.'

She returned to her pastry.

'Anyways, in the end we figured he'd only done it so he'd have a reason for taking the kids up to his bedroom.'

'Do you mean he molested the children?' Crozes said.

'No sir,' she said. 'I can't say he did. But my Angela came back one time and said he touched her funny. And for the life of us we couldn't get her to tell us how.'

Sime said, 'Was she upset?'

Mrs Patton stopped rolling out her dough and raised her head thoughtfully to gaze into the middle distance. 'No, she wasn't. That's the funny thing, I guess. She really liked Norman. Cried for close on a week when we banned the kids from ever going back to the Morrison house.'

'Why did you do that?'

She wheeled around defensively. "Cos he touched her funny. That's what she said, and I don't know what she meant by it, but I wasn't taking no chances. He's not right in the head, and he was far too old to be playing with children.'

There was an awkward silence, then, and she turned back to her pastry.

'Anyways, someone like that should be in a home or a hospital. Not in the community.'

'You think he was dangerous?' Blanc asked.

She shrugged. 'Who knows. He's got a temper on him, I can tell you that. Like a kid throwing a tantrum sometimes. When his mother would call him in at mealtimes and he wasn't ready to go. Or if something didn't just go his way.'

'What about Kirsty Cowell?' Sime said.

She flicked a wary glance in his direction. 'What about her?'

'You told Sergeant Aucoin that Norman was obsessed with her.'

'Well, everyone knew that. When we had summer parties, or dances in the winter, he used to follow her around like a puppy dog. It might have been funny if it wasn't so sad.'

'Used to?'

'Yes . . .' she said thoughtfully. 'It all seemed to stop about six months ago.'

'How did Mrs Cowell react to him?'

'Oh, she humoured him, I guess. There's not a bad bone in that woman's body. She just married the wrong man.'

'What makes you say that?'

'Well, it was obvious, wasn't it? He was never right for her. Or she for him. A marriage made in hell, if you ask me. Only one way it was ever going to end.'

'In murder?'

Her eyes lifted sharply towards Sime. 'I didn't say that.'

'How did Cowell react to Norman Morrison's interest in his wife?'

'Oh, he didn't like it, I can tell you that much. But, I mean, he wasn't a threat to their marriage for God's sake. Norman has the mental age of a twelve-year-old.'

Sime had decided by now that he really didn't like Jackie Patton. 'But you thought he was a threat to your children.'

She banged down her rolling pin on the worktop and turned to face him. 'Do you have children, Mr Mackenzie?'

'No, ma'am, I don't.'

'Then don't judge me. The first responsibility of a parent is the protection of their children. You don't take chances.'

But Sime was unmoved. It seemed clear to him that Mrs Patton had already made that judgement on herself. And guilt read accusation even into innocent questions.

III

The Morrisons' living room had big windows at the front and an archway leading to a dining room at the back. Although most of the furniture in it was dark and old-fashioned, light from the windows seemed to reflect off every polished surface. The patterned wallpaper was almost totally obscured by framed photographs and paintings. Family portraits and groups, black-and-white mostly, with some coloured landscapes. More light reflecting off glass. The air was heavily perfumed, with a background hint of disinfectant. Sime could tell at a glance that Mrs Morrison was someone who had a place for everything, and liked everything in its place.

She was a woman in her sixties, big-boned and carefully dressed in a crisp white blouse beneath a knitted cardigan and a blue skirt that fell just below her knees. Her hair was still dark, with just a few strands of silver in it, drawn back severely from her face and arranged in a bun.

There was little warmth in her blue eyes, and she seemed remarkably composed given the circumstances.

'Would you like tea, gentlemen?' she asked.

'No thanks,' Sime said.

'Well, take a seat, then.'

The three police officers perched uncomfortably on the sofa, and she resumed what Sime imagined to be her habitual seat by the fire, folding her hands in her lap.

'He's never done anything like this before,' she said.

'Done what?' Sime asked.

'Run away.'

'What makes you think he's run away?'

'Well, of course he has. He told me he was going out to the

garden. In that event he'd have been back long before I had to go looking for him. He must have lied to me.'

'Is he in the habit of telling lies?'

Mrs Morrison looked uncomfortable, and withdrew a little further into herself. 'He can be economical with the truth sometimes.'

Sime let that hang for a moment. 'Was there some reason he might have run away? I mean, can you think why he would have lied to you?'

She seemed to consider her response carefully. Finally she said, 'He was upset.'

'Why?'

'He heard what had happened at the Cowell place.'

'Where did he hear that?'

'When we went down to the Post Office to pick up the mail yesterday afternoon.'

'So you both heard the news at the same time.'

'Yes.'

'Why was he upset?'

She shifted uncomfortably in her chair. 'He was very fond of Mrs Cowell. I suppose he was concerned for her well-being.'

'What do you mean, fond of her?' Sime said.

She bristled a little. 'Just that. She was fond of him, too. You must understand, Mr Mackenzie, my son has a mental age of eleven or twelve. We didn't realise that until he began to have learning difficulties at school. It came as quite a shock when the psychologists told us. And it only really became more apparent as he got older. At first I was . . . well, I was devastated. But over the years I've come to see it as a blessing. Most people lose their children, you see, when they grow up. I never lost Norman. He's thirty-five now, but he's still my little boy.'

'So Mrs Cowell was fond of him, as you would be fond of a child?'

'Just that. And, of course, they were at the school together as children.'

'And what did Mr Cowell make of it?'

Her face darkened in an instant, as if a cloud had thrown her into shadow. 'I'm a God-fearing woman, Mr Mackenzie. But I hope that man spends eternity in hell.'

The three men were startled by her sudden, vitriolic intensity.

'Why?' Sime said.

'Because he brought two thugs to this island from across the water and had my boy beaten up.'

'How do you know that?'

'Because they told him to stay away from Mrs Cowell or he could expect much worse.'

'He told you that?'

She nodded, her mouth drawn in a tight line to hold in her emotions. 'He was in a terrible state when he came home that day. Bleeding and bruised and crying like a baby.'

'How do you know it was Mr Cowell's doing?'

'Well, who else could it be?'

'And this was when?'

'Early spring this year. There was still snow on the ground.'

'Did you report it?'

She almost laughed. 'To whom? There is no law on this island, Mr Mackenzie. We settle things among ourselves here.' Echoes of Owen Clarke.

Sime hesitated just briefly. 'Why did the neighbours stop their children from playing with Norman, Mrs Morrison?'

Now her skin flushed red around her eyes and high on her cheeks. 'You've been talking to the Patton woman.'

Sime inclined his head slightly in acknowledgement.

'It was just lies, Mr Mackenzie.' Her cold blue eyes were now filled with the fire of indignation. 'And jealousy.'

'Why would she be jealous?'

'Because this was a house always filled with children, including hers. They loved Norman. They came from all over the island to play with him, to see his little universe on the ceiling. You see he was a grown man, but he was just like them. A child himself.' For a moment her face was lit by the pleasure of recollection. A house full of children. An extended family. It had clearly been a joy for her. But the light went out and her face darkened again. 'And then that woman started putting it about that my Norman was touching the children in a bad way. It was a lie, Mr Mackenzie. Plain and simple. My Norman was never like that. But lies can be contagious. Like germs. Once they're out there people get infected.'

'And the children stopped coming?'

She nodded. 'It was awful the effect it had on poor Norman. Suddenly he had no friends. The house was empty. Silent, like the grave. And I missed them, too. All those bright little faces and happy voices. Life's just not been the same since.'

'And what did your husband have to say about all this?'

'He didn't have anything to say, Mr Mackenzie. He's been dead almost twenty years. Lost at sea when his boat went down in a storm off Nova Scotia.' She shook her head. 'Poor Norman. He still misses his daddy. And after the children stopped coming, well . . . he just spent more and more time in his room. Expanding his little universe.'

'His . . . universe on the ceiling?'

'Yes.'

Sime glanced at Crozes and Blanc. 'Could we see this little universe, Mrs Morrison?'

She led them up creaking stairs to the first floor. There were three bedrooms here, and a large bathroom. But Norman's bedroom was in an attic room built into the roof space. His den, his mother called it as they followed her up steep steps and into the room. There were no windows up here and they emerged from the floor into darkness until Mrs Morrison flicked a switch and flooded the room with yellow electric light.

It was a claustrophobic space, large in floor area, but with low headroom and walls that took a shallow slope in from shoulder height to meet the ceiling. A single bed pushed against the far wall had several teddy bears and a thread-worn panda propped up on its pillows. Bedside tables stood cluttered with toy soldiers and pieces of Lego, crayons and tubes of paint. A dresser set against the right-hand wall was similarly lost beneath a chaos of plastic bricks and packs of Plasticine, a naked dolly with no arms, model cars, a railway engine. The floor itself was strewn with toys and books, and sheets of paper covered with scribbles.

But their eyes were drawn almost immediately to the ceiling, and Sime saw at once what his mother had meant by Norman's little universe. Almost the entire ceiling space was glued with layers of different-coloured Plasticine that formed meadows and roads, ploughed fields, lakes and rivers. Mountains had been moulded out of papier mâché and coloured with paint. Green and brown and grey. There were railway lines and plastic houses, the figures of tiny people populating gardens and streets. Little cars and buses, woolly sheep and brown cows in the fields. There were forests and fences. All stuck into the Plasticine. And everything was upside down.

They had to crane their necks to look up, but it was as if they were looking down on another world. Norman's little universe. So filled with the tiniest detail, that it was almost impossible to take it all in.

His mother gazed up at it with pride. 'It started in a very

small way. With a pack of Plasticine and a few tiny figures. But the children loved it so much, Norman just kept expanding it. Always wanting to surprise them with something new. It just got bigger and bigger, and more ambitious.' She looked away suddenly. 'Until the children stopped coming. Then it ceased being a hobby and became his world. His only world.' She glanced at them, self-conscious now. 'He lived in that world. Became a part of it himself, really. I don't know what went through his mind, but in the end I think he replaced the children who used to come with the ones on the ceiling. If you look you can see that some of them are just faces cut from magazines, or little cardboard cut-outs. And then the tiny coloured plastic figures you get in boxes of breakfast cereal.' She cast her eyes sadly towards his bed. 'He spent all his time up here, and gradually he covered the whole ceiling. When he runs out of space, no doubt he'll start expanding it down the walls.'

Sime gazed up in amazement. A lonely boy trapped in the body of a man, Norman had only found company in a world he created himself on his ceiling. He scanned the mess of the floor beneath it, and his gaze fell on the head of a little girl cut out from an old colour print. She looked familiar somehow. He stooped to pick it up. 'Who's this?'

His mother peered at it. 'I've no idea.' The girl was perhaps twelve or thirteen. She wore glasses that reflected the light and almost obscured her eyes. She was smiling awkwardly, a toothy grin, and her dark hair was cut short in a bob. 'Something he cut from a magazine probably.'

'No, it's a print,' Sime said.

Mrs Morrison shrugged. 'Well, it's no one I know.'

Sime laid it carefully on top of the dresser and turned to Crozes. 'The sooner we find Norman the better, I think.'

CHAPTER FOURTEEN

Sime and Blanc left Crozes and the others to organise the search for Norman Morrison, dividing the island into quadrants and the searchers into groups. Although it was not large, Entry Island was peppered with hundreds of properties, domestic and agricultural, and its coastline was ragged and inaccessible in places. It would not be a simple search.

When they got back to the Cowell place Aitkens and Kirsty had still not returned, and the two investigators set up their monitors and cameras for the interview.

After they had finished, Blanc came through from the back room to find Sime gazing from the window towards the cliffs. 'Do you think Cowell really had the Morrison boy beaten up?' he said.

Sime thought it was odd to hear Norman Morrison described as a boy. But it's what he was, really. A boy in the body of a man. He turned back to the room. 'I think it's what he told his mother. But whether it's true or not . . .' He shrugged.

Blanc said, 'Who else would want to work him over?'

'Depends,' Sime said. 'If there's any truth in the stories about him touching children, then any number of angry fathers. And, of course, that's not something he would want to tell his mother.'

Blanc nodded thoughtfully. 'Hadn't considered that.' Then, 'Listen, I'm going out back for a cigarette.'

'Okay.' Sime walked through the kitchen to the back door with him. 'I might take a look around the big house while we're waiting.'

Blanc seemed surprised. 'What for?'

'I'd just like a better feel for Mrs Cowell before we talk to her again.'

Blanc said, 'I think Marie-Ange is still in there.'

Sime felt a tiny prickle of anger. 'If I get in her way I'm sure she'll tell me.'

Blanc was embarrassed. 'I'm sorry, I didn't mean . . .'

'I know.' Sime cut him off, then regretted his shortness. 'Ignore me,' he said. 'I'm just tired.'

Marie-Ange was in the main room dismantling the lights they had erected to photograph the spatter and smears of blood on the floor. Sime slid open the door of the conservatory and stepped inside.

Without looking up she said, 'Watch where you put your feet. And don't touch anything.' When he didn't respond she raised her head and seemed surprised to see him.

He held up latexed hands. 'I have done this before.'

She relented a little. 'I thought you were one of the patrol-men.' Which was the closest he was going to get to an apology. 'What do you want in here?'

'To look around.'

'Since when did you become a crime scene expert?'

'Not the crime scene, the house.'

She raised an eyebrow and repeated the question that Blanc had asked. 'Why?'

'Professional interest. They say that people and their relationships are reflected in their homes.'

'And you think you can learn something about the Cowells from their house?'

'I'm sure I can.'

She gazed at him for a moment, then shrugged. 'Please yourself.'

Sime walked off along the hall that led to the far end of the house. On his right, stairs descended into a basement. He went down and switched on the lights. Fluorescents flickered on overhead to reveal a guest living room and a further two bedrooms. Cowell had clearly nurtured expectations of many visitors. Sime wondered if they had ever materialised. There was a large storeroom full of files and boxes, and papers stacked on shelves. And through a double door, a sprawling workshop with a pristine workbench that looked as if it had never been used. One wall was hung with myriad tools all neatly arranged in rows and sizes.

Sime plunged the basement once more into darkness and

climbed back up into daylight. Next along the corridor a door leading to a guest bedroom stood ajar. On the far side of it French windows opened into the conservatory. He wondered if any guests had ever slept here. It didn't feel like it. There was a lack of warmth, of anything personal. It was furnished like a five-star hotel room.

Further along, another door led to the master bedroom, and Sime was surprised to find that it was just as impersonal as the guest room. There seemed to be nothing shared in here. No photographs, no mementos of happier times. No paintings on the walls. Not even clothes draped over chairs or lying on the bed, no slippers discarded at the bedside. There were no jars of face cream or make-up on the dresser, no combs or brushes with hair caught in the bristles. Just shiny, dust-free surfaces. The room was as sterile, it seemed, as the relationship it had played host to.

At the end of the hall, a door on the left led to her study, and crossing its threshold Sime at once felt a change in atmosphere. This was Kirsty Cowell's private space and every cluttered surface and crowded bookshelf spoke of her. One entire wall was devoted to books. Everything from classical English literature to the ground-breaking American writers of the twentieth century – Hemingway, Steinbeck, Mailer, Updike; encyclopaedias, books on British and Canadian history, almost a full shelf on the history of Scotland.

There was a well-worn leather recliner with a shawl draped over it, and moccasin slippers beneath it. There were paintings on the walls, amateur efforts that made up for lack of technique in capturing the mood of the island. Crude sea views and clumsy landscapes. One was particularly striking. A line of black crows sitting along an electric cable strung between two telegraph posts, a typical island house behind them, painted a garish green and white, a sky of purple-edged clouds. And Sime realised that he hadn't seen any seagulls on his two trips to the island. Only crows. He glanced from the window and saw them now in black huddled rows, sitting on rooftops and along fences and telephone lines, silent witnesses to an investigation of murder.

He turned back to the walls, and found his eye drawn by a framed black-and-white photograph of a middle-aged couple standing outside the summerhouse across the way. Kirsty's parents, he assumed. Judging from their age, the picture had been taken only a dozen or so years before, yet it felt dated. Not only because it was in black and white, but the couple themselves seemed to belong to another era. The way they dressed and wore their hair. It was taken before the remodelling of the house, and the building looked older, old-fashioned, like the couple themselves.

He saw Kirsty in both of them. She was tall and willowy like her father. But she had her mother's strong features, and her thick black hair, which here had already been invaded by a creeping grey.

He turned then to her desk. A surface cluttered with papers and bric-a-brac. A small wooden Buddha with a fat, laughing face, a mug that hadn't been washed. Scissors, a letter-opener, innumerable pens and pencils in chipped ceramic cups, tissues, reading glasses, endless doodles on a large blotter. A reflection of idle moments of absent thinking. Whorls and stick figures, happy faces and sad. Some just lightly sketched, others worked over again and again until almost cutting through the paper. An indication, perhaps, of darker moods.

A pile of magazines testified to her interest in current affairs. *Time* Magazine, *Newsweek*, *Maclean's*.

In a drawer he found an old family photo album bound in dark-green cracked leather, and sat in her captain's chair to open it on the desk in front of him. Its pages were thick grey paper turned brittle with age. Discoloured black and white snapshots in the early pages were slipped into slits cut to hold them, captions written in faded ink beneath.

The very first photograph in the album was an overexposed sepia portrait of a very old woman, the glaze cracked and flaking in places. Underneath it, written in a copperplate hand, the legend Great-Great-Grandmother McKay, so discoloured that it was almost unreadable. It appeared to have been taken in the late nineteenth or early twentieth century, and Sime thought that perhaps this album had been started by Kirsty's mother collating old family photos. He flipped forward through the pages, taking a journey through time that brought him to the arrival of baby Kirsty, a round quizzical face peering at the camera from the arms of her mother.

And then Kirsty as a little girl, aged seven or eight, staring solemnly into the lens. He flicked forward through the pages, and watched her grow up before his eyes. An awkward smile with two missing front teeth. Older now, with pigtails and braces. Then wearing glasses, hair cut short in a bob.

He stopped mid-turn, a tingling sensation all across his neck and shoulders, and let the page fall back. This was the little girl whose cut-out head he had found lying on the floor of Norman Morrison's bedroom. And he understood now why it was that the child had looked so familiar. In spite of the hair and the glasses and the toothy smile. It was Kirsty.

He turned the next page and saw the dark square left by a missing photograph. The others around it were all of Kirsty at the same age, and he wondered if the absent snapshot was the very picture from which Morrison had cut her head. If it was, then either he had taken it without permission, or Kirsty had given it to him. Though he could not imagine why she would.

He sat staring at it for a long time, before turning the next page to continue his journey. Kirsty stretching through her teens, transformed in a few short years from a cute but gawky ugly duckling to a handsome young woman with knowing blue eyes that seemed to reach through the lens and across the years. And then suddenly the pictures stopped. As she had grown up, so her parents had grown older. And now, presumably, with the death of her mother, the photographic record of a happy family had come to an abrupt end.

He turned back again to the shadow of the missing picture and felt confusion as the sleeplessness of days and weeks washed over him in a wave of almost debilitating fatigue. He rubbed his eyes and glanced at the facing page. A thirteen- or fourteen-year-old Kirsty smiled back at him. Just the age that the Ciorstaidh in his ancestor's journal would have been when next he saw her. And something drew his mind back to the diaries, to the stories his grandmother had read to them as children. And he could almost hear his ancestor's voice.

CHAPTER FIFTEEN

I was, I think, about fifteen years of age when my father came back from the fishing that year.

In his absence I had been going daily to the moor to fetch the peats we cut in the spring and left drying in stacks called *rùdhan mór*. It was hard work loading the dried turves into wicker creels to carry the mile or so back to the village, but I had built a splendid stack behind our blackhouse. Peats laid one on the other in a herringbone pattern that allowed the rainwater to drain through. I had taken a great deal of care over it, because I knew my father would examine it critically on his return.

It had been a fine summer, but the first signs of autumn were in the air. And soon the sun would cross the equator, bringing the equinoctial gales that would herald the start of winter.

My father had been away for two months, as he was every summer for the herring fishing at Wick, and it always took him time to settle back into life on the croft. But he was in good spirits. It was the only season of the year when he had money in his pockets, and already it was burning a hole in them. Old blind Calum said to me that morning that it wouldn't be long before my father would want to be off to Stornoway to spend it. And he was not wrong.

The day was hardly over before my father took me aside and told me to prepare myself for a trip to town in the morning. It was the first time I was to go with him. I knew it would take us a day or more to get there with our old cart and borrowed pony, but I was excited by the prospect. So excited I could barely sleep that night as I lay in my box bed in the dark of the bedroom listening to my sisters beyond the curtains, curled up together in their own bed, fast asleep and purring like cats.

We set off in the morning, a brown pony tethered to our cart and pulling it along rutted and potholed roads till we struck the main north–south highway. It was a touch wider, perhaps, than the roads I was used to, and deeply scarred from so much traffic heading to and from Stornoway.

I sat up next to my father and told him I thought that I could walk faster than our pony. But my father said we needed the cart to bring back our winter provisions, so I should be patient with the beast and be thankful that we had her to bear the load on the road home.

It was the first time I had strayed further from our village than Sgagarstaigh, or Ard Mor, and I was amazed at the size of our island. Once you left the sea behind you, you could walk all day without ever seeing it again. But the land was pitted with wee lochs reflecting the sky, and it broke up the monotony of the landscape.

The thing that amazed me most, though, was the size of the sky. It was enormous. You saw much more of it than ever you did at Baile Mhanais. And it was always changing with the wind. You might see rain falling in the distance from a bank of black cloud. But if you turned your head just a little the sun would be shining somewhere else and there could be a rainbow vivid against the black.

The heather was a wonderful deep purple, punctuated by the yellow heads of the wild tormentil that grew everywhere. At first, as we left the mountains behind us in the south, the land folded over on itself again and again, broken only by the silver-mossed rock that burst through the peat, and the streams and rivers that tumbled from higher ground, teeming with fish.

'Why is it,' I asked my father, 'that we don't eat more fish when the rivers are so full of them?'

His face set and he glowered at the road ahead of him. 'Because those that own the land won't let us take them,' he said. 'The fish in these rivers, boy, are only for those and such as those. And if you're caught taking one, you'll end up in the jail faster than you can say *bradan mór*' – which was the Gaelic for big salmon. And plenty of big salmon there were, too. In just a few weeks they would be fighting their way upstream, jumping the rocks and waterfalls to spawn somewhere up in the hills.

As we got further north the land flattened out, and there was not a tree in sight. You could see for miles across the moor towards the west, and on our right I caught occasional glimpses of the sea. The Minch, they called it, and I knew that somewhere beyond The Minch lay the mainland of Scotland.

As darkness fell we were still some miles from town. My father drew our cart into the lee of a crop of rocks where we were sheltered from the wind and unwrapped the *marag dhubh* that my mother had sliced and fried for us before we left. Blood from the cow, mixed with oatmeal and a little onion. Black pudding they call it now in English, but we knew it then as famine food. Blood drained from the beast in small quantities so that you got at least some protein without having to kill the animal.

And then we slept beneath a tarpaulin, huddled together for warmth, the canvas pulled up over our heads to protect us from the midges, those wee biting flies that come out in black bloody clouds when the wind drops.

It was fine weather when we reached town the next morning and made our way among the carts and traps that rattled along the length of Cromwell Street. There were whitewashed cottages on one side, and tall stone buildings the like of which I had never seen before, gables and dormers and bay windows. On the other side sunlight caught the wind-dimpled waters of the inner harbour where fishing boats were lined up at the quay. A spit of land crammed with shops and houses separated the inner and outer harbours. And anchored out in the bay beyond them, several tall, three-masted sailing ships sat proud on the high tide.

Away to our right, on the hill that rose above the inner harbour, Seaforth Lodge dominated the skyline, a great big two-storey stone house and outbuildings that commanded marvellous views of the town and harbour and the ragged coastline to the east.

'Who owns that?' I asked my father.

'A Mr James Matheson,' he said. 'A very rich man who has just bought the whole of the Isle of Lewis.' He said he had heard that Matheson paid one hundred and ninety thousand pounds for the island. And I could not imagine so much money. 'It means he owns everything, and everybody, on it,' my father said. 'Just like Sir John Guthrie at Ard Mor owns the Langadail estate, and everything and everybody on it. Including us.'

When we reached the centre of the town my father told me to go and explore while he made his tour of the grocery and hardware stores and the ship's chandlers, to buy tools and grain, and a little something for my mother and the girls. He grinned at me. 'And a little baccy for myself.'

I was reluctant at first. I had never seen so many people before, and had no idea where to go or what to do. But he shoved me in the back. 'Go on, son. Time to spread your wings.'

Of all the people in Stornoway that day, it seemed I was the only one who was barefoot. For the first time in my life I felt self-conscious about it, and wished I had come in my Sunday best. I wandered along the quay looking at all the fishing boats, watching my feet on the nets and buoys. The smell of fish was powerful and I turned up a narrow street that led to the outer harbour. Past alehouses and hostels, and down to what they called south beach, where the big boats berthed at the pier.

Most everyone had their heads covered. The men with top hats or cloth caps, the women with all manner of bonnets tied under the chin to stop them from blowing away. The clack of horses' hooves, and the metal of cartwheels on cobbles filled the air, along with the wind and the voices of people that were carried on it.

I heard a Gaelic greeting: *'Ciamar a tha thu?'* A young woman's voice. But I didn't turn, because I couldn't imagine that she was addressing me. Until she said it again, and it seemed as if she were right behind me. I turned and found myself looking into the fine face of a pretty teenage girl, her black hair piled up in pleats, a dark coat open over a long dress that buttoned high up to the neck and trailed almost to the ground. She looked at me with knowing blue eyes that seemed to have a smile in them. 'Bet you don't know who I am,' she said to me in English.

I smiled. 'Of course I do.' And I hoped she couldn't hear the thumping of my heart. 'How could I forget? My arms are still aching from carrying you all that way.'

It pleased me to see her blush, and I pressed home my advantage.

'I thought you couldn't speak Gaelic.'

She shrugged casually. 'I don't. But I learned a few phrases – just in case I should ever bump into you again.'

Now it was my turn to blush. I could feel the colour rising high and hot on my cheeks.

She had regained the advantage and smiled. 'But the last time we met you couldn't speak any English.'

I felt the initiative swing back in my direction, 'I took English at school,' I said. 'Learned the whole language, just in case I should ever come across you lying in a ditch again.' Her eyes widened a little. 'But I haven't had much chance to use it since I left.'

Her face clouded. 'You've left school already?'

'Three years ago.'

Now she was astonished. 'But you couldn't have been any more than . . .' She searched my face, trying to guess my age.

I helped her out. 'Twelve at that time.'

'That's far too young to be leaving school. I'll be tutored until I'm eighteen.'

'I was needed to work on the croft.'

'What kind of work?'

'Well, right now I'm drystane dyking.'

She laughed. 'Are you still speaking English, or what?'

I smiled back at her, enjoying the laughter in her eyes. 'It means I'm building stone walls without mortar. Right now, a sheep fank up on the hill above Baile Mhanais. That's the village where—'

She cut me off. 'I know where you live.'

'Do you?' I was surprised.

She nodded. 'I came once and stood on the hill and looked down at it. I was pretty sure I saw you on the shore. It looked as if you were gathering seaweed.'

I was excited by the thought that she had taken the trouble to come and see where I lived, but tried to hide it. 'That's quite possible.'

She cocked her head and looked at me curiously. 'Why would you gather seaweed?'

'It's good fertiliser. We spread it on the lazy beds.' I could see from her expression that she had no idea what I was talking about, and I didn't want to seem like some peasant boy, so I changed the subject. 'A tutor's a teacher, right?'

'A private teacher, yes.'

'So do you go somewhere to be tutored?'

'No, I'm tutored at the castle. My tutor has a room there.'

A group of boys pushing a cart at the gallop almost knocked us over, shouting at us to get out of the way, and we started walking along the seafront. 'It must be amazing to live in a castle,' I said.

But she didn't seem impressed. 'You live in one of those squat little stone houses with straw roofs,' she said.

'A blackhouse, aye.'

She shuddered. 'I would hate that.'

Which made me laugh. 'They're not so little. There's plenty of room inside for folk in one end and cows at the other.' I knew this would get a reaction and it did.

There was horror on her face. 'You have cows living in your house?'

'It keeps us warm,' I said. 'And there's always fresh milk on tap.'

She shuddered. 'It sounds medieval.'

'Not the same as living in a castle, I imagine, but I like it well enough.'

We walked on in silence for a short time and I stole a glance at her. She was quite tall. Past my shoulder, anyway, and there was a light in her smile that gave me butterflies in my tummy. She caught me looking at her and her face coloured a little, eyes dipping, a tiny smile turning up the corners of her mouth.

She said, 'What are you doing in Stornoway?'

'I came with my father to get provisions for the winter. He's just back from the fishing on the mainland, so we have some money.'

'Don't you make money from your croft?'

I laughed at her innocence. 'The croft barely feeds us.'

She looked at me, consternation in her voice. 'Well, where do you get your clothes?'

'We spin wool from the sheep and weave it into cloth for my mother to make into clothes.' And I had that feeling of self-consciousness again as she looked me up and down, her eyes coming to rest on my bare feet.

'Don't you have any shoes?'

'Oh, yes. But we have to buy them, and they wear out pretty fast. So we keep them for going to church on Sundays.'

I saw in her eyes that she could not even begin to understand how we lived.

'What are you doing in town?' I asked.

'My father brought us. Some friends who are staying at the castle wanted to do some shopping. We'll be lunching at the new Royal Hotel in Cromwell Street. And we're staying over there tonight.' She seemed excited by the idea.

I didn't tell her that my father and I wouldn't be lunching at all. We would eat the last of the black pudding my mother had made and spend the night in our cart, hoping that it wouldn't rain. We stopped and gazed out at the water washing in along the shore, and I saw a tall ship in full sail tacking carefully into the comparative shelter of the harbour through the narrow channel between the rocks.

'I asked the staff at the castle, but no one seemed to know your name.' She glanced up at me. 'Except that you were a Mackenzie.'

I flushed with pleasure at her interest. 'Sime,' I said.

'Sheem?' She frowned. 'What kind of name's that?'

'It's the Gaelic for Simon.'

'Well, it's a silly name. I will just call you Simon.'

'Oh will you?' I raised an eyebrow.

She nodded quite definitely. 'I will.'

'In that case, I'll just call you Ciorstaidh.'

She frowned. 'Why? It doesn't sound that different.'

'Because it's the Gaelic for Kirsty, and I'll see it differently.'

She looked at me with such penetration in those blue eyes that it set my butterflies going again. 'You remember my name, then?'

Caught in that gaze of hers I felt my mouth go dry and I could hardly find my voice. 'I remember every little thing about you.'

'Hey! What do you think you're playing at?'

The voice shouting so close startled me, and I turned to find myself facing a teenage boy, perhaps a year or two older than me. He had a thick head of gingery hair and was tall, a well-built lad wearing fine clothes and a pair of shiny black boots. A slightly smaller boy with short black hair stood at his shoulder. The bigger boy pushed me in the chest and I staggered back, taken by surprise.

'George!' Kirsty shouted at him, but he ignored her, angry green eyes fixed on me.

'What the hell do you think you're doing talking to my sister?'

'It's none of your business, George,' Kirsty said.

'Any cotter boy talking to my sister is my business.' He shoved the flat of his hand once more into my chest. Though this time I stood my ground.

Kirsty stepped between us. 'This is Simon. He's the boy who saved my life the day the trap went into the ditch and Mr Cumming was killed.'

He pushed her out of the way, puffing up his chest and moving close so that his face was just inches from mine. 'Well, if you think that gives you any rights, then you can think again.'

'We were just talking,' I said.

'Well, I don't want you talking to my sister. We don't associate with tenants.' He said the word tenants as if it made a bad taste in his mouth.

'Oh, don't be such an ass, George!' Kirsty tried to insinuate her way between us again, but he held her at bay.

He never took his eyes off me. 'If I ever see you with my sister again, I'll give you such a hiding you'll remember it the rest of your days.'

I felt my honour at stake now, and I lifted my jaw and said, 'You and who else?'

He laughed in my face, and I recoiled a little from his bad breath. 'Hah! I don't need an army to deal with the likes of you.' And from nowhere a big fist swung into my peripheral vision catching me square on the side of my face. Pain and light exploded in my head and my knees buckled under me.

The next thing I knew, the smaller boy was leaning over me, taking one of my hands in his and helping me back to my feet. I was groggy and still a little in shock, and so quite unprepared for the boy suddenly stepping behind me to pull both my arms up my back. George's pale, freckled face ballooned into view, leering at me, and I was helplessly exposed to the fists he pummelled into my stomach. The other boy let me go and I doubled over on my knees, retching.

I could hear Kirsty screaming at them to stop, but her protests were ignored. George lowered his face to mine. 'Just stay away,' he hissed, then turned and, grabbing his sister by the arm, dragged her off protesting, the other boy trailing after them and grinning at me over his shoulder.

I was still on my knees, leaning forward with my knuckles on the ground, when I felt strong hands lifting me to my feet. A fisherman with a woollen hat and a face weathered by sun and wind. 'Are you all right, lad?'

I nodded, only embarrassed that Kirsty should have seen me humiliated like this. Nothing was hurt as much as my pride.

It must have been an hour or more before I met up with my father again. He looked at me, concerned, and saw how the knees were out of my trousers and my knuckles all skinned. 'What happened to you, son?'

I was too ashamed to tell him. 'I fell.'

He shook his head and laughed at me. 'Damn, boy! I can't take you anywhere, can I?'

It was just a few days later that I saw her again. There was very little sunshine that day. The wind was whipping itself up out of the south-west and bringing great rolling columns of bruised cloud in from the sea. But the air was not cold and I liked the feel of it blowing through my clothes and my hair as I worked. Hot work it was, too, moving great big lumps of stone up the hill to chip at them with my hammer so that they fit just right in the wall.

My father had taught me how to build drystone dykes almost as soon as I could walk. 'You'll aye be able to keep some beasts in and others out, son,' he had said. 'Or put a roof over your head. The fundamentals of life.' He liked to use big words, my father. I think he learned them from the Gaelic bible that he read to us every evening and half of Sunday.

The day was waning, but there were still some hours of daylight left and I was hoping to finish the sheep fank by week's end when my father would inspect my work and give it his approval. Or not. Though I would have been devastated if he hadn't.

I straightened up, back stiff and muscles aching, to look down on Baile Mhanais and the shore beyond it, strips of croftland running down the hill to the sea. Which was when I heard her voice.

'*Ciamar a tha thu?*'

I turned, heart suddenly pounding, to find her standing there on the crest of the hill. She wore a long dark cape over her dress, the hood pulled up to protect her hair. But still strands of it managed to break free and fly out like streamers in the wind. 'I'm well, thank you,' I replied in English. 'How are you?'

Her eyes dipped towards the ground, and I could see her hands clasped in front of her, one ringing the other inside of it. 'I came to apologise.'

'What for?' Although I knew fine well, but my pride wanted her to believe that I hadn't given it a second thought.

'My brother George.'

'Nothing to apologise for. You're not his keeper.'

'No, but he thinks he's mine. I am so ashamed of how he treated you, after what you did for me. You don't deserve that.'

I shrugged, feigning indifference, but searching desperately for some way to change the subject. Humiliation ran deep. 'How is it you're not with your tutor?'

And for the first time her face broke into a smile, and she giggled as if I had said something I shouldn't. 'It's a new tutor I have just now. A young man. Just in his twenties. He only arrived a few weeks ago, and I think he's fallen hopelessly in love with me.'

I felt a jab of jealousy.

'Anyway, I can wrap him around my little finger any time I like. So getting away from the castle is not a problem.'

I glanced down the slope towards the village, wondering if anyone down there had seen us. She didn't miss it.

'Ashamed to be seen with me?'

'Of course not! It's just . . .'

'What?'

'Well, it's not normal, is it? The likes of me seen talking to the likes of you.'

'Oh, stop it. You sound like George.'

'Never!' The comparison fired up my indignation.

'Well, if you're so worried about being seen with me, maybe we should meet somewhere that no one can.'

I looked at her, confused. 'Meet?'

'To talk. Or maybe you don't want to talk to me.'

'I do,' I said a little too quickly, and I saw a smile tickle her lips. 'Where?'

She flicked her head beyond the rise to the curve of silver sand below us on the other side of the hill. 'You know the standing stones at the far end of the beach?'

'Of course.'

'There's a wee hollow below them, almost completely sheltered from the wind, and you get a great view of the sea breaking over the rocks.'

'How do you know about that?'

'I go there sometimes. Just to be alone. You'd not have to be scared about people seeing us together if we were to meet there.'

It was late afternoon the day I set off to keep my tryst with Kirsty. I made solitary tracks in sand left wet by the receding tide as I followed the curve of Traigh Mhor north, glancing a little nervously across the machair in case someone was watching. But I might have been the last person on earth. There was not a soul to be seen. I had for company only the sound of the sea breaking on the shore and the gulls that wheeled around the rocks.

At the far side of the beach I climbed up through the cemetery, head and foot stones poking up through the long grass, and I trod carefully, aware that my ancestors lay here and that one day I would join them. I stopped and glanced out over the ocean to see the sun starting its slow descent towards the horizon, edging distant clouds with gold and sending shards of light skimming across the surface of the water. What a view it was from eternity that I would share with the folk who had inhabited this land for all the centuries before me.

The standing stones cast long shadows over the machair. Some of them were more than twice my height. Thirteen primary stones that formed a central circle, with a long approach avenue of stones to the north, and shorter arms to the south, east and west.

A movement caught my eye, and I saw a furl of skirt in the wind, half hidden by one of the taller stones, before Kirsty appeared, turning around the edge of it to stand looking down the slope as I climbed towards her. As I approached I saw that the colour was high on her face. Her skirts and cape streamed out behind her, along with her hair, and she folded her arms and leaned against the grain of the gneiss.

'Did they teach you about the stones at school?' she asked when I reached her, a little out of breath.

'Only that they're about four thousand years old and nobody knows who put them there.'

'My tutor says if we were able to look down on them from above they would form the rough shape of a Celtic cross.'

I shrugged. 'So?'

'Simon, they were put here more than two thousand years before Christ was born.'

I saw her point and nodded sagely, as if the thought had occurred to me long ago. 'Yes, of course.'

She smiled and ran the flat of her hand down the stone that she was leaning against. 'I love the texture of the stones,' she said. 'They have grain running through them like wood.' She tipped her head back and looked up towards the top of it. 'I wonder how they moved them. They must be terribly heavy.' She grinned then and extended her hand towards me. 'Come on.' I hesitated for only a moment, before grasping it, feeling it small and warm in mine. She pulled me away from the stones, and we went running down the slope together, almost out of control, laughing with exhilaration before coming to a halt where the elements had eaten away at the machair and loose, peaty earth crumbled down into a rocky hollow.

She let go of my hand and jumped down into it. I followed suit and landed beside her. Beach grass grew in tussocks and clumps, binding the loose earth and pushing up between cracks in the rock. The wind blew overhead but the air here was quite still, and there was a wonderful sense of shelter and tranquillity. No one could see us, except perhaps from a boat out at sea.

Kirsty arranged her skirts to sit down in the grass and patted the place beside her. I saw her ankle-length black boots and a flash of white calf. I knew she was younger than me, and yet she seemed possessed of so much more confidence. I did as I was bid and sat down next to her, self-conscious again, and a little scared by strange, unaccustomed feelings.

She said, 'Sometimes I look out and wonder if on a clear day it might be possible to see America.' She laughed. 'Which is daft, I know. It's far too far away. But it makes me think about all those folk who set off in boats not knowing what, if anything, lay at the end of their voyage.'

I loved to hear her talk like this, and I watched the light in her eyes as she looked out over the ocean.

'I wonder what it's like,' she said.

'America?'

She nodded.

I laughed. 'We'll never know.'

'Probably not,' she agreed. 'But we shouldn't limit our horizons to only what we can see. My father always says if you believe in something you can make it happen. And he should know. Everything we have, and are, is because of him. His vision.'

I gazed at her, filled for the first time with curiosity about her father and mother, the life she led, so different from mine. 'How did your father get rich?'

'Our family came from Glasgow originally. My great-grandfather made his fortune in the tobacco trade. But all that collapsed with the American war of independence, and it was my father who eventually restored the family's fortunes by getting us into the cotton and sugar trade with the West Indies.'

I listened to her with a sense of amazement, as well as inferiority, aware of all the things of which I was completely ignorant. 'Is that still what he does?'

She laughed. 'No, not now. He's retired from business. Since he bought the Langadail estate and built the castle at Ard Mor that's what takes up all his time. Even if it doesn't make him any money.' She turned the radiance of her smile on me. 'Or so he's always saying.'

I smiled back, engulfed somehow by her gaze, my eyes held by hers, and there was a long silence between us. I heard the wind and the gulls, and the sound of the ocean. I could feel the pounding of my heart like the waves beating on the shore. And without any conscious decision I reached out to run my fingers back through the silky softness of her hair and cradle the back of her head in my palm. I saw her pupils dilate and felt an ache of longing deep inside me.

I remembered the little girl I had lifted into my arms from the ditch and how, as I trotted the long wet mile to the castle, I would look down and see her gazing up at me.

I found her face with my other hand, tracing the line of her cheek so softly with the tips of my fingers, before leaning in to kiss her for the very first time, guided by some instinct which had been aeons in the making. Lips cool and soft and giving. And although I knew nothing of love, I knew that I had found it, and never wanted to lose it.

CHAPTER SIXTEEN

I

Sime returned from memories of his ancestor's diaries to the realisation that he had been sitting staring all this time at the ghostly imprint left in the album by the missing photograph of Kirsty as a child. And he looked up, suddenly startled by the awareness of another presence in the room. Marie-Ange stood leaning against the door jamb watching him. He saw the usual contempt in her eyes, something which had become only too familiar. But there was something else. Concern? Guilt? It was hard to tell.

'You look terrible,' she said.

'Thanks.'

'When was the last time you slept properly?'

He felt grit scratching his eyes as he blinked. 'Sometime before you left.'

She sighed. 'Something else that's my fault, no doubt.' And she pushed herself away from the door and wandered over to the desk, turning her gaze on to the teenage pictures of Kirsty in the album. 'Is that her? The Cowell woman?'

He nodded. 'Aged about thirteen or fourteen I think.'

Marie-Ange leaned over him to flip forward through the pages, casting cold eyes over the growing Kirsty. She stopped at the final photograph. Kirsty with her mother and father, taken in bright sunlight somewhere along the cliffs. Kirsty, a young woman by then, smiling unreservedly at the camera, sandwiched between her mum and dad, an arm around each of them. As she had grown, so they had diminished somehow, and you could see that her mother was not well. 'You'd never guess from this that she'd be capable of killing someone,' Marie-Ange said.

Sime looked at her sharply. 'Is that what you think?'

'Looks more and more that way.'

'And the evidence?'

'Oh, that'll come, for sure. There's bound to be something to give her away. And you can bet I'll find it.' She looked around the study. 'So what did you discover here that tells you about the Cowells?'

Sime thought about it. 'Enough to know that they weren't close. That it was a relationship without warmth. She sought comfort in her own company, her own interests. He found fulfilment elsewhere, and in the end with another woman.'

She gazed at him thoughtfully for a moment. 'I wonder what conclusions someone might have come to about us if they had taken a tour through our apartment.'

'Pretty much the same, I would have thought. Only, in reverse.'

She tutted her annoyance. 'Same old broken record.'

'You were never there, Marie. All those hours when I never knew where you were. And always the same old excuses. Work. A girls' night out, a visit to your parents in Sherbrooke.'

'You never wanted to come. Anywhere. Ever.'

'And you never wanted me to. Always found a good reason why I shouldn't join you. Then made it seem like my fault.' He glared at her, remembering all the frustration and loneliness. 'There was someone else, wasn't there?'

'Oh, you'd love that, wouldn't you? If I'd had an affair. Then it wouldn't have been your fault. No guilt, no blame.' She stabbed an angry finger at him. 'But here's the truth, Simon. If you need someone to blame for the break-up of our marriage, just look in the mirror.'

The clearing of a throat brought both their heads around. Crozes stood awkwardly in the doorway, his embarrassment clear. He chose to ignore whatever it was he might have overheard. 'Just had a call from Lapointe,' he said. 'He'll be taking off for Montreal with the body in about an hour.' He paused. 'The autopsy will take place first thing in the morning.'

'Good,' Marie-Ange said.

'What about Morrison?' Sime asked.

'Still missing. But we'll find him.'

'Is he connected, do you think?' Marie-Ange said. 'To the murder?'

Crozes was non-committal. 'We'll know that better once we talk to him.'

Sime turned the photo album around on the desk so that the page with the missing photograph was facing his superior officer. 'You'd better take a look at this, Lieutenant.'

Crozes stepped into the room and tilted his head to look at the photographs. For a moment he simply seemed puzzled. Then light dawned in his eyes. 'Jesus,' he said. 'That's the kid you found on the floor of Morrison's room.' He looked up. 'Kirsty Cowell?'

Sime nodded. 'Probably cut from the very print that's been taken from this album.'

'Well, how the hell did he get that?'

Marie-Ange looked from one to the other. 'What am I missing here?'

But neither man paid her any attention. Sime said, 'It's the first thing we need to ask him when we find him.'

Crozes exhaled his frustration. 'And maybe you'd better get over there and ask Mrs Cowell.' He tipped his head towards the door. 'She's back.'

II

The heating in the summerhouse had been turned on after the storm and the air was stifling. Sime found himself distracted by Kirsty Cowell's penetrating blue eyes, and an almost irresistible desire to close his own. Concentration was proving difficult in the warmth.

He sat once more with his back to the window, and she seemed cooler, more composed since her long walk with her cousin.

'I want you to tell me about your relationship with Norman Morrison,' he said. Which instantly shattered that composure.

'What do you mean? I have no relationship with Norman Morrison.'

'Are you aware that he went missing last night?'

Now her eyes opened wide. 'No, I wasn't. What happened?'

'He went out after his evening meal and never came back.'

She paled visibly. 'But what does that mean? Is he all right?'

'We don't know. There's a search under way at the moment.' He watched her closely as she tried to evaluate the information he had just given her. 'We understand from more than one source that he was . . . somewhat obsessed by you, Mrs Cowell.'

Anger flashed in her eyes. 'People say all sorts of things. And a place like this is like a hothouse, Mr Mackenzie. Plant a seed of truth and very quickly it grows into a profusion of lies.'

'So what is the truth?'

'The truth is that Norman Morrison is a lovely, gentle, kind man, who stopped growing any older when he was about twelve. And how many of us are there who wouldn't trade all our growing old years to be young again?'

'You had a soft spot for him?'

'I did.' She spoke almost defiantly. 'We were at school

together, here on the island. He always had a crush on me when we were kids. And like everything else it was something he never grew out of.'

'And you encouraged him?'

'Of course not! But he was still a child, and he was still my friend. I could never have hurt him.'

'Can you think of any reason he might have wanted to hurt you?'

She was shocked. 'You're not seriously suggesting that it was Norman who attacked me and killed James?'

'I'm not suggesting anything. I'm asking you.'

'No.' She was adamant. 'There's no way Norman would ever have done something like that.'

'Has he ever been in your house?'

She frowned. 'Here?'

'Here, or the big house.'

'No, he hasn't. At least, he hasn't been here since we were both children.'

'Can you explain, then, how he comes to have a photograph of you in his bedroom, almost certainly taken from the photo album in your study?'

Her mouth fell open slightly in disbelief. 'That's not possible.'

'There is a print missing from your album. One taken of you at the age of about thirteen or fourteen. We found a photograph of you at the same age in his room, the head cut out from the rest of it.'

Her sense of shock was palpable. 'He's . . . he's never been in that house.'

'And you didn't give him a photograph of yourself?'

'Absolutely not.'

Sime drew a slow, deep breath. He wasn't feeling good. 'Are you aware, Mrs Cowell, of your husband's jealousy towards Norman Morrison?'

She was utterly dismissive. 'Jealous? James? I don't think so.'

'According to Norman's mother your husband brought two men to the island to rough him up and warn him to stay away from you.'

'That's ridiculous! When?'

'About six months ago. Early spring.' He paused. 'Have you seen Norman since then?'

She opened her mouth to respond, but stopped herself, and he could see that she was thinking. 'I . . . I don't know. I can't remember.'

Which meant that she probably hadn't, and was replaying events of the past in a new light. But whatever those might have been she wasn't sharing them with him.

'I need a comfort break,' she said suddenly.

Sime nodded. He needed a break himself. A chance to escape the heat of the house and grab some air. As Kirsty went upstairs he went out on to the porch and stood holding the rail, breathing deeply. With all the local cops seconded to the search for Norman Morrison, only Arseneau

182

and a young sergeant called Lapierre were left to continue the search of the area around the house. Sime watched them as they moved methodically through the longer grass with sticks. They were searching for anything that might throw illumination on a dark case. The sun was doing its best to help, sprinkling daubs of watery gold in fleeting patches all along the cliffs. A murder weapon would be good. But if Kirsty had murdered her husband, it seemed to Sime that the simplest thing would have been to throw the knife off the cliffs and into the sea. If Cowell had been murdered by the intruder Kirsty described, then he would almost certainly have taken the knife with him, perhaps thrown it in the sea himself. Marie-Ange's examination of the kitchen had established that all sets of kitchen knives were complete.

Sime was finding it increasingly hard to accept, no matter how much evidence Marie-Ange might find, that Kirsty had murdered her husband. Yet it was his job to get to the truth, regardless. And while the evidence against her was purely circumstantial for the moment, he was in danger of being a minority of one when it came to believing she was innocent. And that in direct contradiction to all of his instincts as a criminal investigator. It was an impossible dichotomy. He turned to go back inside.

III

There was sunlight somewhere. It played in flickering moments of fancy through still air that hung heavy with dust suspended in sharply defined shafts. But there was fog, too, obscuring the light. Rolling in from the sea like a summer haar to obscure all illumination. He heard someone calling. Someone far away. A familiar voice, repeating the same word over and over.

'Sime . . . Sime . . . Sime!'

He was startled awake, but realised that his eyes had not been shut.

'Sime, are you all right?'

Sime turned his head to see Thomas Blanc standing near the foot of the stairs, the oddest expression on his face.

'I'm fine,' Sime said. But knew that he wasn't. A polite cough made him turn to face front and see Kirsty sitting in the armchair opposite. Her head was tilted very slightly to one side, an expression of wary curiosity in her eyes.

'If you want to continue this some other time . . .'

Continue? And it came to him that they had resumed the interview sometime earlier, and he had no idea for just how long he had been sitting in suspended animation. He was breathing heavily.

'No. No, we should carry on.' His disorientation was almost paralysing.

She shrugged. 'Well, I'm waiting.'

Sime glanced at Blanc, who raised an eyebrow. An unspoken question. Sime nodded almost imperceptibly, and Blanc returned reluctantly to his monitors in the back room.

'Where were we?' he said to Kirsty.

'You were asking how James and I met.'

He nodded. 'Tell me.'

'I already have.'

'Then tell me again.'

Her sigh was laden with impatience and frustration. 'James was a guest lecturer on business economics during my final year at Bishop's University in Lennoxville.'

'That's an English-language university?'

'Yes.'

'Just the one lecture?'

'Yes. He'd been invited to talk to us as a classic example of entrepreneurial achievement. A small local business transformed into a multi-million-dollar international success.'

'And your subject was?'

'Economics.' She shrugged her shoulders, and her smile was sad and ironic. 'Don't ask me why. You're forced to make decisions about these things when you're still too young to know. I'd always been good with numbers, so . . .' Her voice trailed away. 'Anyway, there was a drinks reception held for him afterwards and I went along.'

'Why? Were you attracted to him?'

She thought about it. 'I suppose I was. But not in any conventional way. He was twelve years older than me, which is a lot when you are in your early twenties. He wasn't what I would have described as good-looking, or handsome. But he had charm, and knew how to make his audience laugh. And I was impressed by his success, and his confidence, and everything he seemed to know about the world. But what I found, I suppose, most compelling about him was that he came from the Magdalen Islands, just like me. It made me see that no matter who you are, or where you come from, you can be anything you want. If you want it enough.'

'Why would that interest you if your intention was never to leave Entry Island?'

'I wasn't set on that course, then, Mr Mackenzie. The instinct was there, perhaps, but my parents were still alive. They were my anchor. Even if I wasn't there, they would be. So I still felt free at that time to do whatever I wanted. I never dreamt that within twelve months they would both be gone, and that my world would have narrowed to this tiny pinpoint of land in the Gulf of St Lawrence.'

'Do you feel it like a prison?'

'Not a prison, exactly. But I do feel tied to it.'

Sime took a moment to re-examine her. Her expression was weary. Tired eyes heavy from lack of sleep. He knew how she felt. Weird, was the word both Aitkens and Crozes had used to describe her, and he wondered what strange sort of compulsion it was that tied her to this place for no other reason than some vague feeling of missing something if she left. 'So you met him for the first time at the drinks party after his lecture?'

'Yes.'

'And?'

'I was introduced to him as a fellow Madelinot, and I felt his intensity from that first moment. In the way he held my hand for far too long. In the way that he locked me in his gaze and held me there, as if there was no one else in the room.'

'Love at first sight?'

She glanced at him sharply, as if suspecting sarcasm. 'For him, yes. Or so he always said.'

'But not for you?'

'Oh, I was flattered by his attentions, of course. But like I told you, he pursued me relentlessly for the next two years. When I returned to the island after the death of my parents he proposed to me. I told him I wouldn't make much of a wife since I had no desire to leave the island. This was my home, and this was where I wanted to stay.' She smiled sadly. 'And he said in that case he would make it his home, too. That he would build a house here for us. That we would raise a family, establish a dynasty.'

'But you never had any children.'

'No.' Now she wouldn't meet his eye. 'Turned out he was sterile. Children were out of the question.'

This was clearly an emotional subject, leaving her momentarily vulnerable. Sime took the opportunity to switch focus and catch her off balance.

'If it wasn't Norman Morrison, who else might want to kill you, Mrs Cowell?'

She seemed startled. 'What do you mean?'

'You claim that you were the object of the attack, and not your husband. So someone must have wanted to kill you.'

It was almost as if the thought had never occurred to her before, and she seemed flustered, discomposed by the question. 'I . . . I really have no idea.'

'Oh, come on, Mrs Cowell! This is a small community. Is there no one you might have offended, someone who might have a reason to bear you a grudge?'

'No!' Her denial was almost too fierce. 'There's no one.'

'Then why would someone attack you?'

She was at a loss, the colour rising on her cheeks. 'I don't know. Maybe . . . maybe he was a burglar and I just got in the way.'

Sime said, 'Do you know how many instances of burglary have been reported on Entry Island in the last ten years, Mrs Cowell?'

'How would I know that?'

'You wouldn't. Unless you'd asked. As I did. And do you want to know what the answer was?'

She looked at him with naked hostility in her eyes, her lips firmly locked together.

'Exactly zero.' Sime drew a long, slow breath to steady himself. 'But let's assume for a moment that your intruder was a burglar, unlikely though that is. Why would he pursue you across the room, knock you to the floor, as you described, and then attempt to stab you? Apart from the fact that a burglar is unlikely to enter a house where lights are still on and the residents have clearly not gone to bed, wouldn't he be more likely to run if disturbed? And if the real object of his entry into the house was theft, why would he be carrying a knife?'

She glared at him. 'I have no idea.' Her voice was tight and small. 'I told you what happened. I'm not a psychic. I can't explain it.'

'It seems there are a lot of things you can't explain, Mrs Cowell.'

It wasn't a question, and she clearly felt no obligation to respond, and so they sat looking at each other for what seemed like an interminable length of time.

He felt like the school bully, cruelly and relentlessly harassing the class weakling. She seemed crushed and vulnerable, all alone in the world without anyone to stand up for her with the exception of her truculent cousin. He tried to see her again, as he had that first time when he had been so convinced that he knew her. But now it just felt as if he had known her all his life.

He said, 'Kirsty's a Scottish name, isn't it?'

She appeared startled by the question, and a frown of consternation furrowed her brow. 'What's that got to do with anything?'

'Does your family have Scottish roots?'

She sighed her impatience. 'As far as I know, yes.'

'Your mother's great-great-grandmother was called McKay.'

Her impatience gave way to astonishment. 'How do you know that?'

'There's a photograph of her in your family album.'

'You have been busy. I suppose you've been through all my private things.'

'This is a murder investigation, Mrs Cowell. There is no such thing as private.'

Her hands were trembling now, and she wrung them in her lap. 'I don't see the point in any of this.'

But Sime had embarked on his course, and there didn't seem any way back. It had nothing, he knew, to do with the investigation, but he felt impelled to pursue it. 'Just trying to establish your background.'

'Most people on the island are of Scots or Irish, or even English descent,' she said. 'They came here from Nova Scotia, or Prince Edward Island. Some were shipwrecked en route to Quebec City. Great-great-great-granny McKay probably was Scottish. It's a Scottish name. But there's been a lot of inter-marrying since then. My mother's maiden name was Aitkens. Mine was Dickson.' She sucked in a tremulous breath. 'Now are you going to tell me what any of this has to do with the murder of my husband?'

'Sime?'

Sime turned to see Blanc standing in the hallway. He had

a curious expression on his face, the faintest hint of incomprehension creasing around his eyes.

'I think we should wrap this up.'

The shadows of clouds raced across the slopes and hills of Entry Island as the stiffening wind blew them quickly overhead from south-west to north-east. But there was no threat of rain in them.

Thomas Blanc hefted the silver flight cases containing their monitors into the back of the minibus and turned to look at Sime. He kept his voice low. 'What the hell was that all about in there, Sime?'

'What do you mean?'

'Oh, come on, you know what I'm talking about?'

'I don't.'

Blanc's eyes narrowed, clearly suspecting Sime of disingenuity. 'If I didn't know better, I'd say you actually fell asleep sitting upright, with your eyes open, mid-interview.' Sime could hardly deny it, especially since he had no idea how long he'd actually sat like that. 'When's the last time you had a proper sleep? Days? Weeks?'

Sime shrugged.

'You should see a doctor.'

'I already have.'

'Not a medical doctor. A shrink. Someone who can figure out what's going on in your head.' He drew a frustrated breath. 'I mean, what was all that about Scottish roots and great-grannies? Jesus, man! Crozes is going to be reviewing these tapes. And so will others.' He paused and his expression softened. He put a hand on Sime's arm. 'You need help, Sime. You're not up to this. Really. And there's not a single member of the team that doesn't know it. You should be on sick leave. Not attached to a murder case.'

Sime suddenly felt an almost overpowering sense of failure and, like a mask, the brave face he'd been wearing for the world slipped. He let his head drop and couldn't meet Blanc's eyes. 'You've no idea what it's like, Thomas,' he heard himself say. But his voice seemed disembodied, far away. As if it belonged to someone else. 'Night after night after night. Staring at the goddamn ceiling. Counting your heartbeats. Seconds turning to minutes, minutes to hours. And the harder you try to sleep the harder it gets. Then in the morning you're even more tired than when you went to bed, and you wonder how the hell you're going to get through another day.'

He looked up, and the sympathy in Blanc's eyes was almost harder to take than his earlier frustration. Blanc shook his head slowly. 'You really shouldn't be working, man. I don't know what they were thinking of, attaching you to this case.'

He clammed up, suddenly, averting his eyes and stooping to pick up a camera case. Sime turned and saw Crozes approaching.

'How did it go?' he said when he reached them.

Sime glanced at Blanc, but his co-interrogator was ostentatiously busying himself packing camera cases into the minibus. He said, 'She can't explain how Norman Morrison comes to have a photograph of her in his room, or how he got it. And she claims to have no idea why anyone might want to kill her. It didn't even seem to have occurred to her that if she was the object of the attack, then her attacker must have had a reason.'

'Unless, of course, there was no attacker, and she simply hasn't thought it through.' Crozes paused. 'How did she seem to you?'

Sime had no recourse other than to answer honestly. 'Flustered, Lieutenant. Not very convincing.'

'How about you, Thomas? Did she convince you?'

Blanc straightened up. 'Not at all, boss. She's hostile and evasive, and guilty as hell, if you ask me.'

Aitkens stepped on to the porch from inside the summerhouse and they turned as he came down the steps towards them. He shrugged hopelessly. 'She doesn't want me to stay with her overnight.' Then he turned hostile eyes on Sime. 'I don't know what you said to her in there, but you really upset her.'

Sime didn't know what to say, and it was Crozes who rescued him from having to respond. 'A man is dead, Monsieur Aitkens. It's not easy to avoid trampling on people's sensibilities when you're trying to find out why. We appreciate that Madame Cowell has been widowed, but she is also our only witness.' And he closed further discussion on the subject. 'You can come back on the boat with us.'

Aitkens gave him a long hard look, but said nothing before turning and going back into the house.

Crozes turned to Sime and Blanc. 'If Norman Morrison hasn't been found before dark, I'm going to have to leave one of our people to watch over Mrs Cowell. However unlikely it might be, if it was Morrison who murdered Cowell and he's still at large, there's a chance that Mrs Cowell could be in danger.'

Sime said quickly, 'I'll stay.'

Crozes seemed surprised. 'Why?'

'I might as well not sleep here as not sleep back at the hotel.' He was aware of Blanc's head turning to look at him, but he avoided his eye.

CHAPTER SEVENTEEN

The patrolman from Cap aux Meules was in the kitchen fixing himself something to eat before going back over to the big house to stand guard for the rest of the night. Light fell into the living room from the half-open door.

Kirsty was upstairs somewhere, and Sime could hear her moving about. The staircase was lit, but the living room itself was mired in darkness, only one small reading lamp focusing its light in a circle around an armchair in the far corner.

Sime wandered among the shadows in the semi-dark simply touching things. A smiling emerald Buddha with a round fat belly; a calendar comprising two numbered cubes suspended in a brass stand. A ceramic representation of Mr Micawber with a shiny bald head.

A mahogany occasional table by one of the armchairs was covered with a circular lace doily to save it from being scored or scratched by the pewter picture frame that sat on it. Sime turned it towards him and realised that it framed a head-shot of Kirsty. He picked it up, holding it towards the light, and looked at her. She must have been in her early twenties here, a little fuller in the face, her smile infused with the candour and innocence of youth. She was not a prisoner, then. Her parents were still alive, and she had felt free to leave the island.

He gazed for some minutes at the photograph, before running his fingertips lightly over the glass and replacing it on the table. And he wondered if, like Norman Morrison, he was becoming a little obsessed with her.

The patrolman popped his head around the kitchen door to say goodnight, and Sime watched him from the window as he made his way across the grass in the dark. Although the big house was lit up like a Christmas tree and he could sit and watch TV, Sime did not envy him his job. It was a dead man's house, and while the body was gone, his spirit remained in every item of furniture, in the clothes that still hung in his closet, in his blood that stained the floor.

'Where do you mean to sleep?'

Sime spun around, startled. He hadn't heard her on the stair. She was showered and changed, her hair still damp, and she wore a black silk dressing gown embroidered with colourful Chinese dragons.

'The settee is fine,' he said. 'I won't sleep.'

She padded through to the kitchen to put the kettle on, and called back through the open door. 'I'm making tea, do you want any?'

'What kind?'

'Green tea with mint.'

'Sure.'

She came through a couple of minutes later with two steaming mugs and placed one on the coffee table next to the settee for Sime. She took hers to the armchair in the pool of light and folded her legs beneath her as she cradled her mug in her hands, as if cold.

'Well, this is strange,' she said.

He sat down on the settee and took a sip of his tea, nearly scalding his lips. 'Is it?'

'The hunter and his prey calling a truce for the night and sharing a nice cup of tea.'

Sime was stung. 'Is that how you see me? As a hunter?'

'Well, I certainly feel hunted. Like you've already decided I'm guilty and it's only a matter of time before you'll wear me down and catch me out. I have a picture in my mind of a lion and a gazelle. Guess which one I am.'

'I'm just—'

'I know,' she interrupted him. 'Doing your job.' She paused. 'And I'm just someone who saw her husband stabbed to death. I haven't slept since.'

'Well, then, we have that in common at least.'

She cast him a curious glance. 'What do you mean?'

'I haven't slept in weeks.' As soon as he spoke he regretted it, but it was too late to take it back.

'Why?'

He just shrugged. 'It doesn't matter.'

'Something to do with the break-up of your marriage?' She had gone straight to it and he felt almost guilty. Losing your wife did not fall into quite the same category as seeing your husband brutally murdered.

'Forget it,' he said. And he changed the subject. 'Did you ever find that pendant?'

'No.' She gazed thoughtfully into her mug. 'No, I didn't. But I have noticed that there are other things I can't find.'

He replaced his mug on the coffee table, his interest piqued. 'Such as?'

'Oh, little things. A cheap bracelet I got as a student. A couple of hair clips, a pair of earrings. Nothing very valuable. And maybe I've just mislaid them, but I can't seem to find them.'

'Might they not be over in the other house?'

But as if she had decided that she wanted simply to drop the subject, she just shrugged. 'Maybe.' But he knew she didn't believe that. Then, 'You don't really think I'm in danger, do you?'

'From Norman Morrison?'

'Yes.'

He shook his head. 'Not really, no. But the lieutenant doesn't want to take any chances.'

Although she had not nearly finished her tea, she stood up then and carried her mug towards the kitchen, but stopped next to the settee to look at him. 'Why are you the one they left to watch over me?'

'I volunteered.'

The merest widening of her eyes was the only sign of her surprise. 'Why?'

'Because I knew there was no danger of me falling asleep.'

She held his eye for a long moment, then broke contact and went into the kitchen. He heard her pouring her tea down the sink and rinsing out her mug, then she turned out the light and went through to the back bedroom. A few moments later she appeared with a single white duvet and a pillow. She laid the duvet over the back of the settee and dropped the pillow beside him. 'Just in case,' she said. 'Goodnight.'

The light in the stairwell went out when she'd climbed to the landing. He heard her move across the floor above him, and the creak of her bed as she slipped into it. He flirted momentarily with the thought of her naked between cool sheets, but quickly forced it from his mind.

He sat for a long time in the half-light cast by the reading lamp before getting up to cross the room and switch it off. He went to lock the front door then and turn on the outside light in the porch before going through to lock the back door. Locking doors, he knew, was anathema on the island, but he was not going to take any risks.

He went back to the settee and took off his shoes, then lay along the length of it, his head propped on the pillow she had left. The light from the porch shone through the windows, casting long shadows across the room. By its reflection he picked out the cracks and dimples on the ceiling that would become his focus during the long sleepless hours ahead.

From time to time he heard her turning over and wondered if she, too, was failing to find sleep. There was an odd sense of intimacy in his being here, so close to her as she lay in her bed just above him. And yet there could hardly be a greater gulf between them.

After a while he began to feel cold. The heating had gone off, and the temperature outside was dropping. He reached up and pulled the duvet over himself. Its softness enveloped him, and he felt his own warmth reflecting back from it. He took a long, slow breath and closed aching eyes. He thought about his ring. And the pendant. *Don't let her fuck with your mind*, Crozes had said to him. But somehow he believed her about the pendant.

He tried to remember if his father had ever made mention of the ring. Where it had come from. Why it was important. But he had never paid enough attention to family stories. About their Scottish roots. His heritage. Sime had been too busy fitting in. Being a Quebecois, speaking French. All that had really stayed with him were those stories his grandmother had read from the diaries, still so vivid, even after all these years.

CHAPTER EIGHTEEN

It is raining. A fine, wetting rain, almost like a mist. A smirr. It blows in off the sea on the edge of a wind that would cut you in two.

I am with my father. But we are gripped by fear, and running crouched along the line of the hill behind and beyond Baile Mhanais, where it dips down towards the sea loch that I know as Loch Glas. My clothes are soaked and I am almost numb with the cold. I am not sure of my age, but I'm not much older now than when Kirsty and I first kissed by the standing stones beyond the beach.

My father's old torn cloth cap is pulled down low above his eyes, and I see how black they are as he looks back over his shoulder. 'For God's sake keep down, boy. If they see us they'll come after us, and put us on the boat, too.'

We reach an outcrop of rocks almost buried by peat at the top of the hill. And splashing through a stream in spate, we throw ourselves down into the wet grass behind them. I can hear voices carried on the wind. Men shouting. We crawl forward on our bellies, until we have a view down the slope to the shore of Loch Glas, and the village of Sgagarstaigh with its little stone jetty.

My eye is caught at once by the tall, three-masted sailing ship anchored out in the loch. And by the crowd of villagers on the quayside. Before my attention is drawn to the smoke and flames that rise up from the village itself.

The paths between the blackhouses are littered with furniture and other household debris. Sheets and prams, broken crockery, children's toys. A group of men swarms from house to house, shouting and yelling. They carry flaming torches with which they set light to the doors and roof thatch of the houses.

My horror and confusion is absolute, and it is only the restraining arm of my father that stops me from getting to my feet and shouting out in protest. I watch in total stupefaction as the men, women and children of the village are herded on to the jetty by constables in uniform wielding long wooden batons. There are boys I was at school with being struck across the arms and legs by those stout ash truncheons. Women and girls, too. Kicked and punched. They have with them, it seems, only such belongings as they have been able to carry from their homes. And I see for the first time the rowing boat ferrying its human cargo from the jetty to the tall ship.

Finally I find my voice. 'What's happening?'

My father's own voice is grim as he responds through clenched teeth. 'They're clearing Sgagarstaigh.'

'Clearing Sgagarstaigh of what?'

'Of people, son.'

I shake my head, perplexed. 'I don't understand.'

'They've been clearing folk off the land all over the Highlands ever since the government defeated the Jacobites at Culloden.'

'Jacobites?'

My father glares at me in exasperation. 'Jesus, son, did they teach you nothing at school?' Then he shakes his head angrily. 'Aye, right enough, maybe they wouldn't. They say that history is only written by the victors.' He raises his head, drawing phlegm into his mouth, and spitting into the flow of water that tumbles down the hill. 'But I heard it from my father, who heard it from his. And now you're hearing it from me.'

A cheer, carried to us on the edge of the rain, draws our eyes back to the chaos unravelling below, and we see that the roof of one of the blackhouses has fallen in, sending a shower of sparks into the air to be carried off in the wind.

My father turns back to me. 'The Jacobites were supporters of the Stuart kings that once ruled Scotland and England, son. Just about a hundred years ago there was an uprising all across the Highlands. Jacobites who wanted to restore the Stuarts to the throne. With the Young Pretender, Prince Charlie, at their head, they marched south and came within striking distance of London. But in the end they were driven back, and finally crushed at a place called Culloden, near

Inverness.' He sucked in a long, slow breath and shook his head. 'It was a slaughter, son. And afterwards, the government sent a battalion of criminals from English jails on a rampage through the Highlands. They killed Gaelic speakers and raped their women. And in London the government passed laws that made it illegal to wear the kilt or play the bagpipes. If you spoke the Gaelic in a court of law you were deemed not to have spoken at all, and so there was no way of getting justice.'

It is the first time I have heard any of this, and I feel a growing sense of outrage.

'The government wanted to destroy the old clan system, so there could never be another uprising. They bribed some of the old clan chiefs, and sold off the estates of others to wealthy Lowlanders and Englishmen. And the new breed of lairds, like Guthrie, and Matheson, and Gordon of Clunie, wanted the people off their land. You see, sheep are more profitable than people, son.'

'Sheep?'

'Aye, they want to turn over all the land to sheep.'

'But how can they do that?'

My father's laugh was full of bitterness and no humour at all. 'The landowners can do what they like, boy. They have the law on their side.'

I shake my head. 'But . . . how?'

'Because the law is made to keep the powerful in power, and the rich wealthy. As well as the poor in poverty. Tenants like us can barely survive on what we produce on our crofts. Well, you know that! But it doesn't stop us having to pay rent, even though we have no money. So the landlords issue notices of eviction. If we can't pay up we get thrown off. Burned out of our homes so we can't go back to them. Forced on to boats and sent off across the sea to Canada and America. That way they're rid of us once and for all. The bastards even pay our passage. Some of them. They must reckon it's cheap at the price.'

I find it hard to take in everything my father is saying. I am bewildered. I had always thought that Baile Mhanais and everything I know here would be for ever. 'But what if you don't want to go?'

'Pfah!' My father's contempt explodes from his mouth like spittle. 'You don't have any choice, son. Your life is not your own. Like I've told you before, the laird owns the land and everything on it. And that includes us.' He removes his cap to sweep his hair back from his forehead before pulling it back on again. 'Even under the old clan chiefs. If they wanted us to go and fight in whatever war they'd given their support to, we had to drop everything and march off to battle. Give them our lives. Even if it was for some bloody cause that meant nothing to us.'

More shouts from below draw our attention.

'Jesus,' my father almost whispers. 'The poor buggers are jumping off the ship now.'

We crawl a little further around the rock to get a better

view, and I see two men in the water, and a third jumping from the deck of the tall ship after them. The rowing boat is halfway between the ship and the shore, and laden with another load of villagers. So it can't go after them.

The men who have jumped ship strike out for shore, swimming for their lives. But the water is choppy in the wind, and icy cold. I see one of the men struggling now, splashing frantically, before he vanishes beneath the surface. And he is gone, and doesn't reappear. I find it hard to believe I am lying here on the hillside, not half an hour from my own home, watching a man drown in the loch as hundreds of people look on.

A quiet, slow-burning anger takes root inside of me. 'Are you telling me it's our own laird, Sir John Guthrie, who's doing this?' I say.

'Aye, son, it is. He's been clearing villages all up the west coast this last year.' He turns to look at me. 'I reckon if it wasn't for you saving his daughter's life all those years ago, Baile Mhanais would have been long gone, too.'

The two others who jumped ship reach shore below us. One of them can barely stand, and is easy prey for the group of half a dozen constables who detach themselves from the rest and run around the loch's edge. They are on him in a moment, batons rising and falling in the rain, beating him to the ground.

The other is a bigger man, stronger, and he strikes off up the hill, setting a course almost directly for where we lie hidden by the rocks.

'My God,' I hear my father gasp. 'That's Seoras Mackay. A fine man.' And he turns towards me, fear in his eyes. 'For Heaven's sake, son, hide yourself! They're coming this way.'

I don't see where it is my father goes, but in a moment of blind panic I roll through the icy waters of the burn and conceal myself beneath a bank of overhanging ferns. Half of me is still in the water, my nose filled with the smell of damp earth and rotting vegetation, and my teeth are chittering with the cold. I can feel the pounding of feet vibrating through the ground beneath me and then, getting closer, the harsh rasp of lungs desperately gasping for breath.

Seoras Mackay and his pursuers are almost right on top of me when they catch up with him and bring him crashing to the ground. The earth shakes with the weight of the big man, and all the air is forced from his lungs. His face is on a level with mine, no more than eighteen inches away. He looks at me through the ferns. For a moment it seems to me as if those sad brown eyes of his are appealing to me for help. But then they are clouded by resignation as he suffers several blows from the batons of the constables. One of them kneels on his back, pulling his arms behind him, and his wrists and ankles are locked in irons. I hear the dull, brutal clank of metal chains, and he is hauled to his feet to be dragged off back down the hill. Eye contact broken and lost for ever, like Seoras himself.

There is more bad weather on the way. I can see it gathering far out at sea. Behind me the sun sprays yellow light across a fractured landscape, and the wind blows strong enough to knock you off your feet if you don't have them planted right. The tormentil and bog cotton are flattened by it, and I can hear it howling through the standing stones beyond the ridge of the hollow above my head. Even in the shelter of the hollow itself, the tough, spiky beach grasses that bind the sand bend and fibrillate, almost singing in the wind.

I am crouched on a stone, and might be carved out of the same gneiss myself. I don't feel the cold. It would be difficult to be colder on the outside than I am within. I stare out at the whitecaps blowing in ahead of the coming storm, and feel waves of icy emotion breaking over me.

'Hi.' Kirsty's voice rises above the roar of the wind and the sea as she jumps down smiling into the hollow to join me. I can hear the happiness in her voice, and I try not to let it affect me. She stoops to kiss my cheek and I turn my head away to avoid it.

I feel her tension immediately. She stands up straight. 'What's wrong?'

'Your father's what's wrong.'

I don't look at her, but I can hear the immediate anger in her voice. 'What do you mean?'

I stand up and turn to face her. 'Do you know what he's doing?' She just stares back at me, her face a mask of confusion. 'He's forcing people out of their homes and setting their houses on fire so that they can't come back.'

'He is not!'

'And he sends constables and estate workers to force them on to boats to sail them off across the Atlantic against their will.'

'Stop it! That's not true.'

'It is.' I feel my own anger fired by hers. 'I've seen it with my own eyes. Folk I know beaten and kicked. Neighbours at Sgagarstaigh, kids I was at school with, made to leave the houses they were born in, and forced to watch as the bastards set them on fire. I saw them ferried out to a boat in the loch and put in chains if they tried to escape. Just ordinary folk, Ciorstaidh. Folk whose ancestors have lived here for generations. Folk whose parents and grandparents are buried here on the machair. Forced to leave it all and sent off to some godforsaken place on the other side of the world, just because your father wants to put sheep on the land.'

I see the shock on Kirsty's face. Her hurt and bewilderment, her desperate desire for it not to be true. 'I don't believe you!' she shouts in my face, giving voice to that desire, but I have no doubt, too, that she can see in my face that it is.

The tears that have been brimming in her eyes spill from them now, and are spread across her cheeks by the wind. Her hand comes out of nowhere, its open palm catching me squarely on the cheek. I almost stagger with the force of it, and feel how it stings my skin. I see the distress behind her tears. And as she turns and climbs back out of the hollow to run off between the stones that stand proud on the hill, skirt and cape flowing out behind her, I realise that I have just destroyed her world. And mine.

I so dearly wish I could run after her and tell her that none of it is real. But I can't. And I understand fully for the first time how both our lives have changed, and how nothing will ever be the same again.

It is low tide, and the smell of the sea fills the air. A rich, rotting seaweed smell that is so familiar. For once there is no wind and the sea is a placid pewter reflecting a sky that lies low above my head, a sad, unbroken grey. It laps tamely along the shore, licking around the ragged tendrils of Lewisian gneiss that invade it from the shore, ancient hard rock encrusted with shellfish and made slippery by the kelp that grows here in profusion and covers it so abundantly.

I have two wicker baskets that sit at angles on the rock as I hack at the seaweed with a long, curved blade, shredding my fingers on shells like razorblades as I pull it free of the rock to throw in the baskets. My back aches, and my feet, which have been in the water off and on for hours, are frozen numb. The baskets are nearly full and I will shortly make the return trek to the croft once more to spread the kelp on our lazy beds.

I have not been aware of her approach, and only now as I glance up do I see her standing there on the rocks looking down at me. She wears her cape buttoned for warmth, the hood pulled up over her head, and with the light behind her as she stands silhouetted against the sky I cannot see her face. It is some days since our confrontation in the hollow and I had thought I would never see her again.

I straighten up slowly, stepping out of the water and on to the rock. Crabs scuttle about in the pools that gather there, scraps of reflected light scattered randomly amongst the sombre green seaweed.

Now I see how pale she is, dark shadows staining the pure unblemished skin beneath her eyes.

'I'm sorry,' she says, her voice so tiny I can barely hear it above the breath of the ocean. She lowers her eyes. 'It seems I'm always having to apologise to you.'

I shrug, knowing that whatever it is she feels, my remorse is greater. 'What for?'

'For slapping you.' She pauses. 'For not believing you.'

I don't know what to say. I can only imagine the pain and disillusion that would have beset me if someone had dismantled the belief I have in my own father.

'It's still so hard for me to believe that daddy could be responsible for such things. I knew I couldn't ask him straight out. So I asked the serving staff. At first no one would admit to knowing anything. Until I pressed them. It was my tutor who told me in the end.'

She sucks in her lower lip and seems to be biting on it to control her emotions.

'Only then did I finally confront my father. He was . . .' She closes her eyes in wretched recollection, '. . . he was incandescent. He told me it was none of my business and that I simply didn't understand. And when I told him that what I didn't understand was how he could treat people like that, he did what I did to you.' She draws a trembling breath and I see her pain. 'He slapped me. So hard he bruised me.' Her hand moves up to her face instinctively and her fingertips trace the line of her cheekbone. But there is no sign of the bruising now. 'He had me locked in my room for two days, and I'm not sure that I stopped crying once. My mother wanted to reason with me. But I wouldn't even let her in the room.'

She lowers her eyes to the ground and I see defeat in the slump of her shoulders.

'My tutor has been dismissed, and I am confined to the house. I managed to slip out the kitchen door this morning. They probably don't know I'm gone yet, though I'm not sure I care if they do.'

I step close now and take her in my arms, feeling her tremble as I draw her into my chest and hold her there. Her head rests against my shoulder and she slips her arms around me. We stand like this for an age, breathing in time with the slow beat of the ocean. Until finally she releases me and steps back from my arms.

'I want to run away, Simon.' Her eyes fix me in their earnest gaze and I feel the desperate appeal in them. But running away is not a concept that I can easily understand.

'What do you mean?'

'I mean I want to leave here. And I want you to go with me.'

I shake my head in confusion. 'Go where?'

'It doesn't matter. Anywhere but here.'

'But, Ciorstaidh, I have no money.'

'I can get us money.'

I shake my head again. 'I can't, Ciorstaidh. This is my home. My parents and my sisters need me. My father can't manage the croft on his own.' The whole notion of it is alien to me. 'And anyway, where would we go? What would I do? How would we live?'

She stands staring at me, her eyes filled with betrayal and tears. Her face is bleak and hopeless, and suddenly she shouts at me, 'I hate you, Simon Mackenzie. I hate you more than I've ever hated anyone in my life.'

And she turns and strides away across the rocks, both hands pulling her skirt and cape free of the kelp and the pools of seawater, until reaching the grass where she runs off into the morning gloom, leaving sobs of distress in her wake.

And me with a debilitating sense of guilt.

CHAPTER NINETEEN

Sime sat bolt upright and wondered if he had really called out loud in the dark, or just imagined it. In the silent aftermath he listened for any sign that he had disturbed Kirsty. But there was no sound from upstairs. All he could hear was his own rapid breathing and the pounding of blood through his head.

He was perspiring profusely, and he pushed the duvet aside. He remembered the story clearly from his grandmother's reading of it, but dreaming it made it personal in a way that no amount of reading could.

He checked his watch. It was not even midnight. He had slept barely half an hour and all the sleepless hours of the night still lay ahead of him. Endless time to wonder what was sparking these dreams and recollections of his ancestor's journals. What it was that his subconscious was trying to tell him. Something relating to that first meeting with Kirsty Cowell, and his conviction that he knew her. Of that he was certain. And then there was the ring, and the pendant. The arm and sword engraved in carnelian.

There was only one person in the world he knew who might be able to cast light on that. His sister, Annie. And despite his reluctance, he knew that he was going to have to call her tomorrow.

He swung his legs around and planted his feet on the floor, leaning forward on his elbows, his face in his hands. It had seemed chilly earlier, but now he could barely breathe for the heat that he was generating himself. He slipped his feet into his shoes and zipped on his hoodie. He needed air.

A light wind blew high clouds across an inky sky, stars like jewels set in ebony. An almost full moon came and went in washes of colourless silver light. The air was filled with the sound of the ocean, the slow steady breath of eternity.

He walked through the light that fell from the windows of the big house in slabs and rectangles, and stepped up on to the dirt road. For someone raised so far from the sea, the sense of being surrounded by it now was quite unsettling. It lay all around, momentarily at peace, reflecting moonlight in pools and patches, dangerously deceptive in its tranquil beauty. On the far horizon he could see the lights of Havre Aubert and Cap aux Meules twinkling in the dark.

As he walked down towards the lighthouse, his feet crunching on the gravel underfoot, he reflected on the missing man-boy. Why had he run away, and where could he possibly have gone? Did he have any involvement in the Cowell murder? The neighbour claimed he had a temper and was prone to tantrums. Might he simply have taken revenge for the beating he got from Cowell's hired hands, and seen Kirsty as complicit in her husband's actions? Or had he just made the whole thing up?

And then there was the photograph taken from Kirsty's album. How had he got hold of it? If he had been in the house before, might he not have been the intruder who attacked Kirsty on the night of the killing?

Rows of creels, three deep, sat up on a wooden drying platform off to his left. Ahead of him the beam from the lighthouse raked the night sky. The houses dotted about the southern tip of the island lay in darkness, the good people of Entry Island long ago tucked up in bed, getting in practice for the long winter nights that lay ahead. Somewhere in the distance he heard a dog barking, seconds before a swishing sound made him turn to his right and he felt the full force of a blow to the side of his head. Pain and light filled it as his knees folded under him and he hit the ground with force enough to empty his lungs.

Without breath in them he was unable to cry out, and when a boot thumped with sickening force into his midriff he thought he was going to pass out. Instinct took over and he curled up into the foetal position to take the blows on his back and arms and legs. He fumbled desperately for the Glock holstered beneath his hoodie, but even as he pulled it free and tried to swing himself around towards his attacker it was kicked from his hand and spun away into darkness.

His assailant was a shadow against the sky, a big man dressed in black, soaking up the light, blotting out the stars. From where Sime lay retching on the ground, he seemed to fill it completely, eyes burning behind the slits of his mask. He could hear the man's breathing, fast and tremulous, then saw the moonlight reflected on the blade in his right hand. Sime felt as if his insides had turned to liquid. He knew there was nothing he could do to stop this man from taking his life. Plunging the knife into him again and again. Pain, pure and simple, had robbed him of the capacity to defend himself, and in a moment his whole sorry life played itself out before him, filling him with regret for all his wasted years.

An elongated wedge of yellow light fell across the grass, throwing their shadows long into the night. Sime turned his head towards the source of it and saw the silhouette of a stout man standing in the open door of his house, a shotgun held firmly across his chest.

'What the hell's going on out there?' he roared.

And in a moment Sime's attacker was gone, silently sprinting off into the dark, a shadow in the wind, leaving behind him barely a whisper.

Sime very nearly blacked out with relief. He rolled over and emptied the contents of his stomach into the grass, then looked up as a flashlight shone in his face.

'Jesus!' he heard the man say. 'You're one of them cops from Montreal.'

*

Sime had not realised just how far he had walked in the dark, and it took him almost ten minutes to get back to the house, hampered as he was by the pounding in his head and the sharp pain like cramp that gripped his chest with every step.

His gun, retrieved from the grass, was safely back in its holster, but he was unnerved by just how easily he had been disarmed and left at the mercy of his attacker. If it hadn't been for the intervention of a light-sleeping islander, the earth of Entry Island would have been soaking up his blood by now, his body growing cold in the grass.

Now his concern was for Kirsty. He should never have left her alone in the house. The assailant would have had ample time to kill her as she lay sleeping in her bed before coming after Sime. Though why he had attacked Sime at all was a mystery.

Sime hobbled up the steps on to the porch of the summer-house cursing his stupidity. He threw open the door and called her name at the top of his voice.

He was halfway up the stairs in the darkness when the light came on, and a pale and frightened-looking Kirsty stood on the top landing, pulling on her dressing gown, eyes dilated and dark with fear.

His legs almost gave way beneath him from the relief of seeing her. Then her mouth and eyes opened wide as she saw the blood on the side of his head and the mud on his clothes, and she hurried down the few steps that separated them to catch his arm. 'For God's sake, Mr Mackenzie, what happened to you?'

Through his pain and relief, he felt the comfort of the warmth that came from her body, the sureness of her touch. He had not been this close to her before, breathing in her scent, and had to overcome a powerful urge to take her in his arms. 'I was attacked,' was all he managed to say, and he drew himself upright again. 'Are you all right?'

'I'm fine. But you're not. I'm going to call the nurse.'

Downstairs they heard the clatter of footsteps, and the screen door banging open. The patrolman left to guard the crime scene in the big house stood breathing hard at the foot of the stairs, gazing up at them in alarm. 'What's happened?'

CHAPTER TWENTY

I

The harbour was crowded for the arrival of the morning ferry. Pickup trucks with colourful Entry Island licence plates stood idling along the quayside. Men of all shapes and sizes, old and young, in baseball caps and trainers, baggy jeans and T-shirts, hung around in knots smoking and talking. The womenfolk stood apart in groups of their own, conducting quite different conversations. A forest of aerials and masts and radar pods broke the skyline behind them, fishing boats berthed along the pier rising and falling on the gentle grey swell.

Sime stood at the end of the quay beyond the yellow ticket hut, the breeze in his face, watching as the now familiar shape of the blue-and-white *Ivan-Quinn* ferry nosed into the harbour. He was aware of the eyes that were on him, of the lowered voices exchanging the latest gossip that was doubtless spreading like wildfire across the island in the wake of the previous night's attack. He was not looking forward to his meeting with Crozes.

The cut on the side of his head was taped up, the contusion around it angry and inflamed. The nurse had strapped his chest tightly and the support had helped relieve the pain. She thought that he was probably just bruised, but that he should get an X-ray anyway.

He had lain then through all the hours of darkness, feeling the pain ebb away as the paracetamol she had given him took effect. Morning had brought stiffness, and an ache to muscles and joints. After an uncomfortable telephone conversation with Crozes he had taken the minibus to the harbour early and walked along the coast road and back to try to loosen up.

With the ramp down, passengers and vehicles debouched now on to the quayside, locals stepping forward to pick up boxes of groceries and other goods ordered from across the water and beyond. Crozes detached himself from the rest of his team and approached Sime, hands pushed deep into his pockets. He wore dark glasses below the peak of his baseball cap and the only real clue to his mood was in his demeanour. Sime saw Marie-Ange and Blanc glance towards him as they climbed into the minibus to await the lieutenant. The Cap aux Meules cops had brought their own vehicles and set off to resume their search for the missing Norman Morrison.

'What the fuck were you playing at, Mackenzie?' Crozes didn't even look at him. He stood beside him, shoulder to shoulder, staring out across the bay.

'I just went out for some air, Lieutenant. I was only gone a few minutes.'

'A few minutes in which he could have killed her.'

'Then why didn't he?' Sime said.

Crozes turned his head to look at him for the first time. 'What do you mean?'

'Well, he had the chance, but he didn't. He came after me.'

Crozes stared at him thoughtfully. 'You got a look at him?'

Sime blew exasperation through pursed lips. 'Not really. He was wearing dark clothes, and a ski mask. Just like she described.'

Crozes turned away. 'There won't be a single person on this island who doesn't know Mrs Cowell claimed to be attacked by a guy wearing a ski mask. Not very hard to replicate.' He swung his head back towards Sime. 'I don't know why anyone would want to attack you, Sime, but it's just one more complication we really don't need.' He paused. 'Do you have any thoughts?'

Sime shrugged. 'Not really. There's Norman Morrison, I suppose. If he was the one who attacked her.'

'But as you say, why would he attack you?' Crozes took off his baseball cap and scratched his head thoughtfully. 'What about the fisherman you and Blanc interviewed?'

'Owen Clarke?'

Crozes nodded. 'You give him any reason to be pissed off at you?'

'Not that I'm aware of.'

Crozes dragged his cap firmly back on his head, pulled a gob of phlegm into his mouth and spat into the water.

'Let's go talk to him.' Then, as an afterthought, 'Are you okay?'

Sime found it hard to keep the sarcasm out of his voice. 'I'm fine, Lieutenant. Thanks for asking.'

II

Clarke was wearing an oil-stained blue boiler suit open halfway down his chest to reveal a tangle of wiry hair like silvered copper fusewire. The legs of his trousers gathered around a pair of dirty white trainers that were no longer able to contain his big feet and had burst open along either side. He was out with a strimmer, cutting down the long grass around the house. His face was red and beaded with sweat beneath the peak of his baseball cap. His habitual brown-stained roll-up issued smoke from the corner of his mouth. He saw them coming, but made no attempt to stop the motor until Crozes shouted at him and ran a finger across his throat.

He flicked a switch to cut the fuel supply and turned towards them with a bad grace as the motor spun to a halt. 'What do you people want now?'

Sime looked at him carefully. He was a big man, which had not been immediately apparent when he and Blanc interviewed him seated at his workbench two days previously. He was certainly big enough to have been Sime's attacker. Sime glanced at his hands and saw bruised and skinned knuckles, and he realised what had only registered in his subconscious until now. That his assailant had been gloved.

Crozes said, 'Where were you last night around midnight?'

Clarke looked at Sime and flicked his head towards Crozes. 'Do I get an introduction?'

'Lieutenant Daniel Crozes.' Crozes showed him his ID. 'Will you answer the question, please?'

Clarke leaned on his strimmer and leered at them. 'I was screwing this amazing-looking blonde,' he said. 'Tits on her like this.' And he raised his big-knuckled hands to his chest as if grasping imaginary breasts. Then he laughed at the expression on their faces. 'In my fucking dreams! I was asleep. Home in bed. Ask my wife.' He grinned to reveal the remaining handful of brown stumps that passed for teeth. 'Only, don't tell her about the blonde, okay?'

Crozes leaned forward unexpectedly and whipped off the man's baseball cap, exposing the swirls of hair that sweat had flattened to his skull, and a nasty bruise high on his left cheekbone.

'Hey!' Clarke grabbed for his hat, but Crozes held it out of reach.

'Where'd you get the bruise, Mr Clarke?'

Clarke's fingers went automatically to the bruising on his face, and he touched it lightly. His smile had vanished. 'Slipped on the boat and fell,' he said defiantly, as if challenging them to contradict him. He swung his gaze towards Sime and the grin returned, ugly and without humour. 'Where did you get yours?'

There seemed little point in asking Mary-Anne Clarke to confirm her husband's whereabouts of the night before. Wherever he might have been she was going to tell them he was at home in bed with her. But Crozes said he would send someone to take a statement from her later. Just for the record. He was nothing if not punctilious.

As they drove back along the track to Main Street, they could see groups of islanders in the distance, each led by a police officer, working their way methodically across the island in the hunt for Norman Morrison. More than thirty islanders had volunteered, and they were searching old barns and disused sheds, raking through overgrown gullies and creeks. The breeze was getting up now and blew among the long grasses, shifting them in waves and currents like wind on water. The cloud cover was high, allowing only a little hazy sunshine through to lift the brooding darkness of the ocean that moved in restless swells all around the island.

Sime drove, and Crozes stared bleakly out of the window at the searchers. 'I'm going to assign most of our team to help with the search,' he said. 'The sooner we find this guy and rule him either in or out the better. Then we can get back to bringing this investigation to a conclusion.' He dipped his head to peer up towards the near horizon. 'Who the hell's that?'

Sime craned to see, and caught sight of half a dozen quad bikes rising and falling with the contours of the island as they followed a parallel course to the minibus on Main Street. 'Looks like the Clarke boy and his pals.'

Crozes frowned. 'Blanc said you had a run-in with some kids on quad bikes. He didn't say one of them was Clarke's boy.'

'Damn near ran me down and managed to tip himself off in the process.'

Crozes grunted. 'Loss of face in front of his friends. Did you have words?'

'He told us in no uncertain terms to leave his father alone.'

Crozes sat up. 'Let's talk to him.'

Sime swung left and took the road up towards the church, accelerating over ruts and potholes. The minibus rattled and juddered over the uneven surface, and it seemed to take some moments for the bikers to realise it was going to cut them off. Sime pulled the wheel hard left and the vehicle careened across the track to end up side-on to the approaching bikers. They immediately altered course, turning away towards Big Hill. Crozes jumped down and shouted at them to stop. The bikes drew to a reluctant halt in an idling knot of diesel fumes and revving motors. Crozes raised his ID above his head. 'Police,' he shouted. 'Come here.' And he waved them towards him. The kids exchanged glances, then one by one engaged gears and turned to motor slowly towards the minibus as Sime climbed out of it. At the last they fanned out to form a semicircle around the two policemen. 'Which one of you's Clarke?' Crozes said.

Chuck Clarke was in the middle of the group, clearly its leader. The spikes of his gelled hair stood firm against the breeze. 'What do you want with me?' he said.

'Turn off those motors,' Crozes instructed, and in the ensuing silence Sime heard the wind blowing through the grass, and the sound of the sea washing all along the southern shore. Crozes looked at Chuck. 'Get off the bike, son.'

The teenager thrust out a belligerent jaw. 'And what if I don't?'

Crozes slowly removed his sunglasses. 'I'm conducting a murder investigation here, kid. If you want to obstruct me in the course of that I'll have you over on Cap aux Meules kicking your heels in a police cell before you can say quad bike.' He replaced his shades on the bridge of his nose. 'Now get off the fucking bike.'

It was a further loss of face for the Clarke boy, but he had little alternative but to comply. He dismounted slowly and stood with his legs slightly apart, gloved hands on his hips, glaring at Crozes.

The lad was built. Six feet or more, and Sime ran his eyes over the jeans and black leather jacket. He wore scuffed Doc Martens, and Sime thought that they could easily have been the boots that had bruised his ribs. His gaze fell on the expensive, hand-stitched leather gloves. Kirsty had spoken about the gloves of her attacker, and the stitching in the leather.

'Where were you last night?' Crozes said.

Chuck glanced uneasily towards the others. 'Why?'

'Just answer the question, son.'

One of the girls said, 'We had a party last night. My dad's got a barn over the far side of Cherry Hill. We can play music as loud as we like there and don't disturb nobody.'

'How long did that go on for?'

'Oh, I don't know . . .' she said. 'Maybe till about three.'

Crozes cocked his head. 'And Chuck was with you the whole time.'

'He was.' This from one of the other boys. He leaned back on the comfortable leather seat behind him, lacing his fingers together at the back of his head and lifting his feet to cross them on the handlebars of his bike. 'Any law against that?'

'Not unless you were drinking. Or smoking dope.'

An uneasiness stirred among them, and Crozes turned back to Chuck. 'Where were you the night Mr Cowell was murdered?'

Chuck gasped in disbelief and pulled a face. 'You don't think I had anything to do with that?'

'I'm asking you a question.'

'I woss at home wiss my parentss,' Chuck said, mimicking Crozes's strong French accent, and the other kids laughed.

Crozes grinned as if amused. 'That's very good, Chuck. Now if you like, I can have every item of clothing you own confiscated for forensic examination. And I can arrest you and hold you in custody for forty-eight hours while a team of experts pulls your house apart piece by piece. Which I am sure will endear you to your parents.'

Chuck's pale skin darkened. 'I was at home all night. Ask my mother.'

And it seemed to Sime that Mary-Anne Clarke was providing alibis for the whole family.

Crozes's cellphone rang in his pocket and he turned away to fish it out and take the call. He put a finger in one ear and walked several paces away, listening for a moment then speaking rapidly before hanging up. He turned back to the kids and waved a hand toward the far distance. 'Go,' he shouted. 'And if you want to do something useful, join the search for Norman Morrison.'

The kids wasted no time in starting up their motors and wheeling off to snake in an undulating line away across the hillside. Crozes turned to Sime as the sound of the motors faded. 'Ariane Briand just landed at the airport at Havre aux Maisons,' he said. 'You and Blanc take the boat and get over there. I want to hear what she's got to say for herself.'

CHAPTER TWENTY-ONE

I

During the crossing to Cap aux Meules Blanc assiduously avoided asking him about the attack. They passed most of the fifty-five minutes it took to cross the bay in silence. But Sime caught him examining the bruising on the side of his face, and Blanc seemed embarrassed and compelled to say something.

'Are you all right?'

Sime nodded. 'I'll live.'

But there was a tension between them.

They picked up the Chevy the team had left parked at the harbour, and Blanc drove them south on the Chemin Principal before turning off on to the coast road that they had driven two days earlier in the rain. This time there was a vehicle parked outside the Briand house. Ariane Briand was back in residence.

As soon as she opened the door, Sime saw what Aitkens had meant about her. *She was a real looker and still is,* he'd said. *I didn't know a boy at school who didn't have the hots for her.*

She was closer to forty than she would probably want to admit, and was still a good-looking woman. She wore a short-sleeved cut-off top revealing a taut, tanned belly above tight-fitting jeans that showed off her slim hips. Chestnut-brown hair with blonde streaks tumbled in big, loose, careless curls to her shoulders. She had soft brown eyes and fine, full lips, and a jawline that most women would require surgery to replicate.

She wore very little make-up, and her age was only discernible in the finest of lines creasing the skin around her eyes and mouth. She was the kind of woman, Sime knew from experience, that you could only ever admire from afar, unless you happened to be rich, or powerful. Cowell had most certainly been rich. And her ex, he supposed, could be described as powerful. At the very least, a big fish in a small pond.

She stepped back from the door, looking at them without curiosity, and Sime saw that she was barefoot. 'Can I help you?'

Blanc showed her his ID. 'Sûreté, madame. We're investigating the murder of James Cowell.'

'Of course you are. You'd better come in.' She stood aside to let them pass.

They walked into a large dining room that extended up into the roof space where huge Velux windows set into the slope of the roof allowed light to cascade into the room. An arched opening led through to a big, square kitchen with an island set at its centre. They never got any further than the dining room. Ariane Briand stood, almost barring their way to the rest of the house, her arms folded, defensive verging on hostile.

'So . . .' Blanc said. 'Would you like to tell us where you've been for the last two days?'

'Well, maybe you'd like to tell me why that's any of your business.'

Blanc bristled. 'Madame, you can answer my questions here or at the Sûreté. Your choice.'

She pursed her lips pensively, but if she was ruffled showed no sign of it. 'I went shopping in Quebec City. Is that against the law?'

'Even although you knew your lover had just been murdered?'

'I didn't,' she said. 'I had no idea until I flew into the Madeleines this morning.'

Sime nodded towards an expensive oxblood leather suitcase sitting against the island on the floor of the kitchen. 'Is that your suitcase?'

She glanced over her shoulder, but her hostility remained intact. 'That's James's. It's the stuff he brought with him when he moved in.'

'And when was that, exactly?'

'Just over a week ago. The Thursday, or the Friday. I can't remember.'

Blanc said, 'And he never unpacked?'

She appeared momentarily discomposed. 'I've just finished packing it. You can take it with you, if you like.'

Blanc scratched the bald patch on his head. 'If you don't mind my saying so, Madame Briand, you don't exactly sound like the grieving lover.'

She set her fine jawline and thrust it in his direction. 'Grief takes many forms, Sergeant.'

During this exchange Sime let his eyes wander around the room. A man's coat hung on the coatrack beside the front door. A big coat that seemed too large to be Cowell's. But even if it was, why had she not packed it with the rest of his things? On the sideboard stood a large, framed colour photo of Ariane and a man whom he did not recognise. He had an arm around her waist, and both were laughing freely at the camera, sharing a joke with whoever was taking the picture.

He heard Blanc ask, 'Do you have any thoughts about who might have a motive for murdering Monsieur Cowell, madame?'

She shrugged, her arms still folded. 'Well, it's obvious, isn't it?'

'Is it?' Sime said.

'Of course it is. Kirsty Cowell, who else?'

Blanc said, 'Why would you think that?'

'Because she as good as threatened it.'

The ensuing seconds of silence seemed embarrassingly long, before Sime said, 'Explain.'

Ariane Briand set her feet slightly apart as if preparing to stand her ground and defy them to challenge her. 'She turned up at my door the night before the murder.'

Sime felt the shock of her words prickling across his scalp. 'Kirsty did?'

She looked at him, fleeting incomprehension in her eyes. The Kirsty had sounded too intimate 'Yes.'

Blanc said, 'According to everyone we've spoken to she hasn't been off the island in ten years.'

'Well, she was off the island that night.'

'How did she make the crossing?'

'You'd have to ask her that. But I know that she and James kept a small boat at the jetty below their house. And there's a tiny harbour just down the road at Gros-Cap. Presumably that's where she berthed it. She must have walked up in the rain. She was soaked to the skin when I answered the door.'

Sime pictured her standing in the dark at the door, hair wet and hanging in knots over her shoulders, just as he had seen her that first day after she came out of the shower. But it was not an image he wanted to contemplate.

'What did she want?' Blanc asked.

'James.'

Sime frowned. 'What do you mean?'

'She was looking for her husband, that's what I mean. Very nearly hysterical she was, too. And wouldn't believe me when I said he wasn't here. She forced her way into the house and rampaged around the place shouting his name. There was nothing I could do to stop her, so I just stood here until she realised I was telling the truth.'

Sime was shocked. This picture the Briand woman was

234

painting of Kirsty conformed to none of his perceptions of her, or to any of the things she had told him during their several interviews. Nor to the impression that Jack Aitkens had given of her. *Serene* was the word he had used. *Like she had some kind of inner peace. If she has a temper, then I've never seen her lose it*, he'd said. But, then, he had also confessed to barely knowing her.

'When she finally accepted that he wasn't here she went dangerously quiet.' Ariane Briand was lost in a moment of recollection. 'Her eyes were quite mad. Staring. Her voice was little more than a whisper when she told me she had no intention of giving up James without a fight. And that if she couldn't have him she was damned sure no one else would.'

Sime caught sight of his reflection in the mirror above the sideboard and saw how pale he was. And for the first time he allowed himself to contemplate the possibility that maybe Kirsty Cowell had killed her husband after all.

'The night of the murder,' Blanc said. 'Did you know that Cowell was flying back to Entry Island?'

She shook her head. 'No. He was here earlier. But he took a call on his cellphone. I have no idea who the caller was, but it was a fractious call, and he hung up in quite a state of agitation. Said he had something to take care of and would be back in a couple of hours.'

Blanc glanced at Sime, but Sime was lost in a confusion of thoughts. Blanc said, 'You'll have to come to the police station with us, Madame Briand, to make an official statement.' He pushed past her to pick up Cowell's suitcase. 'And we'll take this with us.'

Sime turned to lift the coat from the hanger by the door. 'And the coat?'

Her hesitation was almost imperceptible. 'No, that's not his.'

II

Ariane Briand had repeated her version of events in the interrogation room at the police station. Thomas Blanc had conducted the interview while Sime watched on monitors in the office next door. Under Blanc's forensic questioning she had provided further detail that painted an even more graphic picture of Kirsty's unexpected visit.

Now, as he sat on the edge of the bed in his room at the auberge, Sime found himself sinking into a depression. He had painted a picture for himself of Kirsty Cowell, carefully constructed, layer upon layer, that had been erased in a single wash that coloured her a liar. She had left the island. She had threatened her husband's lover, and implicit in that was a threat to Cowell himself.

The boat which had brought Sime and Blanc across to Cap aux Meules had returned to Entry with more volunteers to help in the search for Morrison. So they had an hour to kill before they could make the return crossing themselves. Sime had declined Blanc's suggestion of a coffee in the Tim

Horton's across the road and retired to his hotel room instead, drawing curtains on the world and retreating into semi-darkness.

He kicked off his shoes and swung his feet up on to the bed. He sat up against the headboard, propped by a pillow to support his back, and took out his cellphone. A growing sense of guilt crept over him. It was time, he knew, to phone his sister. There was no one else he could ask about the ring or the diaries.

He had not spoken to her in such a very long time. Not even on the phone. How long was it? Five years? More? Poor Annie. For some reason he had never felt close to her. Of course there was an age gap. She was four years older. But it was more than that. He had always been a loner, a solitary boy, self-sufficient and never interested in his sister. Even when she had reached out to him after the death of their parents.

As soon as he left school he had gone his own way, heading for the big city. While she stayed behind and married a neighbour, a boy who had been in her class. A French-speaker. And bore him a baby boy and then a little girl. Teenagers now, who spoke no English.

He had been back only once, for their parents' funeral.

The last time he and Annie had met was when she came to his wedding. Without her husband. She had made excuses for him, but Sime knew that Gilles resented the way his brother-in-law had neglected her.

Guilt washed over him again, cold and reproachful. Maybe Marie-Ange was right. Maybe he was all those things she had called him. Selfish, self-centred. They were not pleasant reflections, and he veered away from them, just as these days he avoided his reflection in the mirror.

He found Annie's number in the contacts list of his cellphone and with a great effort of will tapped autodial. He raised the phone to his ear with trepidation. After several rings it was answered by a boy whose voice sounded as if it might be breaking. 'Yeah?'

'Hi. Is your mother there?'

'Who's calling?' He seemed bored. Or disappointed. Perhaps he'd been waiting for a call himself.

Sime hesitated. 'It's your Uncle Simon.'

There was a long silence at the other end of the line that was difficult to interpret. Then the boy said, 'I'll get her.'

He could hear voices distantly in the background. Then more silence. And Sime could actually feel his heart pulsing in his throat. Suddenly his sister's voice. 'Sime?'

'Hey, sis.' He dreaded her response.

But he should have known better. She had never been one to bear grudges. Beyond her surprise, he heard the delight in her voice. 'Oh, my God, little brother! How the hell are you?'

And he told her. Without preamble. The plain, unvarnished truth. His break-up with Marie-Ange, his insomnia. And while he could feel the shock in her silence as she listened, the simple act of sharing everything he had bottled up for so long came as an enormous release.

'Poor Sime,' she said, and meant it, echoing his own thought of poor Annie, just a few minutes earlier. 'Why don't you come home. Stay with us for a while.'

Home seemed like an odd word for her to use. The little military town of Bury, in the Eastern Townships south-east of Montreal, was where she still lived. It hadn't been home to Sime in years. But home had a good sound to it, full of comfort.

'I can't right now. I'm on the Madeleine Islands, a murder investigation.' He hesitated. The moment he asked, she'd know there had been an ulterior motive for him calling. 'Annie, remember those diaries? The ones that Granny used to read from when we were kids.'

If she was disappointed there was no hint of it in her voice. Just surprise. 'Well, yes, of course. Why?'

'Do you still have them?'

'Somewhere, yes. I've still got everything here that we took from Mum and Dad's. And from Granny's. I keep meaning to sort through it all some day, but we put everything in the attic above the garage. And, you know, out of sight . . .'

'I'd like to read them again, sis.' He could tell that she was containing her curiosity with difficulty.

'Of course. Any time you like.'

'I'll come down as soon as we're finished here on the Madeleines.'

'That would be great, Sime. It'll be lovely to see you.' And then she couldn't help herself. 'What's the sudden interest in the diaries?'

'It's complicated,' he said. 'I'll explain when I get there.' Then, 'Annie . . . you know the signet ring I inherited from Dad?'

'Yes. Some kind of red, semi-precious stone, wasn't it? Engraved with a family crest. Not ours, though. It was an arm and sword or something.'

'That's right. Do you know anything about its history?'

She laughed. 'Am I really going to have to wait till you get here to find out what this is all about?'

'Sorry, sis, there just isn't time for me to go into it right now.'

'Well, it got passed down through the male line,' she said. 'Came originally from our great-great-great-grandfather, I think. The one who wrote the diaries. The one you were named after. In fact, I'm sure there's something about the ring in the diaries themselves. Can't remember what, though.'

'Do you remember how or where he got it?'

'I think it was given to him by his wife.'

Sime was deflated. If that was true he couldn't imagine what possible connection it could have with Kirsty Cowell. 'He met his wife here in Canada, didn't he?'

'That's right. She was a serving girl or something in Quebec City.'

A dead end.

240

When he didn't speak for a long time, Annie said, 'Sime? Are you still there?'

'Yes, I'm still here.'

He heard her hesitation. 'It was the tenth anniversary last week, Sime.'

He was momentarily confused. 'Of what?'

'Mum and Dad's accident.'

His guilt returned. He had barely even thought about his parents in all the years since the accident. Of course, he remembered, it had been at this time of year. An autumn deluge which had swollen the River Salmon, washing away the bridge and the cars that were on it at the time. Ironically, it was only their parents who had lost their lives in the accident.

Annie said, 'Someone put flowers on their grave. I visit them often. And I thought it was lovely that someone else had remembered. No idea who, though.'

Sime said, 'Annie, I have to go. I'll call you when I get home, okay?'

He hung up and closed his eyes. There was so much in his life he had simply learned to shut out. Like the death of his parents. He'd always thought there would be time to tell them that he loved them, even if he'd never been quite sure that he did. And then death had stepped in and left him feeling all alone in the world for the very first time.

His ancestor's pain at the loss of his father came flooding back in a surge of childhood memories. It had been a cold winter's night, sometime just after New Year, that their granny had read the account of it to them. Right after dinner, and he and Annie had sat by her feet at the fire while she read. The story had given him nightmares later that night. And he couldn't imagine then what it would feel like to lose a parent. Never mind both of them.

CHAPTER TWENTY-TWO

Even although there was still plenty of light in the sky, it was as dark as a winter's night in the blackhouse. And there was conspiracy in all the faces huddled around the flicker of the peat fire.

I sat among the men listening, but saying nothing.

I still have a clear recollection of the potato crop first failing the previous year. Green, healthy leaves on the lazy beds that turned black and slimy almost overnight. And I remember being sent to the potato store in our barn, pulling aside the tarpaulin to be greeted by a smell like death that rose from the rotting tubers we had so carefully nurtured and harvested twelve months before.

Disaster!

Without the potato there was no way to survive. It was the ever-present at every meal. Our meagre harvest of oats and barley served only to supplement a diet that was totally dependent upon the humble spud. And yet some invisible malady had robbed us of the gift of life that it gave us. A disease visited on us by God. For our sins, as the minister would have it.

There must have been a dozen men or more sitting around the embers of the peat, almost lost in the fug of smoke that hung heavy in the air of the fire room. But I could see the hunger in their sunken cheeks. I had watched strong men grow weak, as I had, and stout men grow thin. I had seen my mother and my sisters wasting away, reduced to scouring the shore for shellfish. Limpets and clams. Food for old women without teeth. They collected nettles for soup, and silver leaf from among the grasses. The roots, when dried and ground, made a kind of flour. But it was a poor substitute for proper grain and we could barely gather enough to sustain us.

The fishermen no longer dried their white fish on the rocks in case we stole them, and we had no boats of our own to take fish from the sea for ourselves.

As always my father led the discussion, old blind Calum squatting at his side, listening intently from within his world of darkness, his head so shrunken now that his Glengarry seemed almost to drown him.

I heard the fettered fury in my father's voice. 'Guthrie hands out grain rations from the Poor Board then charges it against our rents. Earns a name for himself as a man of generosity, while creating the excuse for throwing us off our land. Rents beyond our means, debts we can never repay. And while we're starving, he and his cronies hunt deer and take salmon from the river and eat like kings.'

Discontent rose up from around the fire like smoke. I heard men of God using the language of the Devil. 'Food all around us, and not a damned thing we can eat,' one of the men said.

My father's voice trembled with anger. 'But we could eat. We're just not allowed to. The law that serves the rich forbids it.' It was a favourite theme, and I had heard him vent his anger often on the subject. 'Well, enough's enough. Time to take the law into our own hands and harvest what the Lord provided for all, not just the few.'

Which brought a hush around the fire. For there wasn't a man there who didn't know what that meant.

My father's voice rose in frustration at their lack of gumption. 'It's our job to feed our families. And I for one am not going to stand by and watch my kinfolk waste away before my eyes.'

'What do you propose, Angus?' It was our neighbour, Donald Dubh, who spoke up.

My father leaned in towards the fire, his voice low and earnest. 'The land on the far side of the Sgagarstaigh hill is teeming with red deer. In what the toffs laughingly call a deer forest.' There was no mirth in his own laughter. 'And not a bloody tree in sight!' His face was set, his eyes black, reflecting only the burning of the peats. 'If we set off after midnight tomorrow, there should be enough light for us to hunt by, but not a soul around. We'll kill as many deer as we can carry and bring them back here.'

Old Jock Maciver spoke then. 'We'll get the jail if we're caught, Angus. Or worse.'

'Not if there's enough of us, Jock. A big hunting party. If they catch us it'll make the newspapers. And just think how that'll read. Starving men arrested for trying to feed their families. Guthrie'll do nothing if we're caught. Because he knows the courts would never dare to convict. There would be bloody revolution!'

There wasn't a man around the fire who wouldn't have given his right arm for a haunch of venison. But not one of them who wasn't afraid of the consequences.

When they were gone my mother and sisters came back into the house. They had been out with the other women of the village sitting around a long table between the blackhouses waulking the newly woven tweed to soften it. Usually they sang as they beat the cloth, and the meeting of men around the fire would have been accompanied by the voices of their womenfolk raised in Gaelic song outside. But with the hunger the women had fallen silent. The very first thing that starvation steals is your spirit.

My father took his old crossbow out from the bottom drawer of the dresser and with a cloth started to work oil into the first signs of rust in the iron. It was heavy and lethal. A weapon of war made by a blacksmith, traded to my father years ago by a tinker in return for a hank of tweed. My father was proud of it, and of the bolts he had made himself, short but well balanced with feather flights and flint heads.

When he had finished he laid it aside and started to sharpen the hunting knife he had taken with him on those occasions when the estate had employed him as a gillie. He was skilled with it at the gralloch, the gutting of the deer. The times he had taken me with him I had watched him do it with something like awe. And disgust. It is quite a thing to see the insides of an animal taken out of it almost intact, steam rising from blood that is still hot.

'What knife shall I take?' I asked him, and he turned serious eyes in my direction.

'You're not coming, son.'

I felt anger and disappointment spiking through me in equal measure. 'Why not?'

'Because if for some reason I don't come back tomorrow night, someone's going to have to look after your mother and sisters.'

I could feel my heart pushing up into my throat. 'What do you mean, if you don't come back!'

But he just laughed at me and put a hand on my shoulder. 'I have no intention of being caught, boy, but if I am then they'll probably take me and anyone else they catch to the jail in Stornoway. At least until there is some kind of a court hearing – or they let us go. But either way, it'll be your job to take my place till I get back.'

I watched them leave shortly after midnight. It was still light, and would never get fully dark. It was a clear night, with a good moon that would flood the land when dusk finally came. There was no wind, which was unusual, and meant that they would be eaten alive by the midges. Before he left my father smeared bog myrtle over his hands and face to keep them at bay.

There must have been fifteen men or more in the hunting party, all armed with knives and clubs. And a couple of them had crossbows like my father. I climbed the hill above Baile Mhanais to watch them disappear from view, disappointed not to be with them. At almost eighteen, I was more man than boy now.

I found a sheltered spot to watch for them coming back and settled down to feel the midges in my hair and on my face. I pulled my jacket over my head, and my knees up under my chin, and thought about Ciorstaidh. There was not a day had passed that I didn't think about her with an ache like the hunger of the famine. I had often wondered what would have become of us if I had run away with her as she asked. But it was pointless thinking about might-have-beens. And it was already more than a year since I had last seen her.

It was about two hours later that I heard the far-off sound of men's voices carried in the still of the night. I stood up and could see them huddled together as they came back over the Sgagarstaigh hill at a trot. They were carrying something heavy in their midst. My first thought was that they were back early, and only had the one deer to show for it.

I ran down to the path and struck out across the dry

summer heather, feeling the ground give beneath my feet and sap the strength from my legs. As I got nearer I could hear them breathing, like horses gasping at the end of a race, but not a single voice was raised in greeting when they saw me running towards them.

I scanned the faces for my father, and when I couldn't see him was confused. Had he stayed on to hunt some more on his own? Or had he been caught? I could hardly think of anything worse until I realised that it was not a deer that they carried in their midst, but a man. They came to a stop as I reached them, and I saw that the man was my father. His face deathly pale, his shirt and jacket soaked black by blood.

For a moment we stood in the semi-darkness and no one knew what to say. I was shocked to my core, and couldn't have spoken even had I found the words. I stared at my father, hanging by his arms and legs, sweat glistening on the faces of his bearers.

'They were waiting for us,' Donald Dubh said. 'As if they knew we were coming. The gamekeeper and water bailiff and half a dozen men from the estate. They had guns, boy!'

'Is he . . . ?' I couldn't bring myself to give voice to the thought.

'He's alive,' someone else said. 'But God knows for how much longer. They fired warning shots over our heads. But your father refused to run. As if he wanted them to catch us. Like he wanted to be paraded in front of the public and the press. Like a bloody martyr.' He paused. 'Off he went, walking towards them, shouting like a man demented. And some bastard shot him. Full in the chest.'

'Aye, and then the cowards turned and bloody ran,' Donald Dubh said. 'It's murder, pure and simple. But you can bet your life there's not one of them that'll be held to account for it.'

My mother was hysterical when we carried him into the house and laid him out on the stone floor next to the peat fire. Screaming and tearing at her clothes. Some of the men tried to calm her down. I saw my sisters peering out from the gloom of the back room, faces the colour of ash.

I knelt over my father and cut away his shirt. There was a gaping hole where the bullet had torn through his chest just below the ribcage, shattering bone and flesh. The bullet had not come out the other side, so I could only think it had lodged in his spine. I could tell from the feeble beating of his heart, and the fact that the wound had stopped bleeding, that he had lost too much blood to recover. He was in shock and fading fast.

He opened eyes clouded as if by cataracts, and I am not sure that he even saw me. His hand clutched my forearm. A grip like steel, before slowly relaxing. And a long, hollow sigh slipped from between his lips as the last breath of his life escaped his body.

I had never felt such desolation. His eyes were still open, staring up at me, and I gently placed my hand over them to draw the lids shut. Then I leaned over to kiss him on the lips, and my tears fell hot on skin that was already cold.

The coffin was a crudely made oblong box stained black from the roots of water lilies. It sat on the backs of two chairs set on the path outside our blackhouse. More than a hundred folk were gathered there in a silence broken only by the plaintive cries of gulls driven inshore by bad weather at sea, and the ocean itself sweeping in on a high tide to beat its endless rhythm on the shingle beach.

The men wore caps, and the women covered their heads with scarves. Those of us who could wore black. But we were a ragged collection of dispirited humanity, dressed in little more than tatters and rags, with faces starved of colour and hollowed out by famine.

The wind had swung around to the north-west, banishing the last vestiges of summer. A mourning sky laden with low cloud prepared to weep its sorrow on the land. Old blind Calum, still dressed in his threadbare blue jacket with its faded yellow buttons, stood by the coffin. His face was like putty, and he placed his skeletal old hand on the wood. In the years since he had lost his sight he had committed much of the Gaelic bible to heart. And he recited from it now.

'I am the resurrection and the life, saith the Lord: he that believeth in me, though he were dead, yet shall he live; and whosoever liveth and believeth in me, shall never die.'

And how I wished with all my heart that it would be true.

The coffin was fastened to oars on either side of it, and six of us lifted them, three to each, so that the coffin hung between us as we took my father on his final journey. Up over the hill and down the far side to the sweep of silver sand that curved around to the cemetery.

Only the men accompanied him. Thirty or forty of us. When finally we arrived at the little overgrown patch of machair where stones grew among the grass, myself and two others set about digging a hole in the sandy soil. It took nearly half an hour to make it deep enough for the coffin. There was no ceremony, no words were spoken, no minister present as it was lowered into the ground and covered over. Turf carried from the croft was bedded down on top of the loose soil and small stones placed at the head and foot.

And it was over. My father gone. Placed in the ground with his ancestors, existing now only in the memories of those who had known him.

The men turned away and walked back along the beach, silently retracing their footprints in the sand, leaving me there battered by the wind just below the standing stones where I had made my first tryst with Kirsty. Death comes, but the struggle to live goes on. Beyond the headland I could see women and children on the far shore. Pathetic figures stooped among the rocks and the retreating tide, scavenging for shellfish. And I felt the first spots of rain, like the tears that I could not cry myself.

I turned and was startled to see Kirsty standing there. She

wore a long black gown, a cape with its hood pulled up over her head. Her face was as white as bleached bones. We stood staring at each other for what seemed like an eternity, and I could see her shock at my appearance. She said in a very small voice, 'I wept for you when I heard the news.'

I frowned. 'How did you know?'

'Some of the servants told me a man had been shot during a raid on the deer forest. Men from the Baile Mhanais township, they said.' She paused, struggling to control her voice. 'For an awful moment I thought it might have been you. And then I heard that it was your father.' She sucked in her lower lip and reached out to hold my face in both her hands. Soft, cool hands on my burning skin. 'I am so sorry, Simon.'

And her sympathy, and that moment of tenderness, broke my resolve to be brave, and my tears came at last.

She said, 'The Sheriff-Depute has been to take statements, but it seems no one knows who fired the fatal shot. They say it was an accident.'

Anger flared in me briefly, but quickly subsided. Nothing could change what had happened. Nothing could bring my father back. All I could do now was be who he wanted me to be. I wiped away my tears. 'My family and my village are starving. He was just trying to feed us.'

Concern etched itself deeply in her frown. 'I heard that the potato crop has failed again. But my father is giving you grain, isn't he?'

'Look at me, Ciorstaidh! The grain we get barely keeps us

alive. I haven't eaten properly in months. Children and old people are dying.' Now my anger returned. My father's anger burning in me. 'Ask your father why people are starving to death while there are deer on the hill and fish in the rivers. Ask him!'

I turned away and she caught my arm. 'Simon!'

I wheeled around to face her, tormented by the feelings I had for her, but distanced by everything that separated us. I pulled my arm free. 'My family is my responsibility now. And I'm not going to let them die of hunger.'

'What are you going to do?'

'I'm going to bring home a deer to feed them. Or die trying. Just like my father did.' I hurried off down the slope without a backward glance, and strode out in the rain across the flat wet arc of sand left by the outgoing tide.

When the rain came in off the sea it swept across the hillside like a mist, robbing the land of its summer colours and stealing away its warmth. It was more than an hour since I had left the village, a stout rope coiled across my shoulder, my father's crossbow strapped to my back, a homemade quiver stitched together from an old trouser leg to hold the bolts he had laboured so long to make true.

I was soaked to the skin and shivering. No body fat to protect me from the elements. But I was unaware of my discomfort, wholly focused on the parcel of deer grazing in the valley below me. Five of them, backs to the weather, heads bowed. It had taken me nearly twenty minutes crawling on my belly to get close enough.

The rocks that provided my cover were halfway up the hillside, and I was spreadeagled on a flat slab of gneiss that lay slightly inclined on the slope of the hill. It kept me almost perfectly hidden, but provided the perfect angle for a shot.

I slid back on the rock so as not the break the skyline and armed the crossbow, nocking a bolt into place before sliding forward again to bring the deer into my sights. I wanted a nice clean shot.

Then a movement caught the corner of my eye, breaking my concentration, and I saw a party of five or six men crouched low and moving forward through the glen, downwind of the animals and hidden from their view by a cluster of rocks. They were almost obscured from me by the rain. A hunting party from the castle. I recognised a stalker from the estate, and some way back a gillie holding the pony that would carry the carcass of whatever they shot.

And then with something like shock I realised that among the hunters was Ciorstaidh's brother, George, betrayed by his distinctive red hair.

Their focus was on the deer, and I knew that they had not seen me in my elevated position. I altered the angle of my line of fire, and lowered my head to bring George fully into my sights. I held him there for several long moments, remembering how he had humiliated me in front of Ciorstaidh, my finger dangerously close to lifting the trigger and releasing the bolt that would take his life, just as my father's had been taken by someone in his father's employ. But every fibre of my being fought against it, and in the end I removed the bolt and released the tension from the crossbow.

I rolled out of sight to lie on my back, staring up at the pewter sky, and cursed my luck. Another few seconds and I'd have loosed my shot and the beast would be lying dead in the valley. But then the hunting party would almost certainly have stumbled upon me as I went down to perform the gralloch. So perhaps Lady Luck had favoured me after all.

A single shot rang out in the cold and wet of the late morning and I rolled over and crawled back to my vantage point. One of the hunters had shot the single stag in the group, and in that moment I realised that they were not shooting for food. They were after the trophy. A set of antlers.

But whoever had fired was a poor shot. The beast had been hit high up and towards his back end. He had fallen as the other deer scattered, but was thrashing now and struggling to get back to his feet. Head and front legs first, like a horse. A second shot missed altogether, and the animal was off and running, weaving and distressed, hunched over and clearly in pain. Up the slope and away through the heather. A third shot was fired, and in the time it took the first shooter to reload his flintlock the stag was out of sight.

All caution dispensed with, they were up and after him, running through the peat bog, splashing through the soft,

wet ground. One of them fell, and picked himself up dripping with peaty brown water.

I watched them as they went up and over the rise, George
and the stalker well ahead of the others. But there they
stopped, surveying the wilderness that lay ahead. A deep
valley strewn with boulders, the hills rising steep on both
sides. The valley floor was strength-sapping marsh, and the
primal landscape beyond was quickly lost in the smirr that
drifted through the hills.

From where I lay I could not see what they saw, but it was
clear to me that they had lost sight of the stag. The stragglers
caught them up on the rise, and there was a short and
heated debate before they turned reluctantly and headed
back the way they had come.

I could scarcely believe it. My father would have tracked a
wounded animal to the ends of the earth to deliver it from
pain. And it was clear to me that the poor beast was in agony
as he stumbled off into the next valley.

I waited until they had gone back down the glen before
breaking cover, then ran down the slope to the place the stag
had fallen. The peat bog was churned up where his hooves
had fought for grip to get him back on his feet. There was
blood in the grass. Dark red, almost black. My heart went out
to him. If he had to die, then the least he deserved was a
quick dispatch. Only to wound him, then leave him to die in
wretched torment, was unforgivable.

I knew what I must do, and set off at a trot in pursuit
of him.

Beyond the rise, I picked up his spoor. Although there was a good deal of blood at first, it gradually became less apparent, the wound coagulating, and I was hard pushed to spot any at all. But I knew that the animal would be bleeding inside, and the thought drove me on through the mist and rain, stumbling now, weakened by my hunger and the cold. I looked for broken heather roots and hoofprints in the peat marsh, dropping down to a desperately slow pace, knowing that every wasted moment meant more pain.

After a time I began to despair, not even certain that the water-filled hoofprints I saw were his.

I was close to giving up when I saw him. He had fallen down in a hollow by a small loch. I could hear his distress in the shallow bark of his breathing. I knew that the loss of blood would have starved him of oxygen. He would be dizzy and weak, and in considerable pain if the bullet had clipped the liver.

But I also knew that if he saw me coming he would panic and try to get back on his feet. And if I got too close, those antlers could be lethal. I dropped to one knee and stayed stock-still. He hadn't seen me, and I was still downwind.

Very slowly I approached him from the rear. One soft, careful step at a time I gained on him, until I saw the steam rising from his coat, and his stertorous breathing filled my ears. I laid down my crossbow and quiver and took out my father's long hunting knife. I would have to be quick and accurate.

Close enough now to smell him, I was on him in a single move, my knee pushed hard into the back of his neck, pulling his antlers towards me with my left hand. I reached around under his chin with my knife to draw the blade across his throat, severing both the jugular vein and the carotid artery. What little life there was left in his heart pumped the last of his blood out on to the grass.

I slid off him, to lie in the hollow by his head and watch his big doe eyes cloud over, just as my father's had done. He looked at me now, his life draining away, his pain dying with him. And all I could feel was guilt at the length of time it had taken me to find him.

When he was gone I got to my knees and rolled him on to his back. I grasped the skin of the scrotum and pulled it away from his body to cut it off, and remembered what my father always said when he performed this first, ritual act of the gralloch. *You'll no be needin' these nae mair.* And I ached again at his loss, and the loss too of this fine animal. I was sick of death.

But I forced myself to concentrate now, remembering how my father did this. It was vital, he always said, that the guts be removed intact. Any spillage would contaminate the meat.

I made a small incision and inserted two fingers, palm up, to stop the blade of my knife from catching the intestines, and slid it up towards the base of the sternum, opening up the abdominal wall. And so the gralloch began.

I worked in concentrated silence, with only the sound of my own breathing for company. It was hard, stomach-churning work, and I tried not to think too much about how this had once been a proud, sentient creature.

The fat of the deer was thick and soft when still warm, but it solidified in the cold. It covered my hands and forearms, gore from the cavity congealing in it so that it seemed as if I wore bright red gloves. I grabbed handfuls of sphagnum to try to clean it off, but it was an almost impossible task.

Finally the organs and intestines of the beast lay steaming in the grass and I rested for a while on my knees, leaning forward with my elbows planted in the peat, my forehead buried in the grass. I wanted to weep. But there was no time for self-pity. And just as I had seen my father do before me, I used mosses to wipe out the cavity, and rolled the creature over on to its back. I removed the coil of rope from my shoulder and tied it around the antlers, and along the top of the nose to loop around the jaws, hoping this would keep the head straight and stop the antlers catching on every rock and heather root as I dragged it.

But I had not anticipated just how weak I was. Even with all its insides removed, the beast was unimaginably heavy. I looped the rope around my chest beneath my armpits so that I could lean my whole body weight forward to pull it over the uneven ground, but I managed no more than two hundred yards before falling to my knees, physically and mentally spent. There was no way I could get the beast home.

Tears flowed then, and I gave full vent to my frustration and despair, knowing that both God and my father would be witness to my failure. My anguish echoed around the glen in the rain.

Ten minutes or more must have passed before I started to think what would my father have done. He would never have accepted defeat. Whatever the problem, he used to say, there was always an answer. And when the answer came to me it was simple. If I couldn't take the whole animal, then I would take a part of it.

The best meat is at the rear. The haunches. And I realised that somehow I needed to separate them from the front end of the animal. So I steeled myself to do battle with the beast once more.

But even after I had cut through the flesh and skin and hair along the bottom edge of each of the last ribs, the two halves of the animal were still attached by the spinal ligaments. To expose them to my knife I was forced to twist the rear half in one direction and the front half in the other. Exhausting work, and it took me several minutes to recover before seeking out the ligaments with the tip of my knife to sever them. Then one final push, twisting the haunches through a full 360 degrees to completely disarticulate the spine. And at last, with sweat almost blinding me, I had separated them from the rest of the carcass. They were, of course, still connected at the pelvis, but I hoped that would allow me to use my back and shoulders to carry them, with one leg crooked over each shoulder.

And so it proved. I sheathed my knife and heaved the remains of the creature on to my shoulders, straining my thighs to take the weight as I straightened my legs. I was up and mobile, and from somewhere found renewed determination.

I could not afford to stop, or to think, or to listen to muscles that were screaming at me to give up. I kept my head down, so as not to see the distance still to be travelled. One step at a time.

I thought of Ciorstaidh as I walked, and how I had carried her all that way to the castle in the knowledge that giving up was not an option. And I felt the same thing now. I owed it to my family, to my father, and to the animal whose life I was determined would not be wasted.

I have no idea how long I walked in that almost trancelike state. I had left the glen behind me and was up and over the rise, heading for the Sgagarstaigh hill. I had lost the feeling in almost every part of my body and was amazed that there was still any grip left in my hands.

By mid-afternoon there was a slight break in the clouds, sunlight appearing in transient daubs across the moor. I saw a rainbow, vivid against the blackened sky behind it. And away to my left, a first glimpse of the sea. I was tantalisingly close to home. Which was not a thought that I dared allow enter my mind.

My biggest danger here was in crossing the road to reach the path that led over the hill to Baile Mhanais. For I would be in full view of any passer-by. And there was often traffic on that road going to and from the castle at Ard Mor.

It was only now, as that thought crossed my mind, that I realised, with a sudden stab of panic, that I had somehow mislaid my father's crossbow. That thought alone robbed me of any physical control. My knees gave way, and I dropped to the ground, twisting as I fell to unload the weight of the haunches, and I lay there on the sodden moor with the remains of the stag tipped over at my side.

I tried to recall what I had done with the crossbow. I remembered laying it down with the quiver before leaping on to the neck of the stag. Which was where I must have left it. Lying among the grasses next to the front end of the deer, among all its guts and entrails. How could I have been so careless? It was my father's prized possession, and I knew that I could not go home without it.

I lay for a long time trying to summon the will and the energy to make the long return trek to recover it. And I could hear my father's voice in my head. Don't think about it, boy, just do it.

It took me perhaps twenty minutes to get back to the glen. The crossbow and the quiver lay where I had left them. And not a single bolt fired. I slung both over my back and set off at a trot again towards home.

My spirits lifted now. I felt stronger, nourished by hope and a sense that somehow I was close to achieving the impossible. I took courage from the feeling that somewhere my father was watching me, and that I was making him proud.

I had just come over the Sgagarstaigh hill when I saw them, and dropped instantly to the ground. The hunting party which had shot and wounded the stag was crossing the peat marsh from the road, where a pony and cart waited with the gillie. They had spotted the hind quarters of the deer not a hundred yards away, where I had let it fall, and were approaching it with some consternation. On reaching it, they were suddenly alert. I saw George's head snapping up, sharp eyes quickly scanning the horizon, and I ducked my head and pressed myself into the grass. I knew I daren't look up or I would be seen.

I cursed my stupidity for having left the carcass lying in full view of the road. After all that I had been through, to get so close to home and yet still stare defeat in the face was almost more than I could bear.

Eventually I risked lifting my head, and saw them dragging the rear section of the deer back to the road. The gillie and stalker loaded it on to the cart. I could not imagine what they were doing here, and could only think that the gamekeeper had sent them back out to find and kill the wounded animal. Heads were lifted again towards the horizon, and I pressed myself into the ground once more.

When next I dared to look, the party was heading off along the road in the direction of the castle, the meat that would have fed my family with them on the cart. I let my head fall back into the grass, eyes closed. I wanted to weep, but I had no tears left. My defeat and my exhaustion were absolute, and it was fully ten minutes or more before I found the strength to get to my feet and drag myself off on the weary road home.

I saw smoke seeping up through the thatch of the Baile Mhanais blackhouses as I came over the brow of the hill. I was consumed by two things. Fatigue and failure. And almost wished there were no afterlife, so that my father would not have seen how I had let him down.

It was hard to believe that it was only this morning that we had put him in the ground. A lifetime had passed since then, and I had no idea how I was going to face my mother and my sisters empty-handed.

A voice carried on the wind seemed to call my name. At first I thought it was just my imagination. Then it came again, and I looked up to see Kirsty on the hill. This was the lowest ebb of my life, and I didn't want her to see me like this. But she waved frantically for me to come to her and I could not just walk away.

Reluctantly I left the path and climbed the hill. As I reached her I could hardly meet her eyes, and when I did I saw the shock in them. Covered in the blood and fat of the deer, and soaked to the skin, I must have presented a ghoulish and pathetic figure. 'My God,' she said, her voice little more than a whisper. But she didn't ask what had happened.

Instead she stooped to lift a large wicker basket at her feet. A checkered cloth covered its contents and she held it out to me.

'What's this?' My voice sounded strange to me, oddly disconnected.

'Take it.' She pushed it into my chest, and I grabbed the handle. It was unexpectedly heavy.

'What is it?'

She said, 'There is cheese, and eggs, and cold meat. And a quiche from the kitchen at Ard Mor.'

I had no idea what a quiche was, but all I could feel was shame. I pushed it back at her. 'I can't take this.' And I saw anger fire up her eyes.

'Don't be stupid, Simon. It's your responsibility to feed your family. You told me yourself. And if you knew how much I have risked to bring you this . . .' She cut herself off, and I was unable to meet her eyes again. 'There'll be more. As and when I can get it.'

I felt her hand on my face and looked up, tears brimming along my lower lids. She leaned in to kiss me softly on the lips and turned to hurry away. I stood there watching her go, until she had dipped below the nearest horizon and disappeared from view. I felt the weight of the food in my hands and knew that I had to put my shame aside. I would not go home empty-handed after all.

As I turned to go back down the hill, my eye was caught by a movement. A figure standing at the far end of the path where it cut around the hill towards the road. Two, maybe three hundred yards away. He stood motionless, a black cut-out against a grey sky. And it was not until he turned away, and I saw him in profile, that I realised it was Ciorstaidh's brother, George.

CHAPTER TWENTY-THREE

I

It was Arseneau who met Sime and Blanc at the harbour with the minibus and the news that they had found Norman Morrison.

The wind had felt much stronger on the return crossing and now, as they turned up Chemin Mountain at the end of Main Street, they saw the crowd on the clifftop buffeted by it. A dozen or more police and civilian vehicles were clustered around the Cowell House. Arseneau parked on the road just beyond them and the three detectives walked across the grass to the fence where the crowd was gathered. Perhaps twenty islanders, and several uniformed police officers from Cap aux Meules.

Sime glanced towards the summerhouse and saw a pale-faced Kirsty watching from the porch. He felt a wave of disillusion wash over him and knew that very soon he would have to face her with her lies.

A gate opened on to narrow concrete steps set into the angle of the cliffs, an incongruous grey against the red of the stone. They led down at a steep angle to a tiny jetty, partially formed by a natural arc of rock, and augmented by the same interlocking concrete blocks that made up the breakwater at the harbour. A blue-and-white four-person Seadoo Challenger jet launch was secured to rusted iron rings by weathered ropes and covered over by canvas. It rose and fell violently on the incoming swell. A group of officers wearing orange life jackets was making its way with difficulty across the adjoining outcrop of rocks, carrying among them the lifeless form of Norman Morrison. It brought to Sime's mind the image of his ancestor's father being carried back from the deer hunt. When they finally got to the jetty they laid the body down on the concrete, and seawater foamed out of his mouth and back across his face into open eyes.

Sime could see Crozes down there with the nurse and Aucoin and Marie-Ange. He pushed through the silent group of spectators and started off down the steps. Blanc followed. It was exposed here and he felt the wind yanking at his jacket and trousers and flattening his curls.

The nurse was wearing jeans and a yellow anorak and was crouched over the corpse as they got to the jetty. Morrison had horrific multiple injuries. Most of the back of his head was missing. His skin was bleached white, flesh bloated and straining against what was left of his pullover and jeans. From the abnormal lie of his limbs it appeared that both of his legs and one arm were broken. One shoe was missing, revealing a distended foot that bulged through a hole in his sock.

The nurse stood up. She was unnaturally white, her skin almost blue around the eyes. She turned to Crozes. 'Impossible for me to tell you how he died.' She had to raise her voice above the wind and the sound of the sea breaking all around them. 'But injuries like that . . . I can only think he must have fallen off the cliff. And from the state of the body I'd say he's probably been in the water since the night he went missing.'

Crozes flashed a quick look at Sime then turned back to the nurse. 'No way he was alive last night, then?'

'Not a chance.'

'What in God's name was he doing over here during a storm?' Marie-Ange said.

No one had any answers. Crozes was grim. 'Better get him bagged up and over to the airport. The sooner we get an autopsy the better.' And he turned to Marie-Ange. 'I want to take apart that room of his up in the attic. Piece by piece.'

II

The stillness of Mrs Morrison's sitting room was broken only by the wind whistling around the windows and the sound of a mother softly sobbing for her dead child. The sky outside had grown heavy and the only light in the room, as before, was reflected off all its polished surfaces.

On the drive over, Blanc briefed Crozes on their interview with Ariane Briand, and the lieutenant almost smiled. He looked at Sime. 'I'll sit in with Thomas at the monitors when you interview her,' he said. 'Be interesting to hear how the lamenting widow talks her way out of this one.' But first there was the matter of the man-boy found dead in the water below her house.

Mrs Morrison sat wringing her hands in her armchair by the cold of the dead fire. 'I don't understand,' she kept saying. 'I just don't understand.' As if understanding might somehow bring back her son.

Sime and Crozes sat uncomfortably on the settee, and Blanc emerged from the kitchen with a cup of tea for the grieving mother. He set it down on the coffee table beside her, on top of the book she was reading. 'Here you are, Madame Morrison,' he said. But Sime doubted if she was even aware of him. He sat in the armchair opposite.

Upstairs, Marie-Ange and her crime scene assistant were making a forensic examination of Norman Morrison's bedroom.

Sime said, 'You told us he'd never run off like this before.'

'Never.'

'But he was in the habit of wandering around the island?'

'He went walking a lot. He liked the open air, and he told me once he loved the sting of the rain in his face when it blows in on a strong south-westerly.'

'Did he have any friends?'

She stole a glance at him through her tears. 'Not since the children stopped coming. Folk his own age tended to avoid him. Embarrassed, I suppose. And some of the teenagers used to tease him. He got upset when they did that.'

'He was upset, you said, the night he went missing.'

She nodded.

'Because of Mr Cowell's murder.'

'He didn't care about Mr Cowell. It was Mrs Cowell he was concerned about.'

'Do you think he might have gone to try and see her?'

She tensed at the question, and avoided Sime's eye. 'I have no idea where he went, or why.'

'But he was found at the foot of the cliffs below her house. So he must have gone there for a reason.'

'I suppose he must.'

Sime thought for a moment. To discover the motivation of a man with the mind of a twelve-year-old was not an easy thing, and his mother, he felt, was being less than helpful. 'Did he ever go out at night? After dark, I mean.'

Mrs Morrison turned towards the cup of tea that Blanc had made, as if aware of it for the first time. She lifted it to her lips to take a sip, holding it in both hands, and made the slightest shrug of her shoulders. 'He wasn't in the habit of asking my permission.'

'You mean he did go out after dark?'

'I wouldn't know. I am in my bed at ten sharp every night, Mr Mackenzie. And Norman at times had trouble sleeping. I know he worked on his ceiling into the small hours some nights. He might have gone out for a breath of air from time to time.' She sucked in her lower lip to stop it trembling and fight back more tears. 'But I wouldn't know.'

Crozes said, 'Was Norman depressed, Mrs Morrison?'

She seemed puzzled. 'Depressed?'

'You said when the children stopped coming he retreated into the world of his little universe upstairs.'

'He wasn't depressed, sir. He just refocused his life. As you do. As I did when my husband died.'

'So when you say he was upset, you wouldn't describe him as suicidal?'

Now she was shocked. 'Good God, no. Norman would never have taken his own life. Such a thing would never have entered his mind!'

A soft knocking at the door brought all their heads around. Marie-Ange stood tentatively in the hall at the open door. 'Sorry to interrupt,' she said. 'I think there's something you should see.'

'Excuse me, madame,' Crozes said, and he got up to go out to the hall.

'Simon, too.' Marie-Ange glanced beyond him to her estranged husband, and Sime saw the most peculiar look on her face. He stood up immediately.

They left Blanc with Mrs Morrison and climbed up into the roof of the house. Marie-Ange had brought in crime scene lights and Norman's bedroom was lit up like a film set. Sime and Crozes slipped on plastic shoe covers and latex gloves before entering. It was stiflingly hot up here, and in the glare of the lights the colours of Norman's little universe seemed unnaturally lurid.

The floor had been cleared, and items laid out in some kind of sequence on the bed. Soft toys and model trains, and Norman's dismembered dolly, had been put into plastic bags.

Marie-Ange said, 'I haven't touched the ceiling yet. But we've been photographing it in some detail.' She glanced at Sime. 'There's stuff here that's only apparent when you start examining it minutely. Stuff that seems like it's just a part of the fabric of it until you look more closely.' She used a pair of sprung plastic tweezers as a pointer. 'You see this little group of houses here . . .' She indicated a semicircle of terraced houses around a circular area of grass, like a small park. It was fenced off from the street, and the plastic figures of several upside-down children were gathered around a bonfire. It glowed red at its centre, with a tiny circle of stones around it. 3D smoke had been created by cleverly threading puffs of cotton wool on to a piece of shaped wire that was almost invisible.

Crozes and Sime peered at it closely to try to see what it was they weren't seeing.

Very delicately, Marie-Ange caught a length of fencing with the tips of her tweezers and gently worked it free of the Plasticine. She held it up for the two men to look at. It was a hair clasp, a small arc of comb, the teeth of which had made up the fence posts. 'There's more of them,' she said, and dropped it into Crozes's outstretched hand for him to look at. 'Four in total. But here's the really interesting thing . . .'

She turned back to the ceiling, reaching up with her

tweezers to invade the embers of the bonfire with the tip of them. The stones around the glow appeared to be tiny moulded pieces of Blu-tack. She worked the tweezers, trying to catch hold of something hidden beneath the Blu-tack. Finally she found what she was looking for and moved the tweezers gently back and forth, to pull away the red glow at the heart of the fire. Revealing something much larger than the circle of it which had been exposed. An oval of semi-precious stone set in gold, its coiled-up chain concealed beneath the Plasticine. She turned, and with her free hand took hold of Sime's right hand so that the pendant and his signet ring could be viewed side by side. The arm and sword engraved in each stone were identical. Sime felt a shiver run through him.

III

He emptied the contents of the plastic bag on to the glass tabletop in the summerhouse and looked up to see her reaction. It was clear that Kirsty was shocked. And it was evident to Sime that she was sleeping as little as he was. She seemed to have aged in just three days. The hollows of her face a little deeper, the shadows a little darker. Even the startling blue of her eyes seemed to have lost its lustre.

He leaned over to angle one of the interview cameras down to focus on the items scattered across the table. 'Do you recognise these?'

She went straight to the pendant, lifting it up to run delicate fingers over the engraving of the arm and sword. 'I told you it was identical. Let me see?' And she reached for his hand and his signet ring to make the comparison. 'Where did you get these?'

'Are they all yours?' Along with the pendant there were two pairs of earrings, the four hair clasps used to make the fence, a necklace of paste diamonds that Norman had set along the centre of a road like cat's eyes, a bracelet used to contain a small lake.

She nodded. 'Where were they?'

'Did you ever see Norman Morrison's little universe on his bedroom ceiling?'

'Not personally, no. But everyone knew about it. I think a lot of people went to see it, just out of curiosity.' She frowned. 'What's that got to do with my things?'

'They were all embedded in the Plasticine, a part of his little universe, Mrs Cowell. Unrecognisable for what they were, but performing one kind of landscape function or another.' He paused. 'Do you have any idea how they came to be in his possession?'

Her consternation was evident. She was at a complete loss. 'I . . . I don't know. He must have taken them from the house.'

'When we talked about the missing photograph you said he'd never been in the house.'

'He hadn't.' She caught herself, frustrated by the contradiction. 'At least, not to my knowledge.'

'You think he broke in one night when your husband was away on business and you were sleeping over here?'

'He wouldn't have had to break in. The door's never locked. And he couldn't have taken them all at once. I'd have noticed. He must have been in the house several times over a period.' Her voice caught in her throat, and she fought to hold back tears. 'Poor Norman.' She looked up. 'What on earth was he doing over here on the night of the storm?'

'His mother said he was worried about you.'

She put her hand on her chest and closed her eyes, shaking her head. 'I never realised the obsession ran so deep.' She looked at Sime. 'What happened to him, do you think?'

Sime shrugged. 'Who knows? Maybe he came over here to see that you were okay. Maybe he didn't realise there was a cop in the big house. Maybe he got spooked and lost his way in the dark. It was quite a storm. Well, you know that. And he must have been walking blind in it.'

She let her head fall forward to stare in some distress at the items on the table that he had stolen from her to be a part of his secret world. 'So sad.'

Sime reset the camera to focus on Kirsty once more and sat down facing her in what had become his usual seat. It was raining outside now, and though not dark yet, there was very little light left in the day.

She looked up with a weary expression of resignation on her face. 'More questions?'

He nodded and plunged straight in. 'Why didn't you tell us that you had paid a visit to the Briand home the night before the murder?'

Colour rose on her cheeks and she took a moment to answer. 'Because I knew it would influence your interpretation of events on the night of the murder itself.'

'Your version of events.'

She half-lifted an eyebrow. 'See what I mean?'

'And you didn't think we would find out?'

'I wasn't exactly thinking straight about anything. To be honest it seemed irrelevant to me. All that mattered was what happened that night. Whatever had unravelled, or been said the night before, was beside the point.'

'Unravelled?' Sime frowned. 'That seems a strange word to use.'

'Does it?' And she thought about it herself. 'Maybe that's because it describes the way I felt. Like I was unravelling.'

'You told me that you were glad to discover James was having an affair. That it brought to an end a situation with which you were deeply unhappy.'

'I know what I told you.'

'But that wasn't true.'

'It was!' Indignation flared briefly in her eyes.

'Then how do you explain your behaviour? Turning up at Ariane Briand's door, rampaging about her house looking for James?'

'Rampaging? Is that how she described it?'

'How would you describe it?'

She let her eyes drop to her hands in her lap. 'Pathetic,' she said quietly. 'That's what it was. What I was. Sad and pathetic. Everything I told you about the way I felt was true. But I also felt hurt, and humiliated.' She looked up again, and he thought he saw an appeal for understanding in her eyes. 'I'd been drinking that night.' And now he saw her shame. 'It's not something I'm in the habit of doing. So it didn't take much to tip me over the edge. You know, sitting alone here in the dark, thinking about all the wasted years, remembering every little thing he'd said, all his grand gestures and prom- ises, and wondering if Ariane Briand was the first, or just the latest in a long succession. All those business trips away. I wanted to know. I wanted to confront him.'

'So you took the boat that you keep at the jetty below the cliffs?'

She nodded. 'It was pure madness. I'm not great with boats at the best of times. But the alcohol had me all fired up and I didn't really care. If the weather had been worse I'd probably never have made it. James would still be alive, and my body would have been found washed up on a beach somewhere.' She was looking in his direction, but he doubted that she saw him. She was somewhere else, reliving the madness. 'I was, literally, unravelling.' And suddenly she jumped focus and her eyes seared into him. 'I'm not proud of myself, Mr Mackenzie. God knows what was going through my mind, or what kind of emotional state I was in. I just wanted to have it out with him. Face to face. Clear the air. I just wanted to know. Everything.'

'And when he wasn't there you turned on the next best thing. His lover.'

'I didn't turn on her!'

'According to Madame Briand you said . . .' Sime looked down to consult the notes taken during her formal interview, 'I'm not giving him up without a fight. And if I can't have him, neither you nor anyone else will.' He looked up again. 'Are those your words?'

She shook her head. 'I don't think so.'

'So she paraphrased you?'

'It doesn't sound like me.'

'But was that the sentiment you expressed?'

Her embarrassment was clear. 'Probably.'

'Was it or wasn't it?'

'Yes!' she snapped at him. 'Yes, yes, yes! I lost it, okay? Drink, emotion . . .' She shrugged helplessly. 'Whatever. I was coming apart at the seams. It felt like my life was over. Tied to this damned island. Alone. Almost nobody my own age left. No way I was ever going to meet someone else. All I could see stretching ahead of me were a lot of lonely years in an empty house.'

Sime sat back and let a silence settle between them again, like dust after a fight. 'You realise, Mrs Cowell, that what you said to Madame Briand could be construed as a threat to kill your husband.'

'Well, of course, you'd just love to give it that construction, wouldn't you?' She imbued the word construction with all the sarcasm she could muster.

'You told me that on the night of the murder you didn't know that your husband was coming back to the island.'

She gazed at her hands.

Sime waited for several moments. 'Are you going to respond or not?'

She looked up. 'You didn't ask a question.'

'All right, is it true that you didn't know your husband was coming home that night?'

Her eyes drifted away towards the window behind him, and the view out over the cliffs. And again she made no response.

'According to Madame Briand he received a short, fractious call on his cellphone earlier in the evening and left immediately afterwards. Did you make that phone call?'

Her eyes drifted back in his direction, but all the fight had gone out of them.

'We can check the phone records, Mrs Cowell.'

'Yes,' she said quietly, without further prompting.

'What did you say to him?'

'I told him I wanted to talk to him.'

'To say what?'

'All the things I wanted to have out with him the night before. Only I wasn't drunk anymore. Just kind of cold, you know. Angry. Wanting to know stuff that we'd never had the chance to talk about, so I wouldn't be wondering about it for the rest of my life.'

'And what did he say?'

'That we'd talked enough, and he had no intention of coming to the island. At least, not then.'

'So how did you persuade him?'

'I told him that first I was going to gather together all his clothes and make a nice big bonfire of them on top of the cliffs. And if he still didn't come I was going to set his precious house on fire, his computer and all of his business records with it.' She almost smiled. 'That seemed to do the trick.'

He braced himself for a final onslaught. 'So everything you told us about what happened that night was a lie.'

'No!'

'When you failed to confront him the night before at Ariane Briand's house, you issued a veiled threat to kill him, and the following night lured him to the island by threatening to set his house on fire. When he arrived you fought, verbally at first, then physically.'

'No!'

'Whether it was premeditated or not, you grabbed a knife and in a frenzy you stabbed him three times in the chest.'

'That's not what happened!'

'You immediately regretted it and tried to revive him. And when that didn't work you made up a story about some intruder and ran off to tell it to your neighbours.'

'There was an intruder. I did not kill my husband!' She glared at him, breathing heavily, and he sat back in his seat, aware that his hands were trembling. He didn't dare pick up the papers on his knee for fear that it would show.

She looked at him with hatred in her eyes. 'I think the lion just got the gazelle.'

'It's only what you can expect from a prosecuting attorney if you ever go on the witness stand, Mrs Cowell.' He knew that all the evidence was circumstantial, and accusations alone would not secure a conviction. But just one tiny piece of forensic evidence against her would be enough to tip the balance.

Her face was flushed. Whether from fear, or guilt, or anger it was impossible to tell.

'Are you charging me?'

'No.'

'Good.' She stood up. 'Then this interview is over. And if you want to talk to me again you can do it in the presence of a lawyer.' She strode past him, pushing the screen door open, and went out on to the porch. He got up to look from the window and watched as she ran down the steps and walked off along the edge of the cliffs. Her arms were folded, hair streaming out behind her, and it made him think of Ciorstaidh striding off across the machair after she had told his ancestor that she hated him.

When Sime turned back to the room, Crozes was standing there. He looked exhilarated. 'Just about nailed her,' he said. 'Great job, Sime.'

CHAPTER TWENTY-FOUR

I

The bar shimmered in semi-darkness, light washing down across bottles and optics from hidden overhead lighting. Sime sat at the polished counter on his own, while a bored barman cleaned glasses to keep himself busy. He hadn't felt much like eating with the others, and now they were all in the bowling alley. Friends and colleagues who had worked together on the same team for months, sharing friendship and downtime. Laughing. Cheering when someone made a strike, voices echoing around the cavernous bowling hall. There was a feeling that they were just one step away from cracking this case, and spirits were high. Norman Morrison had been dismissed as a red herring. At worst it seemed that his death had been nothing more than a tragic accident.

Sime had his back to them, but couldn't shut out the noise.

He was on his third or fourth whisky and had begun to lose count. But the oblivion he had been hoping for seemed no nearer than it had when he first sat down. If the alcohol was having any effect on him he wasn't aware of it.

As hard as he tried he couldn't banish from his mind the wounded animal look in Kirsty's eyes when she'd told him that the lion had just got the gazelle. It had left him feeling ruthless and predatory.

He no longer knew what to believe about her. But the fact that she had told him the truth about the pendant was no longer in any doubt, and it left him feeling hugely unsettled. How did they come to possess the same family crest engraved in the same semi-precious carnelian? One a ring, one a pendant. Clearly pieces of a matching set.

Crozes had been dismissive. Nothing to do with the case, he'd said. And Sime was unable to find any grounds with which to challenge that assessment. There was no obvious link to the murder.

And yet still Sime was haunted by that moment he'd first set eyes on the widow and been convinced he knew her. Somehow in that light the arm-and-sword crest seemed less of a coincidence. But he could not for the life of him imagine what it was that connected them.

If there was a connection, and the matching ring and pendant had some significance beyond coincidence, then he could only think that the answer must lie in the diaries. Something in all of this had sparked his dreams and recollections of them. And Annie had thought there was some mention of the ring in them, though he had no memory of that himself. Of course, he knew that his grandmother had not read them everything from the journals. And he vaguely recalled his parents expressing concern about one of the stories. Not suitable for young children, they had said.

He needed to get his hands on those diaries.

'Another one of those, monsieur?' The barman nodded towards his empty glass on the bar. But Sime couldn't face another. He shook his head. It was time to face the night, with all its sleepless demons, and lie on his back to watch the TV screen send its shadow dancers around the walls.

On the walk down the hall he felt as if he were pulling each foot free of treacle. He closed the door of his room behind him and leaned back against it. When he shut his eyes the ground shifted beneath his feet and for a moment he thought he was going to fall over. He opened them again quickly.

He found the remote for the TV in the dark and turned it on. Better to have something meaningless to shut out, than to lie listening to reproachful silence. He kicked off his shoes and lay gingerly on the bed. His ribs were less painful than before. The nurse was right, he thought. Just bruised. And he wondered again who had attacked him the previous night. Not Norman Morrison. And certainly not Kirsty. So who? He spread his hands on the bed on either side of his hips, as if some unseen pressure were bearing down on him and pressing him into the mattress.

His throat felt rough and his eyes were on fire. He closed

them and saw flickering red light through the lids. His breathing was slow but laboured, as if each breath took a conscious effort. His whole body was screaming out for sleep.

The hours passed in an almost fevered delirium, not always fully conscious, but never quite asleep. The passage of time was punctuated by frequent, involuntary glances at the clock. The last time he'd looked it was 1.57. Now it was 2.11. The TV channel had reverted to its nightly diet of tele-shopping special offers. Tonight, a kitchen device capable of chopping any vegetable into a dozen different shapes or sizes.

Sime swung his legs off the bed and stood up. He walked stiffly into the bathroom, avoiding the mirror, and ran the cold tap. Cupped hands splashed icy water on to his face. The shock of it brought momentary relief from the fatigue that numbed him, and he rubbed himself vigorously dry with a towel. In the bedroom he slipped his feet back into their shoes.

Beyond the curtain he slid open the inner glass door, then the fly screen, and unlocked the outer window, sliding it aside and slipping out into the darkness of the car park. The wind blew in across the bay in cold gusts. He zipped up his hoodie, pushed his hands deep into his pockets and started walking. Anything to avoid the excruciating boredom that came with insomnia.

The yellow light of street lamps fell in gloomy patches on the tarmac, reflecting off the roofs of cars in the car park. The main north–south highway was deserted. Lights shining from the windows of the hospital across the way were the only sign of life. Lights that shone for the sick and the dead, and for those who had to deal with both.

He had walked no more than fifty metres when he heard a woman cry out. And then a man's voice. At first he thought that perhaps the woman was being attacked, and he spun around looking for the source of the voices. And then it came to him that these were the sounds of people making love. Voices that drifted out into the night from one of the hotel rooms, issuing from behind curtains drawn across doors left open for air.

Sime closed his eyes. Other people's lives, he thought, and felt the ache of lost love, of moments once shared and now misplaced. Although his marriage was dead and hopelessly beyond resuscitation, he missed the warmth and comfort that comes with being close to another human being.

He stood for a self-conscious moment, listening to the shared experience of the strangers beyond the curtain, almost wallowing in his own misery. Before an ugly thought wormed its way through his self-pity. He looked back along the row of glass doors to his own and made a quick count. And then a moment of pure, incandescent jealousy seared his soul.

Without even thinking, he strode towards the lovers' room and slid the screen door roughly aside, dragging the curtains out of his way. Pale light washed into the room from the street lamps outside, spilling across the bed and startling the man and woman mid-passion. The man rolled to one side, and the woman sat up, wide-eyed and staring towards the figure who stood silhouetted in the doorway. The bedside light snapped on, and Sime gazed in disbelief at the dishevelled figures of Marie-Ange and Daniel Crozes, their nakedness only half hidden by a tangle of sheets.

'Sime!' There was both disbelief and alarm in Marie-Ange's almost involuntary evocation of his name.

So many things passed through his mind in a single moment that not one of them achieved any clarity. His wife and his boss were making love in her hotel room. Two people having sex. People he knew. One he respected, the other he used to love. And when suddenly the fog of confusion cleared he realised with a sickening sense of betrayal that this was not a one-night stand. He saw the half-empty bottle of champagne that stood on the dresser, the two empty glasses. The clothes discarded carelessly on the floor.

'How long?' he said.

Marie-Ange clutched the sheets to her chest to hide her breasts, as if he might never have seen them before. 'It's none of your business. We are no longer an item, Sime. Our marriage is over.'

'How long?'

But she could not maintain her facade of righteous indignation, and turned her head to avoid his eyes, the accusation in them and all his hurt.

Sime switched his focus toward Crozes. 'Lieutenant?' he said, his voice laden with irony, and Crozes couldn't look him in the eye.

'I'm sorry, Sime,' he said.

And Sime went from stillness to fury before his brain could engage in reason. He crossed the room in several long strides and grabbed his superior officer by the shoulders, pulling him from the bed and slamming him hard back against the wall. All the air escaped Crozes's lungs in a single breath, almost at the same moment as Sime's bunched fist sank into his gut, causing him to double up. Without any predetermination, Sime's knee came up into his face, bursting Crozes's lip on his front teeth and spraying blood all over his naked chest and thighs. He heard Marie-Ange screaming, and Crozes's voice gurgling through the blood in his mouth. But Sime was gripped by a rage that wouldn't let him go and he swung Crozes through three hundred and sixty degrees to smash up against the wall again. A chair went flying. The champagne bottle toppled and smashed one of the glasses. Sime swung a fist and caught Crozes on the side of his head. The lieutenant fell to his knees, and only the low, threatening imperative in Marie-Ange's voice stopped him from going for the kill.

'Stop right now or you're a fucking dead man!'

He turned and saw her kneeling on the bed, the sheets and all modesty abandoned now, to be replaced by her standard-issue Glock 26 handgun, held in both hands and levelled at his head.

There were voices outside the hotel room and a frantic banging on the door.

Sime glared at his wife and one-time lover, breathing hard. 'You're not going to shoot me.'

Her eyes were arctic cold. 'Try me.'

And suddenly the madness was over, receding like water after a flash flood. Sime looked at Crozes, bloodied and battered and doubled up on the floor, and for a moment he almost felt sorry for him. He wondered why he had been gripped by such rage. People fall in love, after all. For a thousand different reasons. It chooses them. Not the other way around. And then he realised it was their lies that left him feeling so betrayed, so inconsolably angry.

'For Christ's sake open up in there!' he heard a voice coming from the other side of the door. Fists still pounded on it. He stepped over the prone figure of Crozes and opened the door. Thomas Blanc, Arseneau and two other officers were bunched together in the corridor, wide-eyed in amazement. He saw them switch focus to the room behind him. Crozes lying bleeding on the floor, Marie-Ange stark naked on the bed, the Glock still clutched in her hand.

He pushed through the gaping mouths without a word and stalked off down the corridor, lost in a cauldron of bewilderment, regret, anger, hurt. He needed out, he needed air, he needed time to think, to reappraise. The sound of footsteps in pursuit was accompanied by Thomas Blanc's voice. 'Sime, Sime. For God's sake stop, man!'

But Sime ignored him, pushing open the swing door out to reception and startling the night porter, before slamming through the front doors and out into the cold and dark.

He was halfway across the car park, walking blindly into the night, before Blanc caught his arm and forced him to stop. He turned to be confronted by the alarm and incomprehension in Blanc's eyes, facing him with his own wild stare of what must have seemed like madness.

'Are you insane, Sime!' It wasn't so much a question as a statement. 'Have you any idea what you just did? Crozes is a senior officer, and you've just beaten the crap out of him.'

'He's also been sleeping with my wife for God knows how long.' Sime had no idea what reaction he expected from Blanc, but what he hadn't anticipated was the embarrassment he saw. His co-interrogator seemed at a loss for words. And the truth dawned on Sime with a sickening sense of humiliation. 'You knew.'

Blanc looked at the ground as Sime pulled his arm free of his grasp. His discomfort was acute.

'Which means everyone knew, right?'

Blanc managed to meet his gaze for just a moment before his eyes flickered away again.

'But no one thought to tell me.'

Blanc sucked in a deep breath. 'We thought we were doing you a favour, Sime, protecting you. Really.' There was a plea for understanding in his eyes.

Sime glared at him with anger and dislike. 'Fuck you,' he said quietly. 'Fuck you all.' And he turned and strode off into the dark.

II

The harbour was dominated at its south side by a large rock that towered over the quays. A wooden staircase zigzagged its way up to a viewpoint at the top. Sime stood there, fully exposed to the wind, having made the long slow climb with leaden legs. He had walked aimlessly in an almost trancelike state during all the hours of the night, before pitching up at the harbour. There he had stood at the water's edge staring out across the bay towards Entry Island. Somehow he always seemed drawn back to it. Only a handful of lights twinkled faintly in the distance to betray its presence in darkness.

Now he stood clutching the wooden rail on the viewpoint, braced against the wind that powered out of the south-west. He saw the lights of the islands spread out below him, stretching away to north and south. He knew that sunrise was not far away, and for the first time fully understood the saying that the darkest hour comes just before the dawn.

While walking blindly through the night he had forced himself to think about nothing, entering a nearly zen-like state in which he had allowed none of the events of the last few days to impinge on his consciousness. Only now, overtaken by total exhaustion, did his resolve crumble, permitting those thoughts to flood his brain.

He replayed his life of the last few months in an endless loop, picking up for the first time on all the little details he had missed. The tell-tale signs he had ignored, consciously or otherwise. It seemed to him, looking back, that Marie-Ange and Crozes must have been having an affair for well over a year. She had converted her guilt into an anger that allowed her to blame him. Her infidelity had become his fault. If she had been forced into the arms of a lover, Sime was to blame. It explained so much. How affection had turned to contempt, intimacy to impatience and then anger.

And somehow he understood, for the first time since she had left, what it was he felt. Grief. For the lover he had lost. Almost as if she had died. Except that the body was still there. Walking, talking, taunting, tormenting him.

He clutched the rail, holding himself steady, his body rigid with tension, and he was caught almost unawares by the trickle of hot tears that ran down his cheeks.

It was still dark when he got back to the hotel. The long, low, two-storey building lay silently beneath the yellow glow of the streetlights. There was no hint of the drama which had played itself out there just a few hours before. Sime wondered how many of the team were asleep, what whispered words had passed between them in rooms and corridors. But found that he didn't really care any more. The acute sense of humiliation had passed, leaving him empty of emotion, and indifferent to the opinions of others.

The night porter gazed at him from behind the reception desk with a surreptitious curiosity. In his room, the tele-shopping channel was selling an exercise machine to provide a whole-body workout. Sime locked all the doors and turned the TV off. He kicked away his shoes and slipped between the sheets still fully dressed. It was just after 5.30 a.m., and he lay shivering until gradually he started to recover some heat. A slow-burn warmth began to seep through his limbs, perme-ating his thoughts. He felt his body go limp, the red glow of the digital display on the clock fading to black as lids like lead closed on aching eyes . . .

CHAPTER TWENTY-FIVE

The notices of eviction arrived just days after my father's funeral, but none of us has any intention of leaving.

I feel the wind in my face, cooling my sweat as I toil over this stubborn ground. It is not cold, but the summer sky is laden with rain, and the stiffening of the breeze tells me it won't be long in releasing it. I have a spade in my hands, digging stones out from beneath my feet, trying to make something arable out of this wilderness. The soil here is thin and sandy and full of stones. But if we are to survive this cursed famine then we need to grow more food.

I look up from my labours and catch sight of Ciorstaidh running down the hill towards me. She is pink-faced and breathless, and I am pleased to see her until she gets close and I catch the look on her face.

When she reaches me she takes several moments to recover her breath. 'They're coming,' she gasps.

'Who?'

She is still having troubling finding her voice. 'The Sheriff-Depute and about thirty constables. And a band of men from the estate led by George. They've all been drinking ale at the castle to fortify themselves.'

I close my eyes and in the darkness can feel the end of everything I have known just a breath away.

'You have to persuade the villagers to leave.'

I open my eyes and shake my head slowly. 'They won't.'

'They must!'

'This is their home, Ciorstaidh. They won't leave it. To a man, woman and child, we were born here. Our parents and their parents, and theirs before them. Our ancestors are buried here. There can be no question of leaving.'

'Simon, please.' Her voice is pleading. 'There's no way you'll win. The constables are armed with batons and carrying irons. And whether it's right or wrong, they have the law on their side.'

'Damn the law!' I shout.

She flinches, and I see the hurt in her eyes and regret raising my voice.

She finds control from somewhere and drops her own voice to a whisper. 'The sailing ship *Heather* dropped anchor this morning in Loch Glas. No matter what kind of resistance you put up, they mean to clear Baile Mhanais and put everyone aboard her.' She pauses. 'Please, Simon. At least try and persuade your family to leave before they get here.'

I shake my head, full of foreboding. 'My mother's more stubborn than any of them. And if she won't go, then I won't either.'

She stares at me as if trying to formulate words that will make me change my mind. Before suddenly, quite unexpectedly, she bursts into tears. I am torn between my confusion, and an urge to protect her. I step up the slope to take her in my arms. The sobs that rack her body vibrate through mine. 'It's all my fault,' she says.

I slide my fingers through her hair and feel the smallness of her skull in the palm of my hand. 'Don't be silly. None of this is your fault. You can't be held responsible for the actions of your father.'

She pulls back and stares at me with tear-stained eyes. 'Yes I can. He wouldn't be doing any of this if it wasn't for me.'

I shake my head. 'I don't understand.'

'George saw us together. That day up on the hill, when I gave you that first hamper.' She paused, almost as if she were afraid to go on. 'The bastard told our father.'

I am shocked to hear her use such a word.

'He was furious, Simon. He flew into such a rage I really thought he was going to kill me. He told me he would rather see me dead than be with a common crofter's boy. That's when he ordered the evictions. Baile Mhanais was only spared before because you saved my life. Now he wants to be certain there is no way I can ever see you again. That you'll be on a boat to Canada and lost to me for ever.' There are fresh tears and her voice quivers on the brink of breaking. 'You've got to come with me. You and your mother and your sisters.'

I stare at her in disbelief. 'With you?' I shake my head again. 'How? Where?'

Her breath trembles in her throat. 'I have been locked up in my room for days, Simon. No better than a prisoner in my own house. Until this morning.' She brushes away her tears with the backs of her hands, focused on the telling of her story. 'I persuaded one of the maids to let me out, and while my father was downstairs with the Sheriff-Depute and the factor I went into his study. I've always known he kept cash in there, and I knew I needed money to get away.'

In my mind I picture her feverishly searching her father's study, shaking with fear, and all the time listening for a foot-fall on the stair.

'I found his money box in the bottom drawer of his desk. But it was locked, and I had to force it open with a ceremonial dirk that he uses as a letter opener.' She closes her eyes momentarily, reliving the moment. 'As soon as I did it I knew there was no going back.' Her eyes flicker open to hold me again in their frightened gaze. 'There was two hundred pounds in it, Simon!'

Two hundred pounds! I can barely imagine so much money, never mind holding it in my hands.

'We can get a long way away from here with money like that. All of us. You, me, and your family.' She implores me with her eyes, and I find it almost impossible to resist. She takes my hand in hers, and I feel how cold it is. 'There is no way I can go home again. I have defied my father. I have stolen his money.' She squeezes my hand until it very nearly hurts. 'I can get a horse and trap from the stables at the castle once everyone has left. I'll meet you at the foot of the waterfall near the old Sgargarstaigh crossroads. We can head south and get a crossing to the mainland.'

It is suffocating in the blackhouse. Fresh peat on the fire sends smoke billowing up into the roof of the fire room, stinging the eyes and burning the lungs. But it is my mother's voice that fills the room. A voice full of sound and fury and close to hysteria while Annag and Murdag stand behind her, pale faces blanched by fear.

'You've brought this on us, Sime! You and that foolish girl. God knows, her father is right. There is no place in this world for the two of you together. You belong in different parts of it. Her in hers, and you in yours. How could you have thought for one minute that you would ever be accepted into hers? Or that she would stoop to be a part of ours.'

I have never been close to my mother. Always my father's boy. And since his death she has been strident and whining and always finding fault with me, almost as if she blames me for what happened to him. But I am patient, forever mindful of the responsibility that my father bequeathed me.

'You were happy enough to take the food she's been bringing us these last two weeks.'

But that only sends her spinning off into another tantrum 'If I'd known it had come from the hands of that girl I'd never have taken it!'

And I get angry for the first time. 'Where did you think it came from? God? What did you think it was, manna from Heaven?' I glare at her. 'You're as bad as the laird. He thinks that he and his kind are better than us. And you think that we are better than them. But you know what, we're none of us better than anyone else. We're all God's children, equal under Heaven, and no accident of birth can change that.'

'Don't you bring the name of the Lord our God into this! I'll not have you blaspheming in this house.'

'It's not blasphemy. Read your Bible, you stupid woman!' It's out before I can stop myself, and she hits me across the side of my face with the flat of her hand, nearly knocking me from my feet.

But I stand my ground, glaring at her. My face stinging. 'We're leaving,' I say. And I turn to my sisters. 'Get your things, there's not much time.'

My mother's voice cuts through the smoke. 'Don't you move!' Though she has never taken her eyes off me the girls know that it is them she addresses, and they freeze. 'No son of mine is going to tell me what to do. I was born in this house, as were every one of you. And we're not leaving it.'

Annag speaks up for the first time. But her voice is brittle and uncertain. 'Maybe he's right, *mamaidh*. If there's forty or more of them coming to put us out we'll not stand a chance. Maybe we should go with the laird's girl.'

My mother swings her head around slowly, and the look she gives Annag could have turned her to stone. 'We're staying,' she says, with such finality that not one of us is left in any doubt that there will be no arguing with her. 'Now go and start collecting stones, girls. Good, fist-sized stones that'll crack a constable's skull.' She turns back to me. 'You're a Mackenzie, boy. And Mackenzies don't give up without a fight.'

I wonder what my father would have done.

The wind has dropped, so has the temperature, and the rain has come at last. A fine, wetting rain that drifts like mist over the mountains. When the constables arrive, they seem like wraiths lined up along the top of the hill, grey figures against a grey sky.

The villagers, and all the crofters and their families from the township, are gathered among the houses and along the shore. Nearly two hundred of us. We are a pathetic bunch, diminished by the famine and ill-equipped to stand up to a gang of sturdy, well-fed constables and estate workers. But we are fired up with righteous indignation. These are our homes, and this is our land. Our ancestors have lived here since before anyone can remember, and long before any laird thought that his wealth could buy and sell our souls.

I am resigned to the fight. My heart breaks for Ciorstaidh, but I won't leave my family. Even though I know this is hopeless. I know, too, that before the day is out I will either be dead or on a ship bound for the New World. But I am not afraid anymore. Just determined.

I feel fear moving like a stranger among the others as our enemies gather on the hill, formidable in their dark anonymity, threatening in their silence. And it is the strangest quiet that has fallen over Baile Mhanais. Without the wind the sea is hushed as if it holds its breath. Not even the plaintive cry of the gulls breaches the still of the late morning.

Two figures detach themselves from the group on the hill and walk down the path towards us. It is not until they are close that I recognise one of them as the factor. The laird's lackey. His estate manager, Dougal Macaulay. A man universally despised. Because he was once one of us and now does the laird's bidding. No doubt he thinks that rubbing shoulders with the gentry makes him better than his peers. And you can hear it in his tone as the two men stop no more than a few feet away from the crowd. Me, my mother and my sisters are up there at the front.

He casts a speculative eye over the assembled villagers before he says in Gaelic, 'This is Mr Jamieson, the Sheriff-Depute.'

Mr Jamieson is a man of average height and build, maybe forty-five or fifty years old. He wears leather boots and a long coat that glistens with myriad tiny droplets of rain. His hat is pulled down low over his brow so that we can barely see his eyes. His voice is strong and carries the confidence of the ruling class, and his breath billows like mist around his head as he speaks in English, a language that 90 per cent or more of the people of the township will not understand.

'People of Baile Mhanais. I am here to inform you that the notices to quit served upon you fourteen days since have now expired. I ask you for the sake of peace and good order to leave now, or I shall have no option but to sanction your forcible eviction.' His words might not have been understood, but his tone is.

I feel anger well up inside me. 'And if someone came, Mr Jamieson, and asked you to leave your home, how would you feel?'

He raises his head a little as if to see me more clearly. 'If I were in arrears with my rent, young man, I would have no option but to comply. The law is the law.'

'Aye, your fucking law!' shouts someone with a good grasp of the English vernacular.

'There's no need for that kind of language!' the factor says sharply.

'How can we pay rent when we have no money and no means to earn it?' I turn at the sound of Donald Dubh's voice at my shoulder and see his face as grey as the ocean. I am surprised to hear him speak English.

Mr Jamieson sets his jaw against the tone of the debate. 'I am not here to discuss the social issues involved. Only to enforce the law. I'm warning you that this is an illegal gathering, and that if you do not break it up and leave peacefully I will be forced to read you the Riot Act.'

I have no idea what the Riot Act is, or what the reading of it might entail, but the factor translates his words into

Gaelic and they return an uneasy silence to the crowd. No one moves, and the Sheriff-Depute reaches into an inside pocket to bring out a sheet of paper which he proceeds to unfold.

'For God's sake!' the factor says. 'If he reads you the Riot Act and you pay it no heed, they can hang you for it.'

Which sends a chill through the gathering. But still no one moves. Mr Jamieson clears his throat and his voice rings out. 'Our Sovereign Lady the Queen chargeth and commandeth all persons being assembled, immediately to disperse themselves . . .' A stone comes out of the crowd, striking him on the forehead. His hat spins away and he drops to one knee, his copy of the Riot Act fluttering into the mud. His hand goes to his head, and the blood that oozes through his fingers seems vividly red against the white of his skin.

Macaulay hooks a hand under his arm and pulls him to his feet. 'You bloody fools,' he shouts at us. 'You've brought this on yourselves.'

He drags the Sheriff-Depute away, the man slightly stooped and still clutching his head. His hat lies in the mud where it fell, and I see how thin his hair is, greying and oiled back across his scalp, and he seems less a figure of authority now, than simply a man humiliated. If I did not know what was about to happen, I might even feel sorry for him.

The two men are halfway up the hill when Macaulay shouts to the men at the top of it, and there is the briefest lull before a great yell goes up and the charge begins.

Down the hill they come at a gallop, thirty, forty of them or more. The constables at the front, batons raised, shouting at the tops of their voices as they charge. It is a moment that chills the blood. And the crowd responds. A hail of stones flies through the air towards the advancing policemen. Their helmets offer some protection, arms and batons raised to fend off the missiles, but some are struck about the face or head. Several stumble and fall. But it does not stop the assault.

More stones are hurled, but they are almost upon us now and I hear the first crack of a skull as a baton descends upon a head. A man I know well. A crofter from the beach side. He goes down.

It is mayhem! The voices of men and women in one-sided combat rising up into the still morning air. A bloody cacophony. I see batons rising and falling before my eyes, like the shuttles that fly back and forth across the weave on a loom. I have kept back my stone, but I swing it now, held in my fist, and smash it into the face of a young constable before he can fell me with his baton. I can feel and hear his teeth break, and see the blood spurt from his mouth as he drops.

We are falling back under the onslaught, fending off blows with our arms and hands. I have no idea where my mother and sisters are. I am assailed by the sights and sounds of battle. Those first villagers to have fallen are now being mercilessly kicked and beaten. No matter if they are women or children. I see a teenage girl, who lives three houses away from us, lying screaming on her back as two constables stamp repeatedly on her breasts.

And then I catch sight of the pitiful figure of old blind Calum staggering about, his Glengarry trampled in the mud, arms raised to shield himself from blows he cannot see. A man who once fought for Britain at the Battle of Waterloo. Struck down now by a vicious blow from a young man not even born when Calum was fighting for his freedom. His head divides almost in two and he falls, blood and grey matter oozing from his broken skull. Dead before he hits the ground.

I am so enraged I lose all control, charging at the bastards, screaming at the top of my voice, swinging my fists like a madman, catching one in the face, another in the throat, before there is a crippling blow to the side of my head and I feel my knees fold beneath me. The world goes black and silent.

I have no idea how long I have been unconscious. The first thing I am aware of is a terrible searing pain in my head. And then the light. Blood-red at first, and then dazzling white. And I have to screw up my eyes against it.

I can't move, and for a moment I panic, thinking that I am paralysed. Before realising that a man lies on top of me. I manage to pull my legs from under him, dragging myself up into a half-sitting position against the wall of the blackhouse behind me. And I see that the man who lay on me is Donald

Dubh. He is looking at me, eyes staring. But he sees nothing. There are other bodies on the path. Men, women and children. Most still alive, but dreadfully injured. I hear the muted moans of semi-conscious villagers in pain. Somewhere in the distance a woman is wailing. I roll my head to one side and see her running away across the shore, feet sliding and slithering in the shingle. Two constables chase after her. They catch her near the jetty and beat her to the ground before starting to kick her mercilessly.

It is like my worst nightmare. But there is no waking from it. Further up the slope, between the first two blackhouses at the top of the village, estate workers led by the distinctive ginger head of George Guthrie are dragging an old woman from her house. Old Mrs Macritchie. Eighty if she is a day, and bedridden for months. I remember that she was one of the women who were there the day my mother gave birth to Murdag.

She is still lying on her mattress as they drag her from the house and tip her into the mud. Her nightdress rips open, and I see her pitifully pale wizened old body. Her cries of protest are trapped in her throat like a swallowed whisper. And they start to kick her, these men. I cannot believe I am witnessing such inhumanity, such total absence of compassion. I look away and feel tears searing my cheeks, bile rising in my throat.

I scan the village through my grief. Most of the villagers are gone, it seems, though I have no idea where. And I know that I must get away before George and his crew find me. For then I would be as good as dead, too.

I manage to get to my knees and fall into the narrowest of alleys between two houses. It is damp and dark here and smells of human waste. I crawl along the space on my knees and elbows to where the barns behind the houses are built almost into the side of the hill. The ground rises steeply here, thick with heather and fern, rock breaking through thin topsoil. I get to my feet and pause to draw breath and steel myself. The moment I have climbed above the level of the houses I will be in plain view to anyone in the village. It will take a monumental effort to reach the top of the hill, for there is no path and it is almost vertical in places.

Someone is sure to give chase. But they will likely take the track up from the village, which is the long way round, and if I have the strength for the climb it will give me a good head start.

I reach above my head to grab handfuls of heather root and start pulling myself up the first few feet, searching for footholds. I am propelled by a mixture of both fear and anger, straining muscles in my shoulders and thighs, and I climb quickly. Up now above the roofs of the blackhouses. A quick glance to my left sees one going up in flames. Just as at Sgagarstaigh, the men from the estate are armed with flaming torches, setting fire to roofs and doors.

I hear a shout go up below. I have been spotted. At first I daren't turn to look, and keep climbing, spurred on to even greater effort. Clambering over an outcrop of rock now, before sprawling flat when I get to the top of it, and rolling over to look back down the hill. Flames leap up from more roofs. I see my own blackhouse on fire, and remember all the summers my father and I laboured to strip off the thatch for fertiliser before renewing it for the coming winter. The roof timbers send sparks showering up into the mist as they collapse.

A group of constables have detached themselves from the others and are running up the path to try to cut me off. But not twenty feet below me I see George Guthrie in direct pursuit. His face is upturned, contorted by effort and determination, and is almost as red as his hair.

I am on my feet in a moment, and throwing myself up the slope with renewed vigour, slithering and sliding as my hands and feet search for grip. Mostly I am having to pull myself up with my arms and aching shoulders. When finally I reach the top of the hill I stand up straight on shaking legs and look back down on the village that was once my home. The whole place is ablaze. A cheer going up as another roof collapses.

Away to my left I see a long line of villagers being led up over the rise towards Sgagarstaigh hill. Those who can't walk are crammed on to carts with what few belongings they have salvaged. Many of the men are in irons, stooped and bloodied and struggling to stay on their feet, struck on the shoulders by batons if they stumble.

And there, among them, is my mother. Herself in irons. Her face streaked with blood, staggering, almost running to keep up. Small, rapid steps, limited by the chain that loops between her ankles. Annag and Murdag running at her side, catching her arms to stop her falling.

My sense of guilt is crushing. I have let them down. I have betrayed my father. And worse, I know there is nothing I can do about it.

I hear George's breath now, hard and hollow and tearing itself from his chest. He is no more than ten or fifteen feet from the top. I stoop to pick up several rocks and throw them at him. One strikes him on the shoulder, and he lifts an arm to protect his head. In doing so he loses his grip and slithers back down to the rocks below. But I am distracted by the shouts of the constables on the path, who are heading off across the hilltop towards me.

Their shouts turn heads among the lines of villagers being forced away towards Loch Glas, and I see my mother and sisters look in my direction. But there is no time to dwell on my guilt. I turn and run for my life. Away across the crest of the hill, following a track worn by the hooves of countless deer, winding its way through the heather, circumventing great chunks of rock that lie at odd angles across the slope. Splashing now through a small stream in spate. Arms pumping, head back.

Away to my left, and far below, I see the arc of silver sand that is Traigh Mhor, and the stones that stand as silent witness to the generations who have gone before me. They are a stark reminder that it is my relationship with Ciorstaidh that has brought this calamity upon us.

For the first time I glance back and see George in dogged pursuit. Several hundred yards behind him the constables are losing ground, weighed down by heavy boots and rain-soaked uniforms. But George is fast and fit, well-fed and fuelled by fury. I know that in the end he will catch me.

I grit my teeth and run on, arms and legs pumping air into screaming lungs. Away off to my right now, I catch a distant view of Ard Mor nestling between two hills, the flat leaden calm of the bay beyond almost completely lost in the rain. And I keep going, the slope of the land and the deer path pitching me back towards the coast, where thirty-foot cliffs of black rock have held back the relentless assault of the Atlantic ocean since time began.

I see distant islands through the mist, and in a rare break in the low cloud, a shaft of weak sunlight splashes silver on the surface of the sea.

The machair along the cliff tops is relatively flat, the grass well-grazed and short. Thistles catch my bare feet as I run, skipping over rocks and splashing through patches of bog. My spirit urges me to keep going, but my body is yelling at me to stop. I am almost blinded by sweat, and through it I see the machair fall away to a partially hidden cove where the silver of its tiny stretch of sand is almost phosphorescent in the froth of an incoming tide. I follow the track down to the beach and I know that George is going to catch me there. No sense in expending more energy. As my feet sink into soft sand I realise it is time to stop and face him.

I stagger to a halt, leaning forward for a few moments, my arms taking my weight on my thighs, trying to catch my breath. Then I straighten up and turn around.

George is almost upon me. Just a few yards away when he slows to a stop, breathing hard. His ginger hair is darkened by the rain and his sweat, and falls in lank curls all around his forehead. He looks at me with such hatred and contempt that I very nearly wilt under the force of his gaze.

'You little shit!' he says. 'Did you ever in your wildest dreams really believe you could be with my sister?' He draws a long-bladed hunting knife from a sheath on his belt and extends his arm out to his right, the haft of it firmly grasped in his fist, the blade glinting in my direction. 'I'm going to gut you like the animal you are.' He glances over his shoulder back along the cliffs. There is no sign of the chasing constables. 'And not a witness in sight to say it wasn't self-defence.'

As he advances slowly on me, I plant my feet wide to brace myself for the assault, keeping my eyes fixed on his knife hand. He is so close to me now I can smell him. I feel that he wants me to meet his eye. But I won't take mine off his knife, and decide on an impulse to take the initiative. I hurl myself forward, turning side-on so that my shoulder hits him full in the chest, and I grab his right hand with both of mine.

We crash to the beach, with me on top, and all the air is expelled from his lungs in a short, painful explosion. I twist his wrist and forearm, forcing him to release his grip on the knife, and it goes sliding away across the sand.

But he recovers quickly from his surprise and with his superior strength pushes me away. He gets back to his feet, grimacing with pain and gasping to find his breath. I stoop and scoop up a handful of sand to throw in his face. But he turns his head quickly to avert it, and I see his eyes flicker away towards where his knife lies half buried. We each make the calculation about which of us might reach it first. He dives to his right, tumbling to the ground, and grasping it almost before I can move. He is on his feet again in an instant, the sand in his clothes whipped away by the wind. And his confidence floods back.

He has me now with my back to the sea and no means of avoiding him. I move cautiously backwards as he advances and feel the incoming waves break around my ankles. His lips part in what I imagine he believes to be a smile. But it is more like a wild animal baring its teeth.

He lunges at me and I feel his blade slash the skin of my forearm as I try to grab his wrist again. We come together, faces almost touching, and stagger back through the water. Then fall into the ocean as it breaks over us. I twist and turn trying to avoid the blade, and for a moment we are completely submerged. When I break the surface once more, gasping for breath, I am momentarily confused. The ocean is red. George has released me, and I panic, staggering to my feet and looking for the wound that I cannot feel. Which is when I realise that he is floating face-down in the water, blood bubbling to the surface and eddying all around him.

I grab his jacket, and stumbling through the waves drag him up on to the sand and roll him over. Silver turns red beneath him, blood soaking his clothes from a wound somewhere in his midriff, where he has fallen on his own knife. He is still alive, eyes staring up at me and filled with fear. His lips move but there are no words, and I see his life leave him almost like a physical thing departing.

I feel the sea wash cold around my legs as I kneel beside him, and hear cries from the cliffs. I look up to see three constables looking down at us on the beach. It must be clear to them that George is dead, and with me crouched over his body this way there is only one conclusion that I know they will reach. No point in even trying to explain.

I stand up and sprint away along firm, wet sand. I hear them shout as they begin their descent, but I know now they won't catch me. I turn away from the ocean and pound off into a sandy inlet overhung with soil and razor-sharp beach grass. Up and on to the machair again, heading for the cover of the hills, grateful for the rain that falls like mist and swallows me up to become a vanishing part of the landscape.

I have no idea how long it takes me to reach the crossroads. Water tumbles down the hill over fractured slabs of gneiss to gather here in what I've heard called the drowning pool. The old Sgagarstaigh road passes close by and branches off a little further down the hill towards Ard Mor. But it is little used now, fallen into desuetude since Sir John Guthrie built the castle and the new road leading to it from the east.

Kirsty is waiting in the shelter of the single rowan tree that grows there. She has a horse and trap, the beast stamping its feet impatiently and snorting in the cold. Her relief is almost palpable until she sees the state of me.

'What's happened? Where are your mother and sisters?'

'Taken,' I tell her. 'With everyone else from the village who survived the attack. They're probably all aboard the *Heather* by now.'

'But why didn't you leave before they came?' I see strain all around her eyes.

'My mother wouldn't go. And then it was too late.' I choke back tears and wait some moments to recover my voice. 'Baile Mhanais is in flames. Some of my neighbours are dead. Everyone else was taken away to Loch Glas.' I stare at the ground, afraid now to meet her eyes. To tell her the rest. Then I look up suddenly. 'Your brother's dead, Ciorstaidh.'

I see her eyes blacken with shock in the cold grey of this awful day. 'George . . . ?'

I nod.

'What happened?'

'I got away. He came after me. We fought on the beach beyond the cliffs. He had a knife, Ciorstaidh. He meant to kill me. Gut me like an animal, he said.'

Her voice was little more than a breath. 'You killed him?'

'I didn't mean to. I swear. We ended up in the water and he fell on his own knife.'

I see silent tears run down her face. 'Poor George. I always hated him. I don't know if he deserved to die or not, but one way or another he brought it on himself.' She bit her lip to fight back some inner grief that belied her words. There must have been some moments of affection between them when they were children.

'They'll say I killed him. No matter that he was the one trying to kill me. You can be sure they'll want me for murder. And if they catch me it'll be the gallows.'

I see the quiet determination that sets the line of her jaw. 'They'll not catch you,' she says, and she turns to the trap and opens the trunk at the rear of it. There are two small suitcases inside it. She pulls one out and opens it on the ground. 'I brought some of George's clothes for you, and a pair of his boots. They might be a little big, but they'll do. You can't travel looking the way you do.'

I look at the folded trousers, and the jacket, and the pressed shirt in the case. And George's shining black boots. And I can only imagine how he would have felt at the thought of me stepping into them. 'I can't travel at all,' I tell her.

Her face creases in a frown of incomprehension. 'What do you mean?'

'I can't leave my mother and my sisters.'

'Simon, you told me yourself they are probably already on the boat. There's nothing you can do.'

I close my eyes and want to shout out loud. She is right, of course, but I find it next to impossible to accept.

She grabs my arm and forces me to look at her. 'Listen, Simon. The *Heather* is bound for a place called Quebec City. It's somewhere on the eastern seaboard of Canada. If we can get to Glasgow, then I have more than enough money to pay our passage on the next boat to Quebec ourselves. Once we get there, there's bound to be shipping records or something. You're sure to be able to track them down. But we've got to go. Now. We need to be on a sailing to the mainland before the police come after you.'

CHAPTER TWENTY-SIX

He woke up startled, feelings of pain and regret following him from the dream to his waking consciousness like a hangover. The dream itself had unfolded just as he remembered the telling of the story, but his years of life experience since its reading had coloured it with images and emotions he could not have known as a young boy. And once again Kirsty Cowell had been Ciorstaidh, and he his own ancestor.

Light leaked in all around the drawn curtains of his room and he checked the time. It was a little after seven, so he had not slept long.

These events from his ancestor's life were haunting him now with increasing frequency. When they weren't consciously in his thoughts, his subconscious was dredging them up to fill brief moments of sleep. It seemed there was no escape.

The clearing of Baile Mhanais and his running away with Ciorstaidh had somehow brought him full circle. Back to that first dream, and their separation on the quayside at Glasgow. And that's what filled his mind now. But with a sense of something missing. Although he could not think what. He forced himself to replay the events of that fateful day when the *Eliza* had carried Simon off to the New World, leaving Ciorstaidh behind in the old. The promise his ancestor knew he could never keep. Just as he had dreamt it. Just as he remembered it in the telling from all those years before. And yet still, he knew, there was something he'd forgotten. Something lost in time and just out of reach.

A knock on the door dispersed the dream and its afterthoughts, and his recollection of events the night before came flooding back to replace them. Depression fell on him like snow.

The knock came again. More insistent this time.

Sime felt battered, his eyes full of sleep and still barely focusing. He swung his legs out of bed, his clothes crumpled and damp with sweat, and slipped his feet into his shoes.

'Okay!' he shouted as the knocking started again. He swept his hair back out of his face and rubbed his eyes with the heels of his hands before opening the door.

Crozes stood in the hall. For a moment Sime wondered if he was going to attack him. But he was a pool of dark stillness. The cut on his lip had scabbed over, and there was bruising all around his left eye and cheek. 'Can I come in?'

Sime stood back, holding the door wide, and Crozes pushed past him into the room. As Sime closed the door Crozes turned to face him. 'We can play this one of two ways,' he said.

'Oh?' Sime could determine nothing from expressionless eyes. The pallor beneath Crozes's tan turned his skin almost jaundice-yellow.

'Either we behave as if nothing happened and we just get on with our lives.' He hesitated. 'Or I bring you up on a charge of assault which will see you immediately suspended, and almost certainly dismissed.'

Sime looked at him thoughtfully, his brain slowly clearing. 'Well, let me tell you why you're not going to do that.' Crozes waited. Impassive. 'One, you'd have to admit that you'd been screwing the wife of a fellow officer. Two, you'd have to suffer the humiliation of every single person in the department knowing how I beat the shit out of you.' Still Crozes waited. 'End to both of our careers. And I don't think either of us wants that.'

'So what are you saying?'

'I'm saying that we can play this one of two ways.' He got an almost perverse pleasure from throwing Crozes's words back in his face. 'We can make like nothing happened.'

Crozes contained his anger well. 'Or?'

'Or I can go upstairs with the fact that you've been sleeping with my wife for the last year and we'll see how that plays out.'

'Same result.'

Sime shrugged. 'Maybe.' He was surprised himself just how cool and unemotional he felt. As if it was other people's lives they were discussing. And he realised with something of a shock that he didn't much care any more. About the Sûreté, about Marie-Ange, about Crozes. 'Just depends which of us takes the initiative first.'

'I could arrest you right now. It's not as if there aren't witnesses.'

'And how do you know that I haven't already called Captain McIvir with a full account of what happened. Including your infidelity with my wife?' He saw Crozes stiffen.

'Have you?'

Sime let the question hang for a few long moments. 'No,' he said finally.

Crozes's relief was almost palpable. 'So we're agreed then?'

'Are we?'

'Nothing happened last night. If Marie-Ange and I have a relationship it only began after your marriage broke up. We wrap up this investigation and spend the rest of our careers staying out of each other's way.'

Sime looked hard at the other man. 'In other words you want me to keep my mouth shut.' He could see by the movement of his jaw that Crozes was clenching his teeth.

'You can interpret it any way you like. I'm just laying out the choices.'

It was some time, with silence hanging heavy in the room, before Sime broke eye contact with the lieutenant and sat down on the edge of his bed. 'Whatever you want,' he said wearily.

Crozes nodded, and his whole demeanour seemed to

change in a heartbeat. Suddenly he was the lieutenant again, and it was back to business. The murder of James Cowell. As if nothing at all had passed between them he said, 'The police in Quebec City have tracked down Mayor Briand finally. He's staying at the Auberge Saint-Antoine.' He glanced at his watch. 'There's a flight in forty-five minutes. I want you and Blanc on it.'

CHAPTER TWENTY-SEVEN

I

'Jesus!' Blanc looked up from the folder on his knees. They were somewhere over the Gaspé Peninsula, probably less than an hour from Quebec City. The first hour of their flight had passed in a tense silence, and Blanc had buried his head in Arseneau's briefing notes on Mayor Richard Briand. Now he looked at Sime, squeezed in beside him in the tiny nineteen-seater Jetstream commuter aircraft, unable to contain himself. 'Have you read this stuff?'

Sime was miles away, turning over the traces of his ancestor in nineteenth-century Scotland, and if he thought about the present at all, picking at the scabs of his failed relationship with Marie-Ange. He glanced at his co-interrogator with a cold detachment. 'No.'

Excitement coloured Blanc's normally pale complexion and he flushed pink. 'Everyone knows you don't get to be top dog in politics without money behind you. And Briand's no exception. Even if he is just an island mayor.'

'He's got money. So?'

'It's how he made his money that's interesting.'

'Tell me.'

'Lobsters.' He watched expectantly as Sime absorbed this.

'He was in the same business as Cowell?'

'Not just in the same business, Sime. They were competitors. The whole industry was pretty much sewn up between them. Cowell might have owned half the fishing fleet, but Briand owns the other half. And according to Arseneau's notes the mayor was foiled in a major takeover attempt last year. It seems there was a big bust-up between the two men. No love lost.'

The significance of what Blanc was telling him was not lost on Sime. Dreams and diaries and failed marriages retreated into a distant corner of his mind. 'So with Cowell dead, presumably the widow wouldn't present much of an obstacle to his plans to expand his little empire.'

Blanc nodded. 'Well, exactly. And it must have been a pretty bitter pill to swallow when Cowell moved in with his wife.'

Sime thought about it. 'Which would provide Briand with a very strong double motive for murder.'

'Casts everything in a different light, doesn't it?'

'Except for one little thing,' Sime said.

'What's that?'

'The same thing that's always thrown doubt on Briand as a suspect. If it was Cowell he was after, why did he attack Kirsty?'

'Maybe he wanted to kill them both. Then Cowell's business would have had to be broken up for sure.'

'So why didn't he?'

Blanc frowned. 'Why didn't he what?'

'Kill them both. He had the opportunity.'

Blanc was deflated. 'Maybe he panicked.'

But Sime was shaking his head. 'Having killed one, why wouldn't he kill the other? And think on this. Briand flew to Quebec City the morning after the murder, so it wasn't him who attacked me two nights ago. And the fact that I was attacked by a man in a ski mask would seem to bear out Kirsty Cowell's story about an intruder on the night of the murder. Which would kind of let her off the hook, too.'

Blanc scratched the circle of bald, shiny skin on the crown of his head. 'It also raises the question of why you were attacked at all.'

Sime nodded. 'It does. But it doesn't change the fact that I was.' He paused, recalling only too clearly the moment that he thought he was going to die. He glanced at the file on Blanc's knee. 'Are you finished with that?'

'Yes.'

Sime reached for it. 'Well I guess I'd better read it for myself before we get to Quebec City.' He flipped back through Arseneau's printout and started reading. Only to become aware of Blanc still looking at him. He raised his head and saw embarrassment in the other man's eyes. 'What?'

Blanc said, 'We've got to clear the air, Sime.'

'About what?'

'Last night.'

Sime looked back at the file on his knee. 'Forget it.'

'I can't.'

'Why not?'

'Because I hate to think that you blame me for any of it.'

'I don't.'

'That's not the impression you gave at two o'clock this morning.'

Sime sighed and swung his gaze back towards Blanc. 'Look Thomas, I was a bit emotional, okay? I'd just found out my wife and the lieutenant had been sleeping together behind my back for who knows how long. And if she hadn't pointed a gun at my head I might just have killed him.'

Blanc stared at his hands as he wrung them in his lap. 'But you were right, though. Everyone did know.' He looked up earnestly. 'No one thought it was okay. But you know, you were never that close to anyone, Sime, so no one really felt it was their business to tell you. I certainly didn't think it was any of mine.'

Sime shook his head and almost laughed. How would any of them have phrased it? *Hey, Sime, did you know that Lieutenant Crozes is screwing your wife?* 'If I'd been you I probably wouldn't have said anything either. But it really doesn't matter now. It's done. Over. Time to move on.'

But Blanc clearly had something else on his mind. He said, 'What did Crozes say when he came to your room this morning?'

327

Sime raised an eyebrow. 'You know about that?'

'Everyone knows about it, Sime.'

Sime sighed. 'We agreed to put it behind us.' And he turned back to the file.

There was a long silence before Blanc said, 'Does that mean he's not taking any action against you?'

'It wouldn't work out well for either of us if he did, Thomas. So, no, he's not.' Sime dragged his eyes away from Arseneau's briefing notes and looked up to see Blanc shaking his head. 'What?'

'Doesn't make any sense, Sime.'

'You think he should have charged me?' Sime couldn't conceal his surprise.

'I think he's like a wounded animal. Bleeding and dangerous.' Blanc fixed him with his small dark eyes. 'You gave him a hell of a beating this morning, Sime. In front of his lover. And when you opened the door to that hotel room, there wasn't a single member of the team who didn't see him lying naked and bleeding on the floor. Serious humiliation. He'll feel that for a lot longer than any physical pain you inflicted.' He looked earnestly at the younger man. 'If he says he wants to put it behind him, he's lying. Whatever he said, whatever he promised you, don't believe him. He'll fuck you the first chance he gets.'

II

It took their taxi just under twenty minutes to get from the airport to the Auberge Saint-Antoine in the old port area of Quebec City. For all that he had been brought up in the Eastern Townships, it was Sime's first visit to the provincial capital.

It was an impressive old town, with its walled castle towering over the port and the river, the jumble of ancient houses in narrow streets that clustered beneath the old city walls. Restored now as a tourist attraction and filled with restaurants and hotels.

The St Lawrence river was wide here, and they could see the ferry on its way over from the distant port of Levis on the far bank as their taxi drew up outside Briand's hotel. Although many of its rooms looked out over the river, the entrance was up the narrow Rue Saint-Antoine, stone-built tenements rising all around, trees covering the hill at the top end of the street. Briand had an attic room on the fourth floor, a huge arched window opening on to a view of the river. A man used to getting his own way, he was in a foul mood when he let them into his room.

He closed the door behind them. 'Am I under arrest or what?'

'Of course not.' Blanc's voice was full of reassurance. But Briand was not mollified.

'Well, it feels like it. I had a visit from the local Sûreté last night who told me not to leave my room until you people had spoken to me today. I feel like I'm under house arrest here. I've already missed one meeting this morning, and now I'm going to be late for another.'

'A man is dead, Mayor Briand,' Sime said. He looked thoughtfully at the mayor. He was a tall man, fit and good-looking. He had the sharp, wide-boy look of the politician, polished and well-manicured, but with the cultivated veneer of sophistication that only money can buy. His thick dark hair was gelled back from a tanned face, and Sime had recognised him the moment he opened his door as the man in the photograph with Ariane Briand that he had seen sitting on her sideboard. He wore dark slacks and a white shirt with carefully rolled-up sleeves.

'I know that,' he snapped. 'But I don't see what that has to do with me.'

Blanc said, 'He was your main business competitor, and he was screwing your wife.'

Briand's skin flushed dark beneath his tan. 'Whatever may or may not have occurred between Cowell and my wife was over.' He controlled the anger in his voice by clenching his teeth.

Blanc showed no surprise. 'It is our understanding that Cowell was still living with your wife at the time of his murder. His belongings were still in her house.'

Sime remembered the man's coat that seemed too big for Cowell hanging by her door.

330

'If he'd come back that night he'd have found them on her doorstep.'

'And how would you know that?' Sime said.

'Because I put them there.'

Both detectives were caught by surprise and there was a momentary hiatus. 'You were at your wife's house on the night of the murder?' Blanc said.

'I was.'

Sime said, 'I think you'd better explain.'

Briand sighed heavily and crossed the room to open French windows on to the view of the river. He took a deep breath and turned to face them, his face semi-obscured. by the light behind him. He was a man used to finding the power position in a room. 'If you've never lived on an island,' he said, 'you wouldn't understand how rumours and half-truths grow into full-blown lies.'

'Happens in any small community,' Blanc said. 'Which particular rumour or half-truth are we talking about here?'

Briand was unruffled. 'Contrary to popular opinion, my wife did not kick me out. We had a bust-up, yes. It happens in marriage. We agreed a temporary separation. A sort of cooling-off period.'

'And your wife's affair with Cowell began when?' Sime said.

'After our separation. She's since told me she only really did it to make me jealous.'

Blanc said, 'So that was her only motivation in asking him to move in with her?'

'She didn't.' Briand sounded defensive. 'Cowell invited himself. Turned up one night on her doorstep with a suitcase and said his wife had found out about them.' He ran a hand over the smoothly shaved contours of his jaw, clearly uncomfortable discussing what had undoubtedly been a humiliating experience for him. 'Ariane and Cowell had a fling, yes, but she and I were in the process of making up. She'd been about to end it with him when he turned up that night with his suitcase. It caught her off balance. She didn't know how to deal with it. He was obsessive, she said. Almost creepy. And it had got to the stage she was kind of scared of him. I persuaded her that she had to confront him with the truth. That she and I were getting back together and it was over with him. We were going to face him with it that night. The two of us. The night he was murdered. I came to the house after he left, and we waited and waited, but he never came back.'

Sime said, 'You're saying you spent all night at your wife's house the night Cowell was murdered.'

'Actually, it's my house,' Briand said, his voice tight with annoyance. 'But yes, Ariane and I were home together all night.'

'That's a very convenient alibi,' Blanc said. 'I wonder why your wife never mentioned it to us.'

'Maybe because you never asked her.' His voice was laden now with sarcasm.

'Oh, we will.' Blanc's tone betrayed his annoyance.

Sime said, 'And you both, coincidentally, flew here the next morning.'

'There was no coincidence about it,' Briand said. 'We left together. We'd already planned that, just so she could escape any heat from the break-up with Cowell. I booked the flights and hotel myself just to keep things discreet. I didn't have any meetings until yesterday, so we knew we'd have a couple of days together before she went back.'

Sime was reluctant to admit to himself that there was a ring of truth to all this. The photograph of Ariane and Briand had probably been reinstated to its place on the sideboard the night they planned to break the news to Cowell. The coat left hanging by the door was Briand's. And Ariane hadn't packed Cowell's suitcase on her return from the airport. It had been packed the night he was murdered. But in any event, husband and wife each provided an alibi for the other. And one thing was certain. As he had pointed out to Blanc, it wasn't Briand who attacked Sime on Entry Island. He had been here in Quebec City when it happened.

'When did you hear about Cowell's murder?' he asked.

'Not until Ariane got home. She called to tell me.'

Blanc said, 'It's been all over the news.'

'We weren't watching the news, detective. We were putting our marriage back together. Finding ourselves again. No one knew where we were. We'd turned our cellphones off. It was just us. A hotel room, a couple of restaurants. The world didn't exist.'

'And how did you feel,' Sime said, 'when you heard that Cowell had been murdered?'

A sardonic little smile played about the mayor's lips. 'To be perfectly honest, I gave a little jump for joy. The man was fucking up my personal and business life. His poor wife deserves a medal.'

'His wife?' Blanc said, surprised.

'Sure.'

'Why?'

'For killing him.'

The Château Frontenac with its towers and spires, its green copper roofs and orange brick, dominated the skyline above them. Built on the site of the old Château Haldimand, once home to a succession of British colonial governors, it was now a luxury hotel. Autumn colours on the hill below it painted the slope yellow and fiery red, and a constant traffic of tourists rode the funicular railway up and down to the old city walls.

Sime and Blanc sat in a café beneath yellow parasols watching passengers stream off and on the river ferries at the terminal across the road. An enormous luxury cruise liner, berthed at the dock, almost dwarfed the old port. Cannon that guarded what was once the most important deep-water port on the eastern seaboard of North America poked through the crenellations in the harbour wall, unused in nearly two centuries and painted lacquer-black.

Blanc was on his second coffee and his third cigarette as they sat waiting for their taxi to take them back to the airport. He had already briefed Crozes by telephone. 'He seems happy,' he said. 'It pretty much puts Briand out of the picture and refocuses everything on the wife.'

'But we still don't have any evidence against her. Not real evidence,' Sime said.

Blanc shrugged. 'We should get the pathologist's report sometime today, and early results on the forensics.' He scrutinised Sime carefully. 'What is it with you and her, Sime?'

He felt himself blushing. 'What do you mean?'

'All this stuff with the ring and the pendant, thinking that you knew her. I've seen how you look at her.'

'How do I look at her?' Sime was suddenly self-conscious.

'I don't know. It's hard to say. But it's not how a cop usually regards a suspect. There's something personal there, and it's not right. It's not professional. You know that, Sime.'

Sime didn't respond, and Blanc thought for a moment.

'You asked her the other day about her Scottish roots.'

'So?'

'You're Scottish, aren't you? I mean, that's where your ancestors came from.'

Sime thought about it. 'You know it's funny. When I was growing up I never wanted to be anything other than Canadian. Quebecois. Of course, I knew about my Scottish heritage. My ancestors arrived here speaking Gaelic. And my father was so proud of our Scottish roots. Insisted we spoke English at home. Well, I already told you that.' He smiled. 'He was sure he had a Scottish accent. But I doubt if he did.' He glanced at Blanc. 'Trouble is, I didn't want to be Scottish. I didn't want to be different. Most of the other kids in my class were of French descent. We all spoke French together. I just wanted to be one of them. I was almost in denial about being Scottish. I guess I must have been a real disappointment to my dad.'

Sime turned his gaze thoughtfully towards the port.

'But if you go back five generations, my great-great-great-grandfather arrived here in Quebec City from Scotland without a penny to his name. He and his family had been cleared off their land in the Outer Hebrides, and he got separated from his mother and sisters.'

Blanc sucked a mouthful of smoke into his lungs. 'What about his father?'

'His father was shot dead trying to poach deer on the estate during the potato famine.'

'I thought that was an Irish thing.'

Sime shook his head. 'The famine was just as bad in parts of Scotland.' He nodded towards the port. 'When he got here he went searching records at the harbour master's office, trying to establish when the boat his family came on had arrived. So he could try and find them. A boat called the *Heather*.'

'And?'

'There was no record of it. And he was told it was pre-sumed lost at sea. In those days, if a boat went down no one ever knew.' He recalled only too clearly his grandmother reading that passage from the diaries. How his ancestor had got drunk, and been rescued from the hands of unsavoury characters by an Irishman he'd met. He shook his head. 'Hard to imagine what it must have been like. Thrown off your land and forced on to boats. Arriving in a strange land with nothing. No family, no friends.'

'What happened to him?'

Sime shrugged. 'He did all right for himself in the end. Ended up making a bit of a reputation as an artist, of all things.'

'You got any of his paintings?'

'Just the one. A landscape. I guess it must be the Hebrides. A pretty bleak-looking place. No trees, nothing.' And it occurred to him that the imagery that coloured the back-drop to his dreams must have come from that painting hanging in his apartment. He turned to Blanc. 'What about you? What are your roots?'

Blanc said, 'I can trace my ancestry all the way back to the early Acadians who first settled in Canada. They came from a town in the Poitou-Charentes region of western France called Loudun.' He grinned. 'So I'm a real pure-blood Frenchy. I guess the difference between my people and yours is that mine came voluntarily. Pioneers.'

A taxi pulled up at the kerb and beeped its horn. Both men stood up quickly and Blanc left some coins on the table.

III

They were in the air shortly after midday and would be back on the islands by two. Crozes had told Blanc on the phone that he was calling a team meeting at the Sûreté to assess the evidence gathered to date and decide what further steps to take.

Sime let his head fall back in the seat and closed his eyes only to find Kirsty Cowell's face there, waiting for him, somehow etched on his retinas. He thought about what Blanc had said to him at the café about the way he was with her. *There's something personal there, and it's not right. It's not professional.* And he wondered if he was losing all objectivity in this case.

He felt the plane bank left as it circled over the city below to set a course that would follow the river north towards the Gulf. Blanc nudged his arm. He was in the window seat peering down on the landscape beneath them as they made the turn. It was a beautiful crisp, clear autumn day and the colours of the forest lining the banks of the river were spectacular in the sunlight, as if they had been enhanced by photo-manipulation software. 'Look,' he said. 'See that string of islands in the river?'

Sime leaned over him to try to catch a glimpse. And there they were, standing out in sharp relief against the flow of dark water in the St Lawrence. Grey rock and fall foliage.

338

Nine or ten of them, varying in size, stretched out along the course of the St Lawrence to the north-east of the city.

'Third one up from the Île d'Orléans,' Blanc said. 'That's Grosse Île. That's where they had the quarantine station for immigrants in the nineteenth and early twentieth centuries. You ever hear about it?'

Sime nodded grimly. 'Yes.'

'Poor bastards. It was sheer hell, they say.'

And Sime's recollection of his ancestor's experience there came flooding back.

CHAPTER TWENTY-EIGHT

This voyage is a nightmare beyond anything I might ever have imagined. And it has only just begun! God only knows what miseries lie ahead.

I have learned not to think about Ciorstaidh, for it brings only pain and increases my depression. Had she been aboard with me as planned, we would have been in one of the few passenger cabins above deck. She had our papers, and when it was discovered that I had none, and no proof that my passage had been paid for, I was told by the first mate that I would have to pay my way, and was assigned to the kitchen to cook for the passengers below deck, among whom I would have to find a place.

The kitchen is really just a crude preparation area, and the three of us designated as cooks find it almost impossible to work when the seas are rough, as they have been since we left.

The drinking water in the barrels provided is green. Almost undrinkable. And half the grain in the sacks is mouldy. There is precious little in the way of meat, and it won't keep long anyway. I have no idea how we are going to eke out the potatoes and onions and turnips for the length of the journey.

I have learned that most of the 269 folk in steerage are from the Isle of Skye. Cleared from their land and sent to Glasgow by their landlord, who has paid their passage to Canada. Most of them possess no more than they stand up in. They have no money, and no idea what will happen to them when they arrive at their destination.

The *Eliza* was never intended as a passenger vessel. She is a cargo ship. She will return to the British Isles laden with goods from the New World, and the people in steerage on the way out are little more than paying ballast.

What they call steerage is a cargo hold crudely adapted to take people. Stalls have been constructed along each side of the hull, and down the centre of the ship. The stalls are on two levels, squeezed between the upper and lower decks. They provide little more room on filthy, stained planking than you can lie down on.

Families are squeezed in, eight or ten to a stall. There are no toilets. Just tin chanties that you have to carry, sloshing and spilling, up to the top deck to empty overboard. The air is thick with the stench of human waste and there is no water for washing.

Neither is there privacy when you perform your toilet. Which is embarrassing for everyone, but for the women in particular. Most use blankets held up by family members to screen them.

It is dark down here, and oppressive. In bad weather they batten down the hatches and we see no daylight for days on end. The only illumination comes from the oil lamps that swing overhead, releasing their fumes into already unbreathable air. There are times I cannot even see to write this account of my life, and when the boat yaws and pitches in a storm I am inclined to think that no one will ever get to read it. I have been fortunate to be taken under the wing of the captain's wife, as almost the only passenger in steerage who speaks English. She has provided me with materials to write my journal and a place to keep it safe. The writing of it is the only thing that keeps my sanity intact during these interminable hours and days.

The seasickness is bad, and the music of human misery that I am now used to hearing day and night is almost constantly punctuated by the sound of vomiting. I often think of my mother and sisters aboard the *Heather*, and how it must be for them, too. It is a thought I can hardly bear.

There is another sickness as well. Not caused by the motion of the boat, but by some malady. There is one man, I have noticed, who seems sicker than the rest. A young man, fit and strong, maybe five or six years older than myself. His name is John Angus Macdonald, and he has two young children and a wife pregnant with a third. He has violent sickness and diarrhoea and has not eaten for two days now. And just tonight I noticed an eruption of red spots on his chest and abdomen.

*

We have been at sea for two weeks, and John Angus Macdonald is dead. He and his family were in the stall next to mine and I watched him wither in front of my eyes.

We held a brief funeral service for him this morning. Just a handful of us allowed up on deck for the ceremony. I cannot describe how wonderful it was to breathe fresh air, although in the end it only made it harder to return below deck.

John Angus was wrapped in the sheet he died in. Crudely sewn into it. I was only there because I am one of the few aboard who can read and write, and someone thrust the Gaelic bible in my hand and asked me to read from it. I remembered the passage old blind Calum had recited over my father's coffin. Although it took some time, I found it eventually: John, chapter 11, verse 25. *I am the resurrection and the life, saith the Lord: he that believeth in me, though he were dead, yet shall he live; and whosoever liveth and believeth in me, shall never die.*

And they slid his body over the rail. I saw the tiny splash it made in heaving seas, and realised, possibly for the first time in my life, how utterly insignificant we all are.

I have no idea how many weeks his widow Catriona's pregnancy has left to run, but her bulge is substantial, and it cannot be too long before she will give birth. A baby that will never know its father.

Somehow I feel a responsibility for her now that her man is gone. I am right there in the next stall, and the closest thing to a father her children have. Even as I write this by the feeble light down here, the little boy and girl are curled up at my legs, sharing my sheet now that their father's is gone. All that I can really do for them is try to make sure they each get a little extra food.

The weather continues to be abominable. The hatches have been shut for days to keep the weather out, and I feel that I could cut the air into slices with my knife.

I spoke earlier today with a member of crew who told me the average sailing time is normally four to six weeks. But because of this weather we are already well behind schedule, and he thinks it could take up to two months. I took an immediate inventory of our larder, such as it is, and did a quick reckoning. It seems to me that we will run out of food and water long before we get to our destination.

John Angus Macdonald's sickness has spread. Eleven people have now died and been dropped overboard. Many of my fellow passengers have relentless diarrhoea. It soils the boards we sleep on. It makes a porridge along with vomit to render the floorboards treacherous underfoot. We have no way of cleaning it up, and the stink is beyond unbearable.

I am acutely aware of the symptoms of the sickness that stalks us in steerage, and watch keenly for any sign of it in myself. Thus far I have been spared the malady, but not the misery.

*

Tonight has been one of the most distressing of my life.

Catrìona Macdonald finally went into labour. The ship was pitching violently, and shadows cast by the swinging oil lamps danced among us like demons. It was well nigh impossible to see or focus clearly.

The poor woman was in terrible distress, and the more experienced older women gathered round to help with the delivery. Catrìona's screams rose above even the roar of the storm, and her terrified children clung to me in the stall next door.

It quickly became clear that there was a problem. I led the children to the stall across the way so that they couldn't see, although they could still hear well enough. But even in the semi-dark I could read the body language of the women gathered around the young widow. And their silent panic took me back to that day many years before when Annag and I crouched by the chicken wire at the door to the fire room of our blackhouse when my mother gave birth.

I left the children in the care of a family in the neighbouring stall and went to see for myself. At first the older women pushed me away. This was no place for a man, they said. But I forced my way through, bracing myself against the upright to see poor Catrìona Macdonald lying on her back with her legs held apart. The baby was coming out the wrong way, just as Murdag had done.

There was no experienced midwife on board, and the woman trying to help release the baby was hopelessly out of her depth. I closed my eyes and saw clearly through the smoke of the fire room how the midwife in Baile Mhanais had turned the baby. And when I opened them again it was even clearer to me that if I did not do something this child was going to die.

I pushed the woman out of the way, and I heard the others gasp their surprise as I took her place. I braced my knees against the side of the stall to steady myself against the yaw of the ship so that I could take a hold of the baby. I had seen it done. I knew I could do it.

It was coming arse first, arms and legs still inside. A little girl. I pictured what I had seen the midwife do, freeing the baby's legs one by one, then gently turning and twisting to release first one arm, then the other. The mother's screams very nearly unnerved me. As with my own mother there was a terrible amount of blood, and my confidence started to desert me. The whole body was free now, but the head still trapped inside. Suffocating. The baby was drowning in blood and fluid.

I could feel the life of the child in my hands ebbing away, my own sweat almost blinding me. I tried to remember what it was the midwife had done to free the head, fighting hard to concentrate on what I had seen that day. I recalled how she had felt for the head through my mother's belly. And then pushed down and forward with the palm of her hand.

The women were screaming at me to let go, but I was convinced now that I was the only one who could save the life of this little girl.

My hand slid over the blood on Catrìona's belly, and I felt the head of the baby there, round and hard. I supported the child in the crook of my arm, and pushed down hard, yelling 'Push!' as I did. The head came out so unexpectedly that I staggered and almost fell. I felt the hands of many women grab and steady me. And I smacked that baby's bottom so hard, just as I had seen the midwife do to Murdag.

For a moment, there was nothing. Then a cough and a cry, and I cut through the umbilical with my knife to release the baby into my hands. And there she was, this tiny creature covered in blood and mucus, held to my chest, eyes opening for the first time.

I was very nearly overwhelmed by the emotion of cradling this new life in my arms.

The women gathered around with sheets to try to stop Catrìona's bleeding. But Catrìona was oblivious to whatever pain or peril she might be in. She looked up at me in the half-dark with shining eyes and held out trembling hands for her baby girl. Someone took her from me and wrapped her in a blanket, then handed the child to her mother. Catrìona held her to her breast as if she were the most precious thing on earth. And in that moment, to her mother, I suppose she was.

Catrìona looked from her baby to me, and in a voice barely audible above the storm and the creak of the ship, she whispered, 'Thank you.'

*

We have been at sea for forty-five days now. One of my fellow cooks is dead, the other is sick, and I am doing what I can to feed the remaining passengers. There has been no meat for weeks, the grain is done, and all that remain are a few shrivelled vegetables with which I am doing my best to make a thin soup to go round. Our water, disgusting though it has been throughout, is all but exhausted, too. If we don't succumb to the sickness we will die from starvation.

More and more passengers have come down with the malady that took John Angus Macdonald. And now Catrìona is showing symptoms of it, too.

She has not been well since the birth of her baby, and is deteriorating fast. I spend most evenings comforting her and keeping the children occupied. The baby would have died I am sure had a woman a few stalls away not still been nursing, so I do my best to see that the Macdonalds and the nursing woman get enough food to survive.

Ciorstaidh is a distant memory now. But I know that for the rest of my days I will always regret the moment that I lost her on the quay.

Tonight I had yet another burden of responsibility placed upon my shoulders. Catrìona knows she is going to die. How could she not? I had just wrapped up her children in a blanket and stroked their heads until they fell asleep. I turned to find her watching me with big, sad eyes. She reached out to grasp my wrist and whispered, 'My grandmother always told me that if you save a life you are responsible for it.' She coughed mucus and sputum into her sheet and took a moment to collect herself. 'When I'm gone, my baby is yours to care for. My children, too. Do what you can, Sime. There's no one else.'

I am only eighteen years old. But how could I say no?

Yesterday, we slid three more bodies over the rail. All formalities have been dispensed with by now, although I always whisper Calum's farewell to my father. Even if no one else hears it, I am sure that God is listening.

The weather has improved these last days, and we have been making better speed. I lingered on deck for a while after the burials, and I heard someone shout 'Land!' With others, I ran to the rail on the port side and strained to see beyond the swell of the sea. And there in the distance I saw a small group of islands breaking the horizon. A crewman at my shoulder said, 'Thank God for that. We'll arrive tomorrow or the day after.'

I felt such a sense of relief I wanted to shout out loud and punch the air. I wanted to be there now. I just wanted all this to end. It is strange how it is possible to hold yourself together when you know there is still a distance to go. But as soon as the end is in sight, somehow all your resolve vanishes and you can barely stagger to the finish.

However, my happiness was short-lived. The crewman said, 'Don't get yourself all worked up, son. They'll not let us through to Quebec City just yet. We'll be stopped at Grosse

Île first. And if you thought this was bad . . .' His voice tailed away.

'What do you mean?' I asked. 'What's Grosse Île?'

'It's hell on earth, son. An island in the St Lawrence river, just a few miles downstream from the city. We'll be held in quarantine there. The sick will be treated, and probably die. And the rest of us will be held until they're sure we're not sick. Only then will they let us go on.'

I could have wept.

It seemed extraordinary to see land on both horizons when we sailed into the mouth of the St Lawrence earlier today. But the opposing banks of it are so distant that they barely blur the line between water and sky. I had no idea a river could be this big.

Everyone who could, crowded on deck to watch our progress upriver, banks drawing in on either side. This was the great continent of North America.

But of the 269 passengers who left Glasgow in steerage, twenty-nine are dead and only 240 of us remain.

It was almost dusk when we sailed past a string of dark islands that loomed out of the stream of the river, to drop anchor finally at Grosse Île. There were eight or ten other tall ships anchored there in the bay, all flying the yellow jack of quarantine. It seems that we have brought all our diseases with us to this new world.

Onshore I could see a collection of long sheds, and woods

rising up on the hill behind them. From the wooden pier a long boat set out towards us, water from its oars catching the dying light as it dropped, like liquid silver, back into the stream of the river.

A man came aboard in coat tails and boots and heavy trousers. He wore a hat above a gaunt face with sunken cheeks. One of the crew said to me, 'That's the doctor.'

'Anyone speak English?' the doctor said.

After a moment I raised my hand. 'I do, sir.'

'What language do these people speak?'

'Gaelic.'

'Damn,' he said. 'Our Gaelic translator died two days ago. You'll have to do it.' He took several strides towards me and gave me a good looking at. Then opened my shirt and examined my chest. 'You look healthy enough for the moment.' He spoke a strange, nasal drawling sort of English. 'I'm going to have to examine these folk to see who's sick and needs treatment. The rest of you will be kept in the Lazarettos at the top end of the island.'

'Lazarettos?'

'Just huts, son.' He looked around. 'I guess the sick are still below deck.'

They finally got us all ashore. Ferried on longboats and gathered together on the pier in the dark, lanterns held above us on poles. A collection of miserable souls, dressed in rags, filthy hair long and unkempt, beards tangling on cadaverous faces. Not a single person wore shoes. One man was dressed in a woman's petticoat, given him by the captain's wife to hide his modesty. His humiliation was acute.

Thirty-nine sick people, most of whom could not walk, were taken directly to the hospital sheds. The remainder of us had whatever goods we had brought with us removed by men wearing masks and gloves who moved among us like servants of death. Fortunately, the captain's wife had possession of my diaries, so they were kept safe.

Catrìona Macdonald was taken with the rest of the sick to the hospital, and I was left in charge of her children, holding the baby in my arms. We were herded on to carts then, to make the short journey to the north-east end of the island.

The doctor sat up on the cart beside me and the children. I could almost feel his fatigue. 'I've seen things,' he said, 'that no man should see. I've seen suffering that no human being should have to endure.' He turned to look at me with empty eyes. 'I used to be a religious man, son. But if there's a God, then he abandoned us a long time ago.'

Our sorry convoy moved off through the night, a lantern on each cart. The track cut inland, the sea somewhere away to our right. On our left lay what the doctor described as a mosquito-infested lagoon. Cholera Bay, he called it. Where the *Eliza* had anchored, he said, was known as Hospital Bay.

Nearly a hundred thousand people had come through Grosse Île this year alone, he told me. Most of them off boats from Ireland. He said that people were dying there in their tens of thousands from the potato famine. And I knew just how that must be.

'Five thousand poor souls have died from typhoid on Grosse Île in the last seven months,' he said. 'It's what most of the sick on the *Eliza* have, too.'

'Will they die?' I asked.

'Some of them. The strongest will survive. All things considered, we do not do that bad a job. But our ambulance doubles as a hearse. And it's at work twenty-four hours a day, seven days a week.' He shook his head. 'We've lost two drivers to typhoid already this year, and half of our translators.'

I had no idea what to say to him. Five thousand dead? It was unimaginable. We passed through the only village on the island. Houses and a church set back along either side of the road. I said, 'Who lives here?'

'The quarantine workers and their families,' he told me. 'Doctors, nurses, translators, administrators, drivers. And the men of God, of course. Come to see first hand what hell Heaven has wrought on earth.' His disillusion and lack of faith was almost painful, and I found it hard to meet his eye. And I wondered, too, what kind of people would come and work in a place like this, and bring their families to live here with them.

Beyond the village, the land levelled off, and we were closer again to the sea. Finally we saw the Lazarettos, long shadows in the dark, set in rows overlooking a rocky shore.

When we dismounted, the doctor told me they were sure to call on my services again, and he thanked me for my patience before heading off back to the village. But he is wrong, for I have no patience. I have no desire to be in this place, and will leave it just as soon as I can.

A quarantine worker led us to the last of the huts. It seemed endlessly long, partitioned along its length, open doorways leading from one section to the next. Walls and roof and beams were crudely whitewashed. Oil lamps hung from the ceilings, and shadows lurked and moved like ghosts among the hundreds of people lying side by side on long trestles set against either wall. A double-tier trestle runs down the centre of the hut, groaning with bodies, a single sheet covering eight or ten souls at a time.

This is to be our home for the next days or weeks, until we either come down with the typhoid and die, or survive and move on to the next phase of this hellish journey.

The children clung to my legs as we shuffled in to claim our space on wooden shelves scarred by the graffiti of all those desperate people who have gone before us, and stained by God knows what excretions.

The nursing woman took Catrìona Macdonald's baby to feed her. We would eat shortly, they said. And for that I was grateful. But all I wanted was to be gone.

It is hard to say that I feel better, but after three square meals I am physically stronger.

The doctor who met the boat came looking for me this morning to tell me that the administrator wanted a word. I rode back through the island with him on his cart, and he pointed out the armed guards posted on the edge of the village nearest the Lazarettos. 'There are shifts of them night and day,' he said.

I looked at them in surprise. 'Guards? What are they guarding?'

'Against folk in quarantine straying into the village or trying to escape. It's a dreadful thing, the typhoid, son. The authorities'll do anything to keep it contained.'

There were children playing among the houses in the village as we went through it, and they stopped their games to watch us pass. Dark eyes filled with caution that made me feel like those lepers they speak of in the Bible.

The administration hut was close to the pier, a long shed with windows looking out over the bay. The administrator himself was a Scotsman from a place called Dumfries. He said he had been working here more than ten years. I asked him if he wasn't afraid of catching the typhoid. He just smiled and said the fear never leaves you. But that if he'd been going to catch it he reckoned he'd have got it by now.

'You speak the Gaelic, I'm told,' he said, and I nodded. 'We have translators for most languages here, but we recently lost our Gaelic speaker. Actually, he was Irish, but he seemed able to talk to the Scots well enough.'

The administrator turned to gaze out of the window at all of the boats anchored in the bay.

355

'I wonder if you might be able to help us with a wee problem we have. An Irishman called Michaél O'Connor who arrived here on the fifth. He doesn't appear to speak any English.' He turned back to look at me. 'The man's demented. Even turned violent once or twice. He hitches a ride on the ambulance and comes here two or three times a day shouting and screaming. Maybe you could talk to him for us. Find out what the hell it is he wants.'

I found Michaél O'Connor in Lazaretto No. 3, and was surprised to discover that he was not much older than myself. He was sitting at a table on his own, staring into space. Most men, it seems, shave and get their hair cut after a day or two here, but Michaél had a thick black beard on him, and his hair was shoulder-length, matted and knotted. He looked at me with the palest of blue Celtic eyes, empty of any emotion.

Until I spoke the Gaelic to him, and his face lit up. 'Man, I thought you were another of these bloody people come to jabber at me in English. There's not one of them speaks God's own language, and I can't make myself understood at all.' Then he glared at me suspiciously. 'It's a weird sort of Gaelic you speak, though.'

'Not as weird as yours,' I said.

'Where are you from?'

'Scotland.'

He roared and laughed then and slapped me on the back, and I think it is the first time I have heard human laughter in months. 'Ach, you're a Scotsman!' he said. 'Second-best to an Irishman, of course, but you'll do. Did they send you?'

'Aye,' I said. 'To find out what it is you want from them.'

His face clouded a little as his smile faded. 'My brother Seamus left Cork on the *Emily* more than four months ago. He'd have been quarantined here, so there must be a record of him. They're bloody meticulous about keeping their records. All I want is to confirm that he landed here safely and then passed on to Quebec City after his quarantine.'

'Surely you could have found some way of asking them that?' I said.

And then he shocked me by speaking English with a thick brogue and a foul mouth. 'The fockers don't speak the mother tongue, Scotsman. Just the fockin' English.'

I was astonished. 'But you speak it yourself.' I raised my hands, at a loss to understand. 'So where's the problem?'

His eyes twinkled with mischief. 'I've never given the English the pleasure of hearing me speak their bloody language yet. And I'm not about to start now.'

I laughed and shook my head. 'But these people aren't English, Michaél. They're Canadian. And they only speak English or French.'

He guffawed again. A big, loud, infectious laugh. 'In that case, it looks like I'm going to have to learn the fockin' French, then.'

They gave me access to the arrival and departure records in the administration office this afternoon, and I sat at a table with a great big log that listed the arrival of every boat – where it was from, when it arrived, how many people were aboard, how many had died and were sick.

I looked for the *Heather*, sailing from Loch Glas in the Hebrides. But I couldn't find any record of it. I asked the clerk if every boat that arrived stopped here at Grosse Île. He was a grey little man, with not much hair left, and sad green eyes. He said that every boat got stopped here, but because of pressure of numbers this year if the doctor found no disease aboard then the boat would be allowed to continue without quarantine.

And from that I took heart and hope that my mother and sisters had not faced disease aboard the *Heather*, and that they had passed on directly to Quebec City. I would find out when I got there.

I turned my attentions then to the passenger list for the *Emily*, whose arrival I found had been registered on July 2nd. The crossing had taken fifty-one days, with a hundred and fifty-seven passengers in steerage. Nine had died during the crossing and sixteen were sick on arrival. And there among the surviving passengers was one Seamus O'Connor. The grey clerk with the green eyes raised his head wearily when I troubled him for some further information. 'Seamus O'Connor,' I said. 'Arrived on the *Emily* from Cork, Ireland, on July 2nd. Can you tell me when those passengers left for Quebec?'

He opened another huge ledger, and ran a bony finger with a dirty fingernail down columns of entries. 'Here we are,' he said. 'The *Emily* was held in quarantine for just four days. Six of the sixteen that were put in hospital died.' He ran his finger down another column, then looked up. 'Seamus O'Connor was one of them. He's buried in the mass graves.'

The mass graves are to be found in a flat, grassy area near the south-western tip of Grosse Île. The ground rises up on both sides, rocky and tree-covered. But through the trees beyond the graves, you can just see the sluggish swell of the river. Quebec City is somewhere there, not far upriver. So the dead were almost within sight of it.

Rows of crude white crosses pepper the grass that has grown freshly here over the recently disturbed earth. I found Michaél standing among the trees, sheltering from the drizzle and looking out over the crosses. He wore a blue woollen jacket and torn, baggy trousers held up by braces. The stitching in his boots was rotten and barely held them together. His hands were shoved deep in his pockets.

He nodded towards the graves. 'That's my countrymen buried out there,' he said.

'And mine.'

He looked at me. 'Did you people have the famine, too?'

'Yes.'

He turned away again. And I sensed anger in the way he clenched his jaw. 'There's not one of these poor bastards who would have chosen to leave. But if they'd stayed, they'd have starved to death.' Anger flashed in his eyes now as he turned them on me. 'With not a single landowner lifting a finger to help them.' And then he blurted the question I knew he'd been afraid to ask. 'So what did you learn about Seamus?'

I had been dreading the moment almost as much as he had. I was not at all sure how to tell someone that the person they love is dead. But I didn't have to. He saw it in my face. And he turned away again quickly.

'He's out there, isn't he?' But I knew he didn't expect an answer, and I saw big silent tears running down his cheeks to be lost among his whiskers. 'Why couldn't he have waited for me?' He wiped away his tears with the back of his hands and I could see his embarrassment. 'I pleaded for him to let me go with him. But, oh no. Too risky for his little brother. He wanted to go ahead on his own, establish himself here and make sure I had something worth coming to.'

He stood for a long time trying to contain himself. I had no idea what to say.

Finally he spoke again. 'Looked out for me all our lives, did Seamus. Didn't want to put me at risk. Mam starved to death, you see. And Da died of the cholera. So I was all he had left.' He turned towards me. 'I'd have starved to death too, if it hadn't been for my brother. I never asked where the food came from that kept us alive, but he always came home with something.'

His face cracked open into a mirthless grin to disguise his grief.

'Then he had this bright idea of coming over here. Great things he'd heard about the place. How you could have your own bit of land. Be a free man. Not in the pocket of some fockin' landlord. Left me with an aunt and told me he'd send for me as soon as he'd found us something better. Only, I couldn't wait, could I? Stole a bit of cash and bought my passage aboard the *Highland Mary* from Cork.' His voice choked off, and he fought back his emotions again before gathering himself once more. 'And now . . .' He turned to look at me and I saw the pain in his eyes. 'Now I've no idea what to do with my life.' There was a long pause. 'But I'll tell you one thing.' And suddenly the fire was back. 'I'm not hanging around in this fockin' place.'

I was sitting at the table in our Lazaretto when Michaél came looking for me this morning. I have spent the last few days teaching Catrìona's children to count in English, as well as giving them some basic vocabulary. The Gaelic's not going to take them very far in this land of English and French.

The boy's eight, I think, and the girl about six, but not like children that age I remember from Baile Mhanais. There's no play in them. No sparkle. Hunger and loss have taken their heart. So they sit docile and do what I say, eager simply for the attention. Anxious to please in the hope of some comfort in return. Like pet animals.

All the mischief was back in Michaél's eyes and he could hardly contain his excitement. He grabbed me by the arm and pulled me outside, walking us briskly away from the Lazarettos towards the shore, anxious that no one should overhear us.

His voice was a hoarse whisper. 'I'm getting off Grosse Île tonight.'

I was surprised. 'How?'

He shook his head. 'Don't even ask. It's costing an arm and a leg. And the guards'll bloody shoot us if they see us. There's a boat going to meet us on the north-east shore and take us over to the north bank of the St Lawrence. We can make our way west from there to Quebec City. Me and three others. All Irishmen.' He paused. 'But we might make room for a Scotsman if he wanted to come along.'

My heart was banging in my chest. A chance to escape. 'I do,' I said. 'But I've got no money.'

'You bloody Scots never do!' he said. 'But don't worry about that. You can pay me back sometime. As long as you don't mind travelling second class.' And he grinned at me through his whiskers. 'Are you in?'

I nodded.

Despite my desperation to get off this damned island, by late afternoon I was regretting my impulsive decision to go with Michaél and the Irish. I had promised Catrìona Macdonald that I would take care of her children. And although I told myself it was unfair of her to burden me with that responsibility I still felt guilty at abandoning them. So I decided to go to the hospital to speak to her myself.

It was my first visit to the hospital shed, and when I crossed the threshold I felt as if I had passed from one world to another, from hell on earth to hell below it.

It was long and dark, windows blanked to keep out the daylight. The smell was worse than on the boat. And having breathed God's own clean air for three days it was all the harder to take. Beds were lined up side by side, with the narrowest of spaces between them. Just wooden frames with boards and filthy mattresses.

Nurses in dirty, stained and worn uniforms moved among the dying like angels of mercy, doing what they could to relieve pain and suffering. But they were little more than sanitation workers cleaning up in the wake of death. The strain was clear on pallid faces with deeply shadowed eyes. Even although the doctor had told me there was a reasonably high recovery rate, it seemed hard to believe that anyone could survive this place. The medical practitioners here wore long gowns and hats and face masks to protect them from the miasma of infection that permeated the very air they breathed.

I wanted to turn and go back out immediately. But I steeled myself. The very least I owed Catrìona Macdonald was an explanation. I stopped one of the nurses and asked which bed she was in. She lifted some charts hanging from the wall and riffled through several sheets, running her finger down the names. At length she stopped at one. 'Ah, yes. Catrìona Macdonald. She died this morning.'

363

It was hot outside, the sun showing itself periodically through a broken sky. I stood gulping down fresh air and fighting mixed feelings. A part of me was relieved that I wouldn't have to face her. Another part of me wanted to weep for the woman from whose loins I had torn life. And yet another part of me died a little bit for her children, and her baby who would never know her.

I found Michaél in Lazaretto No. 3, he and a little group of co-conspirators gathered around a table. My fellow escapees. 'I need to talk to you,' I said, and we went outside.

I suppose I must have had something of an aura of death around me, for he gave me an odd look. 'What can I do for you, Scotsman?'

'I need some money.'

He frowned. 'What for?'

'It's a long story. I'll pay you back when I can.' I couldn't tell him I needed it to buy off my conscience. But even in the short time that I have known him, I have realised that Michaél has a way of reading folk.

He looked at me for a long time. A gaze that penetrated my very soul, it seemed. Then he grinned and said, 'What the hell. What we need we'll fockin' steal.' And he dug into an inside jacket pocket and pulled out a small purse with its strings pulled tight and tied in a knot. He took my hand and pressed it into it. 'Ten gold sovereigns in there. I hope they're going to a good cause.'

I nodded open-mouthed, barely able to believe such generosity. 'They are. But I don't know that I can take this much.'

'Take it!' he bellowed. 'And never ask where I got it. The bloody things are far too heavy anyway. And besides, they've got the head of the fockin' English queen on them. No self-respecting Irishman would be found dead with those in his pocket.'

I went straight to the Mackinnon family who had been look-ing after Catrìona's children when I wasn't there. I was blunt with them. Told them that Catrìona was dead and that I was leaving tonight. I produced the coins and laid them out on the table, and said this was to pay for the children's keep. They had three children of their own already, but the hus-band and wife both looked at the money with eyes like saucers. It was more than either of them had ever seen. Or me, for that matter. And for a moment I wondered how on earth I was ever going to pay Michaél back.

The children themselves took the news of their mother's death in a strangely solemn silence. I wondered if perhaps they had just seen so much of it that death no longer regis-tered. They were more upset to learn that I was leaving. They clung to me, silent tears running down their cheeks, little hands clutching my jacket. And I held them both, fighting hard not to weep myself, and wondered how I could be so selfish.

I kissed them, then tore myself free to stand and take the baby in my arms, just as I had that night on the ship. She looked up at me, almost as if she knew that she would never see me again, and gripped my thumb with tiny fingers, such focus in those little eyes staring into mine. I kissed her forehead and whispered, 'Stay safe, little one.' And she smiled.

I can hardly write as I squat here in the dirt, shaking from the cold and wet, sitting as close to the flames as I dare, to warm my bones and light my pages. Michaél watches me with curiosity in his pale eyes. He has no understanding of this compunction I have to put my life on paper. Somehow in these last two months it has become the only thing that gives my existence any point.

I can see the slow movement of the river through the trees below us where we shelter from the rain and the cold beneath this overhang of rock. And somewhere across the water, unseen, lie the horrors of Grosse Île. It hardly seems possible that it is less than two hours since we left the Lazarettos under cover of darkness, and that only Michaél and I remain alive.

There were five of us altogether. Earlier the sky had been clear, but by the time we left after midnight it had clouded over and was threatening rain. The dark seemed impenetrable.

We moved within touching distance of each other, away from the huts, and across the wide, flat, boggy ground that lay between the Lazarettos and the village. It was just possible to see the darker shadow of the tree-covered escarpment that rose away through tangling briar towards the north side of the island. That part of it had never been settled and we knew it would be difficult terrain to negotiate.

We were almost there when God intervened, and a great hole opened up in the sky to let moonlight flood down across Grosse Île. For a moment it was like midday, and there we were, caught in the full glare of the light for anyone to see. And seen we were. By the guards on the edge of the village. A shout went up, voices were raised and a shot rang out in the dark.

We ran for our lives, seeking the cover of the trees, and once there went ploughing through briar and undergrowth that shredded our clothes and skin. Climbing. Up over rock and tree roots, stumbling and tripping, fuelled by panic.

We could hear the soldiers in pursuit, and as we reached the crest of the rise a volley of shots rang out, and one of the Irishmen went down. 'Leave him!' one of the others shouted, but Michaél stopped, crouching beside him to turn him over. I stopped, too, scared as hell and breathing hard. Michaél looked up grimly. 'Dead,' he said. 'Nothing we can do for him.' And he was on his feet in an instant, pulling on my sleeve to drag me running off through the trees.

It got easier as we scampered down the other side, helter-skelter between the tree trunks, almost out of control, until finally we saw moonlight glinting on water through the foliage. And it occurred to me for the first time that if the boat wasn't there, we would be cornered, and either killed or captured.

But there it was, a dark silhouette bobbing up and down between the rocks, waiting for us as planned. We slithered over the rocks and through the water, to be pulled on board by two men whose urgency was clear in the pitch of their voices. 'Quick, quick!' they shouted. Because already we could hear the soldiers crashing down the slope behind us.

In that moment God stepped in again and the moonlight vanished, darkness settling over us like black dust to obscure us from view. We pushed off from the shore, and the boat-men plied their oars to propel us out into the swell and flow of the river. Shots rang out from the shoreline. We could see the rifles flashing in the dark, but their shots went harm-lessly wide or fell short. And soon we were well beyond range. Free.

But not safe. Not yet. The river seemed to move slowly, and yet the current was powerful, and the oarsmen had to fight hard against the drag of it. We had little control, it seemed, over where the river would take us, and we crouched there breathing hard and filled with fear, completely at the mercy of our rescuers and this vast flow of deep, dark water.

It seemed like for ever before we finally saw the black line of the shore, and then suddenly we were there, navigating our way through the rocks to pitch up on a shingle beach. The land rose away steeply from here, trees growing almost down to the water's edge.

The first I knew there was any trouble was the sound of a shot as I stepped out of the boat. I turned around to see one

of the Irishmen collapse into the stern of it. One of the oarsmen held a pistol on the three of us remaining while his
companion went through the pockets of the dead man then
pitched him out into the river.

'Okay, hand over your money.' The gunman's voice was
shaking.

'You've got all the fockin' money you'll get from us,'
Michaél said.

'Well, the way I see it, you've got two choices. You can
hand over the money now, or I can take it off your dead
bodies.'

'We'll be dead as soon as we hand it over,' the other Irishman said.

The man with the gun grinned in the dark. 'That's a
chance you'll have to take.'

The swiftness with which the Irishman lunged at him took
him by surprise. But as the two men went down, the gun
went off, and the Irishman went limp on top of him. The
other oarsman spun around, drawing a second pistol, and I
barely saw the flash of Michaél's blade before it slid up
between the man's ribs and into his heart.

Michaél stooped immediately to pick up his pistol, and as
the first oarsman dragged himself free of the Irishman he
had killed, Michaél shot him point-blank in the chest.

It had all happened so quickly, I had barely moved from
the spot where I stepped ashore. And I stood now, gaping in
horror and disbelief.

'Fockers!' Michaél said. Then, 'Come on, Scotsman, help me go through their pockets. Get all the money you can and let's get out of here.'

We tipped all the bodies into the water when we were finished, and Michaél crossed himself as he said farewell to his friends. Then we pushed the boat out into the river, and started scrambling up the embankment as the rain began to fall.

We have six gold sovereigns and ten Canadian dollars between us, and are lucky still to be in possession of our lives. I have no idea what the future holds, but it seems that mine is now inextricably linked with Michaél's. I glance across the fire to see the flicker of its flames on his bloodless, bearded face. If it wasn't for him, I'd be a dead man now.

CHAPTER TWENTY-NINE

I

The atmosphere in the incident room at the Sûreté on Cap aux Meules was tense. The team sat around an oval table studiously avoiding eye contact with either Sime or Marie-Ange. A map of the Madeleine Isles was pasted across one wall, the yellow-and-green flag of the Sûreté draped in the opposite corner. A blackboard that nearly filled the end wall by the door was covered in chalk scribbles. Names, telephone numbers, dates, places.

Lapointe was back from Montreal, having attended the autopsy. He told them the pathologist had been unable to establish much more than cause of death. Any one of the stab wounds would have been fatal, even without the other two. The knife used had a narrow six-inch blade with serrations along the blunt edge. Possibly a fish-scaling knife, he had thought. Apart from some bruising, the only other injuries the pathologist could find were scratch marks on Cowell's face. His assumption was that they had been made by fingernails during the course of a struggle.

Crozes took a duster and roughly cleared space for himself on the blackboard. At the top of it he chalked up the name of James Cowell, then drew a line from it straight down to the foot of the board. Branching off alternately left and right, he wrote down the names of the suspects.

He began at the bottom with Briand. 'As we've established, Briand has strong motive. His wife had been having an affair with Cowell, and the two men were fierce business competitors. Briand actually had more to gain than any of the others from Cowell's death. Even without taking account of the jealousy factor.' He paused. 'But he has a very solid alibi. He was at home with his wife.' He glanced at Sime and Blanc. 'While you guys were flying back from Quebec City Arseneau and Leblanc reinterviewed her. She confirmed his story.'

Sime found it hard to meet his eye. He said, 'Well, of course she would. She has motive, too, Lieutenant. If we're to believe the two of them, then she was keen to ditch Cowell, but didn't know how to tell him. Her husband said she was actually afraid of him. It's perfectly possible that they both conspired to murder him.'

Crozes nodded his agreement. But beneath his veneer of professionalism his discomfort was clear. 'That's true. But we have not one single scrap of evidence to put either of them at the scene.'

'Then maybe we should be looking for some.'

Now Crozes concealed his irritation with difficulty. 'People have been looking for extraterrestrial life for years, Sime. It doesn't mean it exists. Without evidence to the contrary, and with each providing an alibi for the other, I think we have to rule them out.'

He took his chalk and drew a firm line through Briand's name. The room was silent. Then he tapped the tip of the chalk on Morrison's name.

'I don't think there's one of us who believes that Norman Morrison had anything to do with the murder. He was a sad case. Retarded. The mental age of a twelve-year-old. And while he might have had an obsession with Mrs Cowell, I think his story that James Cowell had him beaten up to warn him off was just that. A story. That he took a beating from someone seems clear, but it's unlikely that we are ever going to find out who. And while his mother can't definitively swear that he was home in bed on the night of the murder, a search of his house has failed to turn up a murder weapon, or any clothes that he might have been wearing during the attack. And certainly no ski mask. In fact, his mother would have known if he even possessed such a thing. And according to her he didn't.'

'And his death?' Lapointe asked.

'A sad accident, Jacques. He was concerned for Mrs Cowell when he heard about the murder. We think he went out in the storm to go and see that she was all right. It was dark. The island was being battered by a force ten or eleven. He must have lost his way and gone over the edge.'

Crozes drew another line through Morrison's name before turning back to the room.

'Then there's Mr Clarke.' He scratched his chin. 'There was clearly antipathy on his part towards Cowell. He blamed him for the death of his father and the loss of their family boat. But his wife swears that he was home in bed, and we have absolutely no evidence to the contrary.' He scored out his name. Then looked up at the one remaining suspect. 'Which leaves us with Mrs Cowell. Who in my view is, and always has been, the most likely killer.'

Sime listened with growing disquiet as Crozes outlined the case against her. It was strong and indisputable, and he knew that in any normal circumstance he could not have found fault with it. But this was different, for one simple reason. He didn't want it to be true.

Crozes said, 'She is the only witness to the murder. She was there when it happened. She doesn't deny that. She was covered in his blood. And, yes, she told us a story to explain that. But there is not one shred of evidence at the scene to support it. There is nothing to suggest that there was in fact a third party.' He drew a deep breath. 'She lied to us more than once. About being happy that her husband had left her. About not leaving the island. About not knowing he was coming back that night. She's admitted to all that. Why would an innocent person lie?'

He looked around all the faces focused on him and knew that his summation was compelling.

'She threatened him. Not directly. But she doesn't dispute that she told Ariane Briand that if she couldn't have him she'd see that no one else could. In his last interview with her, Sime very clearly, very concisely, outlined the most likely scenario. We've all seen the tapes by now. He accused her of luring her husband back to the island by threatening to set their house on fire, and killing him in a fit of jealous rage. He suggested that, immediately filled with remorse, she tried to revive him, and when she failed made up a story about an intruder.' He looked at Sime. 'Powerful stuff, Sime.' There was an edge in his voice.

Sime felt his face colour. He didn't want the credit for any of this. It was almost as if Crozes knew it and was deliberately salting a wound that Sime couldn't even acknowledge. And any praise coming from Crozes had a double edge to it in the light of the previous night's events. Sime stayed focused. 'There are two problems,' he said.

'Oh?' Crozes tried to look interested. 'And what are they?'

'The guy who attacked me two nights ago. You say there's no evidence that Kirsty Cowell's claimed intruder exists. But this guy fitted the description, right down to the ski mask.'

'And that could have been anyone trying to deflect suspicion away from themselves.'

'Like who?'

'Like Owen Clarke.'

'Who has an alibi. And no motive that I can think of for attacking me.'

'His son, then. He might have felt you humiliated him in front of his friends and wanted to teach you a lesson.'

'He also has an alibi.'

Crozes was scathing. 'Yes, if we're to believe his pals. And think about it, Sime. What possible motive could the killer have for attacking you? I think this is a red herring. And I don't want us wasting time on it. What's the second problem?'

'Simple,' Sime said. 'We don't actually have any physical evidence against Mrs Cowell.'

'Oh, but we do.' Crozes's smile was laden with satisfaction. 'Or, at least, we might have. The autopsy report shows that Cowell had scratches on his face, almost certainly made by fingernails.' He paused. 'Mrs Cowell claims that her attacker was wearing gloves. So how could he have left scratch marks? If forensics can match the residue taken from beneath Mrs Cowell's nails with skin from Cowell's face we've got her.'

II

Sime was halfway across the car park to pick up the Chevy and take it back to the Auberge when he realised that he'd left his cellphone lying on the desk in the incident room. He hadn't charged it for several days and needed to plug it in when he got back to his room. He hurried past the cormorant sculpture on the front grass and up to the main door, just as Marie-Ange was coming out. She had been searching for something in her bag as she came through the door and almost bumped into him. A tiny gasp of surprise escaped her lips as they found themselves just inches apart. Her surprise quickly gave way to anger, and he almost withered under its simmering virulence. She glanced quickly behind her. There was no one in the hall. And under her breath she said, 'I should just have shot you. Then we'd both have been put out of your misery.'

'Well, since you're the source of it, maybe you should have turned the gun on yourself.'

Her lips formed themselves into a sneer. 'You're so fucking smart, Simon.'

'At least I'm honest.' Strangely, he felt quite emotionally detached. 'And maybe you should have shot me. You've done just about everything else to me.'

She pushed past him to stride off down the path. But he caught her arm. Her head whipped around. 'Let go of me!'

He said, 'I'm so glad we never had that kid.'

An odd, sick smile flitted across her face. 'Yeah, be grateful. It wasn't even yours.'

She pulled her arm free and hurried away around the side of the building.

He stood staring after her, his face smarting as if she had slapped him. Until now he had thought it impossible for her to hurt him any more than she already had.

CHAPTER THIRTY

The news of Marie-Ange's pregnancy had changed the way he felt about everything. If he had spent his life searching for something, a reason for being, a point to his existence, then suddenly it seemed that he had found it.

But from the start Marie-Ange had been ambivalent. Sime had been unable to understand why she didn't share his excitement. They had been going through a difficult time, and it seemed to him that a child could provide the glue that would keep them together. But looking back on it later, he realised that she had probably only seen it as an impediment to their breaking up. A responsibility to child and family that she didn't want.

They'd had a debate about the scan. Sime had wanted to know the sex of their child. She had not. And, as usual, she prevailed.

Four months into the pregnancy, and having regular appointments with the gynaecologist, she still appeared to have little or no maternal instinct. And yet Sime's sense of fatherhood had been powerful. He had found himself seeing children on their way home from school and imagining how it would feel to be a father. Bringing back memories of his own first day at school, insisting that he could find his way home himself, and then getting lost. He had even caught himself looking at prams and baby seats for the car.

It had stirred memories, too, of the story about his ancestor delivering the baby on the boat, and the moment of parting at Grosse Île when the child had gripped his thumb with tiny fingers. Sime had wanted that feeling. The unqualified and absolute love of a child. The sense that a part of him would live on when he had gone.

At about seventeen weeks Marie-Ange had taken a week's leave to visit her parents in Sherbrooke. Sime was upcountry on a case the day she was due back. That afternoon he got a call to say she'd been rushed to hospital with severe bleeding, but it was twenty-four hours before he was able to get back to Montreal.

Without any idea of what had happened he went straight to the hospital, where he was left sitting in a waiting room for almost two hours. No one told him anything, and he was almost beside himself with worry.

People came and went. Sick people. Worried relatives. Sime was just about to read the riot act to the nurse at reception when Marie-Ange came through the swing door. She was deathly pale, and clutching a small bag of belongings. She seemed oddly hunched, and when he hurried across the room to her she put her arms around him and buried her face in his chest. Sobs ripped themselves from her throat, and when she tipped her face back to look up at him he saw that it was shiny and wet with tears. She didn't need to tell him that they had lost the baby.

Strangely, they had been closer in those next few days than they had in years. Sime pampered her, cooking, doing the washing, taking her breakfast in bed. They sat together at night on the settee with a glass of wine, watching mindless TV.

It was the following week that she had broken the news to him. Her gynaecologist had told her she would no longer be able to have children.

Sime had been devastated. Taking it almost harder than the loss of the baby. He had been revisited by the same sense of bereavement experienced after the death of his parents. Of regret. Of being all alone in the world. Not just then, but for ever. And of somehow failing, not just his parents, but their parents, and their parents before them. It would all end with him. So what point had there been to any of it?

CHAPTER THIRTY-ONE

I

Sime stood smarting in the doorway. She had always claimed that learning she couldn't give him a child had changed him. Changed them. That it had been the beginning of the end. His fault, not hers.

And now the revelation that the baby had not even been his.

But for some reason, something didn't quite ring true. Discovering Marie-Ange and Crozes in bed the night before. Realising that they'd been lovers for months, maybe years. And now replaying that awful time when she had lost the child. All of it brought a sudden reinterpretation of events. As if scales had fallen from his eyes. He felt a surge of anger and disbelief, and started off round the building at a run.

She was sitting behind the wheel of the second rental car, engine idling, but making no attempt to drive away. He ran across the car park and pulled the driver's door open. She looked up at him, her face wet with tears, just as it had been that day at the hospital.

'You liar,' he said.

She flinched as if he had struck her.

'That was my kid. But you figured if you had it you were going to be stuck with me, right?' And when she didn't respond. 'Right?'

There was a singular vacancy in her eyes.

'You didn't go to your parents at all that week. You had an abortion, didn't you? From some back-street quack. 'Cos you couldn't do it legitimately without me knowing.' He stared at her in disbelief. 'You killed my child.'

She said nothing for a very long time, then in barely a whisper she said, 'Our child.' She pulled the door shut, engaged Drive, and accelerated away across the tarmac.

II

Long after she had gone, Sime stood by the *sentier littoral* staring out across the Baie de Plaisance towards the now familiar contour of Entry Island lying along the horizon. Children were playing on the beach, barefoot, running in and out of the incoming waves, screaming as cold water broke over little legs. The breeze ruffled his hair and filled his jacket. He felt hollowed out. His emptiness gnawed at him like a hunger. He was numbed by fatigue.

The longer he stared at this island which had grown to dominate his life these last days, the more compelled he felt to return to it. He had no idea why, except for a powerful sense that whatever answers it was he was seeking were to be found there.

He returned to the car park and got into the Chevy, driving up to the Chemin Principal and then north past the hospital and Tim Horton's to the harbour. There he found the boatman whose fishing boat had been requisitioned by the Sûreté. He was sitting in the back of his vessel at the quayside smoking a small cigar and untangling fishing nets. He looked up, surprised, when Sime climbed down into the boat. 'I need you to take me over to Entry,' Sime said.

'Lieutenant Crozes said I wouldn't be needed till later.'

'Change of plans. I need to go over now.'

When they arrived at Entry Island, Sime told him he could take the boat back to Cap aux Meules. He would make the return trip on the ferry. He stood watching as the fishing boat chugged out of the shelter of the breakwater and back into choppier waters in the bay, then turned to walk past the minibus where they had left it parked up for use on the island. He could have taken it. But he wanted to be on foot, to feel the island beneath his feet. He passed fishing boats with mundane names like *Wendy Cora* and *Lady Bell*, and turned on to the wide, unsurfaced Main Street that swept along the east coast of the island. Sunlight washed across the bay from the distant Cap in moments of broken sky. To the south-west, and much closer, was the Sandy Hook, a long curve of sandbank that extended from La Grave at the eastern point of the island of Havre Aubert. It reached out like a bony finger towards Entry Island.

The breeze was freshening a little, but it was still warm. He headed south past Josey's restaurant. On his left, a chain was strung across the track that climbed to the little airstrip which had once played host to a winter passenger schedule between Entry Island and Havre aux Maisons. The short stretch of runway where Cowell had habitually landed his single-engined aircraft and picked up his Range Rover. The plane was still there, sitting on the tarmac.

At the top of the slope the road cut inland and he followed it up to the Anglican church. A plain white building of clapboard siding with green trim around small arched windows. It stood on the hill with a panoramic view extending west. A huge white cross, held in place against powerful winds by steel cables, cast its shadow across the graveyard.

Sime opened the gate and walked past a ship's bell on a rusted metal mounting to wander among the headstones in the late-afternoon sunshine. Rifleman Arthur E. McLean; Curtis Quinn; Dickson, infant son of Leonard and Joyce. Some of them dated back decades. Others were more recent. But those who had staked their claim to a place here on the slopes of Entry Island were unlikely to be joined by too many more of their fellow islanders as the population dwindled towards extinction.

Sime's shadow fell across an old, weather-worn headstone that stood no more than eighteen inches high and leaned at a slight angle in the grass. He was barely able to make out the name McKay, and he crouched down to brush away more than a century's accumulation of algae and lichen. *Kirsty McKay, he read. Daughter of Alasdair and Margaret. Died August 5th, 1912, aged 82.* Kirsty's great-great-great-grandmother. It had to be. The old lady whose photograph he had seen in the album started by Kirsty's mother. He tried to recall her face, but the detail was gone. There was just an impression left in his mind of a time when people of a certain generation all seemed to look the same. Perhaps the homogenising effect of a popular hairstyle, or a fashion in clothes and hats. Or the limitations of those early cameras. The black, white and sepia prints, the poor lighting. Too dark or too light, too much contrast or too little.

Whatever it was, Sime found something sad in stumbling across the old lady's grave like this. An image in a photo album perpetuates the illusion of life. Long after death, a smile or a frown lingers on. But a hole in the ground, with a stone marking the place where your head has been laid, is for eternity. He placed his hand on the stone. It was cool against his skin, and he felt the strangest sense of affinity with the old woman whose bones lay beneath him. As if somehow she made a bridge between his past and his present. Between him and her great-great-great-granddaughter.

As he stood up he shivered, although it was still warm. And goosebumps prickled all over his arms and shoulders as if someone had just stepped on his grave.

*

Clothes hanging out to dry in the late September sunshine flapped in the wind on a line strung from a characterless modern house next to the Epicerie. Two men in scuffed blue boiler suits and wellington boots interrupted their conversation to stand and watch as Sime walked past the junction. The road surface was broken and stony here. An old golden Labrador, with stiff, arthritic back legs, fell in step beside him.

'Duke!' one of the men called. 'Duke! Here boy.' But the dog ignored him and kept pace with Sime.

Where the path turned right towards the lighthouse, the road swung left, leading towards the Cowell House. Duke took the turn ahead of him and hobbled up the hill, almost as if he knew where it was that Sime was going. Sime hesitated for only a moment. He had no reason or authority to go back to the house. His interviews with Kirsty were over. And in any case, she would no longer speak without a lawyer present. Still, he followed Duke's lead.

The house built by Cowell seemed like a sad extravagance now. It sat up here in cold testimonial to a failed marriage, empty and loveless. He stepped into the conservatory. 'Hello?' His voice reverberated around all the empty spaces within, but brought no response. He crossed the grass to the summerhouse, and found the patrolman from Cap aux Meules making himself a sandwich in the kitchen. The young man looked up, a little surprised.

'I thought you guys had gone back to Cap aux Meules,' he said.

Sime just shrugged. 'Where's Mrs Cowell?'

'You going to question her again?'

'No.'

The patrolman bit into his sandwich and washed it over with a mouthful of coffee. He threw Sime a curious look. 'Last time I saw her she was on the road heading off up the hill there.'

'Where does that go?'

'Nowhere in particular. It peters out after a while.'

Duke was waiting for him as he stepped back out of the house. The Labrador seemed to grin, then turned and started off up the road as if showing him the way. Sime stood and watched as the old dog ambled with his awkward arthritic gait up to the brow of the hill. There he stopped and looked back. Sime could almost feel his impatience.

But Sime turned away and followed the path that led to the cliffs and the narrow steps down to the jetty. The Cowells' motor launch bobbed gently in the afternoon swell.

He imagined Kirsty, half drunk, fired by jealous humiliation, running down these steps in the dark and setting off across the bay in that small boat to Cap aux Meules. What kind of desperation must have driven her?

He turned and walked back towards the house and saw that Duke was still waiting for him on the hill.

Sime had no reason to talk to Kirsty again. And yet he wanted to see her. He wanted to tell her how much he hated this, even although he knew he wouldn't. He started off up the hill after Duke. The dog waited until he was within a few metres, then turned and hobbled on.

The road was rutted and uneven, loose stones skidding away underfoot. When he reached the top of the rise Sime turned and looked back. The house seemed a long way below him already. In the distance, at the southernmost point of the island, the lighthouse looked tiny. And across the water, Havre Aubert seemed almost close enough to touch. The wind was stronger up here, whipping through his hair, filling his hoodie and blowing it out behind him. He turned to find Duke waiting for him again, and he walked on to a point where the road became little more than a path worn through the grass. It divided in a hollow, one branch snaking up towards the summit of Big Hill, the other descending again to the cliffs and the red rock stacks that rose up out of the ocean.

And there he saw her. Standing very close to the cliff's edge, silhouetted against the blaze of reflected sunlight on the ocean beyond. They were facing east here, out across the Gulf of St Lawrence and the North Atlantic towards a far distant land from which their ancestors had once come.

Duke reached her before he did. She stooped to ruffle his neck then crouched beside him. Sime saw her smiling, animated in a way he had not seen her before. Until he entered her peripheral vision and she turned her head to see him approaching. The smile vanished and she stood up immediately. Her whole demeanour became hostile and defensive.

'What do you want?' she said coldly when he reached her.

Sime pushed his hands in his pockets and shrugged his shoulders. 'Nothing,' he said. 'I was just taking a walk. Killing time till the ferry comes.' He flicked his head beyond where she stood. 'You're a bit close to the edge here.'

She laughed, and it seemed to Sime that it was the first time he had seen her genuinely amused. 'I'm not going to throw myself off, if that's what you think.'

He smiled. 'I didn't.' He looked along the ragged line of the cliffs. 'But there's a lot of erosion here. Not safe to get too close, I wouldn't think.'

'I'm touched by your concern.' The sarcasm had returned.

He looked at her very directly. 'I'm only doing my job, Mrs Cowell. I bear you no ill will.'

She gasped her disbelief. 'Accusing me of killing my husband doesn't feel like you bear me much good will either.'

'Just testing the evidence.' He paused. 'A pathologist I know once told me that when he performs an autopsy on a murder victim he feels like that person's only remaining advocate on earth. Someone to find and test the evidence that the body of the deceased has left in his care.'

'And that's what you're doing for James?'

'In a way, yes. He can't speak for himself. He can't tell us what happened. And whatever he might have done, whoever he might have been, he didn't deserve to die like that.'

She looked at him steadily for a long moment. 'No, he didn't.'

An awkward silence settled between them. Then he said, 'Do you really intend to spend the rest of your life here?'

She laughed. 'Well. That depends on whether or not you put me in jail.' He found a pale smile in response. 'But the truth is, Mr Mackenzie, that whatever I might have said in an emotional moment, I really love this island. I played all over it as a child, I've walked every inch of it as an adult. Big Hill, Jim's Hill, Cherry's Hill. Pimples on the landscape really, but when you're young they're the Alps or the Rockies. The island is your whole world, and anything beyond it far off and exotic. Even the other islands in the Magdalens.'

'Not an easy place to live, I wouldn't have thought.'

'Depends what you're used to. We didn't know anything else. At least, not until we were older. The weather is hard, sure, but even that you accept, because it's just how it is. The winters are long, and so cold sometimes that the bay freezes over and it's possible to walk across to Amherst.' And for his benefit, 'That's Havre Aubert.'

'How come you speak English here when the rest of the islands are francophone?'

'Not all of them are,' she said. A gust of wind blew her hair into her face and she carefully drew it aside with her small finger, then shook it back. 'They speak English at the north end, too. At Grand Entry Island, and Old Harry and Grosse-Île. Old Harry is where James came from originally. But, yes, most of the population of the Magdalen Islands are French-speakers. I guess maybe only 5 or 10 per cent of us speak

English.' She shrugged. 'It's our heritage, our culture. And when you're a minority you tend to protect those things, nurture them, defend them. Like the French minority in Canada.'

Duke had wandered off, sniffing among the grasses, and was very close to the cliff's edge. She shouted to him, but all he did was raise his head and cast a dispassionate glance in their direction.

'Come on,' she said to Sime. 'If we head back up the path he'll follow us.' She smiled. 'Duke's made it his lifetime's work to follow every visitor to the island.'

They walked up along the path, side by side, at a leisurely rate. Anyone watching from a distance might have taken them for old friends. But the silence between them was tense.

She said suddenly, 'You probably know, but we still use all the English names for the islands here on Entry. Magdalen rather than Madeleine. Cap aux Meules is Grindstone, Havre Aubert is Amherst – well, I already told you that. Havre aux Maisons is known as Alright Island.' It was as if she felt that by talking about things of no consequence, those things of enormous consequence that were creating the tension, would be somehow dissipated. 'The whole archipelago is surrounded by shipwrecks. I saw a map once that pinpointed them all. Hundreds of them, all around the coast.'

'How come they all washed up here?'

'Who knows? Bad weather, bad luck, and no lighthouse back in the early days. And I suppose we are slap-bang in the

391

middle of the main shipping lane to the St Lawrence River and Quebec City.' She glanced at him and bit her lip. 'How the hell do you make polite conversation with someone who thinks you're a murderer?'

'That's not necessarily what I think,' he said, and as soon as he'd said it, regretted it. Because, on balance, it was what he thought. It just wasn't what he wanted to think.

She looked at him intently. As if those blue eyes could penetrate his outer defences and reach the truth. 'Sure,' she said eventually, unconvinced.

Duke hirpled past them and threw himself into a ditch full of water at the side of the path. He splashed about in it for a while, cooling himself down, then hauled himself out again with difficulty. He shook his coat violently, and sent water spraying all over Kirsty and Sime. She let out a yell and stepped back, almost losing her footing, and Sime was quick to grab her arm and stop her from falling.

She laughed. 'Damn dog!' And then her smile faded as she realised that Sime was still holding her. They were both immediately awkward and he let go of her, self-conscious, almost embarrassed by their unexpected physical contact.

They turned and followed Duke as he ran off with renewed vigour to where the road dipped down over the top of the hill. The wind was stronger here. Below them the bay simmered intermittently in flitting sunlight. Cowell's house stood proud on the edge of the cliffs, the summerhouse where Kirsty had been born just beyond it. The roof of the police patrol car glinted in the sunshine next to Cowell's beige Range Rover.

'Don't you have a car?' Sime said suddenly.

'No.'

'How do you get around?'

'You don't need a car on the island. There's nowhere you can't walk to.'

'But James felt the need for one.'

'He often brought stuff over on the plane with him. I suppose if I'd ever needed one, I could have used his. Except that I don't drive.'

Sime was surprised. 'That's unusual.'

But she didn't respond, her attention caught by his right hand as he ran it back through his hair. 'What happened to your hand?'

He looked at it and saw that the knuckles were bruised and grazed, slightly swollen where he had struck Crozes. He pushed it into his pocket, embarrassed. 'Nothing,' he said. And to his amazement she reached forward to seize his wrist and pull his hand back out of the pocket so that she could examine it.

'You've been in a fight.'

'Have I?'

She was still holding his hand, and pushed up an eyebrow. 'This is a tough island, Mr Mackenzie. There are no policemen here. Men often settle their differences with fists. It wouldn't be the first time I've seen busted knuckles.' She paused, glancing down again at his hand. 'And yours weren't like this yesterday.'

She let him go, and he took his hand back to rub it gently with his other, almost as if trying to hide the damage, and became aware again of the ring with the arm and sword. In spite of a strange compunction to tell her the truth all he said was, 'It's a personal matter.' He avoided her eye.

'Let me guess. Men don't usually hit complete strangers, and since you don't know anyone here it's probably someone you know. One of your co-workers. A fellow investigator. Am I right?'

Now he met her gaze full on. But still said nothing.

'Since I don't see any damage to your face other than the cut you got the other day, it might be fair to assume that you were the aggressor. Which means that you must have had some pretty powerful motivation for attacking a colleague. My guess would be that there's a woman involved?' She raised an eyebrow to ask the question. When there was no response she said, 'And since the only woman on the team is your ex . . .'

'He'd been sleeping with her.' It was out before he could stop himself. And immediately wished he could take it back. He felt his face redden.

'Since before the break-up?'

He nodded.

'And you just found out?'

'Yes.'

394

'And gave him a beating?'

'Yes.'

'Good for you.'

Somehow she seemed to have turned the tables on him. She was the interrogator, he the guilty party defending his actions.

She smiled and said, 'We're really not so different then, are we?' He gave her an odd look. 'Each of us capable of losing our cool in the face of losing a lover.' She paused and sighed. 'You of all people, Mr Mackenzie, should understand what drove me over to Cap aux Meules that night to confront James and the Briand woman.'

His mouth was dry. 'Did it also drive you to kill him?'

She stared at him for a long time. 'I think you know the answer to that.'

Duke had tired of waiting for them and wandered back to drop himself in a huff at their feet.

She said, 'When we first met you thought you knew me.'

He nodded. He wanted to tell her about the diaries. About his dreams. About the little girl called Kirsty whose life his ancestor had saved. The teenage girl he had kissed on a windswept Hebridean island and lost on a quayside in Glasgow. How somehow in his dreams, in his mind, she had become one with the woman who stood before him here on this blustery hill on Entry Island.

She reached out unexpectedly to run fingertips lightly down his cheek and said, 'You don't know me at all.'

Some instinct, or some fleeting movement, made him turn his head. He saw the patrolman from Cap aux Meules approaching on the path, a couple of hundred metres away down the hill. Even from here Sime could see his consternation. How bizarrely intimate this moment must have seemed. Sime the detective, Kirsty the murder suspect, standing so close together on the hill, her fingers extended to touch his face.

She took her hand away, and Sime left her to hurry down the hill towards the policeman. Duke struggled to his feet and ran after him.

The young policeman continued up the slope to meet him halfway. He gave Sime the oddest look, but kept his thoughts to himself. 'Lieutenant Crozes has been trying to reach you, sir.'

'Why didn't he call me on my cellphone?' Sime dug a hand into his pocket to find it, and realised he had never gone back to the incident room to get it. 'Damnit! I'll call him back from the phone at the house.'

And with only the most fleeting of backward glances, he headed quickly off down the road with the patrolman towards the summerhouse. Kirsty stood on the prow of the hill watching them go.

He could hear the contained fury in Crozes's voice. What the hell was he doing on Entry? But he was barely listening. From where Sime stood holding the phone in the living room of the summerhouse, he could see Kirsty walking slowly down the hill. He let Crozes rail at him without response. Until finally the lieutenant ran out of steam and said coldly, 'We'll deal with that later. The preliminary report from forensics is in. Lapointe had them do priority DNA testing. They just faxed the results.'

'And?' Sime knew it would not be good news.

'The samples taken from beneath Kirsty Cowell's fingernails contain skin matching the scratchmarks on her husband's face.' He paused, and Sime heard something that sounded almost like pleasure in his voice. 'Maybe it's just as well you're over there, Sime. I want you to arrest her and bring her back here to be formally charged with murder.'

Sime said nothing.

'Are you still there?'

'Yes, Lieutenant.'

'Good. We'll see you both back here around six, then.' He hung up.

Sime stood holding the receiver for a long time before slowly replacing it in its cradle. Through the window he saw that Kirsty had reached the big house now and was walking across the grass towards the summerhouse. Duke had gone to meet her and was gambolling excitedly around her legs, as enthusiastically as his arthritis would allow. Sime turned to find the patrolman looking at him. 'I'm going to need a witness for this,' he said. The young man flushed with anticipation. It was clear to him that something previously outside of his experience was about to go down.

Sime stepped out on to the porch as Kirsty climbed the steps. She could tell at once that something had changed. 'What's wrong?'

Sime said, 'Kirsty Cowell, you are under arrest for the murder of James Cowell.'

All the colour drained from her face. 'What?' Her shock was clear. Her voice trembling.

'Do you understand?'

'I understand what you're saying, but I don't understand why you're saying it.'

Sime drew a long breath, aware of the patrolman at his shoulder. 'You have the right to retain and instruct counsel without delay. I am taking you back to the police station at Cap aux Meules where we will provide you with a toll-free telephone line to a lawyer referral service if you do not have your own lawyer. Anything you say can be used in court as evidence. Do you understand?' He waited. 'Would you like to speak to a lawyer?'

She stood staring at him for a very long time, every conflicting emotion reflected in her eyes. Until she lifted her hand and slapped him hard across the face where just a few minutes earlier she had touched him with tender fingers.

The patrolman stepped in quickly to grab her wrists.

'Let her go!' The imperative in Sime's voice had almost as powerful an effect on the young man as Kirsty's slap, and he released her immediately, as if she were electrically charged. Sime felt an ache of regret as he met her eye. 'I'm sorry,' he said.

CHAPTER THIRTY-TWO

I

He left her in the care of the patrolman while she packed a bag and he went to get the minibus from the harbour. Which gave him plenty of time to think on the walk there and the drive back. But cogent thought did not come easily. From the moment he first set eyes on Entry Island he had felt something ominous in the dark shadow it laid along the horizon. The sense of destiny he had experienced on arrival had now reached some kind of perverse fulfilment. The woman who had become somehow synonymous in his mind with the girl in his dreams and the Ciorstaidh of the diaries had, after all, murdered her husband. And it had fallen on him to arrest her.

Back at the summerhouse he put her bag in the minibus and she slipped sullenly into the passenger seat beside him. They left the patrolman guarding the scene of the crime, and drove in silence across the island. The sun was dipping low in the western sky, edging pink and grey clouds with gold and lying shimmering like lost treasure across the bay.

It was the last time, he knew, that he was likely to set foot on the island, and he let his eyes wander sadly across its gentle green undulations, its colourfully painted houses, and the mountains of lobster creels piled up along the roadside. As the pitted track that passed for a road wound down below the church, he glanced up the shallow slope where head-stones punctured the grass. Somewhere up there was the lichen-crusted stone that marked the final resting place of Kirsty's many-times distant grandmother, and it seemed to him that he could almost feel the old lady's reproach.

There was a crowd on the jetty to meet the incoming ferry. Sime noticed Owen and Chuck Clarke among them, watching him with sullen eyes. And when the boat had unloaded its cargo of people and goods, they all watched silently as Sime reversed the minibus on to the car deck. Kirsty sat in plain view beside him with dead eyes, a face like stone turning to neither left nor right. This woman who had not left the island for ten years. It could only mean one thing.

He sat with her in the vehicle until the ramp had been raised, hiding them from the view of curious eyes on the quayside. The boat pitched gently as it pulled away to round the breakwater and headed out across the bay. Without a word he reached into his pocket for a pair of handcuffs, and before she realised what was happening took her left wrist and cuffed it to the steering wheel. Her shock was patent, blue eyes blackened by dilating pupils and brimming with hurt and anger. 'What the hell are you doing?'

'I can't risk letting you free on the boat in case you jump overboard.'

She gazed at him in disbelief, her mouth half open. 'You really think I'd commit suicide?'

'It's been known.' He paused. 'Unless you'd rather go up on deck handcuffed to me for all the passengers and crew to see.'

Her jaw set and she turned to gaze sightlessly through the windshield. 'I'll stay in the van.'

He nodded and slipped wearily out of the vehicle to climb the stairs to the top deck, and there make his way along to the prow of the boat. He closed aching, scratchy eyes, and felt the wind in his face like cold water, refreshing, bracing, but not enough to wash away his fatigue or his sense of guilt and betrayal.

He turned to find his way unsteadily back to the stern, and stand holding the rail while he watched Entry Island receding into the gloom of approaching night. He remembered the touch of Kirsty's fingers on his cheek. Could almost feel them still. And everything about what he was doing seemed wrong.

II

As they drove past the hospital and the Auberge Madeli, torn lumps of ragged black cloud blew across the island from the west, underlit by a fiery sunset that burned white hot along

401

the horizon, turning to yellow and red, then purple, all across the underside of the clouds. It looked as if the sky were on fire, and Sime was not sure he had ever seen a sunset like it.

But like all things that burn so brightly, it burned itself out all too fast, and by the time they reached the police station on the Chemin du Gros Cap the sun had gone, leaving behind it only a charred sky.

There was still a little light left in it as Sime led Kirsty into the single-storey building. Yellow electric light fell out in oblongs from the glass doors, and as they pushed through them, heads swung in their direction. From the open door of the general office where secretaries watched wide-eyed. From the incident room next door, where several members of the investigation team were lounging around a table cluttered with papers and open laptops and telephones. They were relaxed now. Job done. Thomas Blanc fleetingly caught his eye then looked away.

Crozes was standing at the end of the hall. He turned, and Sime saw the look of satisfaction on his face, a face still bruised from their encounter in the early hours. 'This way,' he called.

He stood at the door to the cells to let them by. Inside, a uniformed female officer was waiting. Kirsty cast Crozes a dark look as she passed. Sime stopped her in front of the first of two cells and she turned to him. He saw in her expression the same contempt with which he had become so familiar in

Marie-Ange. 'So now we know who was screwing your wife,' she said.

Sime glanced at Crozes, whose eyes narrowed with incredulity, his head half cocked in disbelief. But Sime was past caring. He leaned into the cell to drop Kirsty's bag on the floor by the cot bed set along the right-hand wall.

She looked into it. 'This is it?' she said. 'This is where you're going to keep me?'

'For the time being,' Crozes said.

The walls were painted a pale lemon, the same colour as the sheet on the bed. The vinyl floor was blue, as were the pillow and duvet. 'Very Mediterranean,' she said. 'And colour-coordinated too. What more could a girl ask for?'

There was no door on the cell. Only bars that slid shut on it, so there was no privacy. A stainless-steel unit incorporated a washbasin and toilet in one. Set into the far wall beyond the second cell was a tiled shower. Bleak and depressing. But however despondent she might have felt, Kirsty was determined not to show it.

Crozes said, 'Have you spoken to a lawyer?'

'I don't have one.' And without looking at Sime, she said, 'He told me I could call one from here.'

Crozes nodded. 'Next door.' And he took her through to the interview room. 'No doubt you'll want your lawyer present at all future interviews.'

Kirsty wheeled around, eyes flashing. 'You bet your life I do.' And she stabbed a finger towards Sime standing in the

403

doorway. 'But don't expect me to say a single damned thing if he's even in the building.'

The incident room was empty when they went in and Sime wondered where everyone had gone. It wasn't long until he found out. Crozes closed the door behind them. His voice was low and threatening. 'I'm not even going to ask what the hell you were doing on Entry Island. Or how she knew.'

Sime looked at him disingenuously. 'Knew what?'

'About us.'

Sime held up his fist. 'Busted knuckles. Bruised face. Broken marriage. It doesn't take much to put the pieces together.'

It was impossible to tell from Crozes's face what was going through his mind, but whatever thoughts they were never found voice. He said, 'She'll be charged and held here until a plea hearing can be set up at the courthouse on Havre Aubert. Any subsequent trial will be held on the mainland.' He stopped to draw a thoughtful breath. 'Meantime, I'm taking the team back to Montreal first thing in the morning. And your part in this investigation is over.'

'What do you mean?'

'I mean someone else will be taking over your role as interrogator.'

Sime glared at him. 'In other words you're removing me from the case.'

Crozes turned away to begin casually gathering together

papers on the table. 'Not me, Sime.' He opened a briefcase and stuffed the paperwork inside before turning back to face him. 'You're not well. It's been noted by the brass back at Rue Parthenais. People are concerned for your well-being.' He paused before delivering his *coup de grâce*, barely able to mask his smirk. 'They want you to take sick leave for medical evaluation. An appointment's already been set up with a consultant.'

And Sime realised just how Crozes had fucked him. Exactly as Thomas Blanc had predicted.

III

Sime sat alone in his room while the rest of the team ate in La Patio. All he could think of was Kirsty sitting forlornly on the edge of the cot bed in her cell at the Sûreté. He knew by now that he had lost all objectivity on her guilt or innocence. Though it hardly mattered. She had been charged with murder. And he had been instrumental in bringing the case to that conclusion.

But he remained uneasy. Two nights ago he had lain on the ground in the dark, looking up into the masked face of a man who was about to kill him. A man who matched Kirsty's description of the intruder who she claimed had murdered her husband. Crozes had dismissed it as a red herring. But he hadn't seen the look in the attacker's eyes and understood, as Sime had, that he meant to kill him. This was no kid trying to scare him off. Only fate and a light sleeper had saved Sime from certain death.

More inexplicable still, was why this man should have wanted to kill him. As Crozes himself had pointed out. No matter how much he turned it over in his mind, none of it made sense.

In normal circumstances he would have found it difficult to sleep tonight. But this was no normal circumstance. His bosses at the Sûreté were right. He wasn't fit for duty. In fact he wasn't fit for much of anything. It seemed to him that it wouldn't be long before he was looking for a new job. And washed-up former cops were not exactly the most eligible for employment.

He dropped his face into his hands. The thought of his child that never was fought for space with his grief for the loss of Marie-Ange, and anger at what she had done. He wanted to weep. But tears wouldn't come, and as he sat up again his eye alighted on the signet ring on his right hand. Red carnelian set in gold and engraved with an arm and sword. From the same set as Kirsty's pendant.

He remembered his sister's words. *I'm sure there's something about the ring in the diaries themselves. Can't remember what, though.* And he was almost overwhelmed by the sense that in all his recollections of those stories from so many years before, he was missing something.

Somehow, he knew, it was imperative that he got his hands on those diaries.

CHAPTER THIRTY-THREE

There was none of the usual banter and celebration that accompany the successful conclusion of a case. The detectives assigned to the murder of James Cowell by the Sûreté de Québec at 19 Rue Parthenais in Montreal solemnly presented themselves the following morning at security in the small airport at Havre aux Maisons. They were waved through to the tarmac where their thirteen-seater King Air would take them on the three-hour flight back to the city.

Equipment packed away in the hold, they squeezed themselves into the tiny passenger cabin. Sime once more sat on his own at the front, isolated from his colleagues. As on the flight out he avoided eye contact with Marie-Ange. The tension aboard the small aircraft was almost physical.

They took off into the wind, and as they banked left Sime had a view out across the Baie de Plaisance. The sun was rising beyond Entry Island, casting its shadow long and dark across the bay towards Cap aux Meules. Like a clenched fist with a single finger pointing in accusation.

Sime looked away. It was the last time he would set eyes on it. Just as, the day before, he had set eyes on Kirsty Cowell for the final time. She would be waking now to her first full day of incarceration, awaiting the hearing that would allow her officially to claim her innocence.

He sighed and felt tired. So very, very tired.

CHAPTER THIRTY-FOUR

I

The insomnia clinic was located in the Behavioural Psycho-therapy and Research Unit of the Jewish General Hospital on the Chemin de la Côte-Sainte-Catherine, almost in the shadow of Mount Royal, and just a few streets away from the Jewish cemetery at the foot of it.

There was still warmth in the sun, and leaves on the trees, but an autumn chill on the edge of the wind. The sky was well broken, and Montreal basked in the late September sun-shine. From the office where he had sat patiently answering questions for the last half an hour, Sime could see the traffic heading south on the Rue Légaré. The office was warm, made warmer by the sun streaming in through the windows, and the stop–start movement of the cars below was almost hyp-notic. Sime was finding it hard to concentrate.

Catherine Li was, he guessed, in her early forties. She wore a white, open-necked blouse and black slacks, an attractive woman, slim, with short-cut black hair, and the beautifully slanted dark eyes of someone whose ancestral roots lay somewhere in Asia. Canada was such a melting-pot of differ-ent ethnicities, and although he considered himself a native French-speaker, it nevertheless seemed odd that this woman should speak to him in French.

The plaque on her door had told him that she was a Ph.D. and Clinical Director of the unit.

There had been no preamble. No chit-chat. She had asked him to sit, opened a file on the desk in front of her, and taken notes as he responded to her questions. Wide-ranging questions about his upbringing, his job, his marriage, his feelings on various topics, political and social. She had asked about his symptoms. When they had begun, what form they took, how often he slept. Did he dream?

For the first time she sat back and looked at him. Examin-ing his face, he thought. A face that had grown increasingly unfamiliar to him as he examined it himself in the mirror each morning. Eyes bloodshot, deeply shadowed. Sunken cheeks. He had shed weight, and his hair had lost its lustre. Every time he looked at his reflection he felt haunted by the ghost of himself.

She smiled unexpectedly and he saw warmth and sym-pathy in her soft brown eyes. 'You know, of course, why you are here,' she said. It wasn't a question. But he nodded all the same. 'Your employers at the Sûreté have sent you to me because they fear that your condition is affecting your ability to do your job.' She paused. 'Do you think it is?'

Again he nodded. 'Yes.'

Again she smiled. 'Of course it is. In fact, it's a given. The toxins that have accumulated in your body through lack of sleep are certain to have impaired both your physical and mental performance. As I'm sure you are aware, your concentration and memory will also have been affected. Tired during the day, irritable and fatigued, and yet unable to sleep at night.'

He wondered why she was telling him what he already knew.

She interlaced her fingers on the desk in front of her. 'There are two kinds of insomnia, Monsieur Mackenzie. There is acute insomnia, which lasts for a short period, usually just a matter of days. And then there is the chronic variety, which can be defined as suffering sleep impairment for at least three or four nights a week for a month or longer.' She stopped to draw breath. 'Clearly you fall into the chronic category.'

'Clearly.' Sime was conscious of the sarcasm in his tone. She was still telling him nothing new. But if she was aware of it she gave no indication, perhaps writing it off to the irritability she had just described as one of his symptoms.

'The cause of your condition can also be defined in one of two ways. As either primary or secondary insomnia.'

'What's the difference?'

'Well, primary insomnia is unrelated to any other physical or mental conditions. It is simply a condition in itself. Secondary insomnia, however, means that your sleep problems are related to something else. There are many things that can affect your sleep. Arthritis, asthma, cancer. Pain of any kind. Or depression.' She regarded him thoughtfully for a moment. 'Which is, I believe, your problem. Extreme depression brought on by the break-up of your marriage.' She inclined her head slightly. 'Are you aware of being depressed?'

'I'm aware of being unhappy.'

She nodded. 'The vivid dreaming that you have described to me is frequently a symptom that accompanies anxiety or depression-induced insomnia.'

In an odd way it was almost a relief to have his dreams explained to him in this way. As a symptom. A condition brought on by something outside of his control. But normal, if the symptom of a psychological problem could ever be described as normal.

He became aware of Catherine Li watching him closely. 'Are you still with me?'

'Yes.'

'There is a school of thought which argues that dreams are actually a chemical event. That they are directly affected by modulations in the brain's neurotransmitters. You know what REM is?'

'R-E-M?'

'Yes.'

'A band, weren't they? Losing my religion?'

Her smile indicated anything but amusement. 'You know, I've never heard that one.'

'I'm sorry.' He lowered his eyes, embarrassed.

'REM stands for rapid eye movement. It describes a phase of sleep that you go through, typically, four or five times a night, accounting for anything up to 120 minutes of a night's sleep. It is also when most dreams occur. During REM sleep acetylcholine and its regulators normally dominate, while serotonin is depressed.'

Sime shrugged, incomprehension written all over his face now. 'Which means?'

She laughed. 'It means that I might recommend prescribing you SSRIs.'

'Of course, why didn't I think of that?'

This time her smile was wry. She said, patiently, 'Selective serotonin re-uptake inhibitors. That would increase serotonin levels and elevate your mood.'

Sime sighed now. 'In other words, an antidepressant.'

She shook her head. 'Not just any antidepressant. In fact, most popular antidepressants would probably only make your condition worse. I think this could help.'

Sime was unaccountably disappointed. He wasn't sure what he had expected. But another pill just didn't seem like any kind of a solution to his problem.

II

The apartment seemed colder and emptier since his return. Even just a few days away had robbed it of its sense of being lived in. It smelled stale. Dirty dishes were piled up in the

413

kitchen. There had been no chance to wash them before leaving. Or to empty the garbage. Something in the kitchen bin smelled like it was a long way past its sell-by. Unwashed laundry spilled over from the wicker basket in the bedroom. The bed was unmade, as it always was. Clothes lay on the floor where he had dropped them. Dust gathered in drifts along every surface in every room. Things he had almost stopped seeing. All classic symptoms of a mind kidnapped by depression.

He sat that night in the living room with the television on. But he wasn't watching it. He was cold, but somehow it didn't occur to him to switch on the heating.

He remembered the advice of a lecturer at the academy. Sometimes you can think too much and do too little. And he looked around the apartment and saw the result of thinking too much and doing nothing at all. It was as if somewhere, somehow, he had just given up on life, become paralysed by inertia. He didn't want this, any of it. And yet it was all he had. He was desperate to sleep, but not for the sake of sleeping. He wanted to escape. To be someone else in another place and time. He glanced at his ancestor's painting on the wall. That bleak, dark landscape. And he wished he could just step into it.

The pills they had prescribed were on the shelf above the sink in the bathroom. It was almost time to take them. But he was afraid of going to bed now, in case he still wouldn't sleep. The doctor had said they would take time. But he couldn't face another sleepless night.

He stood up, fuelled by a sudden desire to take back his life. Right here, right now.

He spent the next hour gathering clothes from the floor and stuffing them into the washing machine. While it went through its wash cycle he filled the dishwasher and set it going, then sprayed all the work surfaces in the kitchen with disinfectant before washing them down. He took the garbage down to the disposal unit in the basement. And it was while there that he remembered Marie-Ange's words to him on Entry Island. When he had asked her about her things she had said, *I don't want the stuff. Why don't you just chuck it all in the trash?*

He took the elevator back to the apartment fired with renewed determination, and in the bedroom threw open the doors to their built-in wardrobe. There were the clothes she'd left, hanging on the rail, shoes on the rack beneath them. T-shirts and underwear folded neatly on shelves. Things he remembered her wearing. He reached in to lift out one of her T-shirts and hold it to his face. Though it was clean, somehow it still smelled of her. That distinctive perfume she wore. What was it? *Jardins de Bagatelle*. He had no idea where he had pulled that name from, but the fragrance would be for ever associated with her. And he felt that sense of loss again, like a physical pain in his chest.

Almost in a fury he hurried into the kitchen to retrieve a large black bin bag and went back to the bedroom. He swept all the clothes off the rail and stuffed them into the bag.

Followed by her tees and panties and bras, a nightdress, all of her shoes. He had to get a second bag, and a third. And then he dragged them to the elevator and down to the basement. He hesitated only briefly before emptying the bags down the recyclable chute. Au revoir, Marie-Ange.

On the return trip in the elevator he saw himself in the mirror and couldn't stop the tears from welling in his eyes. He could have been a father by now. He swore at his reflection.

Back in the apartment he was determined not to be diverted by negative emotions. He wiped his face dry and stripped the bed, shoving his dirty linen and used towels into a large laundry bag which he took down to his car. He drove across the bridge to an all-night laundry in Rue Ontario Est and left his washing there to be collected the next day. When he got home he found clean sheets in the laundry closet and made his bed up fresh.

For the next half-hour he took a vacuum cleaner over every carpet in the apartment, then went through a whole packet of static-free dust cloths, wiping over cabinets, shelves and tables, amazed by the dirt that came off them. He sprayed air freshener in all the rooms, then nearly choked on its cloying perfume and opened the windows.

By 1 a.m. the apartment was cleaner and fresher than at any time since Marie-Ange's departure, and there was not a trace of her left in it. Sime stood in the living room breathing hard from his exertions, sweat beading across his forehead. If he had hoped to feel better, he wasn't sure that he did. It was manic behaviour, he knew. Though at least it was something positive. But when he sat down, somewhere deep inside he knew that all he had been doing was avoiding the moment when he would have to lay his head on the pillow and try to sleep.

He went through to the bedroom and stripped off, careful to drop his clothes in the laundry basket. His new regime. Then he padded through to the bathroom and showered. When he came out he stood in front of the bathroom mirror, grateful that it was opaque with steam and that he could not see himself. He took the prescribed dose of SSRIs from their bottle and washed them over with water from his tooth mug, then brushed his teeth.

As he did the steam slowly cleared from the mirror and he saw his ghost staring back at him, hollow-eyed. He had changed everything, and nothing.

Vigorously he rubbed his hair dry with a towel and slipped into a clean pair of boxers. Back in the living room he flicked through the TV channels for half an hour until he turned it off to sit in a silence that screamed. He was so physically fatigued that he could barely stand up. But at the same time his mind was cruising along some astral highway at the speed of light and he felt not the first inclination to sleep.

In spite of warnings to the contrary, he went to the drinks cabinet and took out a bottle of whisky. He poured a large measure, and pulled a face when he took a mouthful. Scotch and toothpaste were a lousy combination. He forced himself to drink it. Then another. And another.

Finally, his head spinning, he went into the bedroom and slipped between the clean sheets. They felt cold, dissipating whatever warmth and sleepiness the whisky had induced. He closed his eyes and let the darkness envelop him. And he lay. And lay. Praying for release.

Nothing happened. He tried hard to keep his eyes shut. But after a time they simply opened and he found himself staring once more at the shadows on the ceiling, tipping his head to one side from time to time to take in the red glow of the digits on the bedside clock, and count away the hours. Sometime, maybe two hours later, the yell of sheer frustration that tore itself from his lips echoed around the apartment.

At 7.30 a.m. there was a line of daylight around the edges of the bedroom blinds, and still he had not slept. Reluctantly, wearily, he drew the covers aside and slipped out of bed to get dressed. It was time to go and face the music at Rue Parthenais.

III

It felt odd riding up in the elevator to the fourth floor of the Sûreté as he had done countless times over months and years. He dreaded the doors opening, the long walk along the corridor past all those familiar black-and-white photo-graphs of old crimes and dead detectives. And when, less than a minute later, his footsteps echoed along its length, he felt completely disconnected.

Faces he knew passed him on the walk along to the detec-tives' room. Faces that smiled and said *bonjour*. Awkward smiles, curious eyes.

At the blue plaque inscribed 4.03 Division des enquêtes sur les crimes contre la personne, he turned into the suite of offices that housed the homicide squad. The door to the incident room lay ajar, and he was aware of heads turning in his direction as he walked past. But he didn't look in.

The offices of the top brass were ranged around an area filled with printers and faxes and filing cabinets, and walkie-talkies on charge. Like fish tanks the offices were open to scrutiny through glass walls.

Captain Michel McIvir emerged from one of them, eyes down, focused on a sheaf of papers clutched in his hand. He looked up as he became aware of Sime standing there. The most fleeting of shadows crossed his face before he managed a smile and waved a hand towards his office door. 'Be with you in a minute, Sime.'

Sime sat in the captain's office. There was a photograph of Paris by night on the wall, and a huge Quebecois flag hung limp from a standing pole. Outside he could see Mount Royal in the distance. Early-morning frost sparkled on the flat roofs of the three-storey brick apartment buildings opposite.

The captain walked in and sat on the business side of his desk. He opened a folder in front of him, and flicked through the several sheets of printed paper it contained. Pure theatre, of course. Whatever their content, he had already read it. He laid his hands flat on the desk and looked up, scrutinising Sime in silence for some moments.

'Catherine Li faxed me her report last night following your consultation yesterday.' His eyes flickered down to the desk and up again, indicating that this was it. He pressed his lips together briefly then drew a breath. 'I've also spent some time reviewing the tapes of your interrogation of the suspect on Entry Island.' Again the characteristic pressing together of the lips. 'Erratic to say the least, Sime.'

Unexpectedly he rose from behind the desk and went to close the door. He stood there holding the handle, looking at Sime, and lowered his voice.

'I am also aware of a certain incident that occurred on the islands during the investigation.' He hesitated. 'An incident which is, and shall remain, off the record.' He let go of the door handle and returned to his desk, but remained standing. 'I'm not without sympathy, Sime.'

Sime remained expressionless. He wasn't looking for sympathy.

'What is clear, however, both from what the doctor says, and from what I have seen with my own eyes, is that you are unwell.' He perched one buttock on the edge of his desk and leaned forward like some patronising physician. 'That's why I am putting you on indefinite medical leave.'

Even though he had been expecting it, Sime tensed. When he spoke his voice sounded far away, as if it belonged to someone else. 'In other words, I get punished and Crozes gets off scot-free.'

McIvir recoiled, almost as if Sime had slapped him. 'There is no question of punishment involved, Mackenzie. I'm doing you a bloody favour here. It's for your own good.'

Which is what people always said when administering bad medicine, Sime thought.

The captain lowered his voice again, confidentially. 'Events involving Lieutenant Crozes have not gone unnoticed. Nor will they be without consequence.' He stood up. 'But that's none of your concern. For now, I want you to go away and get well.'

In the street outside, Sime drew a long, deep breath and despite the news just broken to him by his boss felt free for the first time in years. It was time to go home. Back to the womb.

And, finally, to the diaries.

IV

The drive from Montreal to Sherbrooke took him just under two hours, heading almost directly east into the heart of what had originally been known as the Eastern Townships and was now referred to as the Cantons de l'est. From Sherbrooke he drove down to Lennoxville and took Highway 108 east.

He felt a tightening of his heart and an odd sense of nostalgia as he drove into the forest. For this was where he had been raised, where generations earlier his forebears had carved out a new life for themselves. Literally. Felling trees and clearing land, encouraging virgin soil to grow enough to feed them. So many of the immigrants here had been Scots, and he wondered how many had been victims of the Clearances. He passed a sign for *Le Chemin des Ecossais* – the Scots Road. And as he drove deeper into the woods, he was struck by the Scottish-sounding names of so many of the towns. East Angus, Bishopton, Scotstown, Hampden, Stornoway, Tolsta.

A warm sun slanted out of the autumn sky, transforming every tree into one of nature's stained-glass windows. The golds and yellows, oranges and reds of the fall leaves glowed vibrant and luminous, backlit by the angled rays of the sun, turning the forest into a cathedral of colour. Sime had forgotten just how stunning these autumn colours could be, his senses dulled by years of grey city living.

New highways cut through the forest now in long, straight lines, riding the contours of the land, like the Roman roads in Europe that so represented the single-minded determination of a race. Woodland in full colour stretched out before him as far as the eye could see, like a gently undulating ocean.

And he recalled with great clarity the moment his ancestor had first set eyes on it.

CHAPTER THIRTY-FIVE

It has taken us five days of walking to arrive at our destination, and this is the first chance I have had to update my log. We have been sleeping in the woods, or under hedges, begging for food and water from the houses we passed on the way. Everyone we've met has been incredibly generous. Maybe because they, too, at one time this way passed.

What amazes me most are the trees. Where I come from, you could walk all day and never see a single tree. Here it is impossible to take two steps without bumping into one. And the colours, as the days shorten and the temperatures drop, are like nothing I have ever seen before. It's as if the land is on fire.

As we came further south we started to chance upon villages and townships establishing themselves along the river valleys. Log cabins, some of them little more than huts, built around crudely constructed churches. There were general stores, and sawmills springing up on streams and burns, and little schools where immigrant children were learning to speak a new tongue. Trees were being felled and land cleared, and I was amazed at just how many people there were in what at first had seemed to be such a vast and empty country.

We arrived at the village of Gould in the township of Lingwick, towards noon yesterday morning. Sunday. It was here that we were told we should come if we wanted land. The village is built around a crossroads, with the road dipping away steeply at the north side, towards the valley of the River Salmon. There is a general store, and a church, and a school, and when we arrived there was not a soul to be seen.

That's when I heard the Gaelic psalm-singing coming from the church. It's not like normal singing. More a kind of chanting in praise of the Lord, with the congregation led in their unaccompanied song by one or more precentors. It was so familiar to me, and so redolent of home, that all the hairs stood up on the back of my neck. There is something about that sound, a sort of primal connection with the land and the Lord, that has always affected me.

'What the hell is that?' Michaél said.

And I laughed. 'It's the music of my island,' I said.

'Well, I'm glad I don't come from your island. Sounds bloody weird to me.'

We were standing outside the church when the congregation streamed out into the noonday sun. They cast curious glances our way, two raggedy young men with beards and matted hair standing there in tattered shoes clutching little more than a handful of personal possessions.

When the minister had finished shaking the hands of his flock he walked towards us. A tall, thin man, with dark hair and cautious eyes. He introduced himself in English as the Reverend Iain Macaulay and welcomed us to what he called the Hebridean village of Gould.

'We've come to the right place, then,' I replied to him in Gaelic. And his eyebrows shot up. 'My name is Sime Mackenzie and I come from the village of Baile Mhanais on the Langadail Estate on the Isle of Lewis and Harris. And this is my friend, Michaél O'Connor from Ireland.'

All the caution left the minister's eyes then and he shook our hands warmly. And the congregation, when they heard that I was a fellow Hebridean, began to gather round, each of them welcoming us in turn and shaking our hands.

Mr Macaulay said, 'You have indeed come to the right place, Mr Mackenzie. Gould was established by sixty Hebridean families cleared off their land in 1838. And they were joined by another forty destitute families from the west coast of Lewis just three years later. It's as close to home as you can get without actually being there.' I felt suffused by the warmth of his smile. 'What's brought you to us?'

'We heard that they're giving away free land,' I said.

An old man in a dark suit said, 'Aye, they are that. You've timed it well, laddie. The clerk from the British American Land Company arrives in the morning to start allocating parcels.' He pointed a finger vaguely beyond the church. 'Just to the south there, in what they call the St Francis tract.'

425

Michaél said, 'But why would they be giving away land for nothing?' He was still deeply suspicious of anyone who claimed to own land, but I was relieved that he was at least moderating his language.

Mr Macaulay said, 'If there's one thing there's plenty of in this country, boys, it's land. The company is giving it away so that it will be populated by settlers. That way the government will give them contracts to lay in roads and build bridges.'

We set off from Gould early Monday morning along a track that took us maybe half a mile into the forest. The minister was with us, as well as a large crowd of villagers to accompany twenty or more hopeful settlers and the clerk from the British American Land Company.

We arrived at a small clearing after ten or fifteen minutes. The sun was barely over the tops of the trees and it was still icy cold. But the sky was clear and it looked like we were in for another beautiful autumn day.

Mr Macaulay asked those wanting land to gather round. We were going to cast lots, he said.

'What's that?' I asked him.

'It's a practice that occurs in the Bible, Mr Mackenzie,' he said. 'Most commonly in connection with the division of land under Joshua. I refer you to Joshua, chapters 14 to 21. In this case I will have a bunch of sticks in my hand of varying length. You will each draw one, and he who draws the

426

longest will get the first allocation of land. And so on, right down to the shortest, who will get the last.'

Michaél grunted loudly. 'What's the point of that?'

'The point is, Mr O'Connor, that the first parcel of land will be the closest to the village. The last will be the furthest away, and the most inaccessible. So this is the fairest way to decide who gets what. It shall be God's will.'

And so we drew lots. To my amazement I pulled out the longest stick. Michaél drew the shortest, and had a face like thunder darkening beneath his beard.

We all proceeded then to the starting point of the first parcel, which was to be mine. The minister handed me a short axe and told me to cut a notch with it in the nearest tree. 'What for?' I asked. But he just smiled and told me I'd see soon enough.

So I cut a notch in the closest tree, a tall evergreen pine. 'What now?'

'When we start singing,' he said, 'begin walking in a straight line. When we stop make a notch in the nearest tree, then turn at right angles to it and start to walk when the singing begins again. Another notch when we stop, another turn, and by the time we've sung three times you'll have marked out your parcel.'

'It should be approximately ten acres,' the clerk from the British American Land Company said. 'I'll accompany you to register your land on the official map.'

Michaél laughed and said, 'Well, if you folk would sing a bit slower, and I ran as fast as I could through the trees, then I could have a much bigger piece of land.'

Mr Macaulay smiled indulgently. 'Aye, you could indeed. And you could also break your back trying to clear it of trees and make it arable. Bigger is not necessarily better, Mr O'Connor.' He turned then to the assembled crowd and raised a hand and the singing began. To my astonishment, I recognised it immediately as the 23rd Psalm. I was going to pace out my land to the accompaniment of The Lord is My Shepherd!

The voices grew distant as I marched through the trees with the clerk right behind me. But it carried across the still of the morning, a strange haunting sound pursuing us into the forest. Until they reached the end of the final verse and I cut a notch in the nearest tree during the silence that followed, turning then to my right and waiting for it to start again.

After many stops and starts and a break for lunch, it was nearly dark by the time that Michaél paced out his tract of land. We were almost hoarse with the amount of singing we had done. Never, I was sure, had the 23rd Psalm been sung so often in the course of a single day. As we walked back to the village in the falling dusk Michaél said to me, 'It's too far to my bit of land. So I'll just help you do yours first, and we'll leave mine till later.'

And I was secretly pleased that I wasn't going to have to face the task on my own.

Last night Michaél and I spent our first night in my new home.

We have been working all the daylight hours of every day for the last two weeks to clear an area of land big enough to build a log cabin. Hard, hand-blistering work with saws and axes loaned to us by folk from the village. Felling the trees was simple enough, once you got the hang of it. But moving them once they were down was another matter, and digging out the roots next to impossible. Someone promised to lend us an ox in the spring to help pull out the worst of them, but the priority has been to get a basic cabin up before winter arrives. Temperatures have been falling, and we've been working against nature's clock. One of the older villagers told me that I might have experienced the odd sprinkling of snow on Lewis and Harris, but nothing would prepare me for the snow that would soon fall here.

The last few days we have been stripping trunks and cutting them to length, and then yesterday the whole village turned up for the raising of the cabin. Certainly, we could never have done it on our own, and would have had no idea how to notch and interlock the logs at the four corners.

The walls are seven feet high – which is as high as men can lift a log. The roof is steeply pitched, laid with hand-split shingles and covered with turf.

I would never have believed it possible, but by the end of the day, the cabin was done. A pretty sorry-looking dwelling, but it was a roof over our heads, with a door to shut against the weather.

Someone brought an old box bed on a wagon and reassembled it for me in my newly finished home. On the same wagon came a kitchen table that someone else was donating, and a couple of rickety chairs that might just about take our weight. A bottle of spirit was opened, and everyone took a slug of it to christen the new house. Then a prayer was said as we all stood around the table. The next priority will be the building of a stone chimney at one gable, which is something I might even be able to do myself. Then we'll be able to light a fire and heat the place.

The problem is how to keep ourselves warm in the meantime.

When the villagers had finally gone, and Michaél was hauling water up from the river in buckets, I gathered some kindling and split some logs to build a fire in the centre of the cabin. There are no floorboards yet, just beaten earth, so I made a stone circle to contain the burning wood.

Although the room quickly filled with smoke it would, I knew, soon disperse through all the cracks and crevices between the logs, just as the smoke in our old blackhouse made its way out through the thatch.

But the next thing I knew, the door had burst open, and Michaél came running in, yelling, 'Fire, fire!' at the top of his voice, and threw a bucket of water all over my carefully tended blaze.

'What the hell do you think you're doing?' I shouted at him.

But he just stared at me with big, manic eyes. 'You can't light a fire in the middle of a wooden house, man! You'll burn the fockin' thing down!'

I didn't speak to him for the rest of the evening. And it wasn't long after dark that it became so cold that there was no option but to turn in for the night. It was Michaél who broke our silence finally and wanted to toss a coin to decide who got the bed. But I told him that since it was my house it was my bed, and he could sleep on the bloody floor.

I don't know how much time passed after I extinguished the oil lamp, but it was black as pitch when I became aware of Michaél slipping into the bed beside me, freezing hands and feet bringing all of his cold air with him. I thought long and hard about kicking him out again, but in the end decided that two bodies were likely to generate more heat than one, so pretended that I was still asleep.

This morning, neither of us have commented on it. By the time I was awake, he was up and had built a fire out in the clearing and got a pan of water boiling on it. When I came out with my tin mug to brew a cup of tea, he mentioned very casually that he intended to build a bed for himself today. 'That fockin' floor's far too hard,' he said.

CHAPTER THIRTY-SIX

I

At Chemin Kirkpatrick, Sime turned off to drive north into the town of Bury. It nestled among the trees in the valley of a small river of the same name. Bury had sent men to die in two world wars and commemorated them on plaques at the Bury Armory.

The road that led down to the town was called McIver, and it cut past the Bury cemetery. The last resting place of Sime's parents lay on the slope on the west side of the road. Carefully cropped grass was punctuated by headstones that bore the names of Scots and English, Irish and Welsh. But in the town itself almost all traces of English and Celtic culture had been supplanted by French, with the exception of some street names. And even those were gradually being replaced.

He had arranged to meet Annie at their grandmother's house in Scotstown, but he wanted to stop off first to visit his childhood home. A pilgrimage to the past.

He drove by the end of Main Street and followed the bend out of town, then turned left to cross the river just beyond the timber yard. A restored, bright red fifties pickup truck stood in the drive of a green and cream-painted clapboard cabin with rockers on the porch. A little further on, set back behind the trees, stood the house that had always fascinated him as a child. A folly with turrets and a multifaceted red roof. The house itself was clad with rounded shingles, like fish scales, and painted blue and green, red and grey and peach. Like a fairytale house made of coloured candies. It hadn't always been so colourful. The old lady who lived in it when he was a child had despised children.

It was a strange homecoming. Bittersweet. His had been a happy enough childhood, and yet he had never quite fitted with the rest of his family. He was sure he must have been a disappointment to his parents. He wished now that he could meet his ten-year-old self here on this road that he had walked every day to school and back. The things he could tell him. The advice he could offer.

His old family home stood derelict in an overgrown garden. The sale of it had been left in the hands of a realtor, but there had never been a single enquiry for it. Sime had never quite understood why. It was a fine two-storey house with a front porch and a good bit of land, set in an area of cleared forest on the edge of town. His room had been up in the attic, with a semicircular window looking down on to the road. He had loved that room. It had set him apart from the rest of the house and given him what had felt like a commanding view of the world.

He stood now on the road beside his idling car and looked up at that boyhood window on the world. There was no glass in it. Much of the clapboard siding beneath it had fallen away, or been stripped off. Pigeons were roosting in his old room. Crows lined up along the roof above it like harbingers of doom.

What happened to happiness, he wondered. Did it evaporate like rain off a wet street in sunshine? Was it anything other than a transient moment that existed only in the memory? Or maybe a state of mind that changed like the weather? Whatever happiness he had known in this house was long gone, and he felt only sadness standing here, witness to something lost for ever, like the lives of his parents, and all the generations that had gone before them.

He closed his eyes and almost laughed. The medicine prescribed by the sleep doctor was doing a pretty poor job of cheering him up. He got into his car and set off for Scotstown.

II

Sime had very little recollection of Scotstown. Although he knew it had been founded by Scots colonists in the nineteenth century, in school he and his classmates had been disabused of the notion that it was so called because of the number of Scots who lived there. In fact it had been named after John Scott, the first manager of the Glasgow Canadian

Land and Trust company, which had established the settlement.

It had once been a thriving community, with a lucrative lumber business, and a hydroelectric dam on the River Salmon. The railway had brought freight and trade and people in great numbers. Sime supposed it had probably still been an affluent little town when he was a boy, but its population had dwindled now to a few hundred, most of its industry closed down. Sawmills stood in silent decay with weathered *For Sale* and *To Let* signs tacked on to peeling walls.

It was during his first year at school that his mother had found a job at the *dépanneur* in Bury, and school holidays had become a problem. That first year, and for several thereafter, she had driven Sime and Annie over to Scotstown during summer and winter holidays before she went to work, dropping them off at their granny's house. And it was during those years that their grandmother had read to them from the diaries.

Her house on Rue Albert reflected the decline of the town. It stood, like his parents' home, in a wildly overgrown garden. In its day it had been impressive. Two storeys, with a porch running from the front around both sides, and a large deck at the rear. It was painted in white and yellow, with steeply pitched red roofs. But the paint was faded and flaking and green with moss. The wooden balustrade around the porch was rotten.

A car stood parked in the footprint of two towering pines and a maple tree that cast their shadows on the house. Trees that Sime remembered from his childhood. And he reflected that they had probably outlived by a hundred years or more whoever had planted them. He drew in behind the parked vehicle and stepped out on to the sidewalk. He recalled himself and Annie playing hide and seek here as children, shimmying down the slope to the river behind the house on hot summer days to fish in the shade. The sound of the river itself rose up from beyond the back garden, and he could almost hear the creak of his grandmother's rocking chair as she read to them on the porch.

He walked up the overgrown path and climbed steps to the front door, guilt descending on him now at all the years he had neglected to stay in touch with his sister. While Annie had sent him birthday and Christmas cards religiously each year, he had never responded. Never lifted the phone or sent an email. His apprehension at seeing her again tightened across his chest.

The door swung open as he approached and his sister stood in the doorway, wide-eyed with expectation. He was shocked at how much older she seemed. Grey strands streaked once lustrous blonde hair that was pulled back now in a severe bun. She had put on weight, become almost matronly. But her green eyes were flecked with the same warmth he remembered as a child. Her expression changed the moment she saw him. 'My God, Sime! When you said you hadn't been sleeping, I never imagined . . .'

His smile was wan. 'It's been quite a while since I had a good night's sleep, sis. Not since I broke up with Marie-Ange.'

Shock was replaced by sympathy, and she stepped forward to put her arms around him and draw him close, his years of neglect ignored and forgotten. The sense of relief he felt in that simple moment of affection almost produced tears. He hugged her back, and it felt like years since he had known such genuine warmth.

They stood for a very long time like that on the porch, before finally she held him at arm's length, and he saw how moist her eyes had become. 'It's maybe for the best,' she said. 'You and Marie-Ange.' She hesitated. 'I never did take to her.'

He smiled and wondered why it was that people always seemed to think it might be a comfort to learn that no one liked the person you once loved.

Annie looked beyond him to the mess that was the garden and her embarrassment was clear. 'Gilles used to come and cut the grass every other week,' she said. 'And we tried to keep up the paintwork. At least maintain it to a basic level.' She shrugged. 'But when you have a family . . .' Her voice tailed away. 'It's a fair way from Bury, and when the snow comes . . .' She smiled her regret. 'The winters are so long.'

'No one interested in buying?'

'One or two at first. But you'll have seen for yourself, Sime. The town's dying, so selling's not easy. And when it began to look like it had been lying empty for a while, any interest evaporated.' She smiled, banishing the thought. 'You'd better come in.'

He nodded.

Inside it was dark. It smelled fusty and damp, and felt like stepping back into a previous life. A house that had once been a home, populated now only by the memories of their younger selves. Sime walked slowly over floorboards that creaked painfully beneath his feet, looking around the living room which had occupied most of the ground floor. Although empty, apart from an old picnic table and a couple of chairs, he could conjure up from somewhere a memory of how it had once been. Full of big dark furniture. An old piano, a dresser. Indian rugs on the floor, ornaments on the mantel above a stone fireplace. All around the walls faded wallpaper still betrayed the telltale shadows of the paintings which had once hung there. A large pale rectangle above the fireplace was like the ghost of the picture that had spared the paper from discoloration. But he had no memory of any of the pictures themselves.

They wandered out to the deck at the back of the house and heard the rush of the river rising through the trees. They stood, leaning on the rail, breathing the damp of the woods and feeling the air cool on their skin as a slight breeze whispered through the leaves. Annie turned to look at him. 'What's this all about, Sime?'

And so he told her. About the murder on Entry Island. His certainty, on meeting the widow for the first time, that he knew her. About his ring and her matching pendant. And how that had sparked his first dream, and then his recollections of the diaries. She listened in thoughtful silence as he spoke, and when he had finished she said, 'Come through.'

A large leather satchel lay on the dusty picnic table. Annie picked it up and sat with it on her knee, then patted the seat beside her. As Sime sat down she lifted a bundle of books from the bag. They were small, cracked, leather-bound volumes in different colours and sizes, all held together by yellowed string wrapped several times around and tied in a bow.

'That's them?' His voice was not much more than a whisper. She nodded and he reached out to touch them. Seeing the diaries, touching them, was like being witness to history, like being a part of it.

She untied the string to open the top book as he watched in trembling anticipation. Folding back its leather cover, she revealed the brittle yellowed pages inside. Pages covered with a clumsy handwritten scrawl, faded now with the years.

'This is the first one,' she said. And with cautious fingers flipped back the pages to the inside cover. *Di-ciadaoin 21mh latha de'n t-Iuchair, 1847* was written in a bold, copperplate hand.

'What does it mean?'

'It's the date in Gaelic, Sime. Wednesday, 21st July, 1847.'

'How in Heaven's name do you know that? You don't speak Gaelic.'

Annie laughed. 'Granny taught me the Gaelic numbers, and the days of the week, and the months. I was very little, but they've always stayed with me.'

He was crestfallen. 'Are they all in Gaelic?'

She smiled. 'No. Just the date. He wrote his diaries in English.'

Sime stared at the page. Below the date was a signature. Not easy to read at first. And he canted his head a little and screwed up his eyes. 'Sime Mackenzie,' he read. The man who had bequeathed him his name. *Sime*. So that's where his father had got the spelling. He was tense with emotion. 'Can I hold it?'

She handed it to him and he took it in his hands as if it might break. His ancestor had held this very book. His hand had wielded the pen that formed the letters and words and sentences that told the story of his life. Of the birth of his sister. His rescue of Kirsty. The death of his father. The clearing of Baile Mhanais. That dreadful voyage across the Atlantic. The nightmare that was Grosse Île.

Annie said, 'I thought there might be something symbolic about giving you the diaries here. Since this is where they were read to us.' She put a hand over his. 'But I think we should go home now. The family are waiting to meet you. There will be time enough for reading.'

III

Annie lived in a large, rambling, grey-painted wooden house on Main Street, sandwiched between the town library and the redbrick Bury Armory Community Center. Bury's military history was still evident in the building that housed Branch 48 of the Royal Canadian Legion just across the road, beyond the Post Office. Main Street itself was quiet, leaves falling gently on to manicured lawns from the trees that lined it. There were three churches along its length. Anglican, United and Catholic. Bury had a strong religious as well as military heritage, and the Mackenzies had gone each Sunday to the United Presbyterian Church of Canada, which had absorbed most of the Scottish churches during the Great Merger.

He parked behind his sister's car in the drive and they climbed the steps to the porch. He glanced across the garden. Large maples dropped coloured leaves on to neatly cut grass. A double garage beyond them was almost completely hidden from view. His apprehension returned. While his sister had forgiven him his neglect, he was not so sure that her family would.

She sensed it and took his hand. 'Come on in and say hi to everyone. They won't bite.' She opened the door and led him up a dark hallway and into a much brighter family room with large windows opening on to the garden. He felt the atmosphere as soon as he entered it. His niece and nephew were playing a computer game on the television. His brother-in-law was sitting in a leather sofa pretending to read the newspaper. They all looked over as he came in. 'Luc, come and say hello to your uncle.'

Luc was around fifteen, with a shock of blonde hair gelled back from his forehead. He crossed the room obediently and gave Sime a solemn handshake. There was just the faintest curiosity in eyes that were reluctant to meet his. 'You were just about so high last time I saw you,' Sime said, without any real idea of what else to say.

His sister had trotted along behind him. A gawky girl with braces who gazed at him with unglazed interest.

Annie said, 'Magali couldn't have been much more than a baby.'

Magali presented each cheek and Sime stooped to kiss her awkwardly. Then both teenagers headed back to their game while their father put his paper aside and stood up. He approached Sime with his hand outstretched, but his smile was cold.

'Gilles.' Sime nodded and shook his hand.

Gilles said, 'Nice to see you after all this time. Not sure I'd have recognised you if I passed you in the street.'

Sime felt the sting of the rebuke, and Annie said quickly, 'He's not been well, Gilles.' And the warning in her tone was clear.

It was dark by the time they all sat around the table for their evening meal. The first time Sime had sat down for a family dinner since the death of his parents.

Annie prattled on to fill the awkward silences, bringing Sime up to date on everyone and everything. Luc excelled at sports and was a budding star of the school basketball team. The boy blushed. While Magali, on the other hand, was top of her class at school and wanted to be a doctor. Magali continued to gaze at him with her unselfconscious curiosity. Gilles was now principal of the Bury secondary school, and was even flirting with the idea of standing for political office.

Sime was surprised. 'What party?' he asked.

'Parti Québécois,' Gilles said. Which was the Quebec nationalist party. Sime nodded. He had never been convinced by the idea of an independent state outwith the Canadian federation. But he didn't say so.

Suddenly Magali said, 'How come you never visit?'

An uncomfortable silence fell around the table. It had clearly been a topic of conversation among the family before his arrival, and he felt eyes turning towards him.

He laid down his knife and fork and wanted to be honest. 'Because I've been pretty selfish and self-obsessed, Magali. And I'd forgotten what a wonderful person your mother really is.' He couldn't bring himself to look at his sister. 'But I hope to be a regular visitor from now on, and maybe we can all get to know one another a bit better.' He caught Magali's eye. 'And if you're really interested in medicine, I can take you on a tour of the pathology labs at the Sûreté in Montreal sometime.'

Her eyes opened wide. 'Really?'

He smiled. 'No problem.'

Her mouth fell open now. 'I'd love that.'

'Do you carry a gun?' It was the first time that Luc had spoken since his arrival.

'Usually, yes,' Sime said. 'Not right now, though. 'Cos I'm sort of on sick leave.'

'What kind of gun?'

'Well a patrolman would carry a Glock 17. But detectives like me carry the Glock 26.'

'How many rounds?'

'Thirteen. You interested in guns, Luc?'

'You bet.'

He shrugged. 'Then maybe I can take you to the police shooting range one day and you can have a shot at firing one yourself.'

'No shit?'

'Luc!' his father reprimanded him.

'Sorry,' the boy said. But he wasn't. 'That would be brilliant.'

Sime glanced at Annie and saw the pleasure in her smile. He knew she didn't approve of guns, but anything that made connections and brought the family together had to be good.

He spent the rest of the meal fielding questions about cases he had worked on, murders that they had read about in the papers or seen on TV. From the family pariah he had suddenly become exotic and interesting, at least as far as the kids were concerned. Gilles was more reserved. But just before Annie took him upstairs to show him his room, Gilles solemnly shook his hand and said, 'It's good to have you here, Sime.'

IV

Sime's room was up in the roof, with a dormer window looking out over the garden below. Annie switched on a bedside light and laid out the diaries on the bed in chronological order. He watched her with both apprehension and anticipation. He couldn't wait to read them, but at the same time feared that perhaps they would not provide the illumination he sought. About the ring that had first sparked his dreams, and its possible connections to a woman charged with murder on Entry Island.

Annie lifted the final diary and turned towards him. 'After you phoned,' she said, 'I dug these out and spent most of the next two days reading them. I can't tell you what memories they brought back. I could almost smell Granny's house as I read. And I could hear that distinctive little creak she used to have in her voice when she was reading.' She paused. 'You know she didn't read us everything?'

He nodded. 'I knew there was stuff our folks didn't want us to hear. I can't imagine what, though.'

'You'll figure it out when you read for yourself,' Annie said. 'But you mentioned the ring when you phoned, and that's what I focused on.' She searched his face with dark green, puzzled eyes, then opened up the diary that she held in her hands and searched through it for a page she had marked with a Post-it. 'His entries became more and more infrequent before he stopped altogether. But you should read

445

first from here, Sime. Granny never read us any of this. If she had I'm sure you'd have remembered the significance of the ring.' She handed him the diary. 'When you've read to the end, you can go back and follow the trail from the beginning. I think you'll know where to look.'

She reached up and kissed him softly on the cheek.

'I hope you'll find resolution here.'

When she had gone, Sime stood for a while listening to the silence of the room around him. Somewhere outside he heard the hoot of a distant owl. The diary seemed to grow heavier as he stood there with it in his hands, before eventually he pulled up the chair at a small writing desk below the dormer.

He sat down and turned on the reading light. Then carefully opened the diary at the page she had marked and began to read.

CHAPTER THIRTY-SEVEN

Thursday, 19th May 1853

I have floored the beams now in the pitch of my cabin roof to make an attic. I have built a spare room and indoor toilet at the back, and a covered porch with fly screens at the front. I often sit on the porch at the end of the day and watch the sun set over the trees, and I dream about how things might have been had I not been separated from Ciorstaidh on the quay at Glasgow that fateful day.

I have cleared and ploughed most of my land, and grow enough to feed myself with some left over to sell. At certain times of the year, myself and a few of the other men from Gould walk across the border to earn a bit of cash on the bigger farms at Vermont in the United States. At others I am busy enough on my own land. Especially at harvest time when I have to rush to bring in the crops before the first frosts, which can come as early as September.

Recently I have obtained part-time work teaching English to the Gaelic-speaking children at Gould school. Most of them arrive having spoken only Gaelic in the home, but when it comes to learning to read and write, it's in English that they must do it.

The reason I write about this today is that a remarkable thing happened at the school just yesterday morning.

There is a new teacher this year, Jean Macritchie. She's married to Angus Macritchie, the mayor of the Lingwick municipality. She's a very genteel sort of lady. In her mid-forties, I would say. No airs and graces about her, but polite and softly spoken. She wears print cotton dresses and silk shawls and has a sort of artistic air about her. In fact, art is her great passion, and she has instituted a new art class for the children.

It was lunchtime yesterday when I finally finished marking some papers and I wandered into her classroom. Everyone had gone to eat, but the still-life that Mrs Macritchie had set up for the children to draw was still there. Just a jug and a glass of water and some fruit. And the efforts of the children themselves were still lying on their desks.

I wandered around looking at them. Most were pretty awful. Some of them even made me laugh. And one or two were quite good. I have no idea what impelled me to do it, for I have never drawn anything in my life, but I had a sudden fancy to see what kind of a fist I could make of it myself. So I got a fresh sheet of paper and some charcoal from Mrs Macritchie's desk, and sat down to draw.

It's amazing how I got sucked into it. I don't know how long I sat there following the lines that my eye guided me to draw, using the flat of the charcoal to create the light and the shade, but I didn't hear Mrs Macritchie coming in until she spoke. I just about jumped out of my skin. I looked up and there she was peering down at my sketch. 'How long have you been drawing, Sime?'

'I've no idea,' I said. 'About half an hour, maybe.'

She laughed then. 'No, I mean, is drawing something you've been doing for a long time?'

It was my turn to laugh. 'No, not at all. This is the first I've ever done.'

Her smile faded. 'You're joking, aren't you?'

'Well . . . no,' I said, and glanced at my drawing. 'Is it that bad?' I was hoping to make her laugh again, but she remained quite serious.

'I don't know if you realise it, Sime, but you have a very real talent.' It was news to me. She clasped her hands thoughtfully in front of her face, resting her fingertips on her lips. 'What would you say if I offered to give you lessons?'

I looked at her in astonishment. 'Seriously?'

'Seriously.'

I thought about it for all of two seconds then nodded my head vigorously. 'I'd like that.'

Friday, 7th July 1854

Today was the last day of the school term, and the start of the holidays for the children. Of course, it means that my teaching income will dry up till September, and I'll have to put in a hard summer shift on the land.

It also means putting aside my painting until the start of the new term when I will have time once again. I have taken so much pleasure in the discovery of this unexpected talent. Mrs Macritchie has been very patient this last year, painstaking in teaching me good technique. First in drawing, and then in painting. But it is in the painting that I have found my greatest pleasure. At first I painted the things I saw around me. People and places. And then at some point, I'm not sure exactly when, I began to paint the landscapes that I remembered from home. Baile Mhanais, the castle at Ard Mor. Seascapes, mountains, the bare windswept peat bogs of the Hebrides. These past months I have spent most of my money on materials. Canvas and paints and brushes. I fear it is becoming something of an addiction.

At any rate, I was just packing up my things when Mrs Macritchie came into my classroom. Her behaviour seemed oddly casual, a little unnatural.

'Sime,' she said, 'you remember that painting you gave me? The landscape with the stag, and the hunters shooting at it from behind the rocks.'

'Yes.' I remembered it only too well. The painting of it had taken me right back to the day of my father's funeral when I had hunted down the wounded stag to put it out of its misery. I had taken pleasure in giving it to her as a gift, a small return for all the time she'd invested in me.

'Mr Morrison and his wife from Red Mountain were at our house for dinner last night. He's established a sawmill over there.'

I nodded, a little puzzled. I couldn't imagine where this was leading.

'Mr Morrison is from the Isle of Lewis himself. He saw your painting before dinner, when we were in the drawing room. It hangs above the fireplace there. He was so taken by it that after dinner he went back through to stand and look at it for a very long time. When I asked him what it was that drew him to it, he said simply that it took him home. He said he could almost touch the heather, and smell the peat smoke blowing in the wind.' She hesitated. 'He asked me if he could buy it.'

'Well, he can't,' I said indignantly. 'It was a present to you.'

She smiled. 'Sime, I'd be very happy to hang any one of your paintings on my wall in its place. Besides which, Mr Morrison said he would happily pay five dollars for it.'

I felt my jaw slacken and my mouth fell open in surprise. Five dollars was a small fortune. 'Really?'

'He wants that painting, Sime.'

I didn't know what to say.

'I suggest, if you agree, that I sell it to him for the amount mentioned and hand the money straight over to you.'

'Less a percentage for yourself,' I said quickly. 'Since I would never be doing this at all if it wasn't for you.'

But she just laughed. 'Sime, Sime . . . I didn't give you your talent. God did that. I just helped you harness it. The money is yours. You've earned it. But I have a further suggestion.'

451

I couldn't for the life of me imagine what that might be.

'I think it's time you held a wee exhibition of your work. You've got enough now to make a sizeable presentation. The church hall would be a good venue for it, and if we advertise it properly, it should draw a sizeable crowd. Most folk around here still remember the islands. And you capture the very essence of them in your paintings. You could sell a fair few.'

Saturday, 22nd July 1854

I am so excited that I know there is no point in even trying to sleep. I have no idea what time it is, nor do I care. I have been sitting out here on the porch ever since I got back from town, and I watched the sun go down over the trees a long time ago now.

We held the exhibition of my work in the church hall today, and there must have been two hundred folk or more went round looking at my pictures during the course of the afternoon. And not just from Lingwick. From all over. From as far away as Tolsta in the east and Bury in the west. I had thirty paintings and drawings on display. And we sold every single one of them. Everyone from the old country, it seems, wants a piece of home hanging in their house.

I am sitting here now with nearly forty dollars in my pocket and a list of folk who have commissioned me to do paintings specially for them. It's a small bloody fortune, and more than I could ever have expected to make doing almost anything else. And there is nothing else that I love doing quite as much as this.

For the first time in my whole life I know what it is that I want to do with it.

CHAPTER THIRTY-EIGHT

Sime's immersion in the diary was suddenly broken by a security lamp coming on below his window and he resurfaced to the reality of the attic room in his sister's house in Bury. He felt disorientated, and a little disappointed. He had no idea where events in the diary were leading, nor could he see what possible relevance they might have.

He stood up and leaned over the desk towards the window to peer down into the garden. In the light that flooded the side porch and the grass beyond it, he saw his sister wrapped in a coat and carrying a flashlight. She crossed the lawn towards the trees at the far side.

As the security light behind her went out, only the beam of her flashlight cut through the dark of the garden until another security lamp above the doors of the double garage beyond the trees poured light down on to the path and the turning area in front of it. She opened a door and disappeared from view. A few moments later a yellow light appeared in the attic window above the garage doors, and the security lamp extinguished itself to plunge the garden back into darkness.

Sime sat down again and returned his focus to the diary.

He scanned quickly through its pages, trying to get a sense of the story they told without becoming bogged down by their detail. His ancestor, it seemed, had gone on to great success, exhibiting his work in Quebec City and Montreal. His paintings, in the end, had commanded substantial sums of money. Enough for him to make his living by his art, which must have been rare in those days. But his art was popular. Immigrant Scots appeared to have had an unquench-able appetite for a piece of their homeland, and his ancestor had barely been able to keep up with demand.

It wasn't until an entry made nearly fifteen years later, when his great-great-great-grandfather must have been about forty years old, that Sime found himself halted in his tracks by the opening line.

CHAPTER THIRTY-NINE

Saturday, 26th June 1869

I sit writing this tonight with a real sense that there is some force that guides our lives in ways that we will never understand. I could, I suppose, attribute it to God. But then I would have to credit Him with the bad as well as the good, and to be truthful I am no longer sure what I believe. Life has treated me well and badly in almost equal measure, but it is the bad that always tests our faith. In a strange way we tend to take the good for granted. But I shall never do that again. Not after today.

I have been in Quebec City all this week at an exhibition of my work in the old walled town, almost in the shadow of the Château Haldimand. There are sixty works in the exhibition, and today was the final day, with only two paintings remaining to be sold. It was late afternoon and I was preparing to leave shortly when a young lady entered the gallery.

She was an extraordinarily pretty young woman, which is what immediately drew my eye, although to be honest she was not of the class that one would expect to be visiting an art gallery. I calculated that she was probably in her late teens or early twenties, and while very presentable she was plainly dressed, as you might expect of a maid or a serving girl. But there was something about her that fascinated me, and I could hardly stop myself from watching her as she wandered casually around the gallery moving from one painting to the next. She took some time over each picture, and seemed quite engrossed.

There were others in the gallery at the time, and I became distracted by a potential buyer asking me questions about one of my unsold works.

When he had gone, without buying I might add, the sound of a lady clearing her throat made me turn, and there she was standing at my elbow. There was such an intensity in her eyes that my stomach flipped over. Close up she was even more beautiful than from a distance. She smiled. 'I'm sorry to disturb you, sir. They tell me that you are the artist.'

I felt quite unusually bashful. 'Yes.'

'Scottish landscapes, I think.'

'That's right.'

'They are very beautiful.'

'Thank you.' My tongue seemed to be sticking to the roof of my mouth.

'But they're not just anywhere in Scotland, are they?'

I smiled. 'Well, no. They are all landscapes of the Outer Hebrides.'

'And why did you choose that particular place?'

I laughed. 'It's where I grew up.' I hesitated. 'Are you interested in buying?'

'Oh, good Lord, no!' She almost laughed. 'I couldn't afford
to, even if I had somewhere to hang them.' Her smile faded,
and there was the strangest, most awkward silence between
us. And suddenly she said, 'Why did you come to Canada?'

I was quite taken aback by her directness, but answered
her unexpected question honestly. 'Because my village on the
Isle of Lewis and Harris was cleared by its landlord. I had no
choice.'

'And where did you sail from?'

I frowned now, becoming a little irritated by her questions.
But I remained polite. 'Glasgow,' I said.

She looked at me very directly. 'Aboard the *Eliza*?'

Now I was astonished. 'Well, yes. But how could you possibly know that? You would have been no more than a baby at
the time.'

Her smile seemed to me tinged with sadness. 'That's
exactly what I was,' she said. 'Delivered aboard the *Eliza* by a
Highlander who knew how to recover a baby from the breech
position.'

I swear that my heart stopped beating for a full minute.

'A man who gave me my life,' she said. 'I had always known
that his name was Sime Mackenzie.' Her eyes never left mine
for one moment. 'I first heard about you, maybe three years
ago. An article in the newspaper. And I'd always wondered,
but never dared hope until now that you would be that man.'

I had no idea what to say. A million emotions clouded my thinking, but all I wanted to do was hold her in my arms, as I had done on the *Eliza* all those years before. Of course, I didn't. I just stood there like an idiot.

'The family who raised me gave me their surname, Mackinnon. And the Christian name of my mother.'

'Catrìona,' the name slipped from my lips in a whisper.

'I wanted to give you this,' she said.

And she took out a gold signet ring with an arm and sword engraved in red carnelian. I could hardly believe my eyes. The ring that Ciorstaidh had given me on the quay in Glasgow the day that I lost her. And along with the cash borrowed from Michaél, the ring that I had given to the Mackinnon family into whose care I left the baby at Grosse Île. The only thing of any value that I possessed. My last link to Ciorstaidh, and the greatest sacrifice I could have made.

'I suppose it must have been worth a small fortune,' Catrìona said. 'But they never sold it. Couldn't bring themselves to do it. The money you gave them helped them on their way to a new life, and I grew up with this ring on a chain around my neck.' She held it out to me. 'I'm giving it back to you now as a thank you for the gift of life that you gave me.'

CHAPTER FORTY

Sime was in shock. Tears bubbled up quite involuntarily and blurred his ancestor's handwriting.

He'd had no recollection, from his grandmother's reading of the diaries, of Ciorstaidh giving Simon a ring in Glasgow, or of his ancestor parting with it on Grosse Île to help pay for the baby's keep. As Annie had said, if he'd known how the story completed a circle, that the ring had come back to him in the end, then its significance would surely never have been lost to his memory.

He looked at his hand in front of him on the desk, that very ring shining in the light. He ran the tip of a finger lightly over the engraving of the arm and sword. How could he ever have imagined what history this simple inanimate object had witnessed? How carelessly had he worn it all these years without the least idea of its significance?

He stood up and crossed to the bed and sat down to open and search back through the diaries until he found what he was looking for. And there it was, finally. His ancestor's account of losing Ciorstaidh on the quay, just as he had dreamt it. Except for the gift of the ring she had given him in the moments before their separation. A family heirloom that she had taken in case they needed something to sell. Part of a matching set, including a pendant that hung around her neck.

He searched through the following journals until he found the moment on Grosse Île when his ancestor had given the Mackinnons the ring. Almost as an afterthought. Guilty that the sacrifice had been Michaél's and not his. Sime had not remembered that at all. Then, as he flicked through the pages in front of him, he realised that they were full of detail he did not recall from his granny's reading. Maybe she had paraphrased or edited as she had read. And he knew that someday soon he was going to have to sit down and read them all through from beginning to end. After all, this was his story, too. His history.

Suddenly it occurred to him that he had no idea what had happened to Michaél. Was that the story his parents had not wanted their grandmother to read them? But he would look for it later. There were just two short entries left in the final diary, and he took it back to the desk to settle down in the pool of light and read them.

CHAPTER FORTY-ONE

Saturday, 25th December 1869

On this Christmas day, in the coldest, darkest month of the year, it gives me the most extraordinary pleasure to record that shortly after dinner tonight, I proposed to Catrìona Mackinnon, the child whom I brought into this world twenty-two years ago, and with whom I have fallen deeply in love. To my inexpressible joy she has accepted, and we are to be married in the spring, just as soon as the snows have melted and the warmth of the sun brings life back to the land.

Sunday, 13th August 1871

This is the last entry I shall ever make. I write it to record the birth of my baby son, Angus, named after my father. And the death of his mother, Catrìona, in childbirth. At one and the same time the happiest and the worst day of my life.

CHAPTER FORTY-TWO

I

A soft knocking at his door pierced his emotions. He stood up. 'Yes?' he said, and the door opened. Annie was still wearing her coat. She looked at him with concern, and crossed the room to wipe away his silent tears.

'You've read to the end, then.'

He nodded, not trusting himself to speak.

'So sad,' Annie said. 'To have gone through everything he did, only to lose her in childbirth.'

And Sime thought about his own child, lost even before it had been born. He said, 'What I don't understand is how Kirsty Cowell comes to be in possession of the pendant. They're matching pieces, Annie.'

She took his hand and looked at his ring. 'If only it could speak to us,' she said. Then she looked up. 'Come on, I've got something to show you.'

They climbed creaking stairs to the attic over the garage. Cold electric light from above cast angled shadows across the steps, and dust billowed through it as Annie raised the trap-door to let them into the attic. Almost the entire floor space was taken up with boxes and trunks and packing cases, old furniture covered in dust-sheets, paintings and mirrors stacked against the walls.

'Like I told you, just about everything of value that came from Mom and Dad's place is up here,' Annie said. 'And when Granny died I had all her things brought here too, at least until I could decide what to do with them.' The accumulated detritus of dead people's lives was mired in the deep shadows thrown by a single naked light bulb. 'I hadn't been into the attic in years,' she said. 'Until after you phoned, and I came up here to find the diaries.'

She squeezed her way through tea chests and cardboard boxes, and big pieces of antique furniture loosely covered with tattered bedsheets.

'I noticed the pictures stacked against the far wall at the time. I didn't pay any attention then, but thinking about it again today I realised they must have been the paintings that came from Granny's house. The ones that hung on the walls there when we were kids. And it occurred to me that they might have been Sime Mackenzie's.'

He followed her to the far end of the attic and a stack of a dozen or more framed pictures leaning face-in against the wall.

'While you were reading the diaries I thought I'd come up and take a look.'

She lifted up the nearest of the pictures and turned it to hold in the light. It was an oil painting, darkened now by age. A landscape of a bleak Hebridean vista. Low black cloud hanging over green and purple bog, sunlight breaking through in the far distance, reflecting on some long-lost loch. It was any landscape from any one of Sime's dreams, or like any one of the pictures conjured by his granny's reading of the diaries. Images informed by the pictures that had hung on her walls. It made him think of the painting that hung in his own apartment. Annie tilted it to show him the signature. 'SM,' she said. 'It's one of his.'

One by one she handed the paintings back to Sime. All of them were painted by his ancestor. An arc of silver sand, with the sea rolling in, green and stormy. The view of a blackhouse village from the hill above it. Baile Mhanais. The same village again, with its roofs ablaze, men running between the houses with torches, uniformed constables lined up along the hill. The clearance.

'And this one,' she said finally. 'I remembered it as soon as I saw it. It hung above the fireplace. And it bears his signature.' She hesitated. 'Is this her?'

Sime took it and turned it towards the light, and for the second time in a week his world stood still. A young woman in her late teens gazed at him from the canvas. Blue Celtic eyes, dark hair falling abundantly to her shoulders. The slight quizzical smile that was so familiar. A red oval pendant set in gold hung on a chain around her neck. And although the engraving was not clear, it formed the distinctive V of the crooked arm that held the sword on his ring.

In the deep, soft silence of the attic his voice came like the scratch of horsehair on the strings of a cello. 'It's Kirsty.' Younger, certainly, but unmistakably her. And he, too, recalled now the portrait above the fireplace. All those hours and days, weeks and months over years that they had spent together in their grandmother's house. No wonder he had been so sure he knew her.

He turned it over and wiped away an accumulation of dust and cobwebs to uncover a date. *24th December 1869.* The day before his ancestor proposed to Catrìona. Below the date was the faintest pencil outline of a single word. A name. He read it out loud. 'Ciorstaidh.' A final farewell to his lost love. Painted from memory as he had last seen her.

He looked up and everything was a blur. 'I don't understand.'

Annie said, 'The woman on Entry Island must be a descendant, or related in some way.'

Sime shook his head. 'No.'

'But she has the pendant.'

He had rarely felt so lost. 'I can't explain it, sis. I would have sworn this was her. And, yes, she has the pendant that matches the ring. The same pendant that appears in the portrait. But I've seen her great-great-great-grandmother's grave. Her date of birth. She would have been the same age as Sime's Ciorstaidh from Langadail.' He paused, remembering the cold of the stone when he laid his hand upon it, and pictured the inscription. 'She was even Kirsty, too. But not Kirsty Guthrie. Her name was McKay. Daughter of Alasdair and Margaret.'

II

Even had he not been suffering from insomnia, he would never have slept that night. His brain was in turmoil, trying to make sense of impossible connections. Replaying again and again every conversation he'd had with Kirsty Cowell. Every story from the diaries.

Finally he gave up, letting the night wash over him, and tried to empty his mind of all thoughts, watching the ceiling, and wondering if he was any more than a pawn in some timeless game without start or finish.

At some point during the night, without any real sense of where it had come from, he remembered something that his father had been in the habit of quoting when it came to matters of the family and his Scottish roots. The blood is strong, Sime. The blood is strong. And that refrain remained with him through all the hours of darkness, endlessly repeating until the first grey light fell like dust from the sky, and he rose early hoping not to disturb the rest of the household.

He meant to leave Annie a note in the kitchen, but found her sitting in her dressing gown at the kitchen table nursing a mug of coffee. She was pale and looked up at him with penumbrous eyes. 'I think I've caught your disease, Sime. Haven't slept a wink all night.' Her gaze dropped to the overnight bag in his hand. 'Planning on leaving without saying goodbye?'

He placed his folded note on the table. 'I was going to leave this for you.' He smiled. 'Didn't want to disturb you.'

She grinned. 'As if.' Then, 'I guess you didn't sleep either.'

'There was something going round and round my head all night, sis. Something Dad used to say. The blood is strong.'

Annie smiled. 'Yes, I remember that.'

'I never really understood what he meant, till now.'

'How do you mean?'

'Well, we always knew we were Scottish, right? I mean, Mum's family originally came from Scotland, too. But it never seemed to matter. It was just history. Like the stories from the diaries. Somehow I never really believed these were real people. It never occurred to me that we are who we are now because of them. That we only exist because of the hardship they survived, the courage it took just to stay alive.'

She gazed up at him with thoughtful eyes. 'I always felt that connection, Sime.'

He shook his head. 'I didn't. I always felt, I don't know, sort of dislocated. Not really part of anything. Not even my own family.' He glanced at her self-consciously. 'Until now. In those dreams, I felt Sime's pain, sis. When I read those stories, I feel such empathy. And the ring . . .' Almost unconsciously he ran the tips of the fingers of his left hand across the engraving in the carnelian. 'It's almost like touching him.' He closed his eyes. 'The blood is strong.'

When he opened them again he saw the love in her eyes. She stood up and took both his hands. 'It is, Sime.'

'I'm so sorry, Annie.'

'What on earth for?'

'For not loving you like I should. For never being the brother you deserved.'

She smiled sadly. 'I've always loved you, Sime.'

He nodded acknowledgement. 'Which is why you deserve better.'

She just shook her head, then glanced towards his bag. 'Do you have the diaries?'

He nodded. 'I want to read them, cover to cover. And sort out my head. Somehow I have to try and figure all this out.'

'Don't be a stranger, then.'

'I won't. I promise. I'll be back first chance I get.'

Annie placed her mug carefully on the table and stood up. 'I never asked you yesterday.' She paused. 'Did she do it? Kirsty Cowell. Did she kill her husband?'

He shook his head. 'I don't think she did.'

'Then you have to do something about that.'

He nodded. 'I do. But there's someone I have to see here before I go.'

She waited until he had gone before she opened his note and read the three words he had written on it.

I love you.

469

CHAPTER FORTY-THREE

The road was quiet as he turned on to Highway 108 east, just one or two trucks out early to make up time before the traffic got going. It cut like an arrow through the forest, and as he drove the sun came up over the trees to set their leaves alight. He had to lower his visor to avoid being blinded.

At the village of Gould he pulled off the road into a parking area in front of an old auberge. Next door to it was the Chalmers United Church built in 1892, a plain redbrick building surrounded by neatly kept lawns. There was not much left of the original village, just a few scattered houses set back from the old crossroads. Gone were the schools and churches that had sprung up through the nineteenth century. Most of the plots of land so painstakingly cleared by those early settlers had been reclaimed by the forest, almost all evidence that they had ever existed vanished for ever.

He stood and gazed across the woodland. Somewhere out there was the land that his ancestor had cleared.

Lingwick cemetery was about a hundred metres away on the other side of the road, raised up on a hill that looked out over the trees that smothered the eastern province. An elevated resting place for the dead of a far-off land.

The cemetery itself was immaculately kept. Sime walked up the grassy slope to its wrought-iron gates, their shadows extending down the hill to meet him in the early morning sunlight. He paused by the stone gateposts and read the inscription at his right hand. *In recognition of the courage and integrity of the Presbyterian pioneers from the Island of Lewis, Scotland. This gate is dedicated to their memory.*

The gravestones themselves were set in rows following the contour of the hill. Morrisons and Macleans. Macneils, Macritchies and Macdonalds. Macleods and Nicholsons. And there, in the shade of the forest that pressed in along the east side of the cemetery, was the weathered, lichen-stained headstone of Sime Mackenzie. *Born March 18th, 1829, Isle of Lewis and Harris, Scotland. Died November 23rd, 1904.* So he had lived to be seventy-five, and to see in the new century. He had given life to the woman who bore him his son, and seen it taken away. His love for the woman to whom he had been unable to keep the promise made on that tragic day on the banks of the River Clyde had never been fulfilled.

Sime felt an aching sense of sadness for him, for everything he had been through, for ending up here alone, laid for ever to rest in the earth of a foreign place so far from his home.

He knelt by the tombstone and placed both hands on the cool, rough stone, and touched the soul of his ancestor.

Beneath his name was the inscription, *Gus am bris an latha agus an teich na sgàilean.*

'Do you know what it means?' The voice startled him, and Sime looked around to see a man standing a few paces away. A man in his forties, dark pony-tailed hair going grey around the hairline. He wore a collarless white shirt open at the neck beneath a tartan waistcoat. Black trousers folded over heavy boots.

Sime stood up. 'No, I don't.'

The man smiled. He said, 'It means, Until the day breaks and the shadows flee away. Quite common on Hebridean graves.'

Sime regarded him with curiosity. 'Are you Scottish?'

The man laughed. 'Do I sound it? No, I'm as French as they come. My partner and I own the auberge across the way, but the history of this place is my obsession.' He glanced down at his waistcoat. 'As you can see.' He smiled again. 'I've even been to the Isle of Lewis myself in the company of some local historians. Smelled the peat smoke and tasted the guga.' He reached out to shake Sime's hand, then nodded towards the gravestone. 'Some connection?'

'My great-great-great-grandfather.'

'Well, then, I'm even happier to meet you, monsieur. I have quite a collection of papers and memorabilia over at the auberge. Your ancestor was quite a local celebrity. I think I may even have a photograph of him.'

'Really?' Sime hardly dared believe it.

'I think so, yes. Come on over and have a coffee and I'll see if I can find it.'

As he poured them both coffee from a freshly plunged cafetière, the owner of the auberge said, 'Your ancestor's land and his house were about half a mile out of town on the old road south. All gone now, of course. The fella he came here with never developed his, apparently.'

Sime looked up, interested. 'The Irishman?'

'Yes, that's right. Very unusual for an Irishman to settle in these parts.'

'But he didn't, you said. He never developed his land.'

'No.'

'So what happened to him?'

The man shrugged. 'No idea. The story is that the two of them went off lumberjacking one year, and only one of them came back. But I don't really know.' He stood up. 'I'll see if I can find that photograph.'

From his seat in the window Sime sipped his coffee and gazed with interest around the dining room. The walls were lined by old photographs and stags' heads on one side, and shelves cluttered with bric-a-brac and memorabilia on the other. An antique coffee machine sat on an equally cluttered serving counter and Sime could see through a hatch into the kitchen beyond. The auberge, the owner had told him, was constructed on the site of the original Gould store, built by an émigré from the Scottish mainland.

He returned now with an album full of faded photographs of people long dead and flipped through the pages until he found what he was looking for. 'There,' he said, stabbing a finger at a photograph so bleached by time that it was hard to make out the figure in it.

But Sime saw that it was the portrait of an old man with a long beard sitting on a bench. His hair was pure white and swept back across his head, long and curling around his collar. He wore a dark jacket and trousers. A waistcoat and white shirt were only just discernible. He was leaning forward slightly, both hands resting on the top of a walking stick that he held upright in front of him, his right hand over his left. And there, on his ring finger, only just apparent, was the signet ring that Sime now wore on his.

CHAPTER FORTY-FOUR

I

The flight from Quebec City to the Madeleine Isles took just under two hours in the small commuter aircraft. Sime sat next to an island woman whose two teenage sons fidgeted in the seats in front. They wore baseball caps with upturned brims, listening to iPods and playing computer games. She raised semi-regretful eyebrows at Sime, as if apologising for the behaviour of all teenagers. As if he might have cared.

Some time into the flight he closed burning eyes and very nearly drifted off, before being startled awake by an announcement from the pilot. Above the roar of the engines Sime heard him apologising for any turbulence experienced, and informing passengers that there was a storm on the way. Not on the same scale as the remnants of Hurricane Jess, which had so marked Sime's first visit. But it was likely to hit the islands, the pilot said, with strong to gale-force winds and high precipitation later in the day.

When the plane began its final descent towards Havre aux Maisons, it banked left and Sime saw the storm clouds accumulating in the south-west. And as it swung around for landing, he caught a glimpse once more of Entry Island standing sentinel at the far side of the bay. A dark, feature-less shadow waiting for him in the grey, pre-storm light. He had thought, just a matter of days ago, that he had seen the last of it. But now he was back. To try to resolve what seemed like an insoluble mystery. To right what he believed to be a mis-carriage of justice. Something that, in all likelihood, would lose him his job.

The thought filled him with the same frightening sense of destiny he had experienced on that first visit.

He picked up a rental car at the airport and as he drove along the Chemin de l'Aéroport to join Highway 199 South, the first drops of rain hit his windshield. Worn wipers smeared them across a greasy surface, and he blinked as if that might clear the glass. But he was just fatigued.

His car bumped and splashed through the potholes on the loop of road that bypassed the work on the new bridge, and he crossed over to Cap aux Meules on the old, rusted box-girder construction that had served the islanders for two generations.

By the time he got to the offices of the Sûreté de Police, the rain was blowing across the bay on the edge of a wind that was gaining in strength.

Sergeant Enquêteur Aucoin was surprised to see him. 'She just got back half an hour ago from the Palais de Justice on

Havre Aubert,' he said as they walked down the hall. 'The judge couldn't make it, so it was all done with video cameras. She pled not guilty of course.'

'And?'

'She was remanded in custody for trial in Montreal. They'll fly her out tomorrow to a remand prison on the mainland.' He lowered his voice. 'I don't mind telling you, we'll be glad to see the back of her. We were never designed to host long-term guests. Especially of the female variety.' They stopped in front of the door to the cells. 'What do you want to see her for anyway?'

Sime hesitated. He had no right to be here, no authority to question the accused. But no one in the Sûreté on Cap aux Meules had any reason to suspect that he didn't. 'New developments,' he said. 'I need to speak to her privately.'

Aucoin unlocked the door and let him in. He heard the key turn in the lock behind him. Both cells lay open. Kirsty turned wearily from where she sat cross-legged on her bunk surrounded by books and papers. She wore a simple T-shirt, jeans and white trainers. Her hair was drawn back from her face and tied in a loose ponytail. It had only been a few days, but already she had lost weight. Her skin was almost grey in colour.

Her initial expression of indifference gave way to anger as she realised who her visitor was. 'Come to gloat?'

He shook his head and stepped into her cell. He cleared a space beside her on the bunk to sit down, and she turned to glare at him. 'I want to talk to you.'

'I've got nothing to say.'

'This isn't an official visit.'

'What is it, then?'

He drew a deep breath. 'I saw a painting of you yesterday.'

A frown creased around her eyes. 'No one's ever painted me. At least not that I know of. Where did you see this picture?'

'In the attic of my sister's garage in the town of Bury in the Eastern Townships. It was painted by my great-great-great-grandfather, and it used to hang above the mantel in my grandmother's house when she read us stories as children.' He held up his right hand. 'This was his ring.'

Kirsty exhaled her contempt. 'If this is some kind of trick to get me to admit to murdering my husband, it's not going to work.'

'It's no trick, Kirsty.' And he took out his cellphone and tapped the screen to show her the picture he had taken in his sister's attic the night before.

She turned sulky eyes to look at it, and he saw her expression change. Not in a moment, but gradually. As if the shock of seeing it was slow in penetrating her resistance. Her lips parted and her eyes grew imperceptibly larger. She reached over to take his phone and examine the photograph more closely. Then she looked up. 'How did you do this?'

'I didn't do anything. That's the painting that hung above my grandmother's fireplace when I was a boy.' He paused. 'I knew I knew you. From the first moment I saw you.'

478

Her eyes searched his, and she was remembering perhaps that first encounter when she came down the stairs in the summerhouse to find him waiting to interview her. *I know you*, he had said.

She looked back at the phone. 'Coincidence. Some weird kind of resemblance. But it's not me.'

'If I had just shown that to you and asked if it was you, what would you have said?'

'You just did. And I'm telling you, it might look like me, but it's not.'

'Look again. She's wearing a red pendant.'

Reluctantly she turned her eyes towards it once more. He saw the colour rise high on her cheeks, but her mouth set in a stubborn line. 'That's all it is. A red pendant. Nothing to say it's mine.'

He took back his phone and switched it off, slipping it into his pocket. 'You told me that your great-great-great-grandmother McKay was Scottish.'

'I think I told you she was probably Scottish. I don't know, I've never gone into it. As far as I know her parents came from Nova Scotia, almost certainly Scottish immigrants. But whether Kirsty herself was born in Scotland, Nova Scotia or here, I couldn't tell you. I've never been interested enough to find out. If you want to know about my family history – though God knows why you would – you would need to ask Jack.'

'Your cousin?'

'He's a fanatic on genealogy. Spends hours on the internet going through family records. Recently he was pestering me for access to papers that got handed down through my side of the family.'

'I thought you didn't see much of one another.'

'We don't. He hasn't seen half the stuff I've got up at the house. Not that he really needs to. Apparently there's not much that he doesn't already know.' She smiled sadly. 'He never could understand my lack of interest.'

And Sime thought how she was just like he had been. Indifferent to her past, heedless of her roots. And just as he had done, she had struggled to find her place in a world that lives only for the present, where culture is a disposable commodity, no matter how many generations it has been in the making. 'Where did this obsession with not leaving Entry Island come from?'

She turned her head sharply. 'It's not an obsession! It's a feeling.'

'You said your mother was reluctant to leave, too.'

'As was her mother. Don't ask me why. I have no idea.' She was running out of patience with him. 'Maybe it's in the DNA.'

'And your ancestor, Kirsty McKay?'

'As far as I know, she never left the island once.' She stood up. 'Look, I'd like you to go. They're sending me to prison on the mainland tomorrow. Who knows how long it will take to go to trial? But I can't see any way I can prove my innocence, so I'm probably going to spend the rest of my life behind bars. Thanks to you.'

He wanted to tell her about Sime Mackenzie from Baile Mhanais, and the Ciorstaidh he fell in love with on a remote Hebridean island in another century. Of the struggles that brought him to Canada, and how all these generations later it had brought his great-great-great-grandson to Entry Island and a chance encounter with a woman called Kirsty who was almost identical in every way to the Ciorstaidh he had lost on a quayside in Glasgow.

But he knew how it would sound, and he had no rational way of explaining it to her. Even if she had been halfway receptive. Right now all he felt was her hostility. He stood up and looked into her eyes so directly that she had difficulty maintaining eye contact and looked away.

As a policeman, he knew that all the evidence in the murder of her husband had pointed towards her. But he also knew that most of it was circumstantial, and he had never really believed it. Instinct. Or perhaps something even less tangible. Deep down inside he felt as if he knew this woman, and that there was no way she was capable of murder. 'Kirsty,' he said. 'How did you get your husband's skin under your fingernails?'

'I've no idea. I must have scratched him when I was fighting to pull his killer off him.' She looked at the floor. 'Just go.'

But to her surprise he took each of her hands in his, holding them tightly. 'Kirsty, look at me.'

Her eyes flashed upwards to meet his.

'Look me in the eye and tell me you didn't kill him.'

She pulled her hands away. 'I didn't kill him!' she shouted, and her voice reverberated around the tiny cell.

He continued to stare at her. 'I believe you.'

He saw her confusion.

'I'll fly back with you to Montreal tomorrow, and I'll do whatever it takes to prove your innocence.'

II

The rain was battering his windshield as he turned back on to Highway 199 to head south. He had no idea if Jack Aitkens was still on night shift, but it was closer to drive to his home on Havre Aubert to find out than head north to the salt-mine. Besides which, if he was underground, then he wouldn't be reachable until after six.

It was still just mid-afternoon, but the light was so poor that every car had turned on its headlights, a dazzle of red and yellow lights reflecting on a wet, black road surface.

Sime drove up over the hill, and saw power cables swinging overhead in the wind. He had no idea what drew his attention, but as he passed the car park of the Cooperative supermarket he glanced left and saw a face he recognised. A face caught in the momentary flash of a car's headlights. Pale under a black umbrella, but lit up by a smile. And then it was gone as the umbrella dipped in the wind.

Ariane Briand. And she wasn't alone. Richard Briand had his arm around her, sharing her umbrella.

Sime slammed on his brakes and took a hard left turn into the far entrance of the car park. Car horns sounded in the rain, and he caught the glimpse of an angry face behind flashing wipers. He slowed and cruised among the lines of cars towards where he had last seen the couple, peering past his own wipers through the rain.

There they were, still beneath the umbrella, putting a shopping basket in the trunk of a car, huddled together against the elements. At that final briefing, it was Crozes himself who'd said Briand actually had more to gain than any of the others from Cowell's death. And yet he had never seriously been considered a suspect because his wife had provided his alibi. Even Sime had dismissed him, because on the night that Sime was attacked on Entry Island, Briand had been in Quebec City. Or so he said. No one had actually checked that. He and his wife claimed to have shut themselves away from the world in their hotel, but there was no proof that this was true. All the investigators had was their word for it. The focus had been so much on Kirsty that any other possibility had simply been ignored.

Sime ran through the sequence of events in his mind as the windows inside his car began to steam up. Arseneau had gone looking for Briand on the evening of their first day here. The start of the investigation. Briand's secretary had told him that Briand had left for Quebec City that morning, but that he'd booked his own travel and accommodation, so no one knew where to find him. Had anyone even checked with the airline that Briand had actually left the island?

He wiped the mist from his windscreen in time to catch Ariane Briand and her husband laughing, caught unexpectedly in the rain as their umbrella blew inside out in the wind. Briand stooped to give her a quick kiss before they ran around opposite sides of the vehicle to jump in.

Sime took out his phone and tapped the name of Briand's hotel in Quebec City into Google. Up came the website and a telephone number. He tapped dial, and sat listening as a phone rang somewhere 1,200 kilometres away.

'Auberge Saint-Antoine. Reception. How may I help you?'

'This is Sergeant Enquêteur Sime Mackenzie with the Sûreté in Montreal. You had a guest staying with you recently by the name of Richard Briand. I'd like to check his arrival date, please.'

'One moment, Sergeant.'

Sime watched Briand's car turn out of the car park into a side street and then drive up to the main highway.

'Hello, Sergeant. Yes, Monsieur Briand checked in on the 28th. He left us yesterday.'

Sime hung up. The 28th was the day before he and Blanc had flown to Quebec City to interview him. Where had he and Ariane Briand been for the previous two days if not there? Had Briand left the islands at all before the 28th? Because if not, then he could just conceivably have been

484

Sime's attacker. His flights in and out of Havre aux Maisons could be checked with the airline. Sime would do that first thing in the morning before flying out with Kirsty.

The thought that the Briands might have been lying elevated his pulse rate. But that same old doubt still nagged at the back of his mind. Even if he wasn't in Quebec City as he claimed, why would Briand attack Sime?

III

The rain had eased off a little by the time Sime found himself driving directly south along a narrow strip of land towards Havre Aubert. The sea was breaking all along the Plage de la Martinique on his left. On his right the wind rippled across the surface of the Baie du Havre aux Basques, which was protected from the full force of the storm surge by sand dunes all along its western perimeter. Kite surfers were out in force on this side, taking advantage of the powerful sou'westerly.

He had been preoccupied on the drive south by thoughts of the Briands, but as he approached La Grave, at the southeastern end of Havre Aubert, he forced himself to refocus.

Jack Aitkens's house was a stone's throw from the Palais de Justice, where only a few hours earlier Kirsty had made her first court appearance. It was a typical maroon and cream island home with a steeply pitched roof and overhanging eaves. A covered veranda ran around the front and south side to an entry porch at the south-east corner. Unlike most of the other houses dotted around, it looked in need of fresh paint. The garden, such as it was, had been allowed to go to seed. There was an air of neglect about the place.

Sime parked on the road and hurried up the path to the shelter of the veranda. He couldn't find a doorbell and knocked several times. Nothing stirred inside. There were no lights on, and as he looked around Sime could see no sign of Aitkens's car. It seemed like he was out of luck and that Aitkens had come off nights and was on the day shift.

'Are you looking for Jack?'

Sime spun around to see a middle-aged man working on the engine of an old truck in the shelter of a carport attached to the neighbouring house. 'Yes. I guess he must be at the mine.'

'No, he's on night shift just now. He went down to the marina to secure his boat. Can't take too many precautions with this storm on the way.'

The main street ran along a spit of land that curved around to a tiny harbour sheltered by the crook of the bony finger that was Sandy Hook. A collection of wooden and brick buildings lined each side of the street. Stores, bars, restaurants, a museum, holiday lets. Just behind it, in the shelter of La Petite Baie, lay a tiny marina that played host to a collection of fishing and sail boats. They were tied up along either side of a long pontoon that rose and fell on the troubled water.

Aitkens was securing his boat front and rear to an access pontoon. It was a twenty-five-foot fishing boat with an inboard motor and a small wheelhouse that afforded at least some protection from the elements. It had seen better days.

He was crouched by a capstan and looked up from his ropes as Sime approached. He seemed startled to see him and stood up immediately. 'What's wrong? Has something happened to Kirsty?' He had to raise his voice above the wind, and the clatter of steel cables on metal masts.

'No, she's fine.'

Aitkens frowned. 'I thought you people had gone home.'

'We had,' Sime said. 'But I'm not done here yet.'

'They're sending her to Montreal,' Aitkens said, as if Sime wouldn't know.

'Were you in court?'

'Of course. It's just two minutes from my door.' He paused. 'There's not much evidence against her, you know.'

Sime nodded. 'I know that.'

Aitkens was taken aback. 'Really?'

'I need to talk to you, Monsieur Aitkens.'

He glanced at his watch. 'I don't really have time.'

'I'd appreciate it if you'd make some.' Sime's tone conveyed the strong impression that it was more than a request. But, all the same, he wondered why Aitkens's first response had not been to ask what Sime wanted to talk to him about. Almost as if he already knew.

Aitkens said, 'Well, not out here. Let's get a coffee.'

*

Most of the shops and restaurants on the main street were closed for the season, but the Café de la Grave was open, yellow light spilling out into the sulphurous afternoon. There were no customers. Just rows of polished wooden tables and painted chairs, wood-panelled walls peppered with colourful childlike paintings of fish and flowers. A menu chalked up on a blackboard had earlier offered *Quiche à la Poulet* or *Penne sauce bolognese à la merguez* for lunch. Sime and Aitkens sat by an old upright piano and ordered coffees. Aitkens was ill-at-ease and fidgeted with his fingers on the table in front of him.

'So what do you want to talk to me about?' At last the question.

'Your family history.'

Aitkens swung his head towards Sime, frowning. He thought about it for a moment. 'Is this an official line of enquiry?' His tone was hostile. Sime, after all, was the man who had arrested his cousin for murder.

Sime was caught momentarily off-balance, but couldn't lie. 'My interest is more personal than professional.'

Now Aitkens tilted his head and squinted at Sime with both suspicion and confusion. 'What? About my family history?'

'Well, it's Kirsty's more than yours that interests me. But I guess much of it will be shared. She told me that genealogy was something of an obsession of yours.'

'Not an obsession,' Aitkens said defensively. 'A hobby. What the hell else does a man do with his life when he's not working?

The hours I work, and a geriatric father in the hospital, I'm not exactly an eligible bachelor, am I? Winters here aren't only hard, they're long and damn lonely.'

'So how far back have you been able to trace your lineage?'

Aitkens shrugged. 'Far enough.'

'As far back as your great-great-great-grandmother?'

'Which one?'

'The one buried in the cemetery on Entry Island. Kirsty McKay.'

Aitkens frowned darkly and examined Sime's face for a long time, until the silence became almost embarrassing. Finally he said, 'What about her?'

'What do you know of her origins?'

He smiled now. 'Well that wasn't easy, Monsieur Mackenzie. When people have been shipwrecked and start a new life, the past can be pretty damned difficult to uncover.'

Sime felt his heart rate quicken. 'But you did?'

He nodded. 'Her ship went down just off Entry Island in the spring of 1848. Driven on to the rocks in a storm. The boat had come from Scotland and was bound for Quebec City. She was the only survivor, pulled out of the water by a family living on the cliffs at the south end of the island. There was no lighthouse back then. Seems she was in a bit of a state. They took her in and nursed her back to health, and in the end she stayed with them, almost like a kind of adopted daughter. In fact, she never left the island and five years later married their son, William.'

Sime said, 'Which is how she ended up with the name

McKay, the same as her parents. Only they weren't really her parents.'

'Parents-in-law. But since she had no parents of her own, she was kind of like a real daughter to them.'

Which explained the inscription on the headstone. 'What happened to her real parents? Did they go down with the boat?'

'No, she was travelling alone. Apparently she had some kind of short-term memory loss as a result of the trauma, and no real idea at first who she was or where she'd come from. But her memory did eventually come back. In fragments at first. She used to write things down in a notebook as she remembered them. A kind of way of keeping them real. That notebook came all the way down through the family. I found it in a trunk of memorabilia that my father kept in the attic. I'd no idea it was there until after they'd taken him into hospital.'

Sime was having difficulty keeping his breathing under control and the excitement out of his voice. 'So who was she?'

Aitkens pulled a face and exhaled deeply. 'What the hell does any of this have to do with Kirsty's arrest?'

'Just tell me.' Sime's tone was imperative.

Aitkens sighed. 'Seems she was the daughter of the laird of some estate in the Outer Hebrides of Scotland. Fell in love with the son of a crofter, which was completely taboo in those days. The father opposed the relationship, and when the crofter's boy killed her brother in a fight he fled to Canada. She followed, hoping to find him, and of course never did.'

'Kirsty Guthrie,' Sime said.

Aitkens clenched his jaw and looked at him. 'You knew all along.'

But Sime shook his head. 'No. But a lot of things have just dropped into place.'

Aitkens had returned to fidgeting with his fingers on the table in front of him. 'I've been trying to patch in more detail. Kirsty has a lot of stuff passed down to her by her mother. Stored somewhere down in the basement of the house that Cowell built. I've been at her for ages to let me see it.' He pulled a face filled with resentment. 'But it was never convenient. God knows what'll happen to it now.'

Suddenly Sime said, 'Could you take me over to Entry Island in your boat?'

Aitkens looked at him in surprise. 'When?'

'Now.'

'Man, are you crazy? There's a storm on the way.'

'It won't be here for an hour or two yet.'

But Aitkens just shook his head. 'It's way too rough out there.' He glanced at his watch. 'And anyway, I've got to go shortly. I'm still working the night shift at the mine.'

'Well, do you know someone who could take me?'

'What in the name of God do you want to go there for right now?'

'A couple of things.' Sime was forcing himself to stay calm.

'I'd like to cast eyes on that stuff she keeps in the basement. And . . .' He hesitated. 'I don't think Kirsty killed her husband.'

'Jesus! It was you that arrested her!'

'I know. But I was wrong. We were all wrong. We're just missing something. Something that's probably been staring us in the face all along. I want to take a look at the house again.'

Aitkens stood up, and his chair scraped the floor in the quiet of the café. 'Up to you. But if you're really determined to go out there tonight, Gaston Boudreau might be persuaded to take you. If you cross his palm with silver.'

'And he is . . . ?'

'The guy whose boat you requisitioned during the investigation.'

CHAPTER FORTY-FIVE

Sime braced himself against one side of the wheelhouse as Gaston Boudreau's fishing vessel rose and fell on a swell that was heavy, even within the harbour wall.

Boudreau stood in the doorway unconcerned, it seemed, at the prospect of taking Sime over to Entry Island with the storm so close. But he was perplexed. 'Why can't you just wait till morning, monsieur? The storm'll have blown itself out by then and you can get the ferry over.'

But Sime wanted to be on the plane with Kirsty when it flew out at midday. Tonight would be his last chance to take another look at the house, and to go through the family papers stored in the basement. Besides which, he knew that sleep would probably escape him, and he would be unable to contain himself during the long waking hours of darkness. 'How much will it take?' is all he said.

'How much are you offering?'

Sime's opening gambit of two hundred dollars drew a laugh from the fisherman. 'Take away the cost of the fuel and there's bugger all left for me,' he said. 'Five hundred.'

'Done.' Sime would have paid double. And something about the speed with which he agreed conveyed that to Boudreau. The fisherman pulled a face, realising he could have negotiated more.

'Give me a minute.'

Boudreau stepped inside his wheelhouse and slid the door shut. Sime could see him inside making a call on his cellphone. He had an exchange with someone at the other end that lasted around thirty seconds, then he hung up and slipped the phone back in his pocket. He slid open the door.

'Okay, we've got the green light. Let's get going.'

He turned back inside to start the motor and Sime followed him in. 'Who were you phoning?'

'The owner, of course.'

'Oh, I thought you owned the boat yourself.'

'Hah!' Boudreau smiled wryly. 'I wish.'

'Who's the owner, then?'

GPS and sonar monitors flickered into life. 'Mayor Briand.'

Within fifteen minutes of leaving the harbour, any thoughts that Sime might have had about Briand had deserted him. The commanding sensation of seasickness drove everything from his mind, and by the time they were halfway across the bay he was regretting his foolishness in making the crossing at all.

Boudreau himself stood easily at the wheel, legs apart, somehow moving in time with the boat. Sime took comfort from the fact that he seemed so relaxed. The light was fading fast, the sky ominously black overhead. It wasn't until they were close to Entry Island that he actually saw it, emerging out of the spray and spume to take dark shape and fill their eyes.

The sea was less turbulent in the lee of the island, and they motored easily into the comparative calm of the little harbour as the sea vented its wrath against the concrete breakwaters that protected it.

Boudreau eased his vessel up to the quayside with all the skill of a practised boatman and leaped out to secure it with a rope. He took Sime's hand to steady him as he jumped across the gap between heaving boat and dry land. He grinned happily. 'You want me to stay and take you back?' he shouted above the howl of the wind.

'Good God no, man,' Sime shouted back at him. 'Get home before the storm breaks. I'll take the ferry back in the morning.'

It was only when Boudreau was gone, the lights of his fishing boat devoured by darkness, that Sime was able to take stock for the first time. His entire focus had been on getting here, and now that he was, a flood of emotions drowned all coherent thought. He had forced himself not to think about what Aitkens had told him until this moment, almost afraid to face the implications of what he now knew.

Kirsty Cowell was the great-great-great-granddaughter of Kirsty Guthrie, who had come looking for her Simon and ended up shipwrecked here on this tiny island in the middle of the Gulf of St Lawrence. And she had waited, and waited. Because he had promised, no matter where she was, he would find her. But he never did. And in the end she had married another, as he had. And all that had survived both the time and the generations in between were the ring that she had given his ancestor and the pendant she had kept for herself.

The rain whipped into Sime's face as he stood on the quayside trying to come to terms with the bizarre quirk of fate that had somehow brought him and Kirsty Cowell together.

A group of fisherman securing boats against the storm had stopped what they were doing and gathered now in a knot to stand and watch him from a distance. Aware of them suddenly, Sime became self-conscious and turned to hurry away through the rain-streaked pools of light that lay all along the length of the harbour. A lamp burning in the wheelhouse of the last of the fishing boats caught his eye. A figure stepped out into the stern of the boat as he passed. The face turned towards him and was momentarily caught in the light. A face he knew at once. Owen Clarke. Sime pulled his hood up over his head and lowered it into the wind as he hurried away, following the road up to Main Street.

The thrum of the generators at the top of the road was barely audible above the roar of the wind that he fought against all the way up the hill until he reached the church. A couple of pickups passed him on the road, bumping and lurching through the puddles. Headlights picking him out against the black of the night, then passing with the growl of an engine to be swallowed by the dark. Lights shone in the windows of the few houses dotted around the hillside, but there was not a soul in sight. Sime opened the gate of the church and by the light of his cellphone found his way back to the grave of Kirsty McKay, whom he now knew to be Kirsty Guthrie.

He stood in the wind and rain looking down at her head-stone, knowing that her bones lay beneath his feet.

Just as he had done that morning, Sime knelt in front of the stone and laid both hands upon it. The wet of the earth soaked into the knees of his trousers. The stone felt cold and rough in his hands. And he had a powerful sense of somehow bridging the gap between these ill-fated lovers, bringing them together at last after all these years.

He felt, too, a strong sense of grief. He had lived through passionate moments in the skin of his ancestor. In his dream he had sacrificed everything to try to be with his Ciorstaidh. And here she lay, dead in the earth, as she had done for a very, very long time. He stood up quickly.

Impossible, he knew, to tell tears from rain.

The hoarse revving of a motor reached him above the howl of the wind, and he turned in time to see the shadow of a figure on a quad bike vanishing over the lip of the hill.

By the time he got to the big yellow house on the cliffs it was pitch-dark. He had struggled all the way against the wind, stumbling through the potholes that pitted the road. His clothes were soaked through and he was shivering from the cold.

But he did not go in straight away. He circled the big house and crossed the grass to the summerhouse, the house which had originally belonged to the McKays. The house where Kirsty Guthrie had grown up and in all probability later lived with her husband. The house where, several generations later, Kirsty Cowell had been born and raised. Walking in the footsteps of her ancestor, seeing all the same things that she had seen. Entry Island, almost unchanged in two hundred years. The sun coruscating across the bay towards the other islands of the archipelago stretched out along the horizon. She would have felt the same wind in her face, picked the same flowers from the same hills.

The front door was not locked, and Sime let himself in. He switched on a table lamp and wandered around in the half-dark just touching things. Things that belonged to Kirsty Cowell. An ornamental owl sculpted out of a piece of coal, an old clock that ticked slowly on the mantel. A book she had been reading, laid aside on a coffee table. A mug of tea never returned to the kitchen. And with every touch, the connection between them seemed to grow stronger until he could hardly bear it.

He pushed through the screen door and back out onto the porch, and ran across to the house that James Cowell had built. The last shredded remnants of crime scene tape clung to a wooden stake, fluttering wildly in the wind. The door to the conservatory was not locked and he slid it open to step inside and fumble for a light switch.

Lighting concealed around the conservatory and up into the living area and kitchen flickered and cast warm light among the shadows. Dried blood still stained the floor, and Marie-Ange had stuck down white tape to trace the outline of where the body had lain.

Sime stood dripping on the wooden floor and gazed at it for a long time. He was trying to replay the scene exactly as Kirsty had described it. The clear impression her story had given was that she and not James was the intended target. The intruder had attacked her in the dark of the conservatory, and then chased her across the floor of the living area and tried to stab her.

Which meant that if James were not the object of the attack, it couldn't have been Briand. Because what possible motive could he have had for killing Kirsty?

But then, she had stumbled upon the intruder by accident while James was upstairs. Wasn't it possible that he had simply tried to shut her up, to stop her from raising the alarm? That it only appeared she was the victim?

On the other hand, if she were the target, and her attacker wasn't Briand, he would not have anticipated Cowell being there. As far as anyone knew he had left her and moved in with a woman across the water. His presence would have come as a huge surprise.

Sime turned away from the crime scene, spooked suddenly by a sense of being alone with ghosts, and frustrated by the lack of any real clarity. He headed along the passage that ran towards the far end of the house, and found a light switch on the stairs that led down to the basement.

Here in the bowels of the house you wouldn't have known there was a storm raging outside. Only the occasional deep thudding vibration, as the building soaked up a particularly heavy gust of wind, betrayed the fact that the storm had well and truly arrived.

Sime found a panel of light switches and flicked them all up, flooding the entire basement with the glare of fluorescent light. He went straight to the storeroom he had discovered on his previous visit. It was full of cardboard boxes, a couple of old trunks, a set of leather suitcases. The shelves that lined the walls were bowed with the weight of books and papers and box files.

And everything went dark.

Sime stood stock-still, his heart pounding. He could even have sworn he heard his pulse in the thick black silence. The darkness was profound. He couldn't see his hands in front of his face. For several moments he stood hoping that his eyes would accustom themselves to the dark and he could at least discern something. But still it enveloped him, soft and sight-less, and he felt completely blind.

He reached out to touch the wall and made his way back to the door by touch, reaching it sooner than expected and almost bumping into it. Now he could feel the architrave and the doorframe and stepped cautiously out into what he knew was a large open space with the stairs at the far side of it. He cursed the storm, which seemed louder now, penetrating the layers of insulation that cocooned the house. The chances were that the whole island had lost power, or at least part of it if cables had come down.

A sudden flash of light left an imprint on his retinas of everything around him. Lightning. It had flooded through windows high up on the walls. And vanished again just as suddenly. But with an image in his mind of exactly where he stood, Sime moved quickly in the remembered direction of the stairs. He tripped over the bottom step and gashed his knee on the one above it.

'Shit!'

He waited for several moments for the pain to subside before climbing the stairs, his hands touching the walls on either side to help him feel his way up. Still he could see nothing. And then at the top of the steps, another flash of lightning lit up the whole house. Again he used the lingering image it left to guide himself through to the main room.

There he stopped, and for the first time became aware of an alarm bell ringing distantly in his mind. Through the windows of the conservatory he could see across to the summer-house where the table lamp he had switched on earlier still burned in the living room. He turned around, and through other windows saw the twinkle of distant lights in other houses. Only Cowell's house had lost electricity. Either the fuses had tripped, or someone had switched off the power.

Even if he could find his way to it he had no idea where the fusebox was.

He stood absolutely still, listening in the dark, hearing nothing more than the sound of the storm outside. But something else had every nerve-end tingling. A very powerful sense that he was not alone. Only minutes before the lights went out he had been spooked by the imagined presence of the dead. Now, whether he sensed the warmth of a body or some faint odour, all of his instincts told him there was someone else in the house. Boudreau aside, only a handful of people knew he was here. Aitkens and Briand. The fishermen he'd seen at the harbour, Owen Clarke among them. And was it Chuck he had seen on the quad bike by the cemetery? Of all of them, it seemed to Sime, only Briand had motive. Take away his wife's alibi and he'd also had the opportunity.

Sime cursed himself suddenly for his own stupidity. Just half an hour earlier he had guided himself to Kirsty Guthrie's grave using his cellphone. And he had spent the last several minutes stumbling about in the dark when he had a perfectly usable source of light in his pocket. He fumbled to retrieve it and switch it on.

To reveal a masked face less than half a metre away, a blade rising through the dark.

A startled cry released itself from his throat, and in reaching out to grab the knife hand of his attacker, his phone went clattering away across the floor, its light with it. All that he was left with was the imprint in his mind of two dark eyes glinting behind the slits of a ski mask.

He felt the blade strike his shoulder, cutting through flesh and glancing off the bone. Pain seared through his neck and arm, but he had a hold of the man's wrist with one hand and swung a fist blindly through the dark. He felt the jarring contact of bone on bone and the other man gasped in pain. Sime swivelled side-on and threw all his weight forward, pushing his attacker back until he lost his footing on the two steps leading to the conservatory. Both men fell down into it, Sime on top, the sound of the knife rattling away across the floor. Sime's weight expelled all the air from the other man's lungs, like a long deep sigh, and Sime felt a blast of bad breath in his face.

But he wasn't prepared for the hand that searched for and found his mouth and eyes, fingers like steel tearing at him in the dark. He released his grip on the man's wrist and rolled away, crashing into a reclining chair.

Lightning spiked through the sky outside, and in that moment he saw his opponent stagger to his feet. Sime rolled over on to his knees, trying to control his breathing and steady himself for another attack. But all he felt was the rush of wind and rain that burst into the house as the door of the conservatory slid open. The crack of thunder that exploded overhead made him duck involuntarily.

The fleeting shadow of his would-be killer darted through the light of the summerhouse across the way and vanished into the night. Sime stumbled back up the steps and slithered across the floor, trying to find his phone. Lightning flashed again and he saw it just a few feet away. He dived to get it before the lightning map left his memory, fumbling then with shaking fingers to switch it on, hoping that it wasn't broken. To his relief, it shed an amazing amount of illumination around him. He staggered to his feet and ran over to the kitchen, grabbing a knife from the block. How he wished he still had his Glock. He turned away to pursue his attacker, but stopped suddenly as he saw a flashlight clipped to an electric wall-charger by the door. He tore it free of its charger and with shaking fingers flicked the on-switch. It released a powerful beam of light into the kitchen. He thrust his phone back into his pocket and ran across the room, armed now with blade and light to chase the killer into the storm.

In the conservatory he stopped for a moment to stoop and pick up his attacker's knife by the tip of its blade and lay it carefully on one of the chairs. There was every possibility that this was the knife used to kill Cowell.

And then he was out and into the rain and wind, the sharp pain of his shoulder wound dulling to a pervasive ache. He felt his arm stiffening up. He raised the flashlight and raked it across the clifftops. He saw nothing but the rain that drove through its beam like warp speed on *Star Trek*. He ran around the side of the house and swung the light back down the road towards the lighthouse. Nothing again. The man had disappeared. He turned and directed the beam up the road, and caught the briefest glimpse of a shadow disappearing over the top of the hill.

Sime drew a deep breath and started after him, his torchlight zigzagging around the hillside as he ran. When he reached the brow of the hill he stopped and swung it through an arc of 180 degrees. This was where he and Kirsty had stood just a few days earlier, when they had made some kind of connection for the very first time, and she had touched his face. Just before the call from Crozes that had led him to arrest her for murder.

There was no sign of the fugitive. Then another flash of lightning lit up the hillside, and he saw the man in the hollow below, running along the edge of the cliffs. Sime ran down the hill after him, fighting to keep his feet and his balance in the dark and the wet, buffeted face-on by the wind.

Just metres from the edge of the cliffs he stopped and focused the beam of his flashlight along their ragged contours. Aeons of erosion had eaten away at rock that glowed blood-red in the dark. Columns of it rose almost sheer out of the sea below. The noise of the storm was deafening. The wind threw mountainous seas against the base of the cliffs. Spray rose fifty feet in the air and glowed like silver mist in the light of his torch.

And then he saw him. His attacker had given up. There was nowhere to go. He was unarmed and without light. Sime was sure to catch him. Crouching in the grass to catch his breath, he had extended one arm to his right to keep his balance. And he watched as Sime approached, slow and cautious, keeping the beam of his torch fully focused on him the whole time.

'Give it up, Briand!' Sime shouted above the roar of the wind.

But the man neither spoke nor moved. Sime was within a metre of him now. And suddenly he sprang forward, filling the beam of light, almost snuffing it out, as he powered into Sime and grabbed his knife arm with one hand, punching his wounded shoulder with the other. Once, twice, three times. Sime yelled with pain, and his flashlight went spinning away through the grass. The other man was powerful, and with his weight on top as the two men fell, was able to twist Sime's wrist, forcing him to unclench his fist and release the knife.

Now he had the upper hand, grabbing the knife and turning quickly to get back to his feet. Sime clutched desperately at his face as he did, fingers finding only the slick wet material of the man's ski mask. Which tore off in his hand as the other man rolled away.

The flashlight lay tipped at an angle in the grass. But it cast enough light for Sime to see Jack Aitkens, wild-eyed, his back to the cliffs, the ocean behind him. He stood with his legs apart, slightly bent at the knees, his knife hand extended to his right. He was gasping for breath.

Sime got slowly to his feet, looking at him in astonishment. 'Why?' he shouted.

But Aitkens made no attempt to respond, keeping his eyes fixed on the detective.

'For God's sake, Aitkens!' Sime bellowed. 'Give it up.'

Aitkens shook his head, but still said nothing. Sime glanced towards the flashlight. If he had that, then he could at least blind the man when he came at him. He dived for it at the same time as Aitkens made his move.

Stretched out on his belly, he grasped the torch, half expecting Aitkens's blade to sink itself between his shoulders. He rolled over and shone the light up into Aitkens's face. But there was no one there. He scrambled to his knees and swept the beam of his torch across the clifftops. Nothing. Aitkens had vanished.

The ground beneath Sime started to move, and he scrambled backwards in a panic as the cliff began collapsing along its leading edge. And he realised what had happened. The ground had simply given way beneath Aitkens's feet and dropped him down on to the rocks below.

Soaked and in pain, gasping for breath and sick to his stomach, Sime spread himself out, lying on his belly, and eased himself towards the precipice until he could see down on to the jumble of debris at the foot of the cliffs.

It wasn't a sheer drop, but a steep scree slope that fell in increments to shelves and ledges, before finally plunging down to an ocean thrashing itself against lethal outcrops of rock.

Aitkens lay on his back about fifteen metres down, still some ten metres above the sea, but drenched by the spray it tossed up into the wind. He was alive, one arm reaching up to grasp a ledge of rock above him. But he didn't seem able to move the rest of his body.

Sime wriggled back from the drop and got to his feet, training the light of his torch along the edge of the cliffs until he saw a way down. A gentle cutaway from the top, and a steep seam of rock running downwards at an angle that would lead him to Aitkens. He ran along to it, and carefully lowered himself over the edge, gingerly testing the rock underfoot in case it would give way.

It took him almost ten minutes to make the descent, battered by the explosive breath of the storm, soaked by the salt spray thrown up all along the cliffs.

Aitkens was breathing hard. Short, mechanical bursts of breath. His eyes wide and staring in fear. Sime perched precariously on the ledge beside him. 'Can you move?'

Aitkens shook his head. 'There's no feeling in my legs. My whole lower body.' His voice was feeble. He bit his lip and tears filled his eyes. 'I think my back's broken.'

'Jesus,' Sime said. 'What the hell were you doing, Aitkens? Why would you want to kill Kirsty?'

Aitkens said, 'I thought you already knew. When you came asking questions about our family history.'

'Knew what?'

Aitkens closed his eyes, pained by irony and regret. 'Obviously not.' He opened them again and a tear ran back down the side of his head and into his hair. 'Sir John Guthrie . . .'

'Kirsty's father?'

He nodded. 'He was worth a damn fortune, Mackenzie. All that family wealth accumulated during the tobacco trade, and then sugar and cotton. He didn't just own the Langadail Estate. He had property in Glasgow and London. Investments, money in the bank. And he left all of it to his daughter, since his son was dead.' He closed his eyes again and let out a long, painful breath. He tried to swallow, then looked up at Sime once more. 'Only they couldn't find her. She'd run off to Canada in search of her crofter boy. His wife was dead and there was no other heir.' He seemed to have trouble breathing and speaking at the same time. Sime waited until he found his voice again. 'I did my research. In Scotland, in those days, when a beneficiary couldn't be traced, it had to be reported to the Lord Treasurer's Remembrancer.' He shook his head. 'Stupid name! It's now the Crown Office.' He swallowed to catch his breath. 'In Guthrie's case, the lawyers sold off all his assets and the money was put in the care of the Crown, until someone turned up to claim it. Only no one ever did.'

For the first time, Sime saw how greed had been the motive for everything.

Aitkens screwed up his face in what might have been either pain or regret. 'The only people left alive with a claim on that money were me and Kirsty. Well, my father before me. But since I have power of attorney . . .'

'And you didn't want to share it.'

His eyes fired up with indignation. 'Why the hell should I? She had a big house, a big divorce settlement in her future. More money than she could ever spend on her precious Entry Island. And what did I have? A subterranean life spent in the dark for a pathetic monthly wage. No life, no future. That money could have given me everything.'

And now, Sime thought, if he survived he faced a life of imprisonment, both in a wheelchair and behind bars. And that realisation was writ large all over Aitkens's face, too.

Sime said, 'It was you who attacked me that night.'

Aitkens found his voice again but it was just a whisper. 'Yes.'

'Why, for God's sake?'

'The ring,' he said. 'I'd seen Kirsty's pendant. I knew it came from Kirsty Guthrie. I thought . . .' He shook his head in despair. 'I thought that somehow you might be family, too. Some distant damned relative that was going to come and stake his claim on the money. If you look inside the band of the ring you'll probably find it's engraved with the Guthrie family motto. *Sto pro veritate*.' He closed his eyes, the despair in his sigh conveying all the irony of the words. 'I stand for truth.'

Sime shook his head. 'Jesus.' The ring again. He took out his cellphone and punched in nine-one-one.

'What the hell are you doing?' Aitkens said.

'Getting help.'

'I don't want help. For God's sake, it's over. Just let me die.

I want to die.' He struggled to try and shift his body. If he could move himself just a few centimetres nearer the edge, he could fall away to the oblivion that he saw now as his only escape. But he couldn't do it.

When Sime hung up he found Aitkens staring at him with hate in his eyes. Sime said, 'There should be a rescue team here within an hour.'

Aitkens said nothing and closed his eyes to contemplate the future hell that would be his life.

'One little thing, Aitkens.'

Aitkens opened his eyes.

'You had a watertight alibi for the night that Cowell was murdered. You were on the night shift at the salt-mine.'

Something very like a smile stretched Aitkens's lips across bloodied teeth. 'You people are so fucking stupid. You checked with the mine, of course. And they checked their records. Yes, they told you, Jack Aitkens was on the night shift when Cowell was killed.'

'Obviously you weren't.'

'I swapped with a pal. An informal arrangement. We do it all the time. But it's never recorded. Same guy's standing in for me tonight.' His smile came from lips tinged with the bitter taste of irony. 'You see? I'm not even here.'

CHAPTER FORTY-SIX

Sime opened his eyes, blinking in unexpected sunlight. He felt warm and woozy. It took some moments for him to realise that he was lying stretched out on the settee in the summerhouse, cushions at his head, a thick blanket wrapped around his shoulders.

Something had wakened him. Some noise. He struggled to remember how he had got here.

The police had arrived from Cap aux Meules on the lifeboat with a doctor and a team of medics from the hospital. But in the end they had decided to make Aitkens comfortable where he lay, and wait until the wind dropped to bring in an air–sea rescue helicopter to get him off the cliffs.

The doctor had disinfected and dressed the wound on Sime's shoulder. Sime had been shivering, suffering from hypothermia and exposure, and they had wrapped him in a thermal blanket and laid him here on the settee.

He remembered thinking, before he went to sleep, that just as Crozes had been fixated on Kirsty, he had been so focused on Briand it had blinded him to the possibility of

Aitkens. But then they'd all been blind to that possibility. How could they ever have guessed at such a motive for wanting to kill his cousin?

Sime realised that what had wakened him was the sound of laughter out on the porch, and in that same moment it came to him that he had been asleep. He was almost startled and looked at his watch. It was after 8 a.m. He must have been out for close on ten hours. The first time in weeks that he had slept properly. A long, deep, dreamless sleep.

The door opened and Aucoin poked his head in. 'Ah, you're awake. Good. How are you feeling?'

Sime nodded. 'Okay.' He wanted to shout I've been sleeping. I feel fucking great!

'That's the helicopter away with Aitkens now. They'll probably medevac him out to Quebec City. Helluva job getting him off those cliffs in one piece.'

'Is he . . . ?'

'He's going to live, yes. Live to regret it, too.'

'You got the knife? I laid it on a chair in the house.'

Aucoin smiled. 'Relax. We got the knife.'

'The pathologist should be able to match it up to Cowell's wounds. Might even still be traces of blood where the blade is sunk in the haft.'

'We'll find out soon enough. It'll go off to Montreal this morning.' He nodded towards a pile of clothes draped over an armchair. 'The nurse put your stuff through her tumble-dryer.' He grinned. 'Even washed your boxers for you. I didn't want to wake you before now. But the ferry leaves shortly.'

When he went out again Sime sat up, and Aitkens's words on the cliffs from the night before came back to him. He looked at his hand, then worked the signet ring over his swollen knuckle with some difficulty to turn it towards the light so that he could see inside it. And there, around the inside of the band, almost erased by more than a century and a half of wearing, were the words, *Sto pro veritate*: I stand for truth.

When he stepped out onto the porch he felt how the wind had dropped. The storm had passed, and a watery autumn sun played behind gold-lined cumulus that bubbled up across the sky, shining in patches of precious liquid across a sea that was only now beginning to calm itself after the rage of the night before.

His legs felt shaky as he climbed down the steps and slipped into the back seat of the car that would drive them down to the harbour.

As they drove down the hill the island seemed to unravel slowly on the other side of his window, like a reel of film. Past the épicerie, and the piles of lobster creels, and the church with its giant cross casting a long shadow over the graveyard. He thought he caught a glimpse of Kirsty Guthrie's headstone, but wasn't sure, and it was gone in a moment.

On the ferry he climbed up on to the top deck and stood at

the stern to watch Entry Island lose its features and turn to silhouette against the radiance of the sun rising behind it. Its shadow reached out across the water so that he felt he could almost touch it. His shoulder was aching, and would no doubt require further attention, but he was hardly aware of it.

A patrol car met them at the quay on Cap aux Meules. It was less than a ten-minute drive to the Sûreté. The sun was higher in the sky now, and the wind had dropped to a whisper. It was going to be a fine fall day. When they stepped into the hall, Aucoin caught his arm. 'I guess you'll want to do this?' he said. He was clearly embarrassed and wanted no part of it. Sime nodded.

Kirsty looked up as he came into her cell. She had a jacket on over her T-shirt, all her belongings packed into a sports hold-all that someone in the station must have loaned her. Her hair was not dry yet after her shower, and hung in damp, dark strands over her shoulders. She stood up. 'You're early. I thought the flight wasn't until midday.'

He wanted to put his arms around her and tell her it was over. But all he said was, 'They're dropping the charges.'

He saw the shock on her face. 'How? Why?'

'We've got your husband's killer in custody.'

She stared at him in disbelief, and it was several moments before she found her voice. 'Who?'

He hesitated. 'Your cousin Jack.'

She turned deathly pale. 'Jack? Are you sure?'

He nodded. 'Let's go and get a coffee, Kirsty. And if you'll give me the time, I've got a very long story to tell you.'

EPILOGUE

Sime followed the path back up from the shingle shore, between the remains of the blackhouses that had once made up the village of Baile Mhanais.

How foolish had Jack Aitkens been to imagine that he could inherit any of this? Not just the money, but the history, the lives lived and lost. Even had his claim for the inheritance been upheld, what might have seemed a fortune a hundred and fifty years ago was only worth a fraction of that now. Certainly not worth killing or dying for. Or spending the rest of your life in a wheelchair in a prison cell.

The wind tugged at his hair, and sunlight spilled down the hillside, the shadows of clouds chasing it across the ruins of the old settlement. He wondered in which of these houses his ancestor had grown up. Where his mother had given birth to him and his sisters. Where his father had died, shot to death as he tried to feed them.

It was hard to picture it the way it had been in his dream. As he had seen it in the paintings. Constables beating the villagers to the ground, men setting roofs on fire. All that remained were the ghosts of memories, and the endless wind whistling among the ruins.

At the top of the village, he stopped and looked up. Kirsty was standing on the hill by the remains of the old sheep fank, just as Ciorstaidh had done before her. Her hair blowing out behind her in the wind. It was impossible now for him to separate the two. Almost equally difficult to draw a line between himself and his ancestor. This was not only a pilgrimage to their past, but a journey in search of a future. For him an escape from a life barely lived. For her, release from the prison that had been Entry Island.

She waved, and he climbed the hill to feel the radiance of those blue eyes light up his life. She said, 'The standing stones are over there. At the far side of the beach.'

He smiled. 'Let's take a look, then.' They began their descent towards the beach and he took her hand to steady her as she almost stumbled over the uneven ground.

And he wondered if it had always been his destiny to keep the promise that the young Sime Mackenzie had made so long ago. And if he and Kirsty were somehow meant to fulfil the love that their ancestors never could. Only if you believed in destiny, he thought. Or fate. And Sime had never been quite sure that he believed in either.

POSTSCRIPT

What happened to Michaél

EXTRACT FROM SIME'S DIARY

March, 1848

I sit writing this tonight with fear in my heart. It is my first entry since arriving at the lumber camp four months ago. There has been no time to keep a record. Even if there had been, there is no privacy here, and anyway I've had little inclination.

We live in long sheds that make me think of the Lazarettos on Grosse Île, sleeping on two tiers of bunk beds that range along opposite walls. You can't leave money or personal belongings here. Nothing is safe. You carry everything of value with you at all times.

In the time we have been here we have worked, eaten and slept. It is all we have done. Long, hard, ball-busting days felling and stripping trees, dragging them with teams of horses to the Gatineau River. For the moment the logs sit out on the ice. Great mountains of them. But in the spring the melting iceflows will carry them downstream to the big commercial sawmills at Quebec City.

They feed us well enough, at long tables like animal troughs. They need to fill our bellies to fuel the work we do. It is relentless, and the only day we have to ourselves is the Sabbath. A few of us who hail from the islands gather round on Sundays while I read from the Gaelic bible and we sing our psalms. The French think we are mad. An irreligious lot, they are. Catholics, of course.

The company provides alcohol, too. Their way of keeping us happy. But you daren't drink too much during the week, or you're not fit for working the next day. So Saturday night is the night for drinking. And pretty wild it can get sometimes, too.

From time to time the Scots organise a ceilidh. We have a fiddler among us, and one of the fellas has a squeeze box. No women, of course. Just drinking and gambling and some mad dancing once the booze starts to flow. Which is when the French join in. They're pretty reticent at first, but once they get a drink in them they're worse than the Scots.

There was a ceilidh earlier tonight, and I was sitting playing cards with a bunch of the boys in a corner of the recreation shed when I first became aware of the fight.

The place was heaving, music ringing around the rafters. The bar had been doing a roaring trade, and most of the men had a skinful. But there were voices raised now above the melee, angry querulous voices that cut through the smoke and the noise. A circle had formed, and men were pushing back from the centre of it on all sides. Me and several of the others stood up on the tables to see what was happening.

In the centre of the circle, two huge men were slugging it out. Big knuckled fists smashing into bloodied faces. One of them was Michaél. He's developed a liking for the drink while we've been here, and after a few he gets argumentative, and violent sometimes. He has let his beard grow back, and his hair is longer again, and he presents a scary figure when he gets riled.

But he picked a brute of a man to get into a fight with tonight. A Frenchman called The Bear. At least, that's what we call him. *L'ours* is the French name for him. A giant of a man with more body hair than I've ever seen, a big beard and a shaven head. In a fight with a real bear you wouldn't bet against him.

I immediately jumped off the table and ploughed my way through the crowd. Me and several of the others grabbed Michaél and pulled him away from the swinging fists of The Bear, and the French did the same with their man, both combatants fighting against constraining arms.

Finally the struggle subsided, and the two men stood glaring at each other across the circle at the centre of the storm, breathing like horses after a gallop, steam rising off both of them, and blood on the floor.

'We'll finish this tomorrow,' The Bear growled in his thickly accented English.

'Fockin' right we will!'

'It's the sabbath tomorrow,' I said.

'Fock the sabbath. We'll settle this like men. The clearing at the far side of the old camp. Midday.'

'It doesn't make you men to fight,' I shouted at Michaél. 'More like schoolboys!'

'You keep the fuck out of this!' The Bear glared at me. Then he turned his loathing back on Michaél. 'Midi it is,' he said. 'And you'd better be there.'

'You can fockin' count on it!'

I have tried everything I can to dissuade him. It seems to me that The Bear is the bigger, stronger man, and that Michaél is going to take a beating. And when the blood is up, men like that have no idea when to stop. But honour is at stake, and Michaél won't hear of backing out, though I'm sure he'll regret it in the morning when he sobers up in the cold light of day.

The truth is, I fear for his life.

The old camp is about a mile away from where they built the new one and there is a large cleared area on the far side of it. Just about every man jack of us was gathered there at midday on the sabbath. I went, not to watch the fight, but to look out for Michaél and try to prevent him from being too badly hurt. What a miserable bloody failure I was at it, too!

God only knows what the temperature was. Well below

freezing. But the sun was up in a clear sky, and both men stripped to the waist. If Michaél had one advantage over The Bear, it was his intelligence. The Bear was a big, lumbering idiot of a man. Michaél was blessed with a sharp mind, and native cunning. And while The Bear was stronger, Michaél was faster, lighter on his feet. With space around him he immediately darted in to land a blow on the big man's nose and leap back again before The Bear could swing a fist. Blood spurted from his busted nose and The Bear roared. But Michaél was in again to land two quick blows to the solar plexus and a high kick that caught the bigger man full in the chest and sent him staggering backwards before dropping to his knees.

The crowd was baying and shouting encouragement to both men and the clamour of it rose through the stillness of the trees.

The Bear got to his feet again, breathing stertorously, and shook his head like an animal. Then he advanced on Michaél, arms at his side, eyes fixed like gimlets on his opponent. Michaél retreated, skipping around the circle created by the crowd, darting in to land occasional blows which just seemed to glance off The Bear like water off oiled wood. Until he ran out of space and The Bear closed in on him, oblivious to the punches and kicks being thrown at him.

I barely even saw the glint of the blade as he slipped it from the belt behind his back. One arm closed around Michaél's shoulder, pulling the Irishman towards him, and the other came up from his side in an arc and plunged the knife deep into his abdomen. I heard Michaél's gasp, air escaping from his lungs in pain and surprise. He doubled over, and the crowd went suddenly silent as The Bear withdrew the blade before plunging it in again. Once, twice. Then he stood back as Michaél dropped to his knees, clutching his belly, blood oozing through his fingers, before he toppled forward, face-first into the dirt.

Shock spread through the crowd like fire, dispersing them in silent panic like smoke in the wind. The Bear stood over Michaél's body, breathing heavily, his lip curled in contempt, blood dripping from the knife in his hand. He pulled a gob of phlegm into his mouth and spat on him as he lay on the ground.

His friends immediately grabbed him and pulled him quickly away as I ran to Michaél's side. I crouched beside him and gently turned him over, to see the light dying in those pale-blue eyes I knew so well. 'Focker!' he whispered through the blood bubbling between his lips. His hand clutched my sleeve. 'You owe me, Scotsman.'

And he was gone. Just like that. All that life and energy and intelligence. Vanished in a moment. Stolen by a brute of a man who knew nothing of human dignity. Of Michaél's generosity or his friendship or his courage. And I wept for him, just as I had wept for my father. And I am not sure I have ever felt quite so alone in this world.

*

It didn't seem right that the sun should shine so brightly, falling through the windows of the foreman's office across his desk, reflecting a dazzle of light in our faces while Michaél lay dead outside. The foreman was about forty, and had spent all of his adult life in the lumber business. His jaw was set, and his lips pressed together in a hard line.

'I'm not bringing in the police,' he said. 'We'd have to call a halt to production while they had an investigation. And you can bet your bottom dollar there's not a man in the camp who'll say he saw what happened. Not even your precious Scots.'

'I will,' I said.

He glared at me. 'Don't be a fucking idiot, man. You'd not live to testify.' He shook his head. 'I can't afford a war breaking out between the Scots and the French. Nor can I afford any more delays in production. We're behind as it is.'

He crossed the room to a small safe that stood against the far wall and took out a pile of notes tied in a bundle he'd already prepared. He threw it down on the desk. 'That's your money. Yours and O'Connor's. You can have one of the horses. Just take the body and go.'

So there was to be no justice. Not of the legal kind, anyway.

It was dark by the time I had sewn Michaél up in a canvas sheet and strapped his body to the back of the horse. The camp had been quiet all day, and no one said a word to me when I gathered together all our stuff, mine and Michaél's, to pack into saddlebags. No one came out of the huts to shake my hand or say goodbye as I led the horse off along the lumber trail that tracked away from the river.

Inside I was as icy as I was cold on the outside. But not so numb that I couldn't sense the fear that still hung in a pall over the lumber camp. I didn't go far before I pulled the horse off the track and into the woods to tie her up to a tree.

I had thought long and hard about Michaél's final words to me. *You owe me, Scotsman.* I owed him money, yes. The cash he had loaned me on Grosse Île to pay the keep of Catrìona Macdonald's children. I had been going to pay it back out of my wages. But I knew that's not what he meant. I knew, too, what I had to do. And I knew it was wrong. But Michaél was right. I owed him.

I suppose it must have been about midnight when I sneaked back into the camp. There was no light anywhere. Not a soul stirring. These men worked hard, played hard, and slept the sleep of the dead. There was a new moon in the sky, a sliver of light to guide me as I drifted like a ghost between the long sheds until I found the one where I knew the French slept. The doors were never locked, and the only fear I had was that this one would creak in the silence of the night and waken men from their slumbers. I needn't have worried. It swung open soundlessly, and I slipped inside.

It was profoundly dark here, and I had to wait until my

eyes accustomed themselves to what little moonlight fell through the windows before I moved along between the rows of bunk beds looking for the big, bearded face of The Bear.

His bed was second from the end, the lower bunk. The man above him was breathing gently, purring like a cat, one arm hanging over the edge of his bed. The Bear himself was lying on his back, snoring like the wild boar we hunted in the woods. He slept deep, without a conscience, without a second thought for the life he had taken so gratuitously that day. Of the seconds, minutes, hours, days, months, years of accumulated experience that had made the man who was Michaél O'Connor. Flawed, yes. But a man of generous spirit and good humour, whose very existence he had erased from the face of this earth in the flash of a blade.

I felt anger and grief bubbling up inside me and knelt down beside his bald head. If I were caught, they would kill me for sure. But in that moment I didn't care. I had one thought, one single purpose.

I drew out my hunting knife and clamped my left hand over the big man's mouth as I drew the blade of it across his throat with all my strength. His eyes opened wide in an instant. Shock, pain, fear. But I had severed both the carotid artery and the jugular, as well as his windpipe, and the life fairly pumped out of him as his heart fought desperately to feed blood to his brain.

I clamped both hands over his face as I felt his hands grab my wrists, and summoning every ounce of strength in my body held him fast. His legs kicked feebly, and his eyes turned towards mine. I wanted him to see me. I wanted him to know who had killed him and why. I wanted to spit in his face, just as he had spat on Michaél as he lay bleeding on the ground.

But all I did was fix him in my gaze, and I saw in his eyes that he knew he was lost. The fight went out of him in a matter of seconds, and it was as if I were back on the Langadail estate, watching the life ebb away from the stag whose throat I had cut. His eyes clouded and he was gone. His whole body limp, his grip on my wrists slackening and falling away.

There was a huge amount of blood soaking into the blanket across his chest and staining my hands red. I wiped them off on his pillow and put away my knife, then stood to look down on his ugly, lifeless face before turning away to lose myself in the darkness.

Debt paid.

I have walked the horse through the night to put as much distance between the camp and myself as possible before they find the bastard. But I have stopped here, somewhere deep in the forest, now that first light has come. Not just to rest the horse, but to light a fire and warm my bones. I have never felt this cold, ever, and it is hard to hold my pen without my fingers trembling.

But I think the cold comes from inside, from the Arctic wastes that are my soul. I would never have believed it possible that I could take the life of another human being in cold blood. But cold it was, and calculated, and the only thing I regret is that Michaél is no longer with me.

Friday, 31st March

I arrived home this morning. Rode through the village just before dawn, with Michaél over the back of my horse. He was frozen solid.

The cabin was bleak and cold when I got there, but pretty much as we had left it. I don't think anyone has been in it during the four months we have been away. There's nothing to steal anyway. The notice advertising jobs with the East Canada Lumber Company was lying on the table where Michaél had left it, and I looked at it with a kind of rage inside me. That fate should have dealt us such a tragic hand. I could remember him returning with it from the Gould village store. Had he not chanced upon it that day and suggested it as a way of earning some cash during the winter months, he would still have been alive. We sow the seeds of our own destruction without even realising it.

I lit a fire and made some tea, to thaw out and steel myself for the job ahead. The Frenchman's blood was still on my hands. Turned almost black now. I washed it off in ice-cold water, changed my clothes and lifted the pickaxe we had used to dig up roots, then led my horse off through the trees as the sun rose and angled its first warm light between the branches overhead.

It took nearly half an hour to reach Michaél's plot of land, the notches he had made still there on the trees at the four corners of it. Somewhere near its centre I found a clear area big enough for my purposes and tested the ground. It was rock-hard, still frozen. And I knew it was going to be a long hard job.

After the first eighteen inches the ground began to soften as I broke through the permafrost. But it had taken me over two hours to get there, and it was maybe another three hours before the grave was dug. I had to dig it in an arc to accomodate the curve of Michaél's frozen body, for there was no way to straighten him out. I lowered him carefully into the hole, still wrapped in canvas, and began shovelling the earth over him. When I had finished I laid one stone at his head, and another at his feet, comforted by the thought that at least he would spend eternity on land that was his. It had never been cleared, and probably never would be. But in some office in some city somewhere, this rectangle of land is registered as belonging to Michaél O'Connor. And in it he lies. Master of it for ever.

I stood then, among the trees, with the sun warming my skin, steam rising off me in the cold air, and I uttered my final farewell to him. 'Cuiridh mi clach air do charn.' *I'll put a stone on your cairn.* Then I recited aloud from John, chapter 11, the verse that I knew so well by now. *'I am the resurrection and the life, saith the Lord: he that believeth in me, though he were dead, yet shall he live; and whosoever liveth and believeth in me, shall never die.'*

As I sit here now, writing this, I want so much to believe it, just as I did when old blind Calum recited it over my father's coffin. But I'm not sure that I do any longer, and all I know is that Ciorstaidh is lost, my family is dead, and Michaél is gone.

NOTE

It should be noted that although Baile Mhanais, Ard Mor Castle and the Langadail Estate are all fictitious, the events depicted in relation to the clearance of settlements there are based on real events that occurred during the nineteenth century on the Isle of Barra, the Isles of North and South Uist, the Isle of Harris, and to a lesser extent the Isle of Lewis, during what has become known as the Highland Clearances.

The Highland potato famine was real and lasted almost ten years.

The quarantine island of Grosse Île in the St Lawrence River existed as described, and has been preserved today much as it was when it finally closed down in 1937.

The largest Celtic cross in the world was erected on Grosse Île in memory of the five thousand Irish immigrants who died there in 1847. This book is dedicated to the memory of all the Scots who died there too, and to the very many more who went on to help make Canada the extraordinary country it is today.

ACKNOWLEDGEMENTS

I would like to offer my grateful thanks to those who gave so generously of their time and expertise during my researches for *Entry Island*. In particular, I'd like to express my gratitude to Bill and Chris Lawson, Seallam Visitor Centre, Northton, Isle of Harris, who have been specialising in the family and social history of the Outer Hebrides of Scotland for over forty years; Mark Lazzeri, Land Manager of the North Harris Trust, for his extraordinary historical knowledge of the land and people of North Harris, and his advice on the stalking, killing and gralloching of a deer; Sarah Egan, for guiding me through the remains of cleared settlements in south-west Lewis; Margaret Savage, née Macdonald, and her mother Sarah, for their time and generosity spent in guiding me around the Eastern Townships of Québec; Ferne Murray and Jean MacIver, both of Lennoxville, Québec, for their hospitality and insights into the Scottish community in the Eastern Townships; Lieutenant Guy Lapointe, Capitaine Martin Hébert, Sergeant Ronald McIvir and Sergeant Enquêteur Daniel Prieur, Sûreté de Québec, Montréal; Sergeant Enquêteur Donald

Bouchard, Sûreté de Québec, Municipalité des Îles-de-la-Madeleine; Léonard Aucoin, for his hospitality and help in unravelling the secrets of les Îles-de-la-Madeleine, and allowing me to borrow his house for use in the book; Normand Briand, Canadian Coastguard, les Îles-de-la-Madeleine; Byron Clarke, for his insights into the anglophone community on Entry Island; and Daniel Audet, Auberge La Ruée Vers Gould, for allowing me access to his extraordinary historical records of the settlement of Gould in the Eastern Townships of Québec.

Be the first to hear about
Peter May's next book by signing up at
www.quercusbooks.co.uk/peter-may